The Soviet State

The Soviet State

SECOND EDITION

Ellsworth Raymond

Introduction by
Stanley W. Page

New York • New York University Press • 1978

Library of Congress Catalog Card Number: 76-46138
ISBN: 0-8147-7370-2

MANUFACTURED IN THE UNITED STATES OF AMERICA

To my wife, Anna, and my children,
Cathy, Alan, and Susan

Preface

The Soviet Union is an organic whole, in which politics and economics are closely related. Without knowing Soviet internal affairs, USSR foreign policy is difficult to understand. Soviet institutions and policies have not been static, but developed through trial and error during half a century of history. This book attempts to combine all these elements into an explanation of the present-day Soviet state.

The book is therefore divided into four major sections. Part I describes Russian political and economic geography, Marxist theory, and the historical evolution of the Soviet system. Geography has greatly influenced USSR industrialization and foreign affairs, while Marxism-Leninism is official Kremlin strategy. The historical chapters try to avoid a mere catalogue of events, and concentrate instead on the plans and practices which have molded current Soviet policy. Each historical chapter includes materials on internal politics, economics, and international relations.

Part II analyzes the system of Soviet government, including the complex relationship between the Communist Party, mass organizations, and governmental administration. Separate chapters are devoted to police and propaganda, which *Pravda* has called "pillars of the Soviet state." An attempt is made to assess the political beliefs of the Soviet public.

Part III outlines the main features of the USSR planned economy: industrial growth, communal agriculture, transport, taxation, and the standard of living. A distinction is made between the three forms of Soviet enterprise: state, cooperative, and private. Economic goals, problems, and achievements are analyzed. A separate chapter reviews economic preparation for future war.

Part IV describes the making of Soviet foreign policy, USSR international trade, technical aid, cultural exchange, and methods of Communist expansion. The impact of national communism upon the Soviet orbit is surveyed, including the Sino-Soviet dispute.

A conclusion compares the predictions of USSR citizens and Western experts as to the Soviet future.

The source materials used in this book were compiled over a period of many years. Six of these years, 1938–1943, were spent by the author as an analyst in the US Embassy to the USSR. Another four, 1944–1947, were spent in Washington, DC, where the author conducted research for the War and Navy Departments on Soviet economics, strategy, and political theory. Since then the author has been head of Russian Area Studies at New York University, with guest lectureships at various colleges including the Graduate Institute of International Studies in Switzerland. Two recent trips through the Soviet Union were of great value, as well as research fellowships from the Hoover Institution, Ford Foundation, and New York State Government.

As much as possible, this book is based on primary sources: official USSR publications, US governmental reports, statements by Kremlin leaders, memoirs of Russian refugees, personal observation, and conversations with innumerable Soviet citizens. Though these sources vary widely in political viewpoint, they agree amazingly on the basic features of the Soviet system.

The book is intended primarily as a text for college students, attempting to answer their many questions concerning the USSR. It is hoped, however, that general readers will find the book useful as an introduction to the Soviet way of life.

The author would like to thank Richard Miller and Lawrence Silverstein, two students of New York University, who photographed the Soviet scenes displayed in the front endpaper. Mr. Bernard Koten, Curator of the Russian Library at New York University, was helpful in finding scarce source materials. Raymond Ziminski of the Cosmos Travel Bureau provided technical data on Soviet tourism and transportation. Among Soviet refugees, Colonel Vladimir Shabinsky and the late General Alexei Markoff gave me unpublished military information. And I thank my wife for suggesting the basic organization of this book.

E. R.

Contents

List of Tables

Introduction

I am delighted with this new edition of Ellsworth Raymond's *The Soviet State* which has gone through several printings since its original appearance in 1968. I find the updating of the material to be little short of miraculous. What was in yesterday's paper has by some amazing means been incorporated into the text. However, I hope that another decade will not have to pass before a new revision is made, because Professor Raymond has the extraordinary knack of combining scholarly knowledge with the quality of YOU ARE THERE. Also, things are changing at an ever increasing pace as the Russian empire seems every day more determined to become the greatest of all time.

Not having enjoyed the opportunity to write the introduction for this book the first time around, I am in a position to treat the revised volume as I would a fresh experience. My first impression is that unlike most other college texts dealing with the same material, Raymond's work has a spritely quality, it is full of sparkle and makes for truly enjoyable reading. The tone, moreover, is so objective that none will refer to it as cold war propaganda. The author tells the story the way I myself experienced it in my past visits to the USSR and the way my recent emigré students tell me about its present condition. I have no reservations whatsoever in recommending *The Soviet State* as a text for any course in Soviet history *cum* politics.

Limited by space I can refer only to selected highlights of the book, but they abound on almost every page. The geographic account of the USSR which opens the book is superb and it alone would justify its acquisition. The section on Marxism-Leninism eschews all the usual polemical hairsplitting (thank heaven!) and provides a valuable background to the revolutions of 1905 and 1917. The Civil War is stripped of the complexity that normally baffles all readers, and this allows the major events to stand out. I greatly admire the analysis of the first three Five Year Plans as oriented basically for military-defense purposes, because that, in turn, becomes a credible rationale not only for the mass regimentation which accompanied them but also for the people's toleration of those brutal years. I doubt whether Stalinism in all its horror could ever be reimposed upon the Russians.

Stalin's foreign policy is carefully delineated, and I agree with the notion that the cold war originated in Soviet suspicions concerning the long-delayed second front. I must also sadly concur in Raymond's judgment that Stalin, unlike our own statesmen, made astute use of the weapons' development produced in the course of the war, enabling the USSR to forge ahead while we dragged our feet in the postwar period.

Krushchev's failures, amid buffooning and bombast, are ably contrasted with his successor's triumph via low profile domestic and foreign policies.

The book passes smoothly from the above-outlined historic background into the functioning of the Soviet State. The highly trained bureaucratic specialist, the propaganda apparatus, the industrial and agricultural machinery is thoroughly explored and interpreted. To conclude, I sincerely hope that this book continues to be widely used in our colleges so that Americans may come to understand the powerful antagonist that confronts them. For my own part, I have every intention to use this book in my own courses dealing with the USSR.

Stanley W. Page
Long Beach, N.Y., 1977

The Soviet State

NETH.
The Hague
DENMARK
NORTH SEA
NORWAY
Oslo
SWEDEN
Stockholm
W. GERMANY
Elbe
Berlin
Copenhagen
G. OF BOTHNIA
BALTIC SEA
FINLAND
Helsinki
Prague
CZECH.
Oder
Kaliningrad
LITHUANIAN S.S.R.
LATVIAN S.S.R.
Tallinn
ESTONIAN S.S.R.
Riga
POLAND
Warsaw
Kaunas
Vilnius
Wistula
Pripyat
L. Peipus
Leningrad
L. Ladoga
Petrozavodsk
L. Onega
Minsk
BELORUSSIAN S.S.R.
Vitebsk
Lvov
MOLDAVIAN S.S.R.
Mogilev
Vinnitsa
Gomel
ROMANIA
Kiev
UKRAINIAN S.S.R.
Volga
Kalinin
Moscow
Bryansk
Rybinsk
Yaroslavl
Odessa
Dnepropetrovsk
Orel
Tula
Ryazan
Kursk
Kharkov
Dnepr
Donets
Oka
Gorkiy
Voronezh
Sevastopol
Donetsk
RUSSIAN
Lugansk
Penza
Kazan
BLACK SEA
Don
Rostov
Saratov
Krasnodar
Volgograd
Kuybyshev
ARCTIC
SVALBARD
FRANZ JOSEF LAND
BARENTS SEA
Murmansk
KOLA PEN.
White Sea
NOVAYA ZEMLYA
KARA SEA
Arkhangelsk
Sev. Dvina
Pechora
Vorkuta
Kotlas
Ukhta
Syktyvkar
Pechora
Kirov
SOCIALIST
FEDERATED
Izhevsk
Perm
Ob
URAL
Sverdlovsk
Ufa
Uralsk
Chelyabinsk
Irtysh
Batumi
GEORGIAN S.S.R.
Magnitogorsk
Orenburg
Kurgan
UNION OF SOVIET
Astrak
Ural
TURKEY
Groznyy
CAUCASUS
Tbilisi
Orsk
Petropavlovsk
Omsk
KIRGHIZ STEPPE
AZERBAYDZHAN S.S.R.
CASPIAN SEA
Novosibirsk
ARMENIAN S.S.R.
KAZAKH
Pavlodar
S.S.R.
Barnaul
Aral Sea
Dzhezkazgan
Karaganda
Rubtsovsk
Krasnovodsk
TURKMEN
Teheran
Kzyl-Orda
Semipalatinsk
ALTAI
Urgench
Balkhash
L. Balkhash
Ashkhabad S.S.R.
UZBEK S.S.R.
Tashkent
Bukhara
Dzhambul
IRAN
Mary
Samarkand
Ili
Frunze
Alma-Ata
Andizhan
Dushambe
KIRGIZ S.S.R.
TIEN SHAN MTS.
TADZHIK S.S.R.
AFGHANISTAN
Kabul
PERSIAN GULF
JAMMU AND KASHMIR
Rawalpindi
Indus
WEST PAKISTAN
INDIA
TIBET

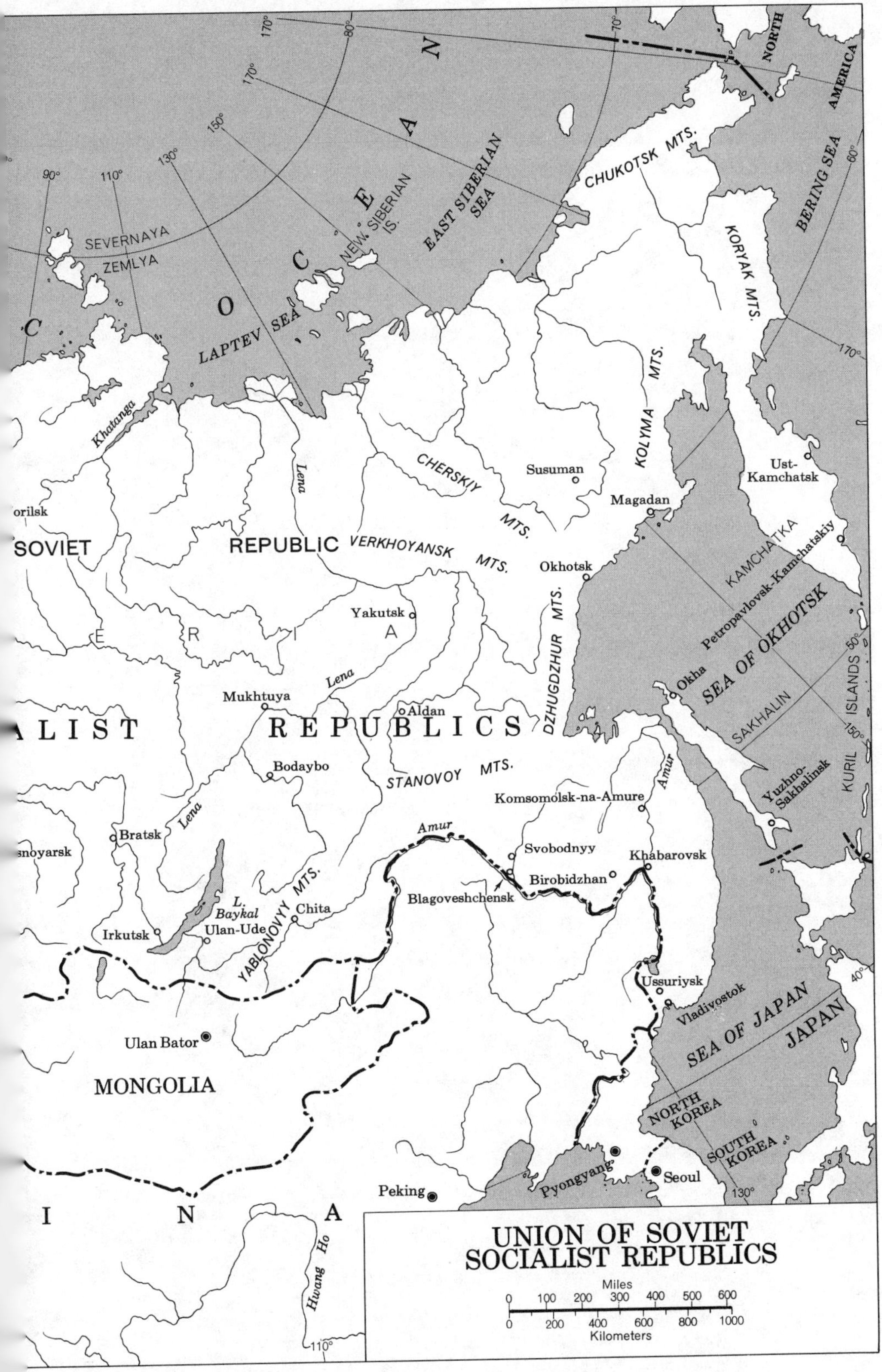

UNION OF SOVIET SOCIALIST REPUBLICS
Miles
0 100 200 300 400 500 600
0 200 400 600 800 1000
Kilometers
O C E A N
NORTH AMERICA
BERING SEA
CHUKOTSK MTS.
KORYAK MTS.
EAST SIBERIAN SEA
NEW SIBERIAN IS.
SEVERNAYA ZEMLYA
LAPTEV SEA
Khatanga
Lena
CHERSKIY MTS.
Susuman
KOLYMA MTS.
Magadan
Ust-Kamchatsk
KAMCHATKA
Petropavlovsk-Kamchatskiy
Okhotsk
SEA OF OKHOTSK
Norilsk
SOVIET
REPUBLIC
VERKHOYANSK MTS.
Yakutsk
E R I A
DZHUGDZHUR MTS.
Okha
SAKHALIN
KURIL ISLANDS
Mukhtuya
Aldan
ALIST
REPUBLICS
STANOVOY MTS.
Bodaybo
Amur
Komsomolsk-na-Amure
Yuzhno-Sakhalinsk
Bratsk
Krasnoyarsk
Svobodnyy
Khabarovsk
Birobidzhan
Blagoveshchensk
YABLONOVYY MTS.
L. Baykal
Chita
Irkutsk
Ulan-Ude
Ussuriysk
Vladivostok
SEA OF JAPAN
JAPAN
Ulan Bator
MONGOLIA
NORTH KOREA
SOUTH KOREA
Pyongyang
Seoul
Peking
I N A
Hwang Ho

Part I

An Unusual Background

Russia is very different from Western nations such as Britain, Germany, or France. Though Western in culture, the USSR is divorced geographically, ideologically, and historically from more familiar European countries. Chapter 1 describes Russian geography, which tremendously influences both the Soviet economy and foreign policy. Since presentday Russia officially is a Marxist state, the ideology of Marxism-Leninism is discussed in Chapter 2. The Soviet way of life was not introduced all at once, but slowly evolved throughout decades of trial and error. An understanding of present government, economics, and foreign policy is impossible without knowing Soviet history. Chapters 3 through 10 are therefore devoted to the historical successes and failures that molded the USSR of today.

Chapter 1

The Largest Country in the World

The USSR occupies a vast subcontinent. Its area of 8,600,000 square miles is as large as that of all North America. One sixth of the world's land surface is embraced by the USSR, which extends 7,000 miles west to east from the Baltic Sea to the Pacific Ocean, and 2,700 miles north to south from the Arctic Ocean to the Afghan Mountains.

The whims of geography have largely isolated this huge land mass from the outside world. Two thirds of the USSR is in Asia, yet the volume of land travel between Asiatic Russia and other Asian nations is amazingly small. High mountain ranges divide the USSR from neighboring Turkey, Iran, Afghanistan, India, Mongolia, and China. Only four railways cross these forbidding mountains to link Russia with Manchuria, Mongolia, Iran, and Turkey. For years at a time, the two latter rail lines have been little used, partly because they are narrow gauge and partly due to frontier tension. Both in the nineteenth and twentieth centuries, most trade between Russia and Asia has traveled the seas.

Yet Russian maritime travel is also precarious, and not to Asia alone. The USSR lies in the far north, and most of the country is in the latitudes of Canada. Moscow, the capital, is as northerly as lower Hudson Bay. Almost all seaports freeze in winter, including the Ukrainian ports on the northern shore of the Black Sea. Only a handful of harbors—south Baltic ports, Caucasian ports on the Black Sea, three Pacific inlets, and Murmansk on the

Arctic—remain open all year. But these are either second-rate harbors or located far from the main centers of Soviet civilization.

Imprisoned by such winter ice, Russia cannot become a great sea power. Neither the Tsars nor the Communists have developed a great surface navy, and there are no overseas Russian colonies. Because of naval weakness, Tsarist Russia in the nineteeth century refused to annex Hawaii (which sought Russian protection) and sold Alaska to the United States. Soviet Russia is remarkably land-minded. Early in World War II, before the USSR and Britain became allies, Moscow's newspaper *Pravda* condemned England in the following unnautical manner:

> Perfidious Albion! You will be overcome by the weight of your sins, and sink into the land!

Another isolating factor has been Russia's harsh climate. Most of the USSR must endure Arctic winters, as cold waves from the north sweep unobstructed down the vast Russian plains. Temperatures of — 40° F are common in midwinter Moscow. North Central Asia is also as cold in winter, despite being much further south. The most frigid town in the world is Verkhoyansk in northeast Siberia, where — 84 ° F has been recorded.

In addition, much of the USSR has little rainfall. High mountains prevent moisture from the Pacific or Indian Oceans from reaching most of Russia. The Arctic Ocean provides few rain clouds, because little water can rise through the ice into the sky. Strange as it seems, most Russian rainfall comes from the distant Atlantic by clouds crossing all western and central Europe. Much of the Atlantic moisture has been lost before the clouds reach the Russian skies.

Thus Soviet agriculture faces an eternal struggle of man against the cruelties of nature. If an early winter does not kill part of the crop, drought will often do the damage.

Because of its harsh climate, Russia has never been troubled by excessive immigration. In past history many tribes and peoples have roamed the vast Russian plains: Scythians, Goths, Huns, Avars, Bulgars, Magyars, Mongols, and Turks. But almost all originated within or near Russia, and desperately tried to escape into better European, Chinese, or Near Eastern climes. The ancient Greeks and Romans founded many colonial cities along the Black Sea coast, but never tried to penetrate deep inland. In more modern times, the 2,000-mile border between Russia and China has not stimulated Chinese immigration. During the past two centuries, millions of Chinese have migrated from their overpopulated homeland into southeast Asia, where at present they are a powerful and troublesome minority. In contrast, only a few tens of thousand Chinese have moved north into cold primeval Siberia.

Asiatic Russia's unkind climate has sometimes averted outside aggression. During the mid-nineteenth century the Chinese Empire signed treaties surrendering East Siberia to Tsarist Russia, partly because of Chinese weakness but also because of China's disinterest in a northern wilderness of mostly frozen soil. Much later, in 1941, Japan rejected Germany's plea to attack the USSR, and thus assist the Nazi invasion of Russia. Instead, Nippon launched an attack upon southeast Asia, thus starting the War of the Pacific. By Japanese logic, the natural wealth of the tropical East Indies was a more tempting prize than the equally great resources of frigid East Siberia.

By the freaks of nature, Russia has largely led an isolated introspective existence. There have been countless wars, but mostly with bordering land-neighbors or among nationalities within Russia itself. Until the present air and rocket age, Russia neither feared nor threatened such distant nations as the United States.

Isolated from the outside world, Russia also has many poorly accessible areas within its own borders. About nine tenths of the USSR consist of sparsely inhabited wastelands. One sixth of the country chills in perpetually frozen tundra north of the Arctic Circle. Naturally there are few inhabitants, the majority being Eskimo-type tribes whose main occupation is raising reindeer. These sturdy animals serve as beasts of burden, provide skins for clothing and tents, are eaten as meat, and yield dung for fuel in an area lacking in trees. The Soviet Union has the largest herds of reindeer in the world.

South of the tundra are the world's greatest forests, extending from the Arctic Circle almost to Moscow in European USSR, and to the Trans-Siberian Railway in south Siberia. These dense woods, mostly evergreen, cover more than half of the USSR and constitute one fifth of the standing timber on our earth. Again there are few inhabitants, a mixture of Eskimos and whites, who live along the rivers and who mainly engage in hunting and lumbering. The forests abound in furbearing animals, so Russia is a major fur-producing and exporting nation. About one third of the furs worn in the United States come from the USSR. Soviet lumber travels south from the forests into the Russian deserts and treeless steppes, and via the Arctic Ocean and Baltic Sea to western Europe. Some timber is also shipped from East Siberia to Japan. Because of its great forests, the USSR is one of the world's largest producers and exporters of lumber.

The airplane is beginning to solve travel problems over the remote tundra and northern forests of Russia, but Arctic shipping and north riverboats meanwhile are the major link to the remainder of the USSR. Of the four Soviet railways that penetrate the northern areas, three are in European USSR. About a dozen highways enter the southern edge of the forests, then stop. Elsewhere, land transport in the tundra and northern forests is dependent on sled, sledge, or pack animal. Many forest areas have yet to be explored by man.

In the south, about one fifth of the USSR consists of the Central Asian desert and semi-desert. On these dry grasslands (north Central Asia) and burning sands (the south), inhabitants are again few. On the northern semi-desert, Mongol nomads drive their herds of cattle, sheep, horses, and camels from one meager pasture to another. In the southern true desert, a more sedentary Turkish population raises cotton, rice, silkworms, and fruit in the river valleys, whose irrigation canals are thousands of years old. Much mining and mineral refining takes place both in the desert and amid the high mountains along the Asian frontier. Otherwise there is little industry. Large quantities of coal, iron, and nonferrous metals are unearthed, then exported to more industrial Soviet areas (the Urals and European USSR) for final use. Only four railways cross Central Asia, where much transport is still by caravans of camels or trucks.

Many Russian rivers flow north into the Arctic Ocean or Baltic Sea. After the winter freeze, the lower reaches of these rivers thaw first, unloosing flood waters to the north. The flood hits the ice of the still frozen river in the north, is blocked, then spreads over the adjacent plain. Thus the USSR contains vast swamps, which are particularly numerous in Belorussia near the Polish frontier, and in west Siberia. Some Belorussian swamps (the Polese) are 50 miles wide. Western Siberian swamps are often covered with trees, and appear like harmless moss. But one false step on this moss may send a man up to his neck in quicksand.

The remaining one tenth of the country, the steppeland, is the home of the vast majority of the Soviet population. The steppes, or prairies, form a rough triangle with one corner at Leningrad on the Baltic Sea, a second at the Rumanian border on the Black Sea coast, and the third in mid-south Siberia. From north to south, the triangle is widest in European USSR, gradually narrowing as it crosses the Ural Mountains into Siberia, and finally vanishing altogether near the central Siberian city of Tomsk.

The steppeland has fertile soil, a geographic blessing attracting large-scale settlement. The northern or wooded steppe is a mixture of broad fields and blocks of dense forest, where medieval Russian settlers partially cleared the lower edge of the northern woods. Huge crops of potatoes, flax, and rye are grown in this forest-field area, which is the region surrounding Moscow. Because of its many green pastures, the wooded steppe has large herds of cattle and is the main center of Soviet dairy farming.

South of the wooded steppe lies the true or treeless steppe, so flat that one can see for miles, often viewing brilliant sunlight on one horizon, while a rainstorm darkens the opposite sky. Though subject to periodic droughts, this sea of land has rich black soil, and is Russia's granary. Black soil results from light rainfall, which cannot wash out natural minerals from the earth. In this area, even the dirt roads are black. Here land is too precious to waste on pasture, so the main livestock are poultry and pigs. Fortunately for Russia, its largest deposits of iron, coal, and oil lie either within the steppes, or border the steppeland frontier. Hence the fertile triangle is the real Russia—the vital industrial and agricultural area of the USSR.

Since most of the triangle spreads through European USSR, the majority of the Soviet people live west of the Ural Mountains —the dividing line between Europe and Asia. According to the latest Soviet census, the total population was distributed as follows: 67 percent in European USSR, 14 percent in Siberia, 14 percent in Central Asia, and 5 per cent in the Caucasus. Concentration of the Soviet population on the steppes creates a paradox. By total territory, the USSR is an underpopulated nation. Yet parts of the Ukrainian treeless steppe suffer from rural overpopulation.

The massing of Russia's people in European USSR links the steppeland internationally with Europe rather than Asia. Most Soviet citizens consider Asiatic USSR a distant colony, not an integral part of the Slavic fatherland. When *Pravda* writes "North," this designates northern European USSR, though most of the Soviet Arctic is located in Siberia. "South" in the press means southern European USSR or the Ukraine, not the far more southerly Central Asia. And "East" officially refers to any place from the eastern bank of the Volga River more than four thousand miles to the Pacific Ocean.

Other attractions turn Russia toward the West. During both Tsarist and Soviet history, Russian mines, forests and fields have been more productive than manufacturing. Therefore Tsarist and Soviet exports have mainly consisted of raw materials. The natural market for such exports is industrial Europe, which is short of raw materials, and which supplies machinery and manufactured goods in return. Non-Soviet Asia similarly exports raw materials, so Russo-Asian trade is difficult to develop, except with highly-industrialized Japan.

Unlike Asia, Europe is easily accessible to Russia. The only mountains along the Soviet European frontier are the low Carpathians. The Polish and Rumanian plains are land gateways into the USSR. Shipping on the Black and Baltic Seas easily connects Russia with all southern and western Europe.

Under both the Tsars and Communists, Russian foreign policy has therefore strived to dominate eastern and central Europe. Examination of the important treaties of nineteenth-century Tsardom and twentieth-century Communism reveal the same pattern: twice as many international agreements with Europe as with Asia. Only when Russia is stopped by superior force in Europe, does it try to expand eastward. Toward the close of the seventeenth century, Tsarist Russia reached the Pacific coast, then concluded the Treaty of Nerchinsk with China recognizing Chinese sovereignty over what now is the Soviet Far East. This treaty was honored by Russia for more than 160 years despite China's weakness, because Tsardom was more interested in the Balkans. When England, France, and Turkey defeated Russia during the Crimean War of the mid-nineteenth century, then Tsardom turned to the East and obtained East Siberia and a Manchurian sphere of influence from China.

Likewise when Soviet Premier Lenin failed to communize east central Europe during 1917–1923, he sought salvation in Asia, declaring that the road to Paris was via Peking. By Lenin's reasoning, if China, India, and Russia—the three most populous countries on earth—went Communist, Marxist socialism would engulf the world. After World War II, when Soviet leaders Stalin, Khrushchev, and Brezhnev were blocked in west Europe by the NATO alliance, they intensified USSR efforts to communize or neutralize underdeveloped Asian, African, or Latin American nations.

The USSR has great natural resources. Arable land amounts to about one billion acres, approximately the same as in the United States. Russia claims to have the world's largest reserves of iron, oil, peat, manganese, platinum, phosphate, and potash, and the second largest deposits of coal (following the USA). There is no question that the world's greatest reserve of standing timber is in Siberia. These resources make the USSR largely self-sufficient. Foreign trade is small for a great power. Tsarist Russia never accounted for more that 3 per cent of world trade. The Soviet share of international trade outside the Communist orbit of nations is about 3 per cent.

The USSR has the second largest industrial base in the world, exceeded only by that of the United States. Russian industrialization started about 1890, later than in West Europe or America. Thereafter Russian industrial growth was rapid, though badly interrupted by two world wars and the civil war of 1918–1920. At present Soviet industry is about 66 per cent as large as American, but is expanding at a faster rate.

There are six major centers of USSR industry. Five of them are inside the fertile triangle, including four in Russian Europe. The Moscow or Central Industrial Region, which includes the capital city and many surrounding districts, is the greatest industrial area in the Soviet Union. Despite great decentralization of industry during the Communist regime, Moscow still remains the largest industrial city in Russia, producing nine per cent of all USSR industrial output. The city contains almost every branch of manufacturing, including huge heavy industries. However, most industries of Moscow and its industrial region are those requiring technical skill, taking advantage of the large pool of skilled labor created by early industrialization. The chief manufactures today are complex and precision machines such as machine tools, watches, radios, and electrical equipment of all types. Moscow itself contains two large automobile and truck factories, and is a major center of airplane design and manufacture. Dating from the Tsarist era is a huge textile industry, which in the past gave Moscow the nickname of "city of calico." Though Moscow today is a city of machines, the Central Industrial Region still produces most of the cotton, linen, and wool cloth of the USSR.

Second in industrial size is the Ukraine of south European USSR. Though flat country is usually lacking in minerals, the Ukrainian steppes rank among the greatest mining areas in the world. Huge deposits of coal and iron lie in close proximity on the treeless plains. The greatest manufacturing industry of the Ukraine is ferrous metallurgy, producing about half the iron and two fifths of the steel in the entire USSR. Based on these metals is the giant Ukrainian engineering industry, which produces mostly heavy equipment like tractors, tanks, trucks, mining machinery, steel mills, locomotives, railway freight cars, barges, and ships. A large chemical industry yields half the coke and and salt. Big mining areas produce one third of the coal and one fourth of the gas of the USSR. Today most USSR sugar comes from Ukrainian refineries.

Third in industrial rank are the low wooded Ural Mountains forming the border between Europe and Asia. Here is the greatest single concentration of mineral wealth in the world. Besides coal, iron, and oil, mountain mines yield huge quantities of asbestos, bauxite (raw material for aluminum), chrome, copper, manganese, nickel, platinum, potash, precious stones, and many other minerals. In Soviet schools the Urals are a godsend for geology students. When a teacher asks where uranium or another obscure mineral is mined in the USSR, a student who doesn't know will simply say: "the Urals." Nine times out of ten, his guess will be right. By virtue of this mineral wealth, the Urals is the largest center for both ferrous and nonferrous metallurgy. There also are huge factories producing nitrates, explosives, heavy machinery, tractors, tanks, artillery, railway freight cars, intercontinental rockets, and nuclear bombs. During World War II the Urals was Russia's main arsenal, producing two fifths of all Soviet wartime munitions.

To the east, where Siberia, Central Asia, and Outer Mongolia triangle together, is the Kuznetsk or Blacksmith's Basin, commonly shortened to "Kuzbas." This mountainous area is located just south of the Siberian end of the feritle steppes. Here is the largest coal field in the USSR and second largest in the world, yielding in size only to the Appalachian deposits in the USA. Gold, iron, lead, zinc, and other metals are also mined in the Kuzbas. As yet there is more mining than manufacturing, but even so the Kuzbas contains a huge nitrate factory and one of the biggest steel mills in Asia. Huge non-ferrous metallurgical plants are under construction in and near the Kuzbas, utilizing the abundance of hydro-electric power.

Comparatively new industrially is the middle and lower Volga valley, which now produces most of USSR oil and natural gas. Besides oil refining, Volga industry concentrates on the manufacture of mobile equipment, like autos, trucks, tractors, short-range rockets, and river ships. During World War II the Volga valley was a whole defense industry in itself, with three huge tank factories and four different cities building warplanes.

The last of Russia's major industrial centers is Leningrad, formerly called St. Petersburg (1703–1913) and Petrograd (1914–1923). Nicknamed the "Venice of the North" because of its many canals and bridges, Leningrad is Russia's second largest city, greatest shipbuilding center, a major seaport, and second only to Moscow in urban industry. Because of its location in the northern forest, Leningrad has no surrounding industrial region as Moscow does. Nevertheless, the northern Venice and its suburbs contain about eight per cent of all Soviet industry. Besides cargo, naval and atomic-powered ships, Leningrad produces large quantities of radios, cameras, precision machinery, electrical equipment, artillery, artificial rubber, and textiles. Because its population has the highest level of education of any Soviet city, Leningrad has often built the pilot plants for new USSR industries, then loaned its experienced personnel for sister factories constructed later in other Russian regions. Most of the incredibly precise equipment for USSR nuclear-bomb plants comes from Leningrad factories.

In contrast to the Soviet Union's industrial strength, its transportation system is inadequate. Even in the steppeland, communications are poor by American or West European standards. There are few intercity highways. Most roads are made of dirt and become impassable during the spring and autumn rains. Even *Pravda* describes the two rainy seasons as "roadlessness." Rivers were the ancient highways, but most Soviet streams are too shallow for large modern riverboats. Furthermore, the rivers are frozen more than half of each year. The backbone of Soviet transportation is the railways, which haul more than three fifths of internal freight.

Yet the railways themselves are insufficient and overburdened. Most of them were built during the Tsarist era, because railway construction has a low priority in Soviet economic planning. Rather than constructing many new lines, the Soviets have mostly improved the old by double-tracking, electrification, and replacing steam engines with diesel locomotives. Vast expansion of the railway system is needed, but would require a large expenditure of steel. The USSR prefers to allocate most of its steel to industrial growth and to the manufacture of machinery and armament.

As a result, much of Soviet farm and factory output is poorly distributed. For example, fruit is abundant and cheap in the subtropical Caucasus, south Crimea, and south Central Asia. But there are constant shortages of fruit in Moscow and Leningrad, simply because transport is poor.

In the late 1970's the USSR had a total population of 257,900,000, which was third largest in the world, exceeded only by China and India. At the time of the Bolshevik Revolution in 1917, the population was 82 per cent rural. Today as a result of greater industrialization, the rural population has decreased to

41 per cent of the total. Thus Communism has changed Russia from a predominantly rural nation into a society of great urbanization.

Because of the large number of male deaths in wars, famines, and prison camps, the Soviet population has a large excess of women over men. According to official Soviet estimates, there are 19 million more females than males in the USSR. Because of the shortage of men, women perform much of the heavy manual labor in the Soviet Union. Many females also rise to governmental posts of medium rank, though men tend to monopolize the highest posts. Today about half the urban labor force, three fifths of collective farmers, most doctors, and half of all scientific workers are women. Many factories, collective farms, and large apartment houses have nurseries to care for children of working mothers.

Today most of the Soviet population is literate. Though constantly rising, the general level of education is lower than in Western Europe or the United States. Four years of grade school were compulsory for all children from 1928 to 1955. Since then, most rural children receive seven years of education, and urban children, ten. The general level of education of the average Soviet citizen is still probably around 8th grade. This is a considerable achievement over the 70 per cent illiteracy when the Communists seized power in 1917.

There are actually four separate school systems operating in the USSR. Only one is private, consisting of a small number of theological seminaries administered by various church denominations. The second is the elaborate network of state schools and colleges managed by the Soviet armed forces. The third consists of special schools of the Communist Party. Fourth and largest is the public school system where most Soviet children study.

The hierarchy of schools of the armed forces can take a corporal and over a period of years train him to be a lieutenant, captain, major, colonel, general, and finally a marshal. Capable draftees are encouraged to remain in the armed forces and become regular army officers. Of course, most corporals don't reach the top, but stop somewhere in the middle officer grades. But many of the present Soviet marshals actually started as noncommissioned officers. In order to achieve such promotion, half of their military service has been spent in army schools.

The Communist party school system is also large. Thousands of night schools teach Marxism, Soviet strategy, and Communist tactics to new party members. They might be best described as high schools of indoctrination. But the party also has its own colleges, whose 150,000 students are mature party members earmarked for promotion. Here the most capable Communists are trained to be party bureaucrats, newspaper editors, and government officials. There are even colleges for industrialists and agricultural administrators. Among the many distinguished alumni of party colleges was former USSR Premier Khrushchev, who majored in industrial management.

Ordinary party colleges are openly advertised. But there also are secret Communist academies which train foreign Communists to spy, sabotage, and lead revolutions. Some governmental and party leaders in the Soviet satellites of East Europe are graduates of these schools, including Marshal Tito of Yugoslavia and Janos Kadar, the first secretary of the Hungarian Communist Party.

But the main education network of the USSR is the huge public school system, including boarding schools. By late 1970's this network consisted of an eight-year grade school, a two- or three-year high school, and college undergraduate programs ranging from four to six years. Both grade and high school are highly technical. When a Soviet youth enters college to major in science, he has already completed algebra, geometry, and trigonometry in high school. He has studied physics since the sixth grade and chemistry from the seventh. Soviet Russia copied this intensive technical education from the German "Real-Schule," which is not like a manual trade school in America but instead is a school of science. So a Soviet student starts his college training at a high level. On the average an American science major in college studies in his junior year what the Soviet student learns as a freshman. Thus the Soviet student completes his five-year college program with a knowledge equal to an American graduate student.

There are no liberal arts colleges in the USSR. Instead, each Soviet college trains its students for a specific profession. Over half of all college students major in science or engineering. This explains why the USSR has more engineers and scientists than the USA. Nor is Soviet engineering exclusively a male profession, as in the United States. On a recent visit to a USSR university, I interviewed three girl students. Two were studying housing construction, and the third was majoring in machine-tool production. When I expressed surprise about such professions for women, the girls laughed and said they liked engineering.

Upon graduating, Soviet college students obtain administrative or professional positions, thus automatically entering the middle class. Soviet Russia in theory is striving to achieve a Marxist classless state, but in fact has a class structure based on income and occupation. Table 1 attempts to compare the class pattern of Tsarist and Soviet Russia. The Tsarist data is presented as published by the Soviets. USSR data is based on rearrangement of Soviet statistics:

Table 1. *Class Structure in Per Cent of Total Population*

Economic Strata	1914 Tsarist Russia	USSR
Upper and middle class	16	22
Manual and white-collar workers	19	56
Peasants	65	22
	100	100

These statistics can be regarded only as approximate. They do, however, reflect the decrease of the peasantry and the increase in workers resulting from Soviet industrial growth. In Tsarist Russia most workers were employed by private firms, and the majority of peasants were small landowners. Today most workers are state employees, and almost all peasants are state or collective farmers. The old upper and middle class consisted mainly of private businessmen, land-owning nobility, and government civil servants. Almost all of the new upper and middle class are officials in the government, Communist party, cooperatives, and mass organizations. The largest subgroups within this class are statisticians, executives, army and police officers, and teachers.

More important politically is the fact that the USSR is a multinational state. There are approximately 150 nationalities in the USSR, of whom 60 are fairly large. According to the latest Soviet census, Russians (or more properly, Great Russians) constitute only 54 per cent of the total population. The next largest Slavic nationalities are the Ukrainians (17 per cent) and the Belorussians (4 per cent). In ancient times the Russians, Ukrainians, and Belorussians were all one nationality. Historical circumstances during the Middle Ages separated them into different areas, where each of the three developed separate languages and cultures. Taken together, these three Slavic nationalities constitute 75 per cent of the total population.

Another 9 per cent of the Soviet population consists of various non-Asian nationalities such as Latvians, Lithuanians, Poles, Moldavians, Armenians, Georgians, and Germans. This group includes 3,000,000 Jews, and the USSR has the second largest Jewish population in the world, exceeded only by the United States.

The final 16 per cent of the USSR population is Mongoloid, consisting of Finno-Ugrians in the north, Mongols in the central regions from the Volga to East Siberia, and Turco-Tatars in south Central Asia and the Caucasus.

Since the USSR is a land of many nationalities, it also is a country of many religions. Altogether 30 different religions are practiced. By far the largest is the Russian Orthodox Church, which today has 50 million adherents. This is the faith of most religious Russians, Ukrainians, Belorussians, and Georgians. When allowed considerable religious freedom from World War II to 1960, the Orthodox Church administered 12 theological seminaries, 89 monasteries and convents, and 22,000 chapels and cathedrals. Today the number of seminaries has been reduced to six, and most monasteries and convents have been closed by the Soviet government.

The next largest religious body is, surprisingly, the non-Christian religion of Muhammadism. The USSR is one of the world's largest Moslem countries with 16,000,000 Mongol and Turkish believers, who live mainly in Central Asia or in nearby Ural, Volga, and Caucasian regions. One of the largest mosques in the entire Islamic world is the headquarters of the Grand Mullah of Central Asia in the Soviet city of Tashkent. The paved grounds, shaded by trees and interlaced with deep gutters of fast flowing water, fill an entire city block. About one quarter of the huge grounds is covered by the four-story blue mosque, surmounted by several domes and a tall slender minaret. Attendance at this mosque is enormous: 5,000 worshipers a day, and 20,000 on Friday, which is the Moslem Sabbath and the only weekday when women can visit church.

Another major religion is the Roman Catholic, with 1,300 churches and a total congregation of about 1,500,000. Most USSR Catholics are Ukrainians, Belorussians, Poles, and Lithuanians residing along the western borderlands. Many belong to the Uniate faith, also called the Church of the Eastern Rite. Uniates formerly accepted the leadership of the Pope of Rome, but their church services are similar to those of the Russian Orthodox. After World War II, the Soviet government forced USSR Uniates to accept the leadership of the Moscow Patriarch of the Russian Orthodox Church.

Exceeding the Catholics in size are the Baptists with 5,000 chapels and almost 3,000,000 believers. Originally introduced into Tsarist Russia by resident Germans, the Baptist faith has attracted many Russians who prefer a simple Christian service to the elaborate ceremonies of the Orthodox Church.

About 3,000,000 Soviet citizens are Lutherans, most of whom are Estonians, Latvians and Germans. Today only about 100 Lutheran chapels remain open, the remainder having been closed by the Soviet government because the Lutheran faith is closely linked with Estonian and Latvian anti-Russian nationalism.

Of the 3,000,000 Soviet Jews, about half a million participate in synagogue services. Worshipers would probably be more numerous, had not governmental closure in the early 1960's reduced the operating synagogues from several hundred to a mere 92. Heavy state persecution of Jews after both World War II and Stalin's death is apparently due to Kremlin fear of Zionism.

Other major religious congregations include a million Armenian Christians, and some 400,000 Buddhists. The latter comprise Chinese and Koreans residing in Soviet Central Asia, plus Mongol communities in East Siberia and the lower Volga valley.

In the 1970's the most persecuted of all Soviet religions were the small but widespread groups of Pentacostals and Jehovah's Witnesses. Comparatively new in the USSR, these faiths are believed to have been introduced by the invading German army during World War II. Both congregations refuse to perform military service, forbid their children to join Communist youth organizations, and in general isolate themselves from Soviet public life.

The Soviet government is officially atheist, and disseminates antireligious propaganda through the schools, press, radio, television, museums, theaters, and the arts. Closed churches are sometimes converted into atheist museums. For example, a former Leningrad cathedral today displays paintings, statues, and documents about past religious cruelty and corrupt priests. The main attraction is a torture-chamber of the Inquisition with a finger-crushing vise, a skull-cracking clamp, and a spike-studded chair. Groups of little schoolchildren are led through by teachers, who carefully explain the grim exhibits.

At one time or another, all USSR religions have been persecuted by the Soviet government. Yet all faiths have survived, because many parents teach religion to their children. Though forbidden to operate Sunday schools, the churches manage to hold special services for children where sermons are couched in simple language. Thus many children grow up to become religious adults.

The 1937 USSR census asked if people believed in religion, and the Soviet government had to suppress the results. The 1939 census omitted this question, and so did the next censuses in 1959 and during 1970. In private conversations with foreigners, Russian priests estimate that half the Soviet population still believes in religion, with church congregations neither growing nor declining.

Racial and religious diversity results in Soviet cultural diversity. Most of European USSR and southern Siberia have one form or another of European culture. But many inhabitants of the Caucasus and Central Asia follow the Moslem way of life, including such anti-Communist customs as veiled women, polygamy, bride purchase, and child brides. Nomads of the Far North live in much the same crude manner as did their ancestors a thousand years ago.

One might expect a country of vast wastelands, poor communications, and many nationalities to have a decentralized government with much local autonomy. Instead, both Tsarist and Soviet Russia have operated highly centralized states, allowing almost no local authority. Both have apparently feared that, without extreme centralization of power, Russia might fall apart into several separate nations. Though politically oppressive, these centralized authoritarian governments have been of economic value, since the vast Russian realm is a natural economic unit. Such is the country which Karl Marx considered unsuitable for socialist revolution, and which established the first Marxist government in world history.

Suggestions for Further Reading

ALLWORTH, EDWARD, *The Nationality Question in Soviet Central Asia.* New York: Praeger, 1973.

CRESSEY, GEORGE B., *Soviet Potentials: a Geographic Appraisal,* Syracuse: Syracuse University Press, 1962.

HUNTER, HOLLAND, *Soviet Transportation Policy,* Cambridge: Harvard University Press, 1957.

KISH, GEORGE, *Economic Atlas of the Soviet Union,* Ann Arbor: University of Michigan Press, 1960.

LANE, DAVID, *The End of Inequality?—Stratification under State Socialism.* Baltimore: Penguin Books, 1972.

MARSHALL, BIRD, and BLANE, *Aspects of Religion in the Soviet Union, 1917-1967.* Chicago: Chicago University Press, 1971.

MATTHEWS, MERVYN, *Class and Society in Soviet Russia.* New York: Walker, 1972.

MEISSNER, BORIS, ed., *Social Change in the Soviet Union: Russia's Path Toward an Industrial Society.* Notre Dame: Notre Dame University Press, 1972.

NOGEE, JOSEPH L., ed., *Man, State and Society in the Soviet Union.* New York: Praeger, 1972.

PARKER, W. H., *The Superpowers: The United States and the Soviet Union Compared.* New York: Halsted, 1972.

SHIMONIAK, WASYL, *Communist Education: Its History, Philosophy, and Politics.* Chicago: Rand McNally, 1970.

Chapter 2

Marxism-Leninism

The official philosophy of the Soviet state is not Marxism, but Marxism-Leninism. This difference in name is quite important. Originally, Marxism was a statement of general principles for militant socialist overthrow of capitalism, but provided little guidance on the countless crucial decisions required for actual organization and administration of a socialist state. Moreover, some early Marxist theories worked out badly when put into practice. Thus Russian Marxists have been forced to amplify and even modify early Marxism in order to adjust to the economic reality and political possibilities of a particular era. These revisions of Marxism are known as Marxism-Leninism, a philosophy which is not rigid and can be further modified in the future.

The founder of this flexible ideology was Karl Heinrich Marx (1818–1883), son of a German Jewish lawyer who had been converted to Protestant Christianity. Well educated in law, history and philosophy, Marx received a degree of Doctor of Philosophy from the University of Berlin, then devoted the remainder of his life to research and writing. Soon he formed a close lasting friendship with Friedrich Engels (1820–1895), the son of a wealthy German industrialist who owned cotton mills in both Germany and England. While Marx and Engels were residing in Brussels, they founded a shortlived Communist League of Dutch, British, French, German, and Swiss workers, and as League propaganda in 1847 co-authored their most famous pamphlet—the *Communist Manifesto.*

During the 1848 German revolution, the two men returned to Germany where they edited a revolutionary newspaper. After the revolution failed, Marx was arrested, tried for treason, and expelled from Germany. He emigrated to England, where he spent the remainder of his life as an impoverished writer, largely financed by monetary gifts from Engels who joined him in exile. In 1864 Marx helped create the International Working Men's Association (First International), which lasted 12 years before disbanding in failure. Meanwhile in 1867 Marx published the first volume of his major work—*Capital.* He died before he completed volumes II and III, which Engels compiled, edited, and published. Engels retired from industrial management, lived on income from his family properties, and wrote several small books explaining in more detail certain ideas of Marx. Without the benefit of Engels' clear and readable literary interpretations, Marx's writings might never have become famous, since Marx wrote with a dull pedantic pen. Engels' will left all his property to Marx's children.

Shocked by the human misery accompanying the British industrial revolution, which was then taking place, Marx devised what he believed to be a system of scientific socialism to replace capitalism and cure capitalist ills. To provide background, Marx rewrote European history in economic terms, since he believed that economic struggle was the main cause of historical events. He divided history into several distinct economic periods, as follows:

In the prehistoric period before civilization, the cavemen lived under conditions of primitive socialism. Each member of a clan worked to the best of his ability, and the products of the work (mostly hunting and fishing) were divided equally among the clan families.

When mankind learned to farm, thus providing the basis for civilization and the rise of cities, primitive socialism disappeared. Instead the human race divided into two basic classes: the exploiters, who owned the means of production such as land, forests, and mines; and the exploited, who performed labor for the exploiters. The exploiters set up a state, or government, whose main purpose was to oppress labor so that the exploiters would retain wealth and power. In the first civilizations, the exploiters were rich landowners and the exploited were their slaves.

According to Marx, a perfect example of an early slave state was the Roman Empire. Landowners and slaves did not live in harmony, but in constant friction or so-called class struggle. Slave rebellions eventually weakened the Roman Empire, which passed away and was replaced by a new civilization.

Medieval feudalism, the new civilization, by Marx's reasoning was an improvement over the slave state. Again there were exploiters (feudal nobles) and exploited (their serfs). But the medieval serf had more rights than a Roman slave. Serfs could not be bought and sold, possessed little tenant farms within an estate, and were required to work on the noble's big fields only half of each week. Thus the exploited class was better off than before. Nevertheless, class struggle continued, as exemplified in the great peasant revolts within England, France, and Germany. Meanwhile in the late middle ages, a new exploiter class arose, which wrested power from the feudal nobles.

The new exploiter class was the urban merchants or so-called bourgeoisie (people of the city). Besides growing rich from trade, the bourgeoisie operated workshops employing artisans who spun cloth, made shoes, or produced other goods by hand labor. Thus began capitalism, a new civilization superior to feudalism. The main exploited class now consisted of free urban workers, who were not slaves or serfs permanently performing labor without pay for a master. The capitalist worker received a salary, could chose his job, and might even change jobs if he disliked his employer. Still there was class struggle, as exemplified by the formation of craft guilds by workers to oppose the merchant guilds of the rich.

Then came the invention of the steam engine, which by the nineteenth century was sufficiently perfected to make possible the construction of factories mass-producing goods by machine. Marx was tremendously impressed by the vast output of factories, which he considered to be the most important means of production. For the first time since prehistoric days, he reasoned, mankind now had the production capacity to satisfy everyone's needs, if the factories worked full blast and their goods were equally distributed among all people.

But he was disheartened when he carefully examined nineteenth-century capitalism. By paying low wages the capitalist factory owners made exorbitant profits, which Marx called "surplus value." Industrial salaries were so meager that many workers could not afford to buy the products of their own factory. In general Marx believed that under capitalism the rich became richer, while the poor became poorer.

Marx also noted that capitalism has periodic recessions and depressions, which in his opinion were caused by low mass purchasing power due to low factory wages. In short, more is produced than can be sold. Then instead of producing at full capacity, many factories close down partially or completely, throwing their workers into unemployment and onto the street. Cut-throat capitalist competition, even in times of prosperity, may also force inefficient factories to suspend operation, with the same grim results.

Since Marx had divided history into economic periods, each an improvement over the previous era, he refused to believe that imperfect industrial capitalism was the final stage of human economic progress. He was certain that another civilization would succeed capitalism, and this bright future must be socialism. Then the capitalists would be dispossessed, and the people themselves would own the factories and other means of production. Everyone would work to the best of his ability, and must be paid in accordance with his needs. Thus all workers would receive equal pay, regardless of the type of work performed. Industry would produce to its utmost, and its goods would be equally divided among the working population. There would be no recessions or depressions, because wages would be high and profits would almost disappear, except for a small planned profit to invest in industrial growth. No cut-throat competition among factories would exist, since all industry would be owned by and would produce for the people.

Personal savings and inheritance would be abolished in a socialist welfare system, since they would be unnecessary and would promote unsocialist inequality. Complete equality would prevail for all workers, regardless of their race, nationality, or sex. Even marriage might be discarded, to make women more equal to men. Atheism would replace religion, which Marx regarded as an "opiate of the people" used by capitalists to reconcile workers to a life of impoverished labor. In Marx's opinion, untrue religious promises of heavenly bliss after death induced workers to accept suffering on earth.

Marx believed that his type of socialism would inevitably succeed capitalism. In some writings he suggested that this transition might be peaceful by election of socialists to government office. In other articles and pamphlets, particularly the *Communist Manifesto,* he urged violent socialist revolution. As a revolutionary force, Marx chose the industrial workers or so-called proletariat. Naturally he realized that capitalist society is complex, not consisting of workers and capitalists alone, but also including such groups as small storekeepers, private artisans, petty private farmers, tenant farmers, clerks, and intellectuals. By Marx's reasoning, all these groups were exploited by the capitalists but lived well during capitalist prosperity, and therefore tended to support capitalism. In contrast the industrial workers lived poorly even during capitalist prosperity, and would gain much by overthrowing the capitalist system. Furthermore, Marx noted that workers usually resided in slums near their factories, and thus were ideally located for seizure of the industries which were the basis of bourgeois power. In the words of Marx and Engels:

> Let the ruling classes tremble at a Communist revolution. The proletarians have nothing to lose but their chains. They have a world to win. Working men of all countries, unite!

The workers should seize their factories, overthrow the capitalist government, and establish a "dictatorship of the proletariat," which would institute socialism by force. This dictatorship would have a workers' parliament, which should legislate quickly rather than debate endlessly, because the deputies are practical laborers instead of professional politicians. Thus each member of parliament would be a "working deputy," who between legislative sessions returns to his workbench. Civil servants of the executive branch of the proletarian government should also be recruited from the working class, and be paid no more than factory laborers. This dictatorship would continue until all capitalist resistance had been crushed, and the entire population became accustomed to living and working under socialism. Then the proletarian dictatorship would "wither away," being no longer necessary.

Hence the central government would disappear, leaving each region to govern itself under worker democracy.

An extreme socialist economy would not be established immediately after the proletarian revolution. Instead, Marx recommended partial socialism, as described in his ten points for a beginning proletarian state:

> 1. Abolition of property in land and application of all rents of land to public purposes.
> 2. A heavy progressive or graduated income tax.
> 3. Abolition of all right of inheritance.
> 4. Confiscation of the property of all emigrants and rebels.
> 5. Centralization of credit in the hands of the State, by means of a national bank with State capital and an exclusive monopoly.
> 6. Centralization of the means of communication and transport in the hands of the State.
> 7. Extension of factories and instruments of production owned by the State; the bringing into cultivation of wastelands, and the improvement of the soil generally in accordance with a common plan.
> 8. Equal liability of all to labor. Establishment of industrial armies, especially for agriculture.
> 9. Combination of agriculture with manufacturing industries; gradual abolition of the distinction between town and country, by a more equitable distribution of the population over the country.
> 10. Free education for all children in public schools. Abolition of children's factory labor in its present form. Combination of education with industrial production.

Obviously a Marxist revolution should occur in an industrial nation which has a large number of factory workers. Marx believed that the United States was too prosperous for revolution, but that West Europe had the properly explosive combination of great industries and mass poverty. However, in Marx's opinion, a revolution would fail in one West European country alone, because surrounding capitalist nations would overthrow the proletarian state by blockade and war.

Therefore, to be successful, the proletarian revolution must occur almost simultaneously in several industrial countries. These nations would form a "Socialist League" which would constitute a common market by eliminating all tariff barriers among member states. Then each nation would specialize in producing what it best produced, and distribute this output equally throughout the League. Thus a League citizen would receive more and better goods than he could obtain from one socialist country alone.

Militarily the League would be strong enough and large enough to survive capitalist attack. The League would slowly expand, partly by force and partly by attracting more nations into the proletarian confederation. Eventually the entire world should be socialist, with the League changing into a "Communist world-state." Then the whole world would produce goods to the best of each area's ability, and share this output equally among all countries. There would be absolute racial equality, because all races and nationalities would have the same standard of living. Residence would be unimportant, since a person should live equally well in Paris, New York, Siberia, or the Congo. And each year the world living standard would rise together with planned expansion of global industry. Economic quarrels leading to war would be eliminated, so mankind at long last could relax in eternal peace. This would be the final stage in human history—the millennium sought by mankind for more than 50,000 years.

Regardless of the love of humanity expressed by the Communist ideal, Marxism is basically impractical and contains countless flaws. Historians question whether cavemen lived as socialist an existence as Marx believed. Presentday primitive tribes in the Arctic, Africa, and South Pacific usually have a class society even if they are ignorant of the use of metals or fire. Though some slavery always existed in Rome, the Roman Empire was originally created on the basis of free labor. Widespread serfdom arose only when this empire was already in decline. Few contemporary historians would share Marx's belief that the Dark Ages of European feudalism were an improvement over the brilliant culture of the Roman Empire.

In analyzing capitalist economics, Marx failed to foresee the rise of labor unions, labor parties, and even labor governments which have vastly improved the living standard of skilled workers. An average American or West European factory worker today considers himself not a proletarian, but a member of the middle-class. Shortly before Marx died, he wrote a letter to a friend explaining the delay of Volumes II and III of *Capital* on the grounds that Volume I should first be revised. In particular, Marx felt that Volume I had been incorrect by predicting that under capitalism the rich become richer, while the poor grow poorer. Marx died before making this revision. Engels either suppressed or knew nothing about this soul-searching letter, which was recently unearthed and published by a German professor.

Very shallow was Marx's belief that government in a slave, feudal, or capitalist system merely existed as a means of oppression to keep the rich in power. Unquestionably tyrants and corrupt politicians convert government into both means of oppression and a source of wealth. But the basic reason for government is need for social regulation—a set of rules enabling groups of people to live together in relative peace and harmony. Some type of authority must compile, update, and enforce these rules. A traffic light on a street intersection is a good example of government. Obviously traffic signals are required where there are automobiles, whether the government of the country be capitalist, socialist, or fascist. Most motorists obey the red and green lights not because of police oppression, but to avoid accidents. And a government is needed to install and maintain the lights, devise traffic rules, and arrest the driver who doesn't stop on red.

Since social regulation was necessary even in prehistoric days, government is as old as mankind. No modern state can wither away unless replaced by a new government, because the need for social regulation will forever remain.

Superficially Marx would appear to be correct in assuming that mankind's main desire is a good or better standard of living. Certainly almost everyone wants to eat well, dress decently, and be comfortably housed. Yet sociologists and psychologists find people seek more than this. Many artists, writers, and musicians live a precarious existence, but are happy as long as they can pursue an artistic career. The immense popularity of sporting contests can hardly be explained in economic terms. Teaching has long been a poorly paid profession, yet countless intellectuals throughout the world prefer the classroom to more lucrative jobs in business.

Marx died before Western capitalist nations introduced the welfare state and governmental operation of some industries. He didn't live to see how semisocialism alleviates certain capitalist ills, only to create new troubles.

When an industry is nationalized in either East or West, the workers in that branch of production often slow down. Apparently the nationalized laborers feel that they now work for a government which is their own, and therefore need not exert themselves. Complaints about the low productivity of labor in state enterprise constantly appear in the newspapers of both semisocialist Britain and ultrasocialist Russia.

Immense paperwork and bureaucratic bungling plague all governments. Interoffice mail from a room in the US Government's Pentagon sometimes takes two days to reach a room across the hall. The more industry is nationalized, the larger the supervizing government must grow, with red tape increasing by leaps and bounds. During World War II, when the US and USSR were allies, the Soviet Foreign Ministry in a formal diplomatic note once refused an American request for certain information on the grounds that wartime official confusion prevented an answer.

Thus Marxism must be objectively described as an intriguing but impractical vision of Utopia. Judging by actual progress since World War II, a mixed system of capitalism and state enterprise seems to be most successful, as in West Europe, Japan, and the United States. Though the Communist nations of East Europe and Asia have achieved great successes in industry and armament, their people live modestly and agriculture is in frequent crisis.

Yet throughout human history, mankind has fought and died for many unrealistic ideals. Truth or untruth of a philosophy is relatively unimportant, as long as there is widespread belief. From Lenin to Khrushchev's successors, all Soviet leaders thus far have been devout Marxists. Many of Marx's ten features of early Comminism have long been practiced by today's USSR.

As Marx decreed, the USSR has nationalized all land. All credit is in the hands of the state, monopolized by national banks. Transport and communications are under central state control. Most factories are state-owned, wastelands are cultivated, and agriculture is planned.

Also as Marx prescribed, all adult citizens are required to work, and armies of urbanites are sent to the countryside to aid agriculture. All children receive free education in public schools, and education concentrates on industrial training. Needless to say, the property of emigrants and rebels has been confiscated.

But on several important points, the Kremlin does not obey Marx. He called for a heavy progressive income tax. Soviet income taxes are light, the highest rate being 13 per cent of a person's annual earnings. The Soviet rich keep most of their income, in contrast to the American rich who pay the bulk of their high salaries into taxes.

Marx also called for the abolition of all right of inheritance. But inheritance is fully legal in today's USSR, though the state insists that the property of the deceased must be divided among close relatives. Marx demanded that child labor be abolished. At the age of 12, according to Soviet law, children on collective farms must work in the fields.

Marx wrote that the products of labor in a Communist society must be used to enrich the life of the laborer. The products of Soviet labor mainly strengthen the industrial might of the Communist state. Far from being enriched, Soviet workers are poorly paid.

Thus the Soviet state has much of the framework of Marxism. Yet such features as low pay, child labor, and small income taxes on the rich are clearly un-Marxist. Under such revision of Marxism, today's Soviet press rarely quotes Marx. Instead, citations from Lenin and other Soviet leaders interpret Marx both for the USSR masses and for Communist believers throughout the world. Over the years, these interpretations have changed Marxism into Marxism-Leninism. The first major Russian revisionist of Marxism was Vladimir Ilich Ulyanov (1870–1924), much better known under his pseudonym of Lenin.

Born in a family of minor Russian nobility and trained as a lawyer, Lenin devoted most of his life to revolutionary activity. He was one of the early leaders of the Russian Social Democratic Workers Party, founded in 1898 as the first Marxist party in Tsarist Russia. In 1903 he split this party by proposing that its members should be under strict discipline. Lenin's opponents in the party took the name of Mensheviks (members of the minority), and his own followers called themselves Bolsheviks (members of the majority). In 1917, taking advantage of mass political and economic dissatisfaction, Lenin's Bolsheviks seized power in Russia. During 1918 they renamed themselves Communists. Thus Lenin was the founder and first leader of the Soviet Communist Party.

Lenin firmly believed in Marxism, but added certain ideas of his own to Marxist theory. He was certain that socialist revolution could only be achieved by force. Unlike Marx, Lenin did not trust the proletariat to seize power. Instead, he believed that a small, highly disciplined party was needed to lead the proletariat into revolution. He therefore organized his Bolsheviks like a civilian army, which recruited only persons who were completely trustworthy to become a revolutionary "élite."

Thus Lenin, even before his 1917 revolution, organized class distinction among revolutionaries; i.e., Bolshevik party members were superior to the rank-and-file nonparty proletarians. Yet class distinction was the very custom which Marx hoped socialism would eradicate.

Lenin described his Bolshevik party as being organized on the basis of "democratic centralism." This meant, in his words, that all party members could vote on party policy. But once the majority had adopted a particular policy, the minority must support this decision even though they had voted against it.

In practice the party was managed like a dictatorship even before the revolution, since the average party member was never consulted on party policy. A group of party leaders debated and decided party issues, while ordinary party members were expelled if they did not obey leadership decisions. As party founder, Lenin himself usually dominated the decisions of the party leadership which he appointed. In brief, he was boss of his party before the Bolsheviks seized control of Russia, whereupon he became dictator of Russia. Yet Marx had desired a socialist dictatorship by the entire proletariat, not by a single party or a single person.

Lenin died in 1924, and was succeeded by a collective leadership of the Communist party Politburo (policy bureau). After five years of intraparty politics, Joseph Vissarionovich Dzhugashvili (better known under his pseudonym of Stalin) won the struggle for power, becoming party leader and consequently dictator of the USSR.

Son of a poor shoemaker and trained for the Orthodox priesthood, Stalin spent his early manhood as a Bolshevik revolutionary, rising from provincial party leadership into Lenin's first party Politburo. As long as Lenin lived, Stalin did little interpretation of Marxism and was not regarded as a Communist ideologist. However, once firmly in power after Lenin's death, Stalin made many changes in the Soviet system and justified this major reorganization in Marxist terms. To carry out the world socialist revolution desired by Marx, Stalin militarized the USSR and built an enormous heavy industry. To make agriculture pay for this industrialization, he collectivized the Soviet peasantry, i.e., forced them into cooperatives operating under severe state control. Instead of weakening the socialist state, or letting it wither away as Marx had desired, Stalin strengthened the governmental dictatorship even more. In particular, he used the secret police not only as a weapon against the general public, but even against dissident members of the Communist party. Art and literature were placed under strict state control, and ordered to produce only works praising or benefiting Communism. Unequal pay accented Soviet class distinctions. Other features of Stalinism included Russification of minority nationalities, almost open anti-Semitism, and at times considerable toleration of religion.

To many western Marxists, Stalinism was a great perversion of Marxism. Stalinists retorted that Stalin simply adjusted Marxism to reality. At any rate, Stalin usually found quotations from Lenin to justify his tremendous innovations, which became part of the official science of Marxism-Leninism.

Stalin died in 1953, and was succeeded by a collective leadership of the Communist party Presidium (formerly Politburo). After five years of Kremlin intrigue, Nikita Sergeyevich Khrushchev (1894-1971) succeeded Stalin as top leader of the USSR. Son of a poor Ukrainian peasant, Khrushchev had little formal education and in his youth worked as both a shepherd and industrial laborer. Joining the Communist party after the 1917 Bolshevik Revolution, he was first a Red Army officer and then a minor party official during the regime of Lenin. But under Stalin, Khrushchev made a spectacular advance to party leadership of the Ukraine and membership in the USSR Politburo by the late 1930's. As long as Stalin lived, Khrushchev appeared to be a devoted Stalinist with few original ideas concerning Marxism-Leninism.

However in 1956, three years after Stalin's death, Khrushchev strongly denounced his former boss as cruel, vain, and tyrannical. In the name of true Marxism-Leninism, Khrushchev then undertook a number of reforms. Police terror was lessened, and regional governments were given more authority over local industries. State censorship over literature and art became milder, and Khrushchev personally promised fast improvement in the meager Soviet standard of living. These changes may have resulted from expediency rather than Marxist theory. Nevertheless they were incorporated into Marxism-Leninism.

Khrushchev ruled the USSR from 1957 to 1964, personally holding the three top offices of governmental premier, first party secretary, and commander-in-chief of the armed forces. Because he was constantly traveling and making speeches both inside and outside Russia, he had to entrust day-by-day control of the government, party, and army to supposed friends. In a fast bloodless coup during October 1964, these friends removed Khrushchev from power, accusing him of making arbitrary unrealistic decisions which upset the USSR government, party, and economy.

The Brezhnev regime succeeding Khrushchev made little change in the Khrushchevian concept of Marxism-Leninism, except to cease criticizing Stalin. The speeches of Leonid Brezhnev, the Communist party secretary-general, at the last two USSR party congresses have become the official program of Soviet internal and global strategy for the next decade.

In the USSR itself, the program claims to have achieved an advanced stage of socialism progressing slowly toward communism. Socialism is defined as representing unequal pay and some shortages of goods, while communism would bring equal pay and an abundance of goods. However, even under full communism the Soviet state would not wither away, but would retain its power until the entire world will be under Communist rule. There would be increasing USSR democracy each year by involving millions of workers and collective farmers in voluntary activities assisting governmental operation, and in mass discussion of proposed state legislation. The program indicated that the USSR Communist party would survive, wielding supreme power even under communism.

The program promises no civil liberties for the Soviet population. Very clearly, no political parties except the Communist party will be permitted, nor will there be freedom of speech, press, or assembly. Communist state propaganda will continue to persuade the Soviet people that idleness, individualism, love of private property, religion, and non-Communist internationalism (such as respect for the United Nations) are evil. As before, the Communist party will dictate the "proper development" of Soviet literature and art.

With regard to the non-Russian nationalities of the Soviet Union, the program promises to respect their national cultures, which however will gradually merge into a common Communist culture. No tendencies toward excessive national pride or secessionism will be tolerated. The program predicts that slowly the many nationalities within the USSR will "draw together" into a single Soviet nationality.

In internal economics, the program clearly indicates that the Stalinist stress on heavy war-potential industry will continue:

> High growth rates in heavy industry fully retain their importance in the present conditions . . .
>
> Without developing heavy industry we cannot maintain our defense capability at the level necessary to guarantee the country's security . . . Much has been done in this respect . . .
>
> The Soviet Army is now equipped with all types of modern weaponry. The further development of the defense industry, its concrete work programmes, depend in many ways on the international situation. The Soviet Union is prepared to support realistic disarmament measures that consolidate peace and do not impair our security.

By 1980, according to the program, this heavy industry should either equal or exceed that of the world's greatest industrial power—the United States. Considerable expansion of light (consumer goods) industry will also occur, but not as fast or as great.

In agriculture the program states that collective and state farms will be the farmsteads of the future. Private gardens of farmers and suburbanites will slowly lose their present importance, as will the peasant private food markets in the cities. State farms are more socialistic than collective farms.

As for welfare, the program promises that average worker wages will increase, with above-average pay raises for white-collar workers, night-shift employees, collective farmers, and the lowest paid labor. Working women, who have young children, will be granted shorter workdays and shorter work-weeks. Pensions will be raised for manual and white-collar workers, collective farmers, and widows with many children. State store prices for basic foods and consumer goods will be held steady, and for some goods will be reduced. More furniture, television sets, refrigerators, cameras, tape-recorders, and vacuum cleaners will be produced and put on sale. The population will have a better diet from larger quantities of meat, milk, butter, cheese, vegetables, and fruit being available in state stores. Many more tailor shops, shoe-repair stores, public laundries, dry cleaners, restaurants, and other services will be provided.

The program also plans a gigantic construction project to be completed by 1990. Secretary General Brezhnev has said:

> In our long-term plans we can provide for the reconstruction of most towns and villages of our boundless country. At the same time, we shall solve the complex problem of providing every family with a well-appointed flat. So far not a single country in the world has been able to solve such a task. But we are tackling it and will solve it.

Also most urbanites will get gas stoves and running water.

According to the program, the countries of the present Soviet orbit of nations should coordinate their economies by a multinational long-term plan, which will gradually equalize their level of development, strengthen them in the struggle against world capitalism, and be the beginning of a future "single world cooperative of working people." Soviet press comments on the program indicate that the long-range goal is to change the Soviet satellite countries of East Europe into Soviet republics within the USSR.

The program clearly states that the overall goal of the USSR Communist party is to make the entire world communist. In this global endeavor, the Soviet Union will aid foreign Communists to seize power in their respective countries. If possible, communization of the world will be achieved without major nuclear war. The Soviet Union plans to avoid atomic devastation by three main devices: First, the Soviet orbit of nations will arm heavily, thus hoping to frighten capitalist opposition from starting major war. Second, the Soviet bloc of nations and the neutral underdeveloped countries will exert their combined political influence to dissuade capitalist governments from warfare. Third, the Soviet Union will support any pacifist movements in the West, even though these groups be religious or bourgeois.

In Western industrial countries, the program encourages Communist parties to form united fronts with labor, peasants, office workers, intellectuals, and socialist parties. The main target of the united front shall be large-scale capitalists (big business). Such a front in democracies might command enough votes to achieve a parliamentary majority peaceably, and thus institute communism. The Soviet press boasts that millions of West Europeans are already voting Communist.

The program expresses concern over the social welfare measures and partial nationalization of industry already in effect in large Western capitalist countries. These mild socialist changes are obviously viewed by the program as competition to Communist revolution. The program therefore rationalizes that monetary inflation wipes out the gains achieved by the Western proletariat through social security. Similarly the program claims that capitalist governments are controlled by the wealthy, so nationalization of industry simply increases the power of the rich.

Though the USSR will attempt to avoid major war, the program approves small wars by dependent nations for "national liberation." The program states that the USSR will support these struggles, which directly or indirectly should weaken the Western great powers, particularly the United States.

The program insists that detente and peaceful coexistence with Western capitalist countries does not lessen Soviet endeavors for world revolution. The Soviet press states:

> Relaxation of international tension does not and cannot cancel out the laws of class struggle. . . . Detente does not give reactionary regimes a safe-conduct. It does not dispense indul-

> gences for the right to suppress peoples' just struggles for their national and social liberation. It would be equally naive to think that the socialist [Communist] countries must pay for detente with unilateral concessions or that in conditions of detente reactionary imperialist circles will be able to do what they could not do during the cold war.
>
> The principle of peaceful coexistence by no means signifies to refrain from revolutionary struggle. Peaceful coexistence is a particular form of the class struggle between two social systems and is taking place in three main fields: economics, politics, and ideology. The main ground in this historical battle is economics. . . .
>
> Peaceful coexistence cannot apply in any way in the ideological arena. Here there may not and cannot be even temporary truces. The battle against bourgeois ideology is the most decisive and acute battle of principle. In this there can be no compromises.
>
> While consistently defending the cause of peace, the Soviet Union considers it to be its highest revolutionary and international duty to support the class actions of workers against the forces of capital and the struggle of nations for their national and social liberation. This is expressed both by profound solidarity and moral encouragement in these just struggles and by immediate material support in the form of financial aid, provisions and other assistance.

Such is present-day Marxism-Leninism, an attempt to impose Marxism upon the USSR and entire world, yet recognizing and trying to solve the practical problems involved. Very clear is the original Marxist ideology, as well as the revisions by Lenin (a strong Communist party), and Stalin (heavy-industry emphasis, militarism, collectivization of agriculture, and state censorship of literature and art). Khrushchev's promises of Soviet prosperity are also evident. In economics the program shows how the Brezhnev regime is striving to improve low living conditions while simultaneously expanding Soviet heavy industry to be the largest in the world.

The program reaffirms Marx's idea that socialism should be spread throughout the world. All USSR leaders thus far have remained faithful to this crusading ideal of world revolution. Such zeal mainly explains why the USSR annexed Estonia, Latvia, and Lithuania in 1940, and forcibly communized Poland,

East Germany, Czechoslovakia, Hungary, Rumania, Bulgaria, and North Korea after World War II. For the same goal, the Kremlin aided Communist seizure of China in 1949, Tibet in 1950, and North Vietnam in 1954.

Some critics of the USSR consider Soviet leaders to be Russian imperialists, little different from the Tsars. This viewpoint fails to explain the increasing USSR socialism, which has caused many economic difficulties, particularly in agriculture. Other critics describe Kremlin leaders as corrupt priests who have forgotten the original humility of their Marxist faith, but use Marxist propaganda as an excuse for seeking total power. As analogy, there have been many corrupt priests in the Christian, Buddhist, and Moslem religions. But history shows that past corrupt priests often considered themselves righteous religious leaders. In the USSR, real or presumed corruption is probably less important than devotion to Marxism-Leninism.

Marxist world revolution is an adventurous foreign policy, always risking a retaliatory major war. As a result, the USSR must maintain large armed forces and a huge heavy industry to supply them. This armament, in turn, requires high taxes which make the standard of living modest for most of the Soviet population.

Of course, most crusading movements in past history eventually lost their zeal. Thus the Moslems, who started out to conquer the world, eventually learned to live in peace with many of their non-Muhammedan neighbors. Marxism-Leninism is such an elastic theory that a future USSR could abandon world revolution and become a mere socialist great power. At present, however, world revolution remains firm Soviet policy.

Suggestions for Further Reading

ARMSTRONG, JOHN A., *Ideology, Politics and Government in the Soviet Union*. New York: Praeger, 1974.

DRACHKOVICH, MILORAD M., ed., *Marxism in the Modern World,* Stanford: Stanford University Press, 1966.

LENIN, VLADIMIR ILICH, *Collected Works,* New York: International Publishers, 1945.

MARX, KARL, *Capital,* Vols. I, II, and III, Chicago: 1909.

LAZITCH, BRANKO, and DRACHKOVITCH, MILORAD M., *Lenin and the Comintern,* Vol. I. Stanford: Hoover Institution Press, 1972.

MARX, KARL, and ENGELS, F., *The Communist Manifesto,* New York: International Publishers, 1948.

STALIN, JOSEPH, *Foundations of Leninism,* New York: International Publishers, 1939.

WEEKS, ALBERT L., *The Troubled Detente.* New York: New York University Press, 1976.

Chapter 3

The Bolshevik Revolution

As the twentieth century began, the Tsarist Russian Empire was ripe for revolution. Economic dissatisfaction was the main impetus for political unrest. Russia was a predominantly agricultural nation, largely self-sufficient, but with a rather low standard of living. Unlike Western Europe, Russia never developed a large foreign trade because there were no overseas colonies, and home production yielded few surpluses for export. Russia was one of the world's leading grain producers and had a growing industry, but most of its farm and factory output was consumed by its own huge population. Lack of extensive foreign trade held down the standard of living, and further isolated a nation geographically difficult to reach from the outside world. Few tourists visited the Tsarist Empire, nor were they encouraged. An Iron Curtain had long been established by the autocratic government, which feared the infiltration of Western democratic ideals. Thus Russia was underdeveloped, not prosperous, and lived in semi-isolation.

Only one fifth of the population lived in cities. The middle class was small, and with the upper class comprised only one sixth of Russia's people. Another one sixth consisted of manual and office workers. A vast two thirds of the population were poor peasants.

The majority of Russia's huge population thus consisted of peasant private farmers, who were extremely discontented. Until 1861 they had been serfs, bound to the soil and bought and sold by their estate-owning masters. Freed by the liberal Tsar Alexander II, they had received only part of the estate land, for which they paid a 49-year mortgage to the government. Their farms were so small that many peasants barely fed themselves from their own produce, and had little or no surplus crop to sell for profit. Hence they wished to seize and divide the already reduced estates, which still held two fifths of Russia's farmland. In peasant thinking, the addition of estate land would increase their tiny private farms to money-making size.

The industrial workers were another discontented class. Though Tsar Peter the Great (1672–1725) founded the world's largest iron industry by building crude foundries in the Ural Mountains, Russia soon lost its industrial lead under Peter's successors. For almost two centuries, industrial development was retarded by the widespread rural serfdom which Peter himself had made more binding. The peasant serfs of the eighteenth and early nineteenth centuries were too poor a market for manufactured goods to encourage businessmen into fast industrial expansion. Also the serfs could not freely leave the estates to form a pool of factory and mine labor. As a result, the industrial revolution in Tsarist Russia came later than in Western Europe, commencing only after 1861 when the serfs were freed.

Once Russia's industrialization began, it progressed very rapidly. On the eve of World War I, Russia had the fifth largest industry in the world, exceeded only by the United States, Germany, Great Britain, and France. Most Tsarist factories were light industry, producing various consumer goods. Heavy industries like mining, metalworking, and machinebuilding were still small. Yet even the fast-growing light industry was insufficient for the needs of Russia's large population.

Much of Tsarist industry was developed by foreign capital, since Russia's wealthy class consisted mainly of landowners who had little cash funds. By the eve of World War I, three fourths of Russia's bank capital was owned by foreigners. Half of all Russian industry was also in foreign hands, including three fifths of oil mining and nine tenths of electric power production. To aid industrialization, the Tsarist government built and operated a large railway system, second in size only to that of the United States. Though extensive, the Russian railways were inadequate for the vast expanses of the Tsarist Empire. Many peasant villages were still hundreds of miles from the nearest rail station.

Most of the new railways were financed by foreign borrowing, so the Tsarist court had the dubious distinction of owing the largest foreign debt of any government in the world. Many patriotic Russians were appalled by this financial enslavement of Tsarist banking, industry, and government to West European banks and state treasuries.

However, economic nationalism was not the main complaint of the new urban working class. As in most countries during early years of industrial revolution, Russia's workers were poorly paid, labored 12 to 14 hours per day, lived in dirty crowded barracks, and possessed almost no social or political rights. Labor unions were few, hounded by the government, and often led by police agents who concealed their true identity by posing as saviors of the working man. Naturally the urban proletariat was searching for fast revolutionary exit from oppressive misery. Instead of easing discontent, the industrial revolution created a new discontented class.

Labor dissatisfaction was more dangerous for the Tsarist regime than the land hunger of Russia's majority peasantry. Illiterate, superstitious, and residing in isolated villages snowbound much of each year, the peasants were a disorganized mass. In contrast, the urban working class was concentrated in Russia's few large cities—the vital administrative, cultural, and commercial centers of a predominantly rural nation. Though small in number, city workers had a high rate of literacy in a basically illiterate country. An apparently natural Russian desire is thirst for education. When illiterate peasants came to cities to seek their fortune as industrial workers, they soon learned to read and write. Often enough, their teachers were impoverished intellectuals preaching socialist revolution against Tsarist tyranny. Not surprisingly, most workers turned to socialism as quick cure for their many ills.

At first glance, the rise of socialism appears unlikely in a semiliterate and mostly rural nation. But Tsarist autocratic suppression of any moderate democratic movement drove many political reformers to extremes. As early as the mid-nineteenth century, socialist groups formed in Russian cities with drastic programs.

The Nihilists demanded abolition of marriage, religion, and national government. By attempting to assassinate monarchs and other government leaders, the Anarchists hoped to shock society into ending all government, law, religion, monopoly capitalism, and war. Meanwhile the Slavophiles believed Russia could save itself only by repudiating Western customs, abolishing the governmental bureaucracy, and returning to pure Christian brotherhood and peasant village democracy. The Populists actually undertook a crusade into peasant villages in a vain attempt to unite the countryside for eventual revolution against Tsarist autocracy. Some of the more militant Populists formed the "People's Will" society, which tried to overthrow Tsarism by killing top government officials. Tsardom was not overthrown, but the People's Will managed to assassinate two national police chiefs, a provincial governor, and Tsar Alexander II—the liberator of the serfs.

In such a radical climate, it was inevitable that some Russian intellectuals would embrace Marxism. In 1898, nine Marxists met in the provincial city of Minsk and founded the "Russian Social-Democratic Workers Party." Thus the presentday USSR Communist Party was born. But in 1898 the party almost died in childbirth, when Tsarist police immediately arrested most of the nine founders.

The tiny party decided to hold a second meeting (or so-called "second congress") in 1903 in the Belgian city of Brussels, safely out of reach of the Tsarist police. The Belgian government took a dim view of this conspiratorial meeting, so the 43 delegates had to complete their deliberations in London. Here Vladimir Lenin split the party by proposing that members be under absolute discipline. Lenin desired a Marxist organization similar to a civilian army, which only the most trusted revolutionaries would be permitted to join. If necessary, a party member must sacrifice his life to fulfill orders from the party leadership.

Other Russian Marxists, including Leon Trotsky, strongly opposed such a military-type party. A majority of the 1903 delegates voted for Lenin, and thereafter became known as Bolsheviks—a Russian word meaning members of the majority. Lenin's opponents took the name of Mensheviks—members of the minority.

The vote was close, and Lenin won only because some of his adversaries went home before the congress ended.

Stalin in 1903 was a Caucasian Marxist leader who did not attend the Brussels-London congress. After learning about the party schism, Stalin quickly joined the Bolsheviks.

At first the Bolsheviks and Mensheviks considered their dispute a temporary family quarrel. Other congresses of the Russian Social Democratic Workers Party were held to bring the two factions together. But the disagreement proved permanent, and soon extended beyond conflict on party organization. In 1912 Lenin made the Bolsheviks a separate party by establishing his own central committee—a small group of 12 men, including Stalin and Tsarist police agent Malinovski. This committee was the start of Stalin's eventual rise to power. The clever Malinovski shared top Bolshevik secrets until Lenin's 1917 revolution, when Tsarist police archives were examined by the victorious Bolsheviks, who quickly executed Malinovski.

Though small in number, the Bolsheviks and Mensheviks were fated to become two of the three most popular political parties in Russia during World War I. Both were Marxist, but widely differed on strategy of revolution.

Bolsheviks advocated violent socialist revolution, with the urban proletariat as the main revolutionary force. However, Lenin considered the city workers too politically immature to revolt by themselves; he believed that the Bolshevik Party must lead them. Peasant support was deemed necessary for revolutionary success, so the Bolsheviks promised to divide among the peasants the lands of the great estates. The Russian revolt would presumably be the first stage in a larger European revolution, which in turn should lead to communization of the entire world.

In contrast, the Mensheviks were more moderate, with faith in gradual socialization by parliamentary means. They trusted the urban proletariat, and desired a large workers' party which could act by itself, rather than under Bolshevik leadership. In Menshevik reasoning, the socialist takeover must be preceded by a bourgeois revolution like the American of 1776 or French of 1789, in which the workers should support the Russian bourgeoisie against Tsarist autocracy. There was little Menshevik interest in either the peasantry or world revolution.

Neither the Bolsheviks nor the Mensheviks were Russia's largest socialist party. Both were outnumbered by the non-Marxist "Social-Revolutionaries"—the successors of the nineteenth-century Populists. The Social Revolutionaries had an agrarian program of land reform, which the Bolsheviks had copied. Most Social Revolutionaries believed in peaceful socialization, but some assassinated governmental leaders in the tradition of the old People's Will.

Democratic parties were organized by the middle and upper classes early in the twentieth century, the two largest being the conservative Octobrists and the liberal Constitutional Democrats (Cadets). The Octobrists desired a strong Emperor assisted by a weak legislature, while the Cadets wanted a constitutional monarchy granting much power to the elected parliament. Neither bourgeois party enjoyed mass support, because there was no large middle class when so much of Russian industry and banking was owned and managed by foreigners. The Tsarist upper class was not only few in number, but divided. Russian merchants and factory owners were a generally despised group of nouveau riche, socially unacceptable to the old landed aristocracy. The latter had originally been a military caste, but by the nineteenth century was no longer required to perform military service. Once their military duty had been abolished, many nobles degenerated into a life of pleasure with little interest in political, social, or economic reform.

Though Tsarist Russia was a deeply religious nation, the clergy failed to halt the rise of socialism. The biggest church, the Russian Orthodox, had been forced to become a virtual branch of government since the reign of Tsar Peter the Great. Village priests even collected some governmental taxes. As a result, the Orthodox clergy had little prestige, and were often viewed by the lower classes as a sort of spiritual police.

Contributing to the mass discontent in the Russian Empire was the racial policy of the Tsarist government. Since the nineteenth century, Tsardom tried callously to Russify its national minorities, who taken together amounted to almost half of Russia's population. For a hundred years, Ukrainians were forbidden to construct buildings in their national architectural style. The periodic Polish rebellions against Russian rule were ruthlessly suppressed.

To avoid Tsarist censorship, much Lithuanian national literature had to be published in Germany, then smuggled into Lithuania.

Russification of minorities became particularly oppressive during the reigns of Alexander III and Nicholas II, the last two Tsars. Suffering the most were the Jews, whose communities had to endure periodic pogroms conducted by "Black Hundred" gangs which were tolerated by the Tsarist government. In self-defense, Jewish workers united in a socialist society entitled the "Bund," which at times cooperated with the Bolsheviks.

Yet with all these weaknesses, and all the mass discontent, the Tsarist court was not seriously threatened by revolution until Russia began losing wars.

Russian military weakness in the twentieth century was first revealed during the Russo-Japanese War of 1904–1905. Angered by Tsarist attempts to infiltrate Korea and create a "yellow Russia" in Manchuria, Japan besieged and stormed Port Arthur, the Manchurian base of Russia's Pacific navy. Retreating Tsarist troops, numbering 300,000, lost 120,000 men in a disastrous battle near the Manchurian capital of Mukden. Arriving in the north Pacific after a troublesome trip halfway around the world, Russia's Baltic fleet was cut to pieces by Japanese torpedo boats while trying to reach Vladivostok by sneaking through the narrow Tsushima Straits between Korea and Japan. Of the 20 Baltic warships, 17 were sunk. Three escaped by fleeing to neutral Chinese ports.

Exhausted financially, Japan concluded a lenient peace, annexing south Sakhalin Island and establishing a sphere of influence in south Manchuria and all Korea. Meanwhile European Russia erupted into a spontaneous revolution. The distant war for alien territories had never been popular, and defeat aroused latent worker and peasant discontent. Widespread strikes started among urban workers, the most dangerous being a nationwide walkout by railwaymen. In many rural districts, peasants began to seize and divide the nobles' estates.

Not one of Russia's three major socialist parties—Bolsheviks, Mensheviks, or Social Revolutionaries—anticipated or was ready for the 1905 spontaneous revolution. Lenin, living in West Europe to avoid Tsarist arrest, returned to Russia only to find that the abortive revolt was over. Stalin helped organize strikes in his native Caucasus, but did nothing of national importance. Of all later Communist leaders, only Trotsky participated actively in the 1905 revolution. During 1905, factory workers spontaneously organized soviets (councils) at their places of work. In turn, factory soviets elected city soviets, which in 1905 challenged urban governments for power. The St. Petersburg soviet in the Tsarist capital claimed to represent all city soviets, and consequently the entire urban proletariat. Trotsky was vice-chairman of the St. Petersburg soviet until his arrest by the Tsarist police.

In an attempt to calm the rebels, a Tsarist Manifesto of October 1905 promised an elected legislature, or so-called Duma. However, the Tsar could veto Duma legislation, and issue his own decrees when the Duma was not in session. Russian troops returning from the Far East after the Russo-Japanese war suppressed the last remnants of rebellion during 1906. The first Duma was elected on a franchise heavily weighted in favor of the upper class and peasants.

Had Tsar Nicholas II realized that his autocracy was obsolete, he would have shared authority with the Duma, gradually converting Russia into a constitutional monarchy. But the Tsar was politically inept and feared any major reduction of court power. This weak, pleasant man, more interested in family pleasures than affairs of state, was completely dominated by his ambitious German wife. She came from minor Teutonic nobility, enjoyed her vast power as Russian Empress, and had no intention of yielding her authority to parliamentary government.

Thus the Duma became a lost opportunity to democratize Russia and stave off future revolution. In May 1906 the first Duma convened with a majority of Cadets. Though this assembly was striving only for constitutional monarchy, it voiced intense opposition to many Tsarist policies. The Tsar became alarmed, and in July dissolved the Duma. A second Duma was elected with many members of the first Duma forbidden to be candidates for legislative office. Yet the second Duma proved to be much more radical than the first. After four months the Tsar dissolved this parliament, arrested its few Social-Democratic members, and disenfranchised large sections of the population for elections to the third Duma.

When the third Duma met in 1907, a plurality was held by

the Octobrists, whose program called for realization of the Tsarist political concessions of October 1905. Far shrewder than the leaders of the first two Dumas, the Octobrists achieved considerable legislative power without overly antagonizing the Tsar. Therefore the third Duma served its full five-year term. Marxist influence on this Duma was negligible, a mere 18 of the total 442 deputies being Social-Democratic. Fear of Tsarist police compelled Lenin himself to flee again to west Europe, and he did not return until 1917.

The fourth Duma was elected in 1912, had a conservative majority, and was still in office when the Tsar abdicated in 1917. This legislature contained only six Bolshevik members, one of whom was Malinovski, the Tsarist police spy. Stalin opened the Bolshevik newspaper *Pravda* in 1912, but was arrested in 1913 and exiled to Siberia, where he remained till 1917. At this point, Bolshevism appeared to have become a lost cause.

Though Russia did not become a constitutional monarchy, the able Premier Peter Stolypin achieved national stability till 1911 by a combination of agrarian reform and brute force. On the one hand, he instituted field court-martials for political rebels, and created such a reign of terror that hangmen's nooses came to be known as "Stolypin neckties." Simultaneously Stolypin tried to break up the antiquated "mir" system, whereby peasant villages owned their land in common, were collectively responsible for paying taxes, and apportioned strips of each type of land to every village family. He issued a series of edicts permitting peasants to withdraw their land from village control, and own it in perpetuity as individual farms. Thus Stolypin hoped to form a new class of independent peasant farmers, who would prosper outside the mir and probably support the Tsarist government which gave the opportunity for this prosperity. This agrarian reform had considerable success. From 1906 to 1915, a total of 2 million peasant households withdrew their land from village ownership, prospered, and joined the ranks of the "kulaks" (rich peasants) who so bitterly opposed Soviet collectivization of agriculture two decades later.

As years of industrial expansion succeeded the economic turmoil of the Russo-Japanese War and 1905 Revolution, labor unrest gradually subsided. In 1906 one million Russian workers went on strike; in 1908, 174,000; and by 1910, a mere 46,000. Meanwhile Russia's foreign affairs in Asia were unusually calm. In the Far East, Russia and its former enemy Japan cooperated to keep other powers out of Manchuria. Outer Mongolia and Tannu Tuva were peacefully converted into Russian protectorates. In the Near East, Russia and its old rival England agreed to carve Persia into spheres of influence.

During late 1911, Premier Stolypin was assassinated by a secret policeman who was a Social-Revolutionary. As he died, Stolypin correctly predicted that his death meant the fall of Imperial Russia. He was succeeded by a series of totally incompetent cabinet ministers.

Revolutionary ferment again arose in the Russian homeland during 1912, when Tsarist troops shot several hundred workers on strike at the Lena goldfields in East Siberia. A wave of sympathy strikes began throughout Russia, and 400,000 laborers left work for May Day demonstrations. Each year thereafter, strikes became more frequent. By early 1914, 1,400,000 workers were striking, and labor unrest was more widespread than during 1905. Russia again was ready for revolution.

Meanwhile, ever since the Russo-Japanese War, Russia had been pursuing an adventurist policy in the Balkans. Attempts were made to block southward expansion of Austro-Hungary, which had annexed Slavic Bosnia-Herzegovina during 1908. Tsarist diplomats helped organize Bulgaria, Serbia, Greece, and Montenegro into a Balkan League, which during 1912 fought a successful war against Turkey. Russia had hoped that the League would also be a bulwark against Austro-Hungary, but in 1913 the League members warred with each other over division of the Turkish territories they had conquered. Above all, Russia was trying to prevent Austria and Germany, two Teutonic allies, from dominating the Turkish Straits, which link the Black and Mediterranean Seas.

After Serbian conspirators assassinated the heir to the Austro-Hungarian throne in 1914, the Tsarist government encouraged Serbia to resist excessive Austrian demands. Because of this Austro-Serbian dispute, Russia ordered a general mobilization as a precautionary measure, since Russian communications were poor and the Tsar feared war might catch his country unprepared. Germany, Austria's ally, viewed this mobilization as an aggressive act, and on August 1 declared war. Russia's allies, France and Britain, then commenced hostilities against Germany. Thus began World War I, in which Russia fought against Germany, Austro-Hungary, Bulgaria, and Turkey.

Tsardom was willing to risk war mainly to block Austrian expansion into the Balkans. But a second major motive was to unite the Russian people in a common war effort, and thus divert the workers and peasants from their discontent. For a short time, this appeal to patriotism was successful. War enthusiasm was great in Russia, strikes subsided, and most political parties—including the Mensheviks and Social Revolutionaries—supported the war effort.

The sole significant exception was Lenin's Bolshevik Party, which opposed World War I from the very start. As early as November 1914, leading Bolsheviks called for a new International of world socialist parties, each to oppose the war in its respective country. As a result of such agitation, the Tsarist government considered the Bolsheviks traitors, arrested the Bolshevik members of the Duma, and exiled them to Siberia for the duration of the war.

Despite this suppression at home, leading Bolshevik émigrés continued the antiwar propaganda abroad. Demanding that the war effort be sabotaged, Lenin helped organize the Zimmerwald Conference of European socialists in 1915, and the second Zimmerwald Conference during 1916, both in Switzerland. His appeal fell on deaf ears. So Lenin and a small group of exile followers printed pacifist literature, unread by socialists but widely used by the German government to dishearten Russian prisoners of war. Meanwhile underground Bolsheviks within Russia created strong conspiratorial organizations at Kronstadt (the large naval base in Petrograd harbor), and among Tsarist troops along the Baltic front.

As World War I progressed, Russia fell into great difficulties which reached a climax at the beginning of 1917. The world's largest Slav state was not conquered, deeply invaded, or overcome by overwhelming military defeat. The Tsarist army fought bravely and well throughout the war. Nothing was lost to the enemy except western borderlands in Poland and the lower Baltic states. Wartime collapse in 1917 came not in the Tsarist army but on Russia's home front, which could neither supply the army nor even keep itself going.

Although Tsarist Russia had the fifth largest industry on earth, factories mainly manufactured consumer goods. Cotton cloth spinning was the biggest branch of industry, and steel mills and metalworking plants were too few for large-scale armament. On the eve of World War I, Russia manufactured neither automobiles nor tractors. Tsarist output of iron ore, the raw material for steel, was below that of Spain, and Russia stood fifteenth in the world in use of electric power. Thus Russian heavy industry was too small and underdeveloped to produce the huge quantities of munitions consumed by modern war. Sensing this deficiency, Tsarism in peacetime had prudently built up a stockpile of military supplies, which were believed to be enough for any war emergencies.

When hostilities broke out in 1914, like all major Powers, Russia was stunned by the enormous munition requirements of the first truly modern war. Soon after the shooting started, Tsarist arms proved sadly lacking in variety. Sole exception to this rule was naval shipbuilding, which won wartime glory by completing four battleships. Yet for a war in which new and better land weapons were vital, Russia could manufacture no more than a few types of guns and ammunition. In the second year of war, Russia began building its first aircraft factories. They still lay unfinished two years later, when the Bolshevik Revolution exploded.

But the main trouble was not lack of variety. It was shortage of even simple weapons. After many years of the most careful stockpiling, Russia's munition reserves were completely consumed during the first three months of war. About 100 government arsenals and private plants tried vainly to fill the gap, and performed real production miracles. From 1913 to 1916, Tsarist output of bullets tripled, while rifle production upped twenty times.

Great as these production achievements were, they could not solve the severe shortage of weapons. For the Russian army numbered a vast 12 million. Four fifths of the large cannon and three fourths of the machine guns used by the Russian wartime army were imported by sea from England, France, and America. Even most shells came from abroad. At the front, the Germans had twenty times as many artillery shells as the Russians. At times, there was only one rifle for every three Tsarist infantrymen. When a rifleman fell in battle, his unarmed comrade grabbed the gun. Russian reinforcements arrived at the front without guns, but no rifles could be found to equip them.

Under these crippling handicaps, the Tsarist army fought the only possible way—with blood. A former American military observer in Russia vividly recalls the battle carnage:

> I believe that Russians are the bravest people in the world. Late in World War I, my station was on the Riga front. The Russian troops there were not the second or third, but the fifth army defending that front. The first four armies had already been slaughtered. I watched the Russians go over the top. They had only one rifle for every four soldiers, not every three. Those brave boys charged the German trenches without a whimper, and fought with bare hands. Russian losses were terrible, but the front was held.

Bad as the situation was at the front, the rear was even worse. Slowly but surely, the whole Russian economy crumbled under the heavy strain of war. With millions of peasants and farm horses drafted into the army, many fields went untilled, and harvests slumped badly. Railways clogged up with war shipments and broke down, unable to carry the extra load. This combination of low harvests and weak transport soon made feeding the cities a real problem. In 1916, less than half the normal amount of grain came to towns from farms to feed urban populations. By early 1917, Russia's largest cities had just two days' supply of bread on hand, a thin margin from famine.

Factories also reached the sad state of having no more than two days' reserves of raw materials and fuel. Plants began to close for lack of supplies, thus creating vast unemployment. By 1917, all industrial production sank to less than half of its prewar level. Meager as munitions output was, the ailing railways could not bring it all from factory to front.

In March 1917, hungry workers rioted against the Tsar in Russia's capital, Petrograd. Petrograd's boulevards had seen many riots, both before and during the war. But this time the revolt could not be suppressed. Instead of whipping, shooting, and sword slashing the mob, the Tsar's trusted Cossacks rode up peaceably. Gently edging their horses into the crowd, they said:

> Don't be afraid. We won't hurt you. We are ordinary people too.

With rioters and riot-breakers uniting in the nerve center of all Russia, imperial autocracy was doomed. Tsar Nicholas II, the last Romanov ruler, had to abdicate his throne. Next day, all Tsarist policemen seemed to have vanished from the face of the earth. None dared don his uniform, once the "little white father" was gone. Russia's parliament, the conservative Duma, then offered the crown to a liberal Grand Duke, the Tsar's brother Michael. He hurriedly declined, seeing little future for Tsarism.

Almost immediately after the Tsar's abdication, workers, soldiers, and sailors established a Petrograd Soviet, such as had existed during the 1905 Revolution. This new soviet and a Duma committee then established a state cabinet headed by Prince Georgi Lvov. This so-called Provisional Government consisted of representatives of the Cadets and Octobrists, plus Alexander Kerenski, a leader of the Social Revolutionaries. France, Britain, and America immediately recognized the Provisional Government, and loaned it arms and money. Partly from belief in Allied duty, and also to gain the Turkish Straits, the Provisional Government recklessly continued the war. And like the Tsar, the new regime was unable to remedy the economic depression caused by World War I. Throughout 1917, peasants began spontaneously and illegally to seize large estates, and the Provisional Government was too weak to stop them. Meanwhile the Tsar's successors were continually threatened by worker demonstrators in the large cities.

Soon after the Petrograd Soviet was formed, other soviets arose spontaneously throughout Russia. Whereas the soviets of the 1905 revolution had been created primarily by city workers, their 1917 counterparts were organized both in the cities and among military units. At first the Social Revolutionaries and Mensheviks held a majority in the soviets, and the Bolsheviks were in the minority. In a spirit of democracy the Provisional Government had legalized the Bolshevik Party, and permitted the Bolshevik Duma deputies to return from Siberian exile. The Bolsheviks were quick to take advantage of their newly found freedom, and developed intensive propaganda against both the war and the Provisional Government.

In April 1917 the German government permitted Lenin and other prominent Bolshevik émigrés to leave Switzerland, cross Germany in a sealed railway car, and thus re-enter Russia via Scandinavia. The Germans hoped that Lenin would help stop the war on the eastern front, leaving Germany free to fight only the Western Allies. Lenin's arrival in Petrograd immediately gave the Bolsheviks a strong leadership, which until then had been lacking under Stalin. In his famous "April Theses," Lenin at once called upon the soviets to overthrow the Provisional Government and establish a "Soviet Socialist Republic." He coined the slogan "All Power to the Soviets," which in fact already shared power with the Provisional Government. Correctly estimating the mood of the Russian people, the Bolsheviks also issued a slogan demanding "Bread, Peace, and Land"—bread for the city workers, distribution of estate land to the peasants, and peace for the war-weary nation.

During April, there were peace demonstrations in Petrograd by mobs of workers. The frightened Provisional Government reorganized itself into a more representative coalition. Mensheviks joined the cabinet, and more Social Revolutionaries were added. In June the First All-Russian Congress of Soviets assembled in Petrograd, with the vast majority of delegates being Mensheviks and Social Revolutionaries. Of the 800 soviet deputies, only 100 were Bolsheviks.

During July 1917, a huge spontaneous demonstration of armed workers and soldiers broke out in Petrograd, demanding that all governmental authority be transferred to the soviets. The Bolsheviks considered this demonstration to be premature, since the soviets were still controlled by Mensheviks and Social Revolutionaries. Yet the Bolsheviks dared not oppose the mob, and halfheartedly supported the demonstration, which was suppressed by the Provisional Government with much bloodshed. After this uprising, Prince Lvov resigned the governmental premiership, which was assumed by the Social Revolutionary, Kerenski. Blaming the guiltless Bolsheviks for the demonstration, Kerenski suppressed the Bolshevik Party. The Bolsheviks were falsely branded as German agents, and Lenin fled into a Finnish forest to avoid governmental arrest.

In August a half-secret Bolshevik Party congress was held in Petrograd, with Lenin absent and Stalin presiding. This congress welcomed Leon Trotsky into the Bolshevik Party, and elected him a member of the party's Central Committee. Trotsky, recently arriving from New York via Canada, had finally decided at this critical time to join forces with Lenin, whom he had previously opposed.

Soon after this congress a counter-revolution was attempted by Tsarist general Lavr Kornilov, commander-in-chief of the Russian armies on the Baltic and Polish fronts. Not bothering to conceal his plans, Kornilov sent troops toward Petrograd to overthrow the Provisional Government and establish a military dictatorship. Fearing that the Petrograd garrison was not strong enough to resist Kornilov, Premier Kerenski asked the Bolsheviks for help. By this time the Bolsheviks had armed large numbers of Petrograd workers (the so-called Red Guards) for insurrection against Kerenski, and also wielded great influence among the sailors of the Kronstadt naval base. After a stormy argument as to whether Kerenski was worth saving, the Bolshevik Central Committee decided to defend the Provisional Government against Kornilov. Lenin reasoned that Kerenski had publicly revealed governmental weakness and thus would appear ridiculous following Kornilov's defeat. Then the Bolsheviks could easily overthrow the Provisional Government.

In practice the Kornilov counter-revolution was almost comic. Railway workers refused to transport his troops, who began to desert as the military crusade neared Petrograd. He was easily defeated, dismissed, and later died fighting the Bolsheviks during the Russian Civil War.

Yet this comic opera put the Bolsheviks in a very strong position, as Lenin had expected. Since the Bolsheviks had helped save Kerenski's government, he no longer dared oppress them. Lenin's prestige was high, and his Bolshevik Party falsely claimed full credit for preventing a military coup d'état. In the autumn of 1917, the Bolsheviks won majorities in the soviets of Moscow, Petrograd, and other key cities. Many left-wing Social Revolutionaries and radical Mensheviks began to support Bolshevik appeals. The Bolshevik Party itself had grown sixfold from a small membership of 40,000 in March 1917 to 240,000. The rural villages were in anarchy, with peasant seizures of landowners' estates multiplying rapidly. Bolsheviks had also infiltrated and gained control of the Petrograd military garrison, the Kronstadt naval base, and many governmental troop units on the front.

Under these favorable circumstances, Lenin decided to seize power by force. The Bolshevik-dominated Petrograd Soviet established a Military Revolutionary Committee to be the rebel general staff. Trotsky, head of both the soviet and the committee, gave secret instructions to Petrograd's soldiers, sailors, and Red Guards to be ready. Bolshevik couriers were dispatched from Petrograd to Helsinki, the Ukrainian front, and the Ural and Donets Basin industrial regions to prepare a coordinated uprising. Learning about the widespread plot, Kerenski on November 6, 1917, tried to suppress a Bolshevik newspaper in Petrograd. This defiant gesture served as a signal for Bolshevik action, and on November 7 local soldiers and sailors seized Petrograd almost without bloodshed and overthrew the Provisional Government. Premier Kerenski fled from the capital, disguised as a female nurse. This Bolshevik revolution was so quick and easy that little shooting could be heard, the city was calm and quiet, and in the suburbs people shopped, strolled, and dined as if nothing unusual had happened. Moscow fell to the Bolsheviks a few days later, and the rest of Russia quickly followed suit.

World War I had hurled Russia into such chaos and despair that a small military revolt was enough to put Lenin into power. The world was stunned, and so were the Bolsheviks.

Suggestions for Further Reading

CONQUEST, ROBERT, *V. I. Lenin*. New York: Viking, 1973.

CURTISS, JOHN S., *The Russian Revolution of 1917*, New York: Van Nostrand, 1957.

GOLDER, FRANK A., *Documents of Russian History, 1914–1917*, New York: Century, 1927.

KERENSKY, ALEXANDER, *Russia and History's Turning Point,* New York: Duell, Sloan and Pearce, 1965.

PARES, BERNARD, *The Fall of the Russian Monarchy,* New York: Knopf, 1939.

ROBINSON, GERARD T., *Rural Russia under the Old Regime,* New York: Macmillan, 1949.

SCHAPIRO, LEONARD, *The Communist Party of the Soviet Union.* New York: Random House, 1970.

SETON-WATSON, HUGH, *The Decline of Imperial Russia, 1855–1914,* New York: Praeger, 1952.

TROTSKY, LEON, *History of the Russian Revolution,* New York: Simon and Schuster, 1936.

TUCKER, ROBERT C., *Stalin as Revolutionary, 1879-1929.* New York: Norton, 1973.

WEEKS, ALBERT L., *The First Bolshevik. A Political Biography of Peter Tkachev.* New York: New York University Press, 1968.

WOLFE, BERTRAM D., *Three Who Made a Revolution,* New York: Dial, 1949.

Chapter 4

The Russian Civil War

"My God, we won! What do we do now?" said Lenin and Trotsky to each other across a desk in Petrograd's Smolny Girls Institute, which the Bolsheviks used as revolutionary headquarters, dispossessing the aristocratic girls.

What they did, after recovering from the shock of revolutionary victory, was a combination of expediency and Marxist idealism. The Provisional Government was abolished, and workers' soviets became the central, regional, and local state parliaments. A governmental cabinet was established with Lenin as premier, Trotsky foreign minister, and Stalin—minister of non-Russian nationalities. Since "minister" was considered an obsolete bourgeois word, the new cabinet ministers were called "People's Commissars." Former courts and police were also dismissed, and they were replaced by people's courts (mass meetings) and workers' militia (armed civilians). All authority in the army and navy was transferred to soldiers' and sailors' soviets, who elected their officers. Similarly, teachers lost control of schools and colleges, which were now managed by committees of students and janitors.

The nobility were deprived of their ranks and titles. Parochial and Sunday schools were forbidden. The church was divorced from the state, and all church buildings and sacred decorations were nationalized. If a congregation wished to conduct services, the chapel and its interior furnishings had to be rented at high prices from the state.

Church marriage became illegal, and only civil weddings were recognized by the law. The "postcard divorce" was instituted, by which, after a petition by one spouse to a court, his or her mate received a postcard announcing legal separation. A Baltic sailor took advantage of these regulations to marry and divorce 20 times during one month. Such marital freedom was intended to grant equality to women, who also were permitted to receive the same jobs and pay as men.

To cope with Russia's numerous racial minorities, the Soviet government issued a "Declaration of Nationalities", drafted by Stalin, promising regional autonomy, racial equality, respect for minority cultures, and the right of minorities to secede. Finland immediately requested freedom, which Stalin personally granted in a speech at Helsinki. Though Poland was under German occupation, a group of Polish refugees obtained a Soviet treaty proclaiming Polish independence. Thus at first, Soviet Russia actually permitted minorities to secede.

These innovations might be described as Marxist idealism, producing radical social transformations. In contrast, the economic policy of the new Bolshevik government was cautious. The banks, communications, foreign trade, and natural resources were slowly nationalized. But in industry and commerce, only the larger enterprises were taken over by the state. Great difficulty was encountered in establishing state control over nationalized enterprises, because of the lack of skilled industrial administrators among the Bolshevik revolutionaries. Lenin's government even requested former Tsarist owners and managers of nationalized plants to act as Soviet administrators. In many factories and mines, committees of plant workers took control and operated the enterprise for the sole benefit of its personnel, regardless of the industrial needs of the central government. This so-called "workers' control" created virtual economic anarchy. Many factories manufactured only goods easily sold on the local market. A Soviet merchant ship struck a reef, while its sailors were arguing which course should be steered to avoid shipwreck.

In theory, all land was nationalized in the rural regions. But in fact the peasants seized and divided the estate land, adding it to their small private farms. Thus Russian agriculture changed in a few weeks from a mixture of great estates and small farms to almost complete farming by smallholders. The Soviet government set up committees of poor peasants to make an equitable distribution of the estate lands. In practice, however, peasants living near the estates simply divided the confiscated land among themselves, while distant peasant households received little or no land. Meanwhile the Bolsheviks made no attempt to socialize farming, except for a few model state and collective farms organized on estates which government officials managed to seize and keep from the peasants.

In foreign affairs, at first Marxist idealism prevailed. A peace appeal was issued to all governments and all nations fighting World War I for an immediate armistice without annexations and without indemnities. Among other statements, the peace appeal said:

> The (Soviet) Government considers it the greatest crime against humanity to continue this war for the sake of dividing among the powerful and wealthy nations the weaker nationalities which they have conquered. . . .
>
> The Government abolishes secret diplomacy and on its part expresses the firm intention to conduct all negotiations absolutely openly before the entire people; it will at once begin to publish in full the secret treaties concluded or confirmed by the (Provisional) Government of landowners and capitalists from February to October 25, 1917. The Government denounces absolutely and immediately all the provisions of these secret treaties designed, as they were in the majority of cases, to secure profits and privileges for Russian landowners and capitalists, and to retain or increase the territories annexed by the Great Russians.

The most important of these secret treaties was the Anglo-French agreement for Russia to control the Turkish Straits after the war. Denunciation of this aggressive pact pleased Turkey, but the general peace appeal was greeted by deaf ears throughout the capitalist world.

Meanwhile the Soviet Government issued a special "Manifesto to the Moslems" promising an end to mistreatment of Russia's 30 million Mohammedans, and abrogation of Tsarist special privileges in Near Eastern countries such as Iran. The manifesto solemnly declared that Istanbul should forever remain Moslem.

These promises created a favorable impression in Turkey and Iran, but were largely ignored by the Moslems of Russian Central Asia.

When the general peace appeal failed, the Bolsheviks concluded an armistice with Germany and other Central Powers on December 15, 1917. Then Marxist idealism was confronted with power politics in the first major diplomatic negotiations of the Soviet government early in 1918 at the Polish city of Brest-Litovsk. A Soviet delegation headed by foreign minister Leon Trotsky, including two workers and two peasants to be properly proletarian, attempted to make peace with the Central Powers. Because Russia was losing the war, and also because of socialist pacifism, the Bolsheviks requested peace without annexations and without indemnities. The German delegation cynically replied that defeated Russia must pay indemnities and surrender its western borderlands. Since the peasant backbone of the Russian army had gone home to share in the division of estates, the Soviet government was in no position to continue the war. On the other hand, the German demands seemed too harsh to accept. So Trotsky made his famous "no peace, no war" declaration that Russia would not continue fighting, yet refused to sign a peace treaty on German terms. The naiveté of this Soviet attitude soon became painfully obvious. German armies advanced with no opposition, soon overran the Ukraine, and reached the Caucasus—1,000 miles beyond the line of farthest Teutonic advance against the Tsarist army.

The Soviet government was thrown into temporary confusion. Lenin and Trotsky frantically offered to continue the war in alliance with the Western democracies, if they would aid Soviet power. Though France, Britain, and the United States had broken diplomatic relations with Russia after the Bolshevik revolution, unofficial representatives had been left behind such as commercial consuls, Red Cross donors, or seemingly nonpolitical businessmen. So desperate were the Bolshevik leaders that they even proposed repayment of the Tsarist and Provisional governments' foreign debts, which had been repudiated by the Soviet authorities. Compensation was also offered for Western property nationalized within Russia by the Bolshevik revolution. This offer of alliance was refused by the West, because the Soviet government appeared to be temporary and weak.

To compound Soviet uncertainty, Politburo member Bukharin argued that Russia should continue fighting the Central Powers even without an alliance with the Western democracies. Bukharin predicted that Germany and Austro-Hungary would soon be defeated by the West, throwing Central and Eastern Europe into revolutionary chaos. Amid postwar confusion the Soviet army could easily march to Berlin, communizing both Poland and Germany.

Lenin angrily retorted that further warfare would overthrow the fragile Soviet government. After much bitter debate, the Central Committee of the Russian Bolshevik party defeated Bukharin by the slender margin of just one vote.

Trotsky resigned as foreign minister. A second Soviet delegation, including no peasants and no workers, traveled to Poland and on March 3, 1918, signed the humiliating Treaty of Brest-Litovsk, which freed Finland, Estonia, Latvia, Lithuania, Poland, western Belorussia, and the Ukraine from Russian rule. Several border cities were ceded by Russia to Turkey. Germany was promised a huge indemnity in cash, copper, and iron. Should Allied troops invade Russia, and the Russians be too weak to repel this aggression, German troops would fight the Allies on Russian soil.

The Brest-Litovsk Treaty had grave repercussions. First, Germany did not abide by the treaty terms. Besides occupying Russia's western borderlands, German troops advanced beyond the Ukraine into the Azov seacoast and the Caucasus. Fortunately for the Bolsheviks, the Central Powers lost World War I on the western front during late 1918, surrendering to the Allies. German armies had to demobilize and withdraw from Russia. The Soviet government took advantage of this turn of events by annulling the Brest-Litovsk Treaty, and trying to establish Communist regimes in Finland, the Baltic states, Belorussia, and the Ukraine.

Another Brest-Litovsk result was the Allied decision to invade Russia for the purpose of overthrowing the Soviet government. This undeclared war was motivated by a variety of reasons. The Allies wanted to punish the Bolsheviks for making peace with Germany, to bring Russia back into World War I, and to establish a friendly Russian government which would not be a dangerous center for dissemination of socialist and pacifist ideas. Also the Allies hoped to recover their large arms shipments to the former

Provisional Government, before Soviet Russia delivered these munitions to Germany. Actually Lenin had no intention of sending this valuable armament to Germany, but the Allies didn't know his views.

Another Allied military motive for intervention was to rescue the so-called "Czech Legion," which had been formed by the Provisional Government among Czechoslovak prisoners of war captured from the Austro-Hungarian army. Originally intended to fight on the Russian front against the Central Powers, the Czech Legion was marooned by the peace of Brest-Litovsk. To get rid of the Legion, the Soviet government permitted the Czechs to cross Siberia for embarkation at Vladivostok on Allied boats bound for West Europe.

Other reasons for Allied intervention were to protect Western investments in Russia, and to set up an honest Russian government which would repay Tsarist foreign debts. Japan also hoped to take advantage of Russia's weakness by seizing East Siberia, while Britain and France concluded a secret treaty dividing the Ukraine into British and French spheres of influence.

Thus Allied invasion of Russia began shortly after the Brest-Litovsk treaty, before World War I had ended. When German surrender during November 1918 terminated World War I, Allied intervention in Russia continued and expanded.

Meanwhile internal tensions were leading Russia into civil war. In January 1918 was held the only meeting of the Constituent Assembly, the sole freely elected parliament in all Russian history. While still in power, Premier Kerenski had ordered this assembly to be elected, because he considered the Provisional Government to be unrepresentative. The Bolsheviks had permitted the election to take place, believing that they would obtain a majority. But the Bolsheviks were an urban party in a predominantly rural country. Whereas city soviets showed a Bolshevik majority, the heavy peasant vote in the elections to the Constituent Assembly gave a large majority to Social Revolutionaries. When the assembly met on January 18 it refused to support the Bolshevik government, which ordered the legislature to be dispersed by force. Russian troops refused to obey this Bolshevik command, and the assembly was actually closed the next day by Mongol and Latvian soldiers loyal to Bolshevism.

Angry Social-Revolutionaries retaliated by assassinating several high-ranking Bolsheviks, and a frantic woman tried to kill Premier Lenin. Though she failed, Lenin received a severe bullet wound which hastened his death a few years later.

More important than these individual acts of violence were the innumerable anti-Bolshevik revolts started in provincial cities by disgruntled members of the dispersed Constituent Assembly. Leadership of this so-called "White Russian" rebellion quickly passed into the hands of Tsarist army officers, who had troops and arms needed for civil war. Soon the White Russians joined forces with the Allied interventionists, who gladly supplied munitions, money, and moral support to the anti-Bolshevik Whites.

Meanwhile the Soviet Declaration of Nationalities had backfired. Instead of gratefully accepting the Bolshevik offer of racial equality, many non-Russian minorities seceded from Soviet Russia. First with German help, later with Allied aid, Finland, Estonia, Latvia, Lithuania, Poland, Belorussia, the Ukraine, and Caucasus declared their independence. The Moslems of Turkestan revolted too, hating any Russian, Tsarist or Soviet.

Born as a result of one disastrous war, the Soviet government was now confronted by another. For three difficult years, 1918–1920, the Soviet government fought three groups of enemies: many White Russian armies, guerrilla bands of the seceding national minorities, and small troop units from 14 Allied countries: Belgium, Britain, China, Czechoslovakia, Estonia, Finland, France, Greece, Japan, Latvia, Lithuania, Poland, Rumania, and the United States.

Faced with this opposition, the Bolsheviks mobilized their infant government for total war. The Soviet capital was hurriedly transferred from vulnerable Petrograd to the safer interior Moscow. Instead of Bolshevik, the ruling party assumed the Marxist name of "Communist," because—as Lenin explained—the eventual goal was establishment of Communism. A Red Army was hastily created, first of Communist and young Communist volunteers. Half of the Communist Party joined the Red Army. Soon the supply of Communist volunteers was exhausted, so the Red Army conscripted masses of workers and peasants. Since few Communists, workers, or peasants were skilled in military tactics, 50,000 Tsarist officers were induced by persuasion, patriotism, or force to lead the fast-expanding Red Army. To prevent treachery, a Communist political commissar carefully watched each former Tsarist officer. Soldiers' soviets no longer were permitted to give commands, nor were the new officers elected by troops. Iron discipline was instituted by Trotsky, who after Brest-Litovsk became Soviet minister of war. A so-called "Military Opposition" of Communist guerrilla leaders against Trotsky's "spit and polish" was suppressed by Premier Lenin.

As in all civil wars, atrocities were abundant. To combat White terror, the Soviet Cheka (Extraordinary Commission to Combat Counter-Revolution) unleashed a wave of Red police terror against the Social Revolutionaries, Mensheviks, national minorities, and other anti-Communist groups. Formed in late 1917, the Cheka expanded greatly during the Russian Civil War. When the Red Army captured a Russian city or village, Cheka troops would immediately enter to arrest or execute real and suspected anti-Communists. Stalin spent the war at various fronts, partly as a high-ranking army political commissar but often as local Chekist commander.

An example of Red terror was the assassination of Tsar Nicholas II, the Tsarina, and most of the royal family. They were being held prisoner by the Communists in the Ural city of Yekaterinburg (now Sverdlovsk). When Czech troops approached the city, the local Communists became panic-stricken, fearing that the Tsar would be freed and become a leader of the entire White Russian movement. So in great haste, without Lenin's permission, the royal family was shot. Their fate stunned all Europe.

With battlefronts sprouting like mushrooms, mild economic socialism was short-lived. All industry and commerce were nationalized, even artisan workshops and tiny private stores. Worker control of factories was ended, and each plant became strictly subordinate to the Supreme Council for National Economy. As early as 1918, all factory technicians were compelled to stay on their jobs. Soon agricultural specialists, railwaymen, water transport personnel, and coal miners met the same restrictions. Postal, telegraph, and telephone workers were militarized. By 1920, this labor draft embraced every worker in every industry.

Many radio stations were taken over by the Red Army. The War Ministry had to give permission before a private citizen could send a telegram or make a long-distance phone call. Automobiles were repeatedly mobilized by the Red Army. For the 1920 invasion of Poland, half the civilian autos and trucks in Russia were sent to the front.

The whole railway system was put under martial law. Less important railroads were torn up, and the old rails used to build new strategic lines. Half the locomotives that still ran hauled troop trains. Government permits had to be obtained before a civilian could take a train trip. If an ordinary citizen tried to ride the rods, he might be shot. A Russian refugee professor in America has described to me what happened to him during the Civil War in the Ukraine. Finding himself a hundred miles from home without a train permit, he hauled out his wallet and counted his wartime change—a dozen million badly depreciated rubles. Peeling off several million, he bribed the conductor to let him sit on a passenger car step. Thus the professor rode the hundred miles, shivering both from cold and fear of a firing squad.

There was no time for careful organization of army and urban food supply. Soviet officials confiscated all marketable crops from the farms, leaving the peasants barely enough for their own needs. Farmers were paid off in worthless currency. When peasants resisted this forced sale, buried their grain in the ground or sold food on the black market, Red Army troops seized the farm surplus by force.

Even so, cities were on malnutrition food rations throughout the Civil War. For months, the entire food ration for a staff member of the important Soviet Foreign Ministry was just half a loaf of bread per day. Once a month, as a special treat because of the ministry's prestige, each employee was doled out one tiny lump of sugar. This was such a momentous event that the Foreign Minister personally distributed the precious sweets.

"Send everything to the front" became the Soviet slogan, and it was obeyed literally. The Red Army was given a free hand to loot its supplies from any government organization or private home. All rifles, revolvers, bullets, and even swords had to be given to the troops. Arbitrarily the War Ministry grabbed goods from state warehouses, completely disrupting civilian trade. This military robbery was all the more chaotic, since several poorly coordinated civilian and army agencies shared the work, all quarreling jealously among themselves. The Red Army also quartered troops in buildings without permission of the owners. Soldiers barged into schools and apartment houses, crowding students or tenants into a few rooms, or putting them out on the street. For all this the Red Army paid nothing.

No matter how much the rear was robbed, the Red Army was armed even worse than that of the Tsars. Already shattered by World War I, Russian industry was in no shape to withstand this new war blow. Many factories were wrecked by Civil War battles, which raged throughout the length and breadth of Russia, not just on the western frontier as in World War I. Undamaged industrial plants remaining in Soviet hands had been nationalized too fast, and there were few Communists with the engineering skill needed for efficient industrial operation. Both men and machines of armament industry were exhausted from working 24 hours a day, seven days a week throughout World War I.

As in World War I, weapons were lacking in variety. Three factories tried to build crude tanks. Yet the few dozen tanks in Red Army hands by the war's end were almost entirely captured from enemy White Russian or foreign armies. The airplane factories, which Tsarism was never able to complete, lay unfinished and idle throughout the Civil War. Naval shipyards shut down, and did not reopen until the mid-1920's. Most of the meager Tsarist navy was lost forever. Part was sunk, and part sailed away under White Russian command to French North African ports. By 1921, the Black Sea, Pacific, and Arctic naval fleets had vanished.

Even the crudest infantry weapons were in critically short supply. Inadequate as Tsarist munitions output had been for World War I, the Communists produced even less for the Civil War. By 1920, Soviet production of machine guns was less than half of peak Tsarist output, and of rifles and bullets, a mere one third.

Again Russia had to fight a war not with military hardware, but with human sacrifice. At the start of the Civil War, the Red Army was a tiny force of 350,000 men. By the war's end, it had mushroomed to a huge army of 5,300,000—outnumbering all White Russian and Allied expeditionary forces combined. But winning battles by sheer manpower took a terrible toll of Communist lives. An old Red Army officer has described this battle to me:

> You may not believe it, but people can actually stop a tank. I've seen it done several times. In the Civil War, the Whites and foreigners had tanks. We Reds had none. If a tank attacked us, our men surrounded it in a solid mass. The tank would try to escape, crushing many Red soldiers, but the mob still squeezed the machine. Finally the caterpillar treads and wheels were clogged with human bodies, and the tank could not move. That's how we stopped and captured enemy tanks!

The Civil War campaigns began during the spring and summer of 1918, when the British, French, and Americans landed troops in northern European Russia and aided a counter-revolutionary "Government of North Russia." Japan sent an army into the Siberian Far East, helping a bourgeois Russian local administration. American troops occupied the Pacific port of Vladivostok to prevent excessive Japanese aggression, send munitions to Admiral Kolchak's White Army in west Siberia, and rescue the Czech Legion. Meanwhile the Czechs turned against the Soviet government, and seized most of the Trans-Siberian Railway, thus taking control of western and central Siberia. Tsarist generals raised revolts in the North Caucasus and Don river valley; a Social Revolutionary government arose in the Volga valley; and a White Russian administration was set up at Omsk in western Siberia. During this turmoil, all Central Asia rebelled. By late 1918, three fourths of the vast Russian land mass and three fifths of the population were in the hands of White Russians, foreign interventionists, or seceding nationalities.

All Russia was thrown into hopeless confusion. The tide of battle surged back and forth across the whole country, with cities and regions changing hands overnight. Many towns had a new government every week. Russians carefully peeked through the window each morning to see which flag was ruling them that day. When a White army approached, peasant villages brought forth the traditional greeting of bread and salt, and produced the rural priest to prove they were still religious. If the Red Army came, the peasants still offered bread and salt, but hid the priest.

During 1919, the military situation of the Communists began

to improve, though the Allied Powers completely blockaded Russia, while Anglo-French troops landed in the Caucasus and on the Black Sea coast. The first great White Russian setback was the defeat of Admiral Kolchak, who had proclaimed himself "Supreme Ruler of Russia" with strong Allied support. Kolchak's forces crossed the Urals from Siberia and threatened to capture the Volga valley. But the Red Army drove the Whites back into Siberia, where they were finally defeated. Kolchak himself was shot by the Bolsheviks in east Siberia at the close of 1919.

During the summer of 1919, Tsarist general Yudenich attempted to attack from Estonia and seize Petrograd. His forces were defeated in Petrograd suburbs and driven back. Meanwhile Tsarist general Denikin seized the Ukraine and advanced northward upon Tula, whose large armament factories supplied the Red Army. But the Communists defeated Denikin's army near Moscow, and by the end of 1919 the Ukraine and North Caucasus were recaptured by the Soviet forces. At the height of the battles with Denikin, General Yudenich again tried to storm Petrograd, but was thrown back into Estonia a second time.

Discouraged by these White Russian failures, Britain and America began to withdraw their troops from north European Russia and the Soviet Far East. After a mutiny of French naval sailors in sympathy with the Communists, France sent home its navy from the Black Sea coast.

The Allies abandoned their blockade of Russia early in 1920, the last American troops quitting Siberia on April 1. Later that year the Moslems of Central Asia were reconquered by the Red Army in just six months, though Tsardom had intrigued and fought 44 years for the original Russian annexation of the same territory. This Soviet "campaign for cotton" was one of the bloodiest offenses of the entire Civil War. More Asians were killed than during the four decades of Tsarist invasion.

During 1920, two strong military threats to Communism arose in European Russia: Poland and Tsarist general Wrangel. Although granted its independence by the Bolsheviks, Poland decided to take advantage of Communist weakness by seizing Belorussia and the western Ukraine, lands which in medieval times had been under Polish rule. Soon the western Ukraine was captured by the Polish army. Meanwhile Wrangel's forces, equipped with Allied weapons and aided by Ukrainian nationalist guerrillas, seized the north Caucasus and the lower valley of the Don River. But the Red Army quickly drove the Poles out of the Ukraine and Belorussia, and neared the Polish cities of Lvov and Warsaw. In this attack the Red Army overreached itself, and was driven back by a Polish counter-offensive. Meanwhile the Western Allies became alarmed at Polish military weakness, and offered Poland military aid. To avoid further trouble, Poland and Soviet Russia concluded the Peace of Riga, drawing a boundary line that left large Ukrainian and Belorussian minorities under Polish rule.

After this truce, the main forces of the Red Army turned against Wrangel, whose White army was driven into the Crimean peninsula. The narrow Perekop isthmus linking the peninsula with the mainland was heavily fortified, and the Reds lacked the naval ships to land on the Crimea. Here Soviet general Frunze, conqueror of Kolchak and Central Asia, planned and won the most brilliant battle of the Russian Civil War. At night large groups of Red Army infantry waded down the calm Putrid Sea shore of Perekop past the White entrenchments. Up to their armpits in water, the soldiers held rifles and ammunition above their heads to keep the weapons dry. Cannon were sent too, hauled on ropes underwater by gangs of men. Red cavalry also forded the shallow Putrid Sea. In the morning the White defenders of Perekop were dumbfounded to find themselves attacked from both front and rear. Perekop fell, and the Crimea soon followed. Wrangel's White army was literally driven into the Black Sea, embarking on ships and sailing away forever to Turkey, the Balkans, and North Africa. In November 1920, the Russian Civil War ended.

During the Civil War, as might be expected, Communist rule of Russia became more direct. In late 1917, to avoid the appearance of one-party rule, several left-wing Social Revolutionaries had been made members of the Soviet cabinet. These Social Revolutionaries left the cabinet during 1918 in protest against the Brest-Litovsk Treaty, and thereafter only Communists could become cabinet ministers. Another governmental change in 1919 was the official sanctioning of the presidium system, whereby a soviet when not in session delegated its full power to a small standing committee, the presidium of trusted Communists and

Communist sympathizers. By 1920 the soviets were no longer legislatures containing both Communists and members of other socialist parties. To be elected to a soviet, one either had to be a Communist, or nonparty. Thus Russia fell under complete one-party rule, which has continued ever since.

A diplomatic event of 1919, which is now omitted from Soviet history books, was Lenin's peace offer to William Bullitt, who later became the first American ambassador to the USSR. President Woodrow Wilson sent Bullitt to Moscow in 1919 as his personal emissary to discuss peace terms with the Communists. At the time Kolchak, Yudenich, and Denikin were still undefeated, and Lenin was extremely pessimistic about Communist prospects. Premier Lenin offered to give away most of Russia, providing that the Communists could keep and rule in peace the territory they then controlled. Bullitt returned with Lenin's offer, which the White Russian generals rejected, believing the Communists would eventually be defeated. Soon afterward, the Soviet military situation improved, and Lenin never again made such a peace offer.

Early in 1919, in order to gain left-wing support abroad, a congress of international radicals was held in Moscow, founding the Communist International (Comintern, or Third International). Most of the foreign delegates represented themselves rather than existing political groups. But upon returning home, the delegates organized Communist parties loyal to Soviet Russia. Lenin hoped to strengthen the weak Marxist revolutions he had already helped start in Central and Eastern Europe. If these revolts succeeded, the chances for Communist survival in Russia would be vastly improved.

To Lenin's dismay, all the foreign Communist revolutions failed—in Finland, Estonia, Lithuania, and Germany during 1918; Latvia, Hungary, and again Germany in 1919; and Poland during 1920. The most successful revolt was in Hungary, where a Communist government was in power for four months, only to be overthrown by the Rumanian army.

Discouraged by European Communist failures, Lenin turned his revolutionary attention toward Asia. In late 1920 the Russian Communists reconquered the Caucasus, overthrowing the nationalist governments of secessionist Azerbaidzhan, Armenia, and Georgia. The Comintern immediately organized a Congress of

Peoples of the East at Baku, the biggest Caucasian city. Delegates attended from Asiatic Russia, the Near East, Far East, and Africa. Again the delegates were individual radicals rather than group leaders, but began to found Communist parties upon returning home. And no immediate Asian revolutions occurred. Yet the congress was a landmark in Comintern history. Soviet appeals to the congress for overthrow of colonialism were enthusiastically applauded, but the delegates disapproved of the Communist call for a revolt against native feudal governments. From this reaction the Russian Communists learned that nationalism has stronger appeal for colonial revolutionaries than socialism, a lesson of value for later Comintern intrigue in Asia.

Despite economic collapse, underarmament, and the failure of external revolutions, the minority party of Communists won the Russian Civil War. Not a single prominent Western military writer had predicted this Red victory. Yet in retrospect, there were sound reasons for Soviet military success: White Russian generals opposing the Communists were often extreme reactionaries, who tried to restore the great estates to their former owners. They were hated by the peasant majority of Russia's population who had fallen heir to these lands. Other White leaders were democratic but unrealistic, believing in reforms but not wishing to introduce them until approved by a freely elected government. In contrast, the Communists sanctioned the peasant division of estates, and made other long-overdue reforms such as separating church from state and granting equality to women. Also the Communists were accepted as Russian nationalists, since they had no foreign backing like the Allied support to White generals.

The Communists were also the best organized political party in Russia, remaining tightly united in wartime while their numerous enemies quarreled jealously among themselves. Communist Party membership grew fast from 270,000 in 1918 to 612,000 by 1920. Many Communist leaders proved to have surprising military ability. War minister Trotsky was an outstanding military organizer, who created a fairly efficient infantry and cavalry army literally from rabble. The former prison laborer, Mikhail Frunze, who conquered Kolchak, Wrangel, and Central Asia, proved a better strategist than his highly trained White officer opponents.

Of great advantage to the Soviets was their continual control of Petrograd and Moscow, Russia's two largest cities, longtime capitals, and greatest industrial centers. Thus the Whites were forced to attack Russia's populous industrial nucleus from less-developed rural provinces, much like the agricultural South against the industrial North during the American Civil War. The centrally located Communists stayed in constant communication, while the far-flung White armies had great difficulty receiving messages from each other. More important, thanks to the fine railway network out of Moscow, the Red Army could quickly shift troops from front to front, concentrating against the most dangerous White enemy of the moment. Meanwhile the White armies had to depend on sparce provincial rail lines.

Composed largely of officers and cadets, most White armies were too small to win. Allied intervention troops were also few in number, with servicemen tired of battle after four years of fighting World War I. French naval sailors even mutinied and had to be sent home from the Black Sea. Anyway the Allied detachments usually did not fight, but merely served as supply troops for the nearest White army.

Had the Allies invaded with large armies which fought hard, the Soviet government might not have survived. But the Allies had the limited objective of helping Russia to achieve a pro-Western government. Complete conquest of Russia would have required a huge, long, and expensive military campaign, which the war-weary Allies were unwilling to undertake.

The Civil War made a profound impression upon the Soviet leaders, who thereafter feared and mistrusted the outside world. The Soviet government now believed itself surrounded by a hostile capitalist world, which could be expected to attack Russia in the future. Relations with Poland long remained tense because of the 1920 Russo-Polish war, which left substantial Ukrainian and Belorussian minorities under Polish rule. Though the Communists could not stop Rumania from seizing Bessarabia, the Soviet government never recognized this annexation, and its maps showed this borderland as Russian. Despite freeing the Baltic states, the Bolsheviks had attempted to establish Communist regimes there, an omen that Soviet Russia might try to control those small countries in the future. Annexation of several Caucasian frontier towns by Turkey created a basis for future disputes with that Near Eastern neighbor. Moreover, the Communists noted the disadvantage of Turkish control of the Dardanelles, when during the Russian Civil War, Turkey had permitted Allied warships to enter the Black Sea. Premier Stalin during the 1950's and Premier Khrushchev in the 1960's both justified Soviet armament because of lessons learned from Communist near defeat during the Russian Civil War.

Suggestions for Further Reading

BUNYAN, JAMES, *Intervention, Civil War, and Communism in Russia, April–December, 1918,* Baltimore: Johns Hopkins University Press, 1936.

BUNYAN, JAMES, and FISHER, HAROLD, *The Bolshevik Revolution, 1917–1918,* Stanford: Stanford University Press, 1934.

CARR, E. H., *The Bolshevik Revolution, 1917–1923,* New York: Macmillan, 1953.

CHAMBERLIN, W. H., *The Russian Revolution, 1917–1921,* New York: Macmillan, 1935.

DEGRAS, JANE, ed., *Communist International Documents, 1919–1922,* New York: Oxford University Press, 1956.

GANKIN, OLGA H., and FISHER, HAROLD, *The Bolsheviks and the World War: Origin of the Third International,* Stanford: Stanford University Press, 1940.

GERSON, LENNARD D., *The Secret Police in Lenin's Russia.* Philadelphia: Temple University Press, 1976.

HOVANNISIAN, RICHARD G., *The Republic of Armenia: Vol. I: The First Year, 1918-1919.* Berkeley: California University Press, 1971.

MORGAN, MICHAEL, *Lenin.* Columbus: Ohio University Press, 1972.

MORLEY, JAMES W., *The Japanese Thrust into Siberia, 1918,* New York: Columbia University Press, 1957.

PAGE, STANLEY W., *Lenin and World Revolution,* New York: New York University Press, 1959.

PIPES, RICHARD, *Formation of the Soviet Union, Communism and Nationalism, 1917–1923,* Cambridge: Harvard University Press, 1955.

RESHETAR, JOHN S., *The Ukrainian Revolution, 1917–1920,* Princeton: Princeton University Press, 1952.

SILVERMAN, SAUL N., ed., *Lenin.* Englewood Cliffs: Prentice-Hall, 1972.

STEINBERG, I. N., *In the Workshop of the Revolution,* New York: Rinehart, 1953.

VARNECK, ELENA, and FISHER, HAROLD H., *The Testimony of Kolchak and Other Siberian Materials,* Stanford: Stanford University Press, 1935.

WARTH, ROBERT D., *The Allies and the Russian Revolution,* Durham: Duke University Press, 1954.

Chapter 5

The New Economic Policy

By early 1921, Russia was in chaos. The Civil War had plunged the country into the worst economic depression of any nation in modern history. Soviet factories and mines yielded barely one tenth of Tsarist prewar industrial output. Three fourths of all coal mines and electric power stations were out of operation. Smelting of iron and steel, the basic metals of modern industry, had slumped to a mere 5 per cent of Tsarist peak production.

To make matters worse, half the farmlands lay untilled and half the railways were not operating. Therefore only one fourth as much grain reached the cities from the farms as before the war. City populations had shrunk in half because millions had gone "back to the farm," where at least they could find something to eat.

Great too was the loss in human lives. Without counting losses from secession of Finland, Poland, Bessarabia, and the Baltic states, the Soviet population had decreased by several million during the three years of civil war. And victory was accompanied by a deadly combination of flu epidemic and famine.

Peasant uprisings began against governmental grain requisitions in Siberia, the Ukraine, and in central European Russia not far from Moscow. As if this were not enough trouble, the Communist government was thunderstruck in March 1921 by a naval mutiny at Kronstadt, an island near Petrograd in the Finnish Gulf serving as the main base of the Baltic fleet. Hoping to inspire a nationwide rebellion, the Baltic sailors proclaimed the slogan: "For the Soviets, but without Communists." They demanded free elections, freedom of operation for all proletarian political parties, free trade unions, liberation of anti-Communist political prisoners, restoration of small-scale private manufacturing, and an end to governmental regulation of peasant farmsteads.

Red Army units crossed the ice of Petrograd harbor, stormed Kronstadt, and slaughtered the rebellious sailors. But the Communists were shocked by such opposition coming from Kronstadt, an old revolutionary center which had helped the Bolsheviks seize power. While the Kronstadt mutiny was being suppressed, Premier Lenin hurriedly introduced the New Economic Policy (NEP) to prevent both further revolts and complete economic collapse.

Created hastily as a stopgap without previous planning, the NEP was intended to save socialism by encouraging petty capitalism. These were the main NEP innovations: Instead of the government purchasing all of the peasants' marketable crops, the state now bought only a fixed proportion of the harvest. Any farm surplus above and beyond the government levy could be sold by the peasantry on the private market. Successful private farmers could eventually lease land from poorer peasants, and hire the latter as farmhands. Thus the rich peasants, or kulaks, could legally organize small private estates.

In the cities petty private trade and small-scale private manufacturing were again permitted, as long as the store or workshop did not hire more than ten employees. Cooperatives were encouraged in both handicraft production and in retail trade as a form of socialism offering opportunities for individual profit. Foreigners were invited to finance and manage industries in Russia on a concession basis, with the foreign businessman and the Soviet government dividing the profits. However, foreign trade remained a government monopoly. Also the Soviet government never relinquished its ownership of large industrial enterprises, the banks, the wholesale trade system, railways, sea and river ships, telephone and telegraph communications, and all natural resources.

At the outset, the NEP was intended to permit only a small amount of private retail trade, with most commerce remaining in state stores. But by 1923, three fourths of all retail trade had been captured by the hardworking Nepmen (small private businessmen). The Nepmen never succeeded so strongly in industry, but in the mid-1920's produced as much as one fifth of all industrial output.

External peace, decentralized management of state economic enterprises, and the official encouragement of private profit brought about a slow recovery of Russia's war-shattered economy. By the close of the NEP in 1928, the grain harvest was near the prewar Tsarist level, and more cotton and sugar beets were raised than in Tsarist times. Total herds of cattle, sheep, goats, and hogs also surpassed those of prewar Russia.

By 1928 industry had also recovered to the prewar Tsarist level. Fuel and power production even exceeded the Tsarist output. Meanwhile inoperative railways had been restored, unfinished Tsarist railway construction was completed, and some new lines were built. By 1928, Russia had more rail trackage than in 1913.

The USSR had great difficulty in establishing normal commercial relations with Western countries and foreign businessmen, who still resented the Soviet cancellation of Tsarist debts and nationalization of alien property. Nevertheless, foreign trade made a partial recovery, with NEP imports and exports closely resembling those of Tsarist days. Nine tenths of Russia's exports were products of the farms, forests, and mines such as grain, timber, furs, chrome, manganese, and oil. Four fifths of NEP imports were deficit raw materials and machines.

Some success was achieved in reducing Russia's dependence on supplies from abroad. No longer did Petrograd heat its homes with coals from Newcastle. Railways from the Ukraine to Petrograd were improved, so the city could burn Ukrainian coal instead of British. Under the Tsars, Russia imported most of its copper and cotton. By 1928, most cotton and copper consumed in the USSR were homemade.

The Soviet government was pleased with the economic revival caused by the New Economic Policy, but did not wish to continue the NEP indefinitely. The strength shown by private enterprise worried the Communist leaders. The USSR was still predominantly a rural country, with the vast majority of the population consisting of small private farmers. During the late 1920's heavy taxation had driven many Nepmen out of business. Yet in 1928 one fifth of retail trade and 13 per cent of manufacturing still remained in private hands. Despite intensive official support of urban and rural cooperatives, only 3 per cent of the working population had joined them. Small farmers and petty private businessmen had comprised about 70 per cent of the Tsarist population. The NEP raised this proportion to almost 80 per cent. Thus socialism had dispossessed the Russian rich, only to increase the ranks of a second antisocialist class—the self-employed and smallholders. Against such widespread private enterprise, Soviet leaders feared that socialism could not long endure.

Another NEP disappointment was the failure to attract many foreign businessmen to provide capital and engineering skill for expansion of Russian industry. Few foreigners were willing to accept the harsh concession contracts offered by the Soviet government, which severely limited the concessionaires' profits. During the NEP, only a small percentage of Soviet industrial output was produced by concessions. Thus the Communists realized that the USSR had no hope of attracting large amounts of foreign capital, and that future industrial expansion must be financed from Russia's slender monetary resources.

A third governmental worry was that NEP heavy industry was too weak for modern war. Russian armament industry in 1927 manufactured only a few types of armament, and their quality was worse than West European or Tsarist weapons. Cannon made in the land of Communism shot only two thirds as far as the artillery of capitalist world powers. Both soldiers and officers of the Red Army preferred to carry old Tsarist rather than new Soviet revolvers.

No Russian tank factories existed. To train an army of half a million men in mechanized warfare, the Soviet Union had only a few dozen tanks. These mostly were outmoded models captured during the Civil War from White Russians and foreign invaders. Every May Day, this handful of ancient wrecks creaked across Red Square in the Moscow military parade, a pitiful spectacle of lack of mechanized might. Army trucks were also conspicuous by their absence, and horses were the backbone of military transport. The Soviet auto industry was a sickly infant, manufacturing a grand total of 500 cars and trucks in 1927.

Soviet shipyards in 1927 could launch only half as much shipping as the Tsarist docks of 1913. The Red Navy was less than one fourth the size of the naval fleet of the Tsars.

As early as 1921, the first year of NEP, all half-built Tsarist aircraft factories had been repaired, completed, and put into operation. By 1923, Russia was fourth in the world in number of civilian and army planes, trailing only France, England, and the USA. Yet even this aircraft industry, the lone armament success, constructed virtually no military airships except scouting planes. Thus intensive industrialization was an urgent military need.

Agriculture was the greatest NEP failure. Though overall crop production made a good recovery, by 1928 only half as much grain as in 1913 was moving off the farms to feed the cities. This decrease in the marketable share of the harvest had several causes. The farm population had increased over its prewar size without a comparable expansion of cropland. As the number of farm families grew, parents divided their land among their children. Thus Soviet arable land became more and more subdivided into ever smaller farms. There were 23 million small private farms in 1924, and 26 million by 1928. Most of these tiny farms produced barely enough to feed their peasant owners. Only the kulaks consistently raised enough surplus for the market.

But the kulaks disliked the low prices the government paid the farmers for food; whereas, the prices of industrial goods needed by the peasants were very high. This price difference caused the so-called "scissors crisis" early in the NEP, forcing the government to raise prices paid for farm produce. However, the state never fully satisfied peasant monetary demands, because it wished to keep food cheap for the city workers, who were the chief supporters of governmental socialism. Hence by the end of the NEP, the kulaks began to hoard grain and to refuse to sell to the government. As a result, bread rationing had to be introduced in the larger Soviet cities. The NEP economic system can hardly be considered a success, when it resulted in rationed food.

Such economic difficulties and the generally unsocialistic nature of NEP induced the Soviet government to seek another economic program to replace the New Economic Policy. As early as 1925, the Communist Party approved a future of forced industrialization to expand Soviet industry far beyond the Tsarist level. In the later NEP years, both collectivization of agriculture and national economic planning were adopted as official policy. The State Planning Commission was ordered in 1927 to draft a First Five-Year Plan, which was approved and put into operation during late 1928. Not surprisingly, this Plan concentrated on abolition of Nepmen's stores and workshops, collectivization of the small private farms, and fast expansion of heavy, war-potential industry.

During the Russian Civil War many schools had closed, and education stagnated. At the start of the NEP, Russia was still a country where less than one third of the population could read and write. During the relatively peaceful 1920's, the Kremlin undertook a widespread campaign against this illiteracy. An attempt was made to force every child to attend early grade school. Young children were told to teach their parents the three R's after school. Brigades of Communist youth opened literacy schools for adults in city slums and rural villages. Every large industrial enterprise organized a "Factory-Worker School" to give its employees at least the rudiments of education. Khrushchev received his early education during the 1920's in a school operated by a coal mine.

This educational campaign paid dividends. By the late 1920's, half the Soviet population could read and write. Yet although literacy increased, formal schooling deteriorated. The little red schoolhouse became a laboratory for progressive educational experiments. Examinations and marks were abolished. School-teachers had little authority, and students largely managed their own school. Instead of taking regular courses, the students formed brigades working on projects which would include a variety of subjects. Thus at fall harvesting time, the brigade might study a "complex" of agriculture, weather, botany, and food distribution. They learned a little of everything, and not much of anything.

An elderly Russian refugee professor has vividly described to me these early years of ultraprogressive education. His Soviet university was managed by a board of students and janitors. The students passed rules that girls could attend the university, smoking was permitted in all classrooms, and a college dance would be held every evening. Even great Tsarist literature, such as the world-famous writings of Tolstoi, was condemned as obsolete bourgeois drivel. No new course could be taught, unless the janitors first gave permission.

Similar modernism ran riot in literature and art, which during the NEP were only mildly censored by the Soviet government. In every artistic field a "Proletarian" group arose, striving to create alleged true art of the people. Music was written imitating the sound of factory machinery, while books appeared describing no individuals but only masses of people. Occasionally the government had to restrain the Proletarians from dominating other artistic circles.

The latter bore various names but were known collectively as "Fellow Travelers," who were non-Communists willing to cooperate with socialism. The Fellow Travelers were modernists of great ability, who refused to proletarianize their artistic creations. From them came bold literature and daring music, plus such innovations as office buildings on stilts and the theater in the round.

Near the close of the NEP, the Kremlin became worried about the independence displayed by fellow-traveler artists and authors. Zoshchenko, the most popular NEP writer, specialized in short stories ridiculing Soviet daily life. Even worse was Evgeni Zamyatin, who fled abroad where he published *WE,* a novel picturing the future of socialism as a society of planned marriage, dull work, and planned exercise by people bearing numbers instead of names.

Therefore as NEP ended, the Soviet government ordered the Proletarians to assume control over literature and most fields of art. The Proletarian triumph was short-lived, for they too were suppressed in the early 1930's for unwillingness to produce state propaganda.

The official NEP treatment of organized religion was a combination of extreme repression and semitolerance, depending on the particular church. In the early 1920's, the main governmental offensive was aimed against the Russian Orthodox and Roman Catholic faiths. Many of their churches were closed, and thousands of priests were imprisoned or executed.

During 1922, more than 50 bishops and archbishops of both churches were tried and convicted for alleged counter-revolutionary activity. A worldwide reaction of anger occurred in the foreign press, and thereafter Soviet religious persecution became more subtle. In 1925 a society of the Militant Godless was organized among young Communists. The Godless converted many churches into antireligious museums, published atheist magazines, and printed crude posters depicting Christ as an evil merchant. On religious holidays, society members would often dress in clerical costumes, then stagger down city streets as if drunk. These coarse tactics antagonized many religious people, and the Godless never achieved a large membership or widespread success.

Meanwhile the Kremlin tried to favor minor religions against the majority Russian Orthodox Church. Thus the 30 million devout Moslems in and around Central Asia were left relatively undisturbed. The humble Baptist religion was even encouraged in an official attempt to fight Orthodox pomp with Christian simplicity.

As a result the Baptists thrived, conducting illegal Sunday schools, organizing large charitable and social activities, and creating a "Christomol" youth society whose size began to rival the Komsomol (Young Communist League). Baptist ministers even preached on the streets, openly appealing to the passing crowd.

At the end of the NEP the Soviet government had to face the fact that its antireligious campaign had largely failed. Somehow, both the Russian Orthodox and Roman Catholic churches had survived under persecution. The Godless society was unpopular, while both Moslems and Baptists were stronger than before. Drastic persecution of all religions therefore occurred after the NEP ended.

Though differences of opinion on party strategy and tactics had often arisen among Communist leaders in 1917 and during the Russian Civil War, the introduction of the New Economic Policy in 1921 aroused the first widespread Bolshevik opposition to the party leadership. Lenin obtained party approval of the NEP with great difficulty, because many Communists interpreted condolence of private trade and private manufacturing as a betrayal of socialist ideals.

During 1921, various party factions formed in opposition to

other Leninist tactics. The "Democratic Centralists" demanded more democracy in the Communist Party, with real election of local party officials rather than their appointment from above. Trotsky urged a military-type mobilization of industrial workers to speed economic recovery. In contrast to Trotsky, Russia's trade union leaders wanted organized labor to take over the Soviet government. This so-called "Workers' Opposition" argued that Russia was a workers' state, and therefore should be ruled by labor unions.

Lenin opposed all these party factions, considering Trotsky too extreme, and defending the authority of the Politburo (top party committee) against both the Democratic Centralists and Workers' Opposition. The factions were defeated, but Lenin ordered the Communist Party to be purged of Nep opponents and factionalists who refused to repent. Thus began the first great purge of the Russian Communist Party, reducing its membership from 732,000 in 1921 to 386,000 by 1923.

Along with this purge, the Kremlin of the early 1920's used other devices to consolidate its power. When the Red Army reconquered most minorities at the end of the Civil War, the Ukraine, Belorussia, and the Caucasus had each been permitted to become Soviet republics separate from the Russian republic. During 1923–1924 the loose alliance of the Russian, Ukrainian, Belorussian, and Caucasian republics was changed into a tightly knit federation—the Union of Soviet Socialist Republics (USSR). Since the Russian republic had much more territory and population than the other three republics combined, formation of the USSR actually meant Russian absorption of the Ukraine, Belorussia, and Caucasus. Thus most of the old Tsarist empire was reunited under direct Moscow control.

In 1922, Lenin suffered a stroke, went to the countryside to rest, and largely left the Soviet government in the hands of three Politburo members: Kamenev, Zinoviev, and Stalin. Meanwhile Stalin was appointed as secretary-general of the Communist Party, a post which was considered to be routine administrative work. But the secretary generalship controlled party patronage, and Stalin quickly took advantage of his new position to place his personal followers in key posts throughout the party regional and central hierarchy. Largely absorbed in a quarrel with Trotsky,

Kamenev and Zinoviev were unaware that Stalin was stealthily gaining control of the Communist Party, and hence of the Soviet government. But the sick Lenin was suspicious, and dictated the following message to be given the party Central Committee after his death:

> Comrade Stalin, having become Secretary-General, has concentrated an enormous power in his hands; and I am not sure that he always knows how to use that power with sufficient caution. . . .
>
> Stalin is too rude, and this fault, entirely supportable in relations among us Communists, becomes insupportable in the office of Secretary-General. Therefore, I propose to the comrades to find a way to remove Stalin from that position and appoint to it another man who in all respects differs from Stalin only in superiority—namely, more patient, more loyal, more polite and more attentive to comrades, less capricious, etc.

After several strokes Lenin died on January 21, 1924. His request for Stalin's removal was read, ignored, and kept secret by a party Central Committee packed with Stalin's supporters.

Meanwhile Stalin maneuvered against his Politburo rivals. During 1924 he sponsored the "Lenin Enrollment"—a vast recruiting of new party members to commemorate Lenin's death. As a result, Communist party strength almost doubled from 386,000 in 1923 to 736,000 in 1924, most new members being carefully chosen adherents of Stalin. Having flooded the Communist Party with his own supporters, Stalin then instituted a second party purge, which expelled opposition Communists and reduced membership from 736,000 in 1924 to 643,000 in 1925.

Against such shrewd tactics, Stalin's Politburo rivals inevitably lost the struggle for the dead Lenin's throne. Kamenev, Zinoviev, and Stalin teamed together against Trotsky, who was dismissed as War Minister in 1925, removed from the Politburo during 1926, expelled from the USSR Communist Party in 1927, and exiled from Russia during 1929. After defeating Trotsky, Stalin allied with Politburo members Bukharin and Tomski against Kamenev and Zinoviev, who were removed from the Politburo during 1926. In turn Bukharin lost his Politburo seat in 1929, and Tomski in 1930. All these rivals eventually died violent deaths. Kamenev and Zinoviev were executed for alleged treason during 1936, and Bukharin in 1938. Tomski committed suicide in 1936, and Trotsky was assassinated four years later.

Soon after Lenin's demise, Stalin introduced major changes in Soviet policy. The most revisionist change was his new slogan of "Socialism in One Country." According to Marx and Lenin, a Communist revolution could not long survive unless it seized power almost simultaneously in several countries. Stalin discarded this theory as impractical, arguing that Russia alone could achieve socialism. Thus he virtually abandoned the previous Soviet goal of "immediate" world revolution. Stalin carefully explained that Russia must be built up into a fortress of socialism, to serve as a citadel for "future" world revolution. Partly this policy was a question of money, since Soviet Russia had wasted considerable funds by subsidizing unsuccessful foreign revolts. The same funds could have been used constructively to strengthen the military-industrial power of the USSR. One-country socialism was violently but unsuccessfully opposed by Trotsky, who desired a "permanent revolution" abroad.

To give Russia time to become a fortress, Stalin proclaimed "peaceful co-existence" with capitalist countries. Temporarily Communism and capitalism would live in armed truce, with relatively normal commercial and diplomatic relations. During this truce, both the Comintern and Soviet foreign ministry would try to weaken the capitalist world by aggravating existing frictions such as: labor versus business, small versus large capitalist nations, and colonies versus colonial powers. Stalin managed thus to live in peace with capitalism while undermining the capitalist system.

No time was wasted in starting Russia on the long road to becoming a fortress. In 1925 a Soviet law ordered the adult civilian population to be trained in rifle-shooting, and the entire national economy to be organized in peacetime for future war. Another edict made it a crime for any Soviet citizen to collect economic data forbidden for publication. A 1926 decree defined unpublished economic, diplomatic, and military data as state secrets. Simultaneously, war mobilization bureaus were organized in all governmental ministries. A year later, similar mobilization units existed in many large factories. Several engineering colleges added military departments to their faculties for the purpose of training new armament engineers.

During the early NEP years, there were several important Soviet moves in the international arena. In 1921, Red Army troops entered Outer Mongolia in pursuit of a White Russian army, and after defeating the Whites, organized a Mongol Communist government which founded the Mongolian People's Republic—the first Soviet satellite. Tannu Tuva, a small mountainous territory between Outer Mongolia and Siberia, was also invaded in 1921 by Soviet troops, which established a second satellite—the Tuvan People's Republic. Because of their common Mongol nationality the two satellites soon wished to unite. The cautious Kremlin forbade unification, because it might start a pan-Mongol movement arousing Russia's own numerous Mongols.

Also during 1921 Russia abandoned its attempt to create a people's republic in northern Iran, which had been invaded by Soviet troops late in the Russian Civil War. Iran got the Red Army out by signing a treaty allowing Russian troops to return, whenever the USSR believed Iran to be threatened by external aggression. With renewals, this treaty is still in force today, and Iran dares not denounce it.

In 1922, Soviet delegates were invited by the European powers to participate in the Genoa Economic Conference, despite the fact that the host countries had not recognized the Soviet government. The purpose of the conference was to alleviate the world economic depression of the early 1920's. Western conferees immediately demanded repayment of the Tsarist debts and compensation for the foreign property nationalized in Communist Russia. The Soviet delegates were willing to comply, if Western nations paid for the damage they inflicted by invading Russia during World War I and the Russian Civil War. By Soviet calculations, Western war damage in Russia exceeded what the Kremlin owed the West.

An impasse immediately developed, so the Soviet delegation conducted secret negotiations with the envoys from the German Weimar Republic, which like Russia was an outcast to the victorious Allies of World War I. The result was the Treaty of Rapallo, by which Germany recognized Soviet Russia and concluded a trade agreement. More important, Germany accepted the Soviet proposal that German war damage in Russia equaled Russian debts to the Weimar Republic. This established a sound precedent for Russia never to repay Tsarist or revolutionary debts to other capitalist nations.

Ensuing from Rapallo was an agreement for secret collaboration between the German and Soviet armies. The Weimar Republic, which was limited by the Versailles Peace Treaty of World War I to a token military force, sent large numbers of army officers into Russia to train with the Red Army. Since the same treaty also limited Weimar armament industry, German engineers operated a few Soviet enterprises producing tanks, parachutes, shells, submarines, warplanes, and poison gas. Part of this binational production was smuggled into Germany, with the remainder staying in the USSR. Thus Russia succeeded in learning Germany's superb military tactics and skilled armament techniques. This Communist-capitalist marriage of military convenience survived from 1922 until 1933, when Hitler seized power in Germany.

Russia achieved two further international successes during 1922. A harvest failure due to drought created a famine in south European Russia. The Soviet government managed to obtain much food and extensive medical aid from the American Relief Administration, headed by Herbert Hoover, future President of the United States. When first requesting this aid, the Kremlin insisted that only pro-Soviet Russians be fed. The American Relief Administration replied that its duty was to help all postwar depression victims, regardless of politics. Confronted by famine which might cause revolt, the Soviet government had to accept aid on American terms. Several million Soviet citizens were saved from starvation by American food, and USSR President Kalinin expressed the fear that the United States might win too many friends among the Russian people by such generosity. After American aid ended, all Soviet employees of the American Relief Administration were in official disrepute. But as late as World War II, old Soviet citizens of south European Russia displayed fond feelings for the distant, rich, benevolent USA.

Also during 1922, Allied pressure forced Japanese troops to evacuate Vladivostok, thus ending the last remnant of Civil War intervention on the Russian mainland. Shortly afterward, Soviet Russia annexed the Far Eastern Republic, which had arisen in East Siberia during the Civil War.

After these Soviet successes, 1923 was a year of trouble and failure. At the Lausanne Conference on rules for the Dardanelles, Soviet delegates requested Russian participation in the control of the Turkish Straits. Allied opposition was very great, so Russia unwillingly signed the Lausanne Convention leaving administration of the Straits in Turkish hands.

During the same year Britain's Foreign Minister, Lord Curzon, sent an ultimatum demanding that Russia not interfere in the Near East. Though rejecting the ultimatum, the Soviet government was badly frightened. Huge fund drives were conducted, inducing the Russian public to contribute money for "anti-Curzon" tanks and planes. Meanwhile a Soviet envoy to Italy was assassinated in Switzerland by a White Russian émigré.

Perhaps the most discouraging blow was the failure of the 1923 Communist revolt in Germany, where the population was expected to turn toward Communism in anger against French occupation of the Rhineland. This half-hearted rebellion was easily suppressed by the German government, which was annoyed by Russian support of the revolt only a year after Rapallo. However, Soviet-German commercial and military cooperation continued.

Dismayed by the weakness of the German Communists, the Fifth Comintern Congress in 1924 abandoned hope of achieving quick revolution in Europe. Western Communists were ordered to struggle against European moderate socialists, who were now considered almost worse enemies of Communism than European capitalists. The Comintern assumed that Communist uprisings in Central and Eastern Europe had failed mainly because of lack of support from the large European socialist parties, which considered Communists too extreme. Comintern opposition to European socialists continued until 1933, when Germany fell under Nazi rule.

Meanwhile the Communist International devoted its major attention to the Far East. If Communist revolutions were impossible in Europe, perhaps they might succeed in underdeveloped nations of Asia. Then Europe would be weakened by losing its Asian raw materials and markets. Such was the new Comintern strategy, and the last major attempt at immediate world revolution before Russia withdrew into "Socialism in One Country."

Hence in 1924 the USSR and Comintern conducted a series of intricate negotiations in China. First, Russia established diplomatic relations with the Peking government of the Chinese Republic. By recognizing Peking suzerainty over Outer Mongolia, the USSR regained the Chinese-Eastern railway. This strategic rail line crossing northern Manchuria had been built and owned by Tsarist Russia, then seized by China during the Russian Civil War.

Next the Comintern allied with Sun Yat Sen's Kuomintang, a national reform movement in south China trying to overthrow the reactionary Peking government. After failing to obtain support from Western democratic powers, Sun requested aid from Moscow which sent him arms, money, and both military and political advisors.

Then the Chinese Communists joined the Kuomintang, with secret Kremlin instructions to infiltrate and gain control over Sun's revolution. If the plot succeeded, the Communists might win power in China by riding on the coattails of the Kuomintang. Should the scheme fail, the USSR still had diplomatic relations with China's legal government at Peking. Meanwhile Outer Mongolia remained a Soviet satellite, despite Russian recognition of Peking's Mongolian claims.

By 1927 this grandiose double-cross of China failed in a manner Russia had not expected. The Kuomintang broke its alliance with the Comintern, expelled its Soviet advisors, suppressed the Chinese Communists, then marched north to eventual victory over the Peking government. After great losses, the remaining Chinese Communists fled into China's southeast mountains and barely survived. But Russia still managed to keep control of Outer Mongolia and the Chinese-Eastern railway.

In contrast to Soviet intrigue in China, Russia dared not attempt to double-cross powerful aggressive Japan. Japanese invasion troops remained in the Russian north of Sakhalin Island four years after the Russian Civil War. In 1925 they finally withdrew, at a very high price. The USSR had to allow Japanese ships to fish in Soviet Pacific waters, and Japanese companies to mine north Sakhalin coal and oil.

Meanwhile "peaceful co-existence" was gaining results in the West. During 1924, Britain, France, and Italy established diplomatic relations with the USSR. Austria, Denmark, Greece, Norway, Sweden, and Mexico quickly did the same. Soviet nonaggression pacts were concluded with Turkey in 1925; Germany, Lithuania, and Afghanistan in 1926; and Iran during 1927.

As the NEP ended in 1928, Soviet delegates began attending disarmament conferences of the League of Nations. However, Russia still refused to join this international organization, which Communist propaganda described as a "league of capitalist robbers."

Also in 1928, Russia adhered to the Briand-Kellogg pact, which supposedly outlawed war forever. This international peace treaty was authored by French foreign minister Briand and US Secretary of State Kellogg, and signed by most nations of the world. At first the USSR demanded US recognition as the price for signing. When the United States refused, Russia signed anyway.

The NEP was a controversial period, meaning different things to various people. Official Soviet histories describe it as a temporary retreat into semicapitalism, until Russia was ready for intensive socialism. Trotskyites view the NEP as change of the Communist Party from a semi-democracy into a Stalinist bureaucracy. Older Soviet citizens have fond memories of NEP artistic freedom and the well-stocked private stores. The NEP was all of these, and also a period of great state decisions setting Russia's future course in agriculture, industry, armament, and diplomacy for many years to come.

Suggestions for Further Reading

ANDERSON, P. B., *People, Church and State in Modern Russia,* New York: Macmillan, 1944.

BAYKOV, ALEXANDER, *The Development of the Soviet Economic System,* New York: Macmillan, 1946.

CARR, EDWARD H., *The Interregnum, 1923–1924,* New York: Macmillan, 1954.

CARR, EDWARD H., *Socialism in One Country, 1924–1926,* New York: Macmillan, 1960.

DEUTSCHER, ISAAC, *Stalin, a Political Biography,* New York: Oxford University Press, 1967.

DEUTSCHER, ISAAC, *The Prophet Unarmed—Trotsky, 1921–1929,* New York: Oxford University Press, 1959.

EUDIN, XENIA, FISHER, HAROLD H., and JONES, F., *Soviet Russia and the West, 1920–1927,* Stanford: Stanford University Press, 1957.

EUDIN, XENIA, and NORTH, ROBERT C., *Soviet Russia and the East, 1920–1927,* Stanford: Stanford University Press, 1957.

KOCHAN, LIONEL, *Russia and the Weimar Republic,* New York: Praeger, 1955.

SCHAPIRO, LEONARD, *The Communist Party of the Soviet Union,* New York: Random House, 1960.

STALIN, JOSEPH, *Foundations of Leninism,* Moscow: Foreign Languages Publishing House, 1939.

STRUVE, GLEB, *Soviet Russian Literature, 1917–1950,* Norman: University of Oklahoma Press, 1951.

TROTSKY, LEON, *Stalin,* New York: Harper, 1946.

WEISSMAN, BENJAMIN M., *Herbert Hoover and Famine Relief to Soviet Russia: 1921-1923.* Stanford: Stanford University Press, 1974.

Chapter 6

The Soviet Industrial Revolution

In the spring of 1927, the international situation suddenly changed for the worse. Scotland Yard raided Arcos, the Soviet trading company in England, and found evidence of espionage. The British government angrily broke off relations with Russia, which feared that England might even declare war.

Meanwhile the Peking government raided the USSR Embassy and consulates in China, finding evidence of Soviet help to the Kuomintang and Chinese Communists. In reprisal, Russia severed diplomatic relations with the Chinese government in Peking.

During the summer the Soviet Ambassador to Poland was assassinated by a Ukrainian nationalist who wanted to stir up trouble between Poland and Russia. In early winter, disaster arrived in south China, which by then was controlled by the Kuomintang led by Sun Yat Sen's successor, Chiang Kai Shek. Discovering that the Chinese Communists were infiltrating the Kuomintang to gain control, Chiang broke the Comintern-Kuomintang alliance, slaughtered thousands of Communist Chinese, and exiled his Soviet military and political advisors.

As these troubles piled up abroad, USSR leaders became alarmed. In late December 1927, the Fifteenth Congress of the Soviet Communist Party ordered the State Planning Commission (Gosplan) to prepare a Five-Year Plan of industrialization to begin the next year. As the official explanation stated:

> Technical and economic backwardness and the constant threat of intervention on the part of the aggressive imperialist powers

made the industrial development of the Soviet state at high speed a matter of necessity.[1]

Thus from the very start, the Five-Year Plans were not "peaceful economic construction" or routine industrialization. They were inspired by war danger, and concentrated on construction of heavy industry whose enterprises are either convertible to munitions or produce the raw materials of war. The First Five-Year Plan of 1928–1932 assigned 78 per cent of its industrial investments to such heavy industries as mining, metallurgy, chemicals, machinebuilding, and munitions. This First Plan, as well as the Second (1933–1937) and Third (1938–1941), also built a vast number of new mines and heavy-industry factories in the Ural Mountains and Soviet Asia, so they would be safe from foreign invasion. In addition, there was a frantic race for autarky, trying to produce every type of mineral, raw material, machine and armament within Russia itself, the goal being to assure economic self-sufficiency in case of future wartime blockade.

Of course, there were also sound nonmilitary reasons for the Five-Year Plans. Russia leads all other countries in mineral resources, but its industry of the 1920's was too small to develop them. Even by 1927, the slender output of Soviet factories was no match for the huge crops of Russia's farms. Peasants obtained too few manufactured goods in payment for their products of the soil. Then too, the Marxist philosophy of USSR leaders demanded industrialization to create an abundance of goods for all to share. But more important than these other motives was the search for safety through military-economic power.

The First, Second, and Third Five-Year Plans are officially described as the second Soviet revolution, because the immense speed of industrialization required great public sacrifice and wrought changes in every aspect of Soviet life. Quickly a major transformation occurred in mass education. Hundreds of thousands of engineers and millions of skilled workers were needed for the growing industry, but the undisciplined progressive schools were not providing them. Hence in the early 1930's, the Soviet

---

[1] *Outline History of the U.S.S.R.*, Moscow: Foreign Languages Publishing House, 1960, pp. 290–293.

school system was drastically overhauled. Janitor-student control of the schools was abolished. Instead, teachers were given almost dictatorial powers. Courses were taught as thoroughly and severely as in Tsarist days, and the student brigades and study "complexes" of the 1920's vanished. No longer was prerevolutionary culture ridiculed. In the desperate search for knowledge, Tsarist culture was not only studied but almost revered.

To solve the shortage of skilled workers, long years of advanced mathematics and laboratory science became part of grade-school and high-school programs. These technical courses were compulsory. The best students went into colleges and universities, where they studied prescribed programs for practical professions. The entire school system became highly technical, to fill the acute shortage of industrial personnel.

At the start of the First Five-Year Plan in 1928, only one sixth of the USSR population lived in cities. By 1941, when Hitler's attack interrupted the Third Five-Year Plan, one of every three Soviet citizens was urban. The cities more than doubled their population, as millions of Soviet peasants moved into urban areas to work in the newly built factories. But the government built insufficient new urban housing to shelter them. As a result, more people were squeezed into the same space. On the average during the 1920's about two people occupied each city room. By the end of the 1930's this ratio had risen to three.

Factory laborers worked under much greater discipline than during the 1920's. As the First Five-Year Plan began, unions lost the right to strike. In the early 1930's, they were forbidden to bargain with government industry over wages and hours. Almost all industrial workers began to be paid according to piecework norms set by the state. If a worker failed to fulfill his norm, he didn't receive full pay. The Kremlin abandoned even lip service to the Marxian ideal of equal pay for all types of work. Instead, salaries for foremen, engineers, and administrators were vastly higher than for ordinary workmen, thus rewarding skilled personnel and encouraging their rise in the economic hierarchy.

Because of low real wages and bad housing, workers drifted from one factory or city to another, searching for better living conditions. At first the Kremlin made no attempt to stop this mass labor turnover, which reached the incredible peak of 150 per cent of all industrial workers during 1930. In that year, statistically all workers changed jobs once, and half changed twice. By 1938, when labor turnover still ran as high as 80 per cent, labor passports were introduced for all government employees. The passport listed the employee's work record—all promotions, commendations, and pay raises, and every demotion, dismissal, or reprimand. To obtain a new job, the worker had to display his labor passport. Even this measure proved insufficient, so a law of 1940 forbade all state employees to quit their jobs without permission from their manager. For trying to run away, the punishment was six months' forced labor at their old place of work.

Besides controlling the economy, labor, and education, the State Planning Commission attempted to plan literature and art. The majority of news in the Soviet press became industrial. Artists and writers were ordered to glorify industrialization. Creative people who refused were sometimes imprisoned or shot. As a result Soviet art and literature declined, producing dull paintings and statues of worker enthusiasm, and dreary propaganda novels like *Cement.*

As heavy industry increased dramatically during 1928–1940, so did armament production. At the start of the First Five-Year Plan, the USSR manufactured no submarines, no tanks, and only harmless scout planes. The tiny war industry struggled hard to make even inferior guns and bullets. Then came the great change.

During the First Plan of 1928–1932, Soviet shipyards expanded, and more than quadrupled their previous output. By 1932–1933, Stalin had enough warships to replace the Russian Pacific and Arctic naval fleets, which had vanished with the downfall of the Tsars. By 1940 the Red Navy had the largest fleets of motor torpedo boats and submarines in the world. Stalin guarded his shores mainly with a mosquito fleet, a poor man's navy of small, easy-to-build boats. At the time Russia had neither the steel, the technique, nor the shipyards to match Britain, America, or Japan in capital ships. But a mosquito fleet is good naval defense, since even one submarine is a threat to a surface navy. In 1940 one hundred Soviet subs patroled the Sea of Japan alone, as a gentle warning to Nippon's aggressive admirals.

Soviet aircraft industry tripled its output during the First Plan, and quintupled during the Second. No longer did the aircraft industry limit its production to scout planes. Fighters, strafers, and bombers began to pour out of aircraft factory gates. By 1940 Russia had an annual plane production almost as large as the United States. When Hitler attacked Russia in 1941, the USSR had one of the two largest fleets of combat aviation in the world, almost matching the huge Nazi Luftwaffe.

Neither did the first three Five-Year Plans neglect the land battleships, army tanks. For Soviet military strategy had little or no faith in fixed fortifications like the Maginot Line. The Red Army trained for mobile war, maneuvering fast-moving troop columns over a wide fluid front. Tankbuilding factories sprung up during the First Plan. During 1934–1939, the Red Army's fleet of tanks tripled. When the Soviet-German war finally began, USSR tank output was up to 12,000 a year, and total tanks numbered 24,000. Stalin entered World War II with the largest tank fleet in the world.

While building up its huge fleets of submarines, planes, and tanks, the Soviet government did not neglect artillery, which Stalin called the "god of battle." During the First Five-Year Plan, old gunmaking workers were rounded up and given laboratories to design new models. This invention by order was soon crowned by success. In the early 1930's, Soviet-designed heavy, anti-aircraft, and light artillery were put into mass production. By 1940, the last year of peace, the defense industry was producing nearly four times as much heavy ammunition, and almost five times as many cannon as Tsarist Russia produced annually at the height of World War I. When the Soviet-German war erupted in 1941, Stalin's Red Army had more ammunition and artillery on the front than its formidable opponent, Hitler's Wehrmacht.[2]

Backing this immense peacetime armament output was a heavy industry which since 1928 had quadrupled, and was third largest in the world, yielding in size only to its American and German competitors. Impressive gains had been made in civilian output. For example, pre-Plan USSR had imported most of its autos and tractors. On the eve of World War II, the Soviet Union manu-

---

[2] Raymond, Ellsworth, *Soviet Preparation for Total War* (doctoral dissertation), Ann Arbor: University of Michigan, 1951, pp. 133–138.

factured all its autos and tractors, led the world in production of grain harvesting combines, and was first in Europe in output of tractors and trucks. Giant factories built during 1928–1940 included Europe's biggest railway carbuilding plant and the world's largest tractor factory, in the Ural Mountains; Europe's largest auto factory, in the Volga valley; the third largest steel mill in the world, also in the Urals; and the world's greatest copper mill, in Central Asia on the shores of Lake Balkhash.

All this was expensive to build, requiring immense taxation and public sacrifice, since the USSR in the 1930's could obtain no large, long-term foreign loans. Yet vast quantities of Western machines had to be imported for such fast industrialization. To obtain the foreign currency to pay for foreign machines, Russia exported raw materials, food, and fuel which it could ill spare, even shipping out grain during a farm famine of 1932. Though all types of machinery were imported, Soviet purchases were largest for machine tools, the machines that make machines. As the Plans progressed, the USSR used the imported machine tools to build more and more of its own machinery, gradually reducing its dependence on foreign technical aid. Just like the Japanese, the Russians were clever copyists. A few models of each new foreign machine were imported. Soviet engineers studied them, then soon manufactured good imitations. Thus the dozens of electric locomotives operating on Moscow's suburban rail lines were all copied from one imported engine sent to Russia from the General Electric Company in the United States.

If imitation was too difficult, the USSR simply bought foreign patents. Many American companies cooperated. Thus most Soviet passenger planes in the late 1930's were DC-3's, mass-produced in Central Asia from blueprints provided by the Douglas Aircraft Corporation. Almost all passenger automobiles on Moscow streets were Soviet-built Buicks and Fords. In the annual military parades across Moscow's Red Square, one could see hundreds of Christie light tanks, also produced from US patents.

Throughout the prewar Plans, twice as many machine tools were purchased from abroad than produced in the USSR itself. These tools in turn manufactured such imitations as the GE locomotive, DC-3 plane, Buick, Ford, and Christie tank. Imports were so great during the early 1930's that the American, British and German machine-tool industries largely survived the world-wide economic depression by filling huge Soviet orders.

Politically the prewar Plans were an era of internal repression, which increased each year to a climax in the mass purge of 1937–1938, then diminished from 1939 onward. There were many reasons for this repression and purge: to instill public discipline during high-speed industrialization, to stifle mass complaints about the hardships accompanying industrialization, to expand state control over all aspects of daily life, to crush real and suspected enemies of Soviet progress, and to create a new, more obedient and more practical Soviet bureaucracy. Repression also became a vested interest for power-seeking police, and for ambitious young officials who gained fast promotion by inheriting the jobs of purge victims.

In 1928, a group of Tsarist engineers was arrested at the Donbas coal-mining town of Shakhty. In a show trial they confessed to mine mismanagement, sabotage, and espionage for Germany to help restore capitalism in the USSR. Other oldtime specialists and technicians made similar confessions in the trials of the Industrial Party (1930), Menshevik professors (1931), and Vickers engineers (1933). The Industrial Party was a Soviet group allegedly aiding France, the professors supposedly conspired with Mensheviks abroad, while the Russian and English engineers in the Vickers trial were accused of spying for England. Britain immediately retaliated by ceasing to purchase Soviet exports, forcing the USSR to release the English engineers.

All four trials created mistrust in the old Russian intelligentsia, which was non-Communist but had faithfully served the Soviet regime for many years. As a result, countless oldtime specialists were arrested or dismissed during 1928–1933, just when their skills were sorely needed for the start of fast industrialization. Apparently the accusations against those on trial were false, for many then convicted were later pardoned. Professor Ramzin, a leader of the Industrial Party, received the highest USSR decoration during World War II for inventing a new steam boiler. But fear of the West and desire to find a scapegoat for the many Soviet industrial accidents evidently induced the Kremlin to stage these unnecessary trials.

The only positive result of disgracing the old Russian intelligentsia was that engineering courses were hurriedly organized for thousands of young Communists, who otherwise would not have received technical education so quickly. As fast as the Communist engineers were trained, they replaced the old specialists.

Meanwhile Stalin continued to demote and disgrace old Politburo rivals who had contested his rise to power. During 1929 Trotsky was exiled from the USSR, while Bukharin was dismissed from both the Comintern and USSR Politburo. In 1932, Kamenev and Zinoviev were expelled from the Communist Party, and Bukharin, Rykov, and Tomski publicly apologized for opposition against Stalin's policies.

Repression of Tsarist intellectuals, old engineers, and Stalin's Kremlin rivals hurt small but important groups of the Soviet people. But the entire USSR population was affected by the drastic state persecution of religion during the First and Second Five-Year Plans. In 1929 the Soviet Constitution was amended to forbid freedom of religious propaganda. In practice this meant that churches no longer could operate charities, recreation facilities, social organizations, or Sunday schools. Nor could priests visit parishioners' homes, preach on the streets, or publish religious literature. No faith was spared from these restrictions. Both the Moslems and Baptists, who previously had been left undisturbed, were now persecuted as strongly as the Russian Orthodox Church. Thousands of priests were arrested on charges of conducting religious propaganda, while others hid from arrest in peasant villages or were forced to perform humiliating manual work such as sweeping the streets.

Religious congregations were still free to worship, if they could find a church building open for services. But the Soviet government closed most churches. A new road would be built straight through churchyards. Chapels were blown up overnight to make way for Communist construction projects. For example, the largest Moscow Orthodox cathedral was dynamited to clear the ground for erection of a "Palace of Soviets." Or most often, church buildings were simply confiscated by the government for failure to pay exorbitant state rent and taxes. Governmental ownership of all land, and of church buildings and sacred ornaments, legally facilitated these closures. Reliable statistics are absent on the extent of this antireligious campaign. But by the mid-1930's, available evidence indicates that four of every five churches, temples, and mosques in the USSR had been closed, destroyed, or converted into secular buildings such as warehouses, factories, garages and antireligious museums.

Private enterprise fared even more poorly. During the First Five-Year Plan, all the half-million private stores in the USSR were closed by the Soviet government. These small commercial establishments were taxed out of business, because their owners were officially deemed to be undesirable petty capitalists. Unfortunately the government did not have the personnel and equipment ready to open enough new state and cooperative stores to replace the private tradesmen. As a result, the USSR in 1932 had only one third as many stores as in pre-Plan 1927. Throughout the 1930's, despite a slow increase in the number of state and cooperative retail establishments, the long customer queues so common outside store doors were caused not just by scarcity of goods, but also by lack of sufficient stores. Thus daily shopping became a time-consuming chore.

While private stores were being taxed into oblivion, the Soviet government tried to collectivize Russia's 26 million small private farms by inducing the peasants to join large agricultural cooperatives. The peasants were disinterested, and by 1929 only 4 per cent of all peasant households had voluntarily entered collective farms. So Stalin made a violent speech demanding liquidation of the kulaks as a class by depriving them of their land. Local Soviet officials interpreted his speech as an appeal for fast gunpoint collectivization. By early 1930, 55 per cent of all peasant households had been forced into collective farms, though the First Five-Year Plan had only called for 20 per cent by 1932. The peasants resisted by hoarding food and killing their livestock rather than surrendering it to the collectives. By February 1930 there were widespread peasant disturbances, and government officials were shooting 40 peasants a day. Stalin then intervened, made a speech accusing the collectivizers of being "dizzy with success," and ordered a halt to the collectivization brutality for which he himself was responsible. Collectivization was made voluntary, kulaks were allowed to join the collectives, and collective farmers were permitted to retain their houses, gardens, and some livestock as private property. Millions of peasants immediately withdrew from the collective farms, and within a few months only 25 per cent of peasant families were collective farmers. Heavy taxation forced them back, so 61 per cent were on collectives in 1932, and 93 per cent by 1938. But gunpoint collectivization was never attempted again.

Crops slumped during the collectivization excesses, so Soviet cities had to undergo food rationing until 1935. Livestock herds declined much more than field crops, and required much longer to revive. During 1928–1933, the USSR lost over half its horses and cattle, two thirds of its pigs, and seven tenths of its sheep and goats.

As the hardships of industrialization and collectivization multiplied during the First Five-Year Plan, small opposition groups formed within the Communist Party. These groups apparently united into a loose anti-Stalin coalition, led by Stalin's disillusioned friends rather than his past Politburo rivals. According to post-Stalin Soviet histories, by 1934 the majority of the Central Committee of the Communist Party were conspiring to dismiss Stalin from his key post of party secretary-general.

Sensing political danger, Stalin in 1933 began a routine reduction of the Communist Party to weed out members of dubious background. About 800,000 persons were expelled from the party, but usually not arrested. Then a spectacular murder either terrified Stalin, or gave him the excuse for a truly titanic purge. In late 1934, Politburo member Sergei Kirov was assassinated in Leningrad party headquarters by a young Communist named Nikolaev, the husband of Kirov's secretary.

Strange circumstances preceded this apparent crime of passion. Leningrad police knew that Nikolaev was armed and vindictive, yet failed to disarm or arrest him. The endangered Kirov received no extra guards. A key witness to the murder died soon afterward in an auto accident which spared all other passengers. The post-Stalin Soviet press has hinted that Stalin possibly made the murder easy, using Nikolaev as an unsuspecting pawn. For Kirov was young, handsome, ambitious, and more popular with the masses than the Georgian dictator.

A few weeks before Kirov's demise, he was condemned to death by the Labor Solidarists (N.T.S.), a Russian émigré organization with headquarters in Yugoslavia. At the time N.T.S. planned to assassinate all Politburo members, starting with Kirov. When Kirov was shot, the Labor Solidarists proudly assumed full credit for the assassination, though Nikolaev was never an émigré. At first the Soviet press accepted this N.T.S. claim.

Soon however, the Kirov murder was reexplained as part of a vast treasonous plot by Stalin's old Politburo rivals. Gradually the former rivals were arrested, along with other high officials who were supposed accomplices. At three Moscow show trials during 1936–1938, these prominent men publicly confessed to such crimes as organizing the Kirov murder, planning to assassinate all other top Soviet leaders, sabotaging USSR military power, blowing up Soviet factories, plotting to restore Russian capitalism, and intriguing to surrender the Ukraine to Germany, Belorussia to Poland, and the Soviet Far East to Japan. By court decision Kamenev and Zinoviev were executed in 1936, and Bukharin and Rykov in 1938. Trotsky, alleged mastermind of this high-level conspiracy, was sentenced to death in absentia, the sentence being fulfilled by a Spanish Communist who murdered Trotsky in Mexico City during 1940.

As Stalin's old rivals were executed within the USSR, their relatives, office staffs, protégés, and friends were also executed or imprisoned. Anyone who ever crossed the path of all those alleged criminals was under suspicion and often purged. Meanwhile the police used the opportunity of mass purges to arrest almost every person of dubious political background: former Tsarist bourgeoisie, priests, former kulaks, Russians with relatives abroad, foreigners who immigrated into the USSR and became Soviet citizens. Finally no one was safe. Millions of loyal Soviet citizens were demoted, arrested, or imprisoned.

At first the great purge did not harm the army officer corps, which lived in comfortable isolation from the Soviet civilian masses. Then in 1937 the Nazi Gestapo and Czechoslovak secret service informed the Soviet police that Marshal Tukhachevski, assistant USSR minister of war, allegedly planned a military coup. Kremlin guards were to kill Stalin, while Moscow garrison troops would seize the police ministry. The list of Tukhachevski's coplotters read like a *Who's Who* of the Red Army, and included the Leningrad garrison commander, the chief political commissar of the army, the assistant commander of all Red cavalry, and many others.

The marshal and six other generals were tried and shot a month after their arrest, without public trial or confessions of guilt. Afterward the Soviet police methodically purged all bureau chiefs in the war ministry, all commanders and most assistant commanders of USSR military districts, and even most officers of medium rank who were friends of Tukhachevski.

By 1938 all Soviet life was paralyzed by fear, and the humblest bureaucrat was afraid to make decisions because he might be accused of sabotage. *Izvestia,* the chief governmental newspaper, revealed that most Soviet officials made three copies of every order they issued. One was officially dispatched, the second filed in the office safe, and the third was carried in a personal briefcase day and night, "just in case." Because of this bureaucratic fear, and mass arrest of countless skilled engineers, growth of heavy industry was slowing down. War clouds were looming in West Europe, and a terrified nation is not the best human material for battle. The purge had to be ended.

Yagoda—the police minister who started the 1930's purge—was arrested in 1937 for insufficient harshness, and executed in 1938 as an alleged member of the vast Trotskyite conspiracy. Yezhov, his successor, was too harsh and had to be removed to stop the purge. In 1939 he quietly disappeared, and is rumored to have died in an insane asylum. The police was then heavily purged, and most assistant ministers were shot. A few thousand political prisoners were released from forced labor camps, on the grounds that they had been falsely accused. Local party organizations in 1939 were told to abandon mass purging. Church persecution was eased, and the head of the Militant Godless Society admitted that half of all Soviet citizens were sincerely religious. Stalin publicly announced that "life was better, life was gayer." The great purge was over.

The purge toll was fantastic. Dead were six members of Stalin's own Politburo, 70 per cent of the 1934 Central Committee of the Communist Party, and most ministers of the USSR governmental cabinet. Three fifths of all regional leaders, almost three fifths of the 1934 party congress, and half of all army officers had been arrested. About half the rank-and-file members had been expelled from the party. Almost every family in Russia had a relative killed or imprisoned by the great purge.

The post-Stalin Kremlin condemns the excesses of the 1930's purge, and has exonerated more than 7,700 high-ranking purge victims, many posthumously. But no full explanation has been offered for the Kirov murder, and Soviet histories still claim that Trotsky, Bukharin, Kamenev, and Zinoviev were dangerous traitors. Under the circumstances, impartial explanation of the purge can only be speculative.

Nikolaev, Kirov's murderer, apparently was influenced by Zinoviev's writings, but didn't belong to a widespread anti-Stalin conspiracy. The conspiracy was probably not a loose association of defeated Trotskyites, but a group of powerful disillusioned Stalinists. For example, many Russian émigrés believe the Tukhachevski plot to have been real, regardless of Gestapo or Czech machinations. Yet at first, Stalin struck against bogus opponents, his old Politburo rivals, who were already broken and therefore confessed under police torture to the most traitorous crimes. Their confessions on internal intrigue cannot be checked, but careful examination of Nazi and Japanese records has revealed no collusion between Tokyo, Berlin, and Stalin's old rivals.

Soviet military power was weakened not by a Trotskyite conspiracy, but by Stalin's own purge of army officers. The many industrial accidents during the purge probably resulted more from incompetence than sabotage. And purge brutality aroused much fearful hatred of Stalin, his police, and Communism itself.

What did the Kremlin gain from the great purge? First, the arrest of millions probably liquidated all dangerous opposition movements. Second, because Soviet mankind was paralyzed by fear and no one trusted his neighbor, new opposition groups were almost impossible to form. Third, Lenin's old bureaucracy was largely replaced by youthful officials who owed their careers to Stalin. Thus the purge built Stalin's personal political machine.

Soviet foreign policy during the prewar Plans combined limited warfare with intricate diplomatic maneuvers to postpone major war. The first limited war came in 1929, when the Manchurian government seized the Chinese-Eastern Railway. Soviet troops immediately invaded Manchuria, defeated the Manchu army, and returned the railway to USSR control.

A real international danger arose during 1931, when the Japanese army conquered all of Manchuria, converting it into the puppet state of Manchukuo. This time there was no invasion from the USSR. Soviet Russia was not ready to fight the formidable Japanese Army, and made the best of a bad situation by selling the Chinese-Eastern Railway to Manchukuo.

Other Soviet reactions to the Japanese aggression came quickly. A number of Soviet factories were converted to armament production, so that USSR munitions output would increase. Belts of light fortifications were built along both the Far Eastern and western frontiers, as well as on exposed seacoasts. The entire Red Army was equipped with gas masks, mass parachuting became a Soviet sport, and "Ready for Defense" tests were instituted for organized athletics. To ensure better police control of the population, the old Tsarist practice of internal passports was revived.

In the early 1930's, the USSR concluded nonaggression pacts with two European powers, France and Italy, as well as with four countries along the western frontier: Finland, Estonia, Latvia, and Poland. Stalin in 1933 explained these pacts as reflecting foreign respect for the fast growth of USSR industry, but actually the Soviet government was anxious to sign them for additional security.

In the same 1933, the USSR finally succeeded in establishing diplomatic relations with the United States. The main American motives for recognizing Communist Russia were desire for increased trade and fear of Japan. Russia was so delighted that two of the finest Moscow buildings were assigned to the new U.S. Embassy.

However, a new foreign threat to the USSR arose in 1933. Hitler was elected to power in Germany. At the time the Kremlin obviously misunderstood and underestimated the Nazi movement, because German Communists had been ordered not to cooperate with Weimar socialists. Russia soon realized its mistake, when Hitler crushed the German Communist Party and began rearming Germany for all-out war against the USSR. Now Russia was threatened from the east and west by highly aggressive Japan and Nazi Germany, who soon united in an Anti-Comintern Pact openly aimed against the Soviet Union.

Stalin responded to this double danger of the late 1930's by a threefold foreign policy: alliance and friendship with Western democratic nations, armed resistance to the Axis, and attempts to gain the friendship of Axis powers. Russia tried to divide the non-Soviet world, to prevent another capitalist encirclement like the one in the Russian Civil War. The USSR joined the League of Nations in 1934, and until 1939 vainly appealed for League members to take collective action against Axis aggression in Ethiopia, China, and Austria. The Comintern stopped its revolutionary propaganda in non-Axis nations, ordering foreign Communists to form united fronts with Western socialists and liberals. Soviet diplomatic relations were established with Czechoslovakia, Rumania, Bulgaria, and Albania. Soviet military alliances were concluded with France and Czechoslovakia in 1935, and with Outer Mongolia during 1934 and 1936.

In direct opposition to Axis countries, the USSR in 1933 terminated the Soviet-German army cooperation which had existed since 1922. From 1935 Russian frontier forces fought 300 to 400 skirmishes each year against Japanese troops along the Manchurian border. Both sides started the skirmishes, testing each other's strength. During 1936–1938, Soviet military advisors, tanks, trucks, and planes were secretly sent to the Spanish Republic, aiding the latter in its unsuccessful civil war against the Fascist protégé, General Francisco Franco. This aid proved insufficient for republican victory, but at least forced Germany and Italy to concentrate on helping Franco until he won in 1939. As long as Hitler and Mussolini were diverted toward Spain, Russia was more secure from Axis attack.

On Moscow orders in 1936, the Chinese Communists allied with the Kuomintang to fight the Japanese invasion striking into China proper. Then in 1937 Russia concluded a nonaggression pact with Chiang Kai Shek, and began sending him arms along the old Silk Road through Sinkiang. Much as the Kremlin disliked Chiang for his anti-Communism, Russia had to save Kuomintang China from the much more dangerous Japan. The Soviet Far Eastern army fought a large-scale battle against Japanese troops in 1938 at Lake Khasan on the Siberian-Korean frontier, and a small undeclared war against Japan in 1939 along the Mongolian-Manchukuo border. Both engagements were won by the USSR, and Japan was greatly impressed by the strength of Soviet armed forces.

On the other hand, Soviet attempts were made throughout the 1930's to come to agreement with Japan and Germany. The USSR offered Japan nonaggression pacts in 1934 and 1937, but was refused. Nazi-Soviet treaties guaranteeing peace in the Baltic area were proposed unsuccessfully by Russia in both 1934 and 1936. During 1936 the USSR also suggested that the Third Reich join the Soviet-French alliance, which had been concluded in 1935 against Germany.

In 1938 Hitler created an international crisis by demanding the German-inhabited Sudetenland (west Bohemia) from Czechoslovakia. At first the Kremlin promised military aid to the Czechs, if France would honor its alliances with Czechoslovakia and the USSR. But when France asked if Russia would fight, the USSR suggested referring the Czech crisis to the impotent League of Nations.

During the autumn of 1938, the Munich conference of British, French, German, and Italian leaders solved the Czech crisis by ceding the Sudetenland to Nazi Germany. Russia was frightened, not so much by the Munich agreement, as by Soviet exclusion from a crucially important summit meeting. According to the Soviet press, both Fascist and democratic great powers of west Europe were allying against the Soviet Union.

Desperately trying to split this nonexistent alliance, Russia in early 1939 simultaneously offered a trade agreement to Hitler, and an anti-Nazi alliance to Britain and France. The two great Western democracies were disinterested, describing the Soviet offer of alliance as premature. But Nazi Germany, which had refused USSR cooperation during 1934–1936, immediately began cautious negotiations. German occupation of all Czechoslovakia during 1939 spring failed to disrupt the Nazi-Soviet exploratory conversations. In contrast, Czechoslovakia's disappearance frightened Britain and France into seeking the Soviet alliance they had previously spurned. Russia was dismayed when the two Western democracies sent to Moscow third-ranking negotiators, who rejected Soviet demands for military bases in the Baltic states, and

Red Army admittance into Poland if the Poles were attacked by Hitler. Meanwhile Germany was willing to make many concessions to the USSR, so Russia would not aid Poland against forthcoming Nazi invasion.

After concluding a trade agreement, Russia and Germany on August 23, 1939, signed a nonaggression pact which superceded the old Soviet-German neutrality treaty of 1926. Ostensibly the new treaty was a strong nonaggression pact, even providing for mutual consultation on matters of common interest. Much more important than the pact, however, was its secret protocol dividing East Europe between the Soviet Union and the Third Reich. Russia's share was Finland, Estonia, Latvia, East Poland, and Bessarabia, with Lithuania being added a month later.

The Nazi-Soviet pact had immediate worldwide repercussions. First, Germany felt safe from two-front war, and attacked Poland on September 1, 1939. Britain and France responded by declaring war against Germany on September 3, so World War II started with Russia remaining comfortably neutral. Second, Japan was frightened by the pact, and hurriedly stopped the undeclared Soviet-Japanese war in Outer Mongolia. Third, Moscow ordered Communist parties throughout the world to abandon anti-Fascism, and to adopt a neutral attitude toward World War II. As a result the British and French parties opposed their nations' war effort, while American Communists demanded U.S. neutrality with the slogan "the Yanks aren't coming!" Fourth, Britain and France semiblockaded Russia to prevent strategic materials from reaching Germany via the USSR. Fifth, Russia itself supplied Germany with large quantities of grain, cotton, oil, and minerals useful to the Nazi war effort.

Worldshaking as the Nazi-Soviet pact was, the Kremlin had little faith in it. The standing Red Army sharply increased from 1,960,000 men in 1939 to 3,240,000 in 1940. Meanwhile the Soviet General Staff drafted war plans against Britain, France, and Nazi Germany. Having helped start World War II, Stalin apparently planned to intervene later in the war (when both sides would be exhausted), and share the spoils of victory. However during 1939–1940, the Kremlin was uncertain which side Soviet future intervention should assist.

Taking advantage of its neutrality during the first two years of

World War II, the USSR made large-scale annexations along the Soviet western frontier. Deprived of German support because of the secret protocol of the Nazi-Soviet pact, and unable to receive aid from far-off beleagured Britain and France, the small nations of East Europe usually offered little resistance. During the autumn of 1939, Russia annexed eastern Poland after Hitler's Wehrmacht had conquered the western part of that unfortunate country. When Poland disappeared from the map, Russia demanded and quickly obtained military bases in Estonia, Latvia and Lithuania. The three Baltic states also signed military alliances with the USSR, ostensibly aimed against Britain and France but actually against Nazi Germany.

During the winter of 1939, Russia requested naval bases, some frontier adjustments and a military alliance from Finland, which with unexpected stubbornness refused part of the Soviet demands. The exasperated USSR invaded Finland on November 30, 1939, anticipating easy victory. A Communist cabinet claiming to be the legal government of Finland was even organized at Terioki, the first sizeable Finnish town captured by the Red Army. But Finnish ski troops cut Soviet mechanized columns into ribbons along the narrow roads through the frontier forests. The Red Army had to pause and regroup, not defeating the main Finnish forces until March 1940.

Most Western nations were angered by the Soviet aggression against small democratic Finland. Before 1939 ended, Russia was expelled from the League of Nations. Planes from Fascist Italy manned by Italian aviators fought the Red Army on the Finnish front. The United States almost broke diplomatic relations with the USSR. Hamstrung by the Nazi-Soviet pact, Germany could not intervene, but promised Finland postwar assistance. Most dangerous to Russia was the formation of Anglo-French special troops, training for Arctic warfare in Finland. Confronted by such international opposition, the USSR gave Finland a lenient peace treaty, taking little more than originally demanded.

During the summer of 1940, the Kremlin was frightened by the German strength and French weakness proven by Hitler's conquest of France in a mere 20 days. The Soviet reaction was to extend the USSR frontier westward by annexing Estonia, Latvia, Lithuania, and the Rumanian lands of Bessarabia and

Northern Bukovina. Because of the Nazi-Soviet pact, Germany did not protest, but occupied Bulgaria and the remainder of Rumania to protect them from further Soviet advance.

Meanwhile Russia pursued a diplomacy of isolation. Stalin ignored a British offer to cede the Turkish Straits to the USSR, if Soviet material aid to Germany would cease. In the autumn of 1940, when Hitler offered Iran and India to the USSR to induce Russia into joining the Axis alliance, Molotov demanded Bulgaria. Hitler refused, and soon ordered his Wehrmacht to plan a 1941 invasion of the USSR.

Soviet friction with Germany became open in the spring of 1941, when the USSR concluded a treaty of friendship with Yugoslavia just before the latter was invaded by the Wehrmacht. When a Nazi attack on Russia appeared imminent, a Soviet neutrality treaty was concluded in April 1941 with Japan, so the USSR would be spared a two-front war. Japan was also pleased by this pact, which safeguarded the Japanese rear from Soviet attack during most of the forthcoming Pacific war.

The war danger forced Stalin in May to become Premier, retaining former premier Molotov as vice-premier and foreign minister. In a final attempt to appease Hitler, the USSR broke diplomatic relations with the exile governments of Belgium, Norway, and even Yugoslavia. But the appeasement was too little and too late for Germany, which invaded the USSR on June 22, 1941.

Suggestions for Further Reading

Adams, Arthur E., *Stalin and His Times*. New York: Holt, Rinehart and Winston, 1972.

Baykov, Alexander, *The Development of the Soviet Economic System*, New York: Macmillan, 1947.

Beloff, Max, *The Foreign Policy of Soviet Russia, 1929–1941*, New York: Oxford University Press, 1949.

Heymann, Hans, *We Can Do Business with Russia*, Chicago: Ziff Davis, 1945.

Hyde, H. Montgomery, *Stalin: The History of a Dictator*. New York: Farrar, Straus and Giroux, 1972.

JASNY, NAUM, *The Socialized Agriculture of the USSR,* Stanford: Stanford University Press, 1949.

KHRUSHCHEV, NIKITA S., *The Crimes of the Stalin Era,* New York: The New Leader, 1956.

KLINE, GEORGE L., ed., *Soviet Education,* New York: Columbia University Press, 1957.

LEVYTSKY, BORYS, *The Stalinist Terror in the Thirties.* Stanford: Stanford University Press, 1974.

MEDVEDEV, ROY A., *Let History Judge: The Origins and Consequences of Stalinism.* New York: Knopf, 1972.

Nazi-Soviet Relations, 1939–1941, Washington: U.S. Department of State, 1948.

STRUVE, GLEB, *Soviet Russian Literature, 1917–1950,* Norman: University of Oklahoma Press, 1951.

ULAM, ADAM B., *Stalin: The Man and His Era.* New York: Viking, 1973.

USSR GOVERNMENT, *Documents and Materials relating to the Eve of the Second World War,* New York: International Publishers, 1954.

Chapter 7

The Nazi-Soviet War

Four o'clock in the morning, Sunday, June 22, 1941, black Nazi bombers roared out of the twilight over western Russian cities. The largest army that Hitler ever assembled attacked across the USSR's European frontier. At half past five, the German Ambassador handed a declaration of war to Vice-Premier Molotov, who quietly complained: "Do we deserve this?"

Hitler caught the Kremlin by surprise. Stalin wasn't even in Moscow. He had so misjudged the situation that he was resting in the Caucasus. That morning the reins of Soviet government were in the hands of slow methodical Molotov. Russia was not told of war for eight hours, because Molotov first had to contact Stalin, then draft a speech which would break the news gently.

By noon, all was ready. Molotov went on the radio and tried to read a stirring speech. But the effect was spoiled by his own stammering and stuttering. After his last nervous shout, "victory will be ours," massed trumpets blew bugle calls and the Red Army chorus roared out marching songs. Unforgettable was the sharp contrast between that impressive music and Molotov's voice.

Well might he worry. Nazi tank columns knifed through Soviet troops like butter. Minsk, capital of Belorussia, was captured by a Panzer group numbering no more than five hundred men. Every day another Soviet city fell. At the end of the first half-year of war, Hitler ruled Bessarabia, the Baltic states, Belorussia and the Ukraine. Leningrad was encircled, and Moscow besieged.

In six months the Red Army lost one fourth of all European USSR.

Never has the Soviet government fully explained this 1941 military disaster. One excuse is that Hitler caught Russia by surprise with his overnight betrayal of the 1939 Nazi-Soviet non-aggression pact. Yet Wehrmacht invasion could hardly have been a complete surprise. For two months before the attack, Hitler massed troops on the Soviet frontier. About two weeks ahead of the invasion, the Luftwaffe ended mass air raids on England—a clear sign that German planes were moving east. Just in case, the Red Army massed most of its men and planes also on the Soviet-Reich frontier. Weeks before war began, anti-aircraft guns were installed on the roofs of large Moscow buildings, and detailed air raid instructions were published by the Moscow press.

But the absence of a Nazi ultimatum seems to have lulled the Kremlin into false security. Complete military preparations were never made, and suicidal mistakes occurred on the very eve of war.

The Red Army was prepared for offense, not defense, and if attacked, planned to fight the war on enemy territory. So the 180 USSR divisions along the west frontier in June 1941 had no defensive plans and no defense in depth. Most Soviet troops were massed into a thin ribbon just inside the border. Giant supply depots were filled to bursting with arms, ammunition, and oil—not in the safe rear, but so close to the frontier that they could be shelled by German long-range artillery.

No Soviet fortifications existed. In the early 1930's, the "Stalin line" of barbed wire, machine gun nests, tank traps, artillery emplacements, and pillboxes had been built along the western frontier. But in 1939–1940 Russia had seized East Poland, Bessarabia, and the Baltic states, moving the Soviet border one hundred miles or more to the west. It was decided to build new fortifications on the new frontier, bringing up wire and equipment from the old Stalin line. Hitler struck at just the right moment when the old fortifications had been dismantled, and the new were not yet built.

When war began, face to face across the frontier were 180 divisions on each side. But the German divisions were fully manned, while the Russian divisions were skeleton forces not mobilized to full strength. At first the Wehrmacht actually outnumbered the Red Army in both men and machines.

To make matters worse, Russia had armed too soon, and its weapons were out of date. Hitler's blitzkrieg in west Europe compared to Soviet setbacks in the Finnish winter war of 1939–1940 convinced the Kremlin that it was time to rearm. In the spring of 1941, the Red Army was retooling with new and better tanks, guns, and planes. Hitler picked the perfect moment for attack. The Red Army had abandoned its old military hardware, and had not yet learned to use the new. When war first came, hundreds of Soviet planes were destroyed on the ground, because pilots were not trained to fly them. More USSR tanks were lost from bad driving than in battle.

To all this, add widespread wartime sabotage by racial minorities in USSR western borderlands. Ukrainian peasants welcomed German troops with the traditional offering of bread and salt. Lithuania revolted, freeing two cities from Soviet rule before the Wehrmacht arrived. Sabotage was so great in Estonia and Latvia that the Red Army issued a pleading appeal in the Baltic press: "Don't blow up bridges. Don't wreck railways. Don't cut telegraph and telephone wires!"

Once military retreat started, it snowballed. Thousands of Soviet planes and tanks, and millions of soldiers were lost. In six months Hitler captured one third of Russia's industry, and two fifths of its farms and railways. Sixty-five million Soviet citizens (one third of the nation) went under Nazi rule. Thus the USSR began its war with a crippling handicap. No wonder Hitler proudly proclaimed in October 1941: "The enemy is already beaten, and will never rise again."

To salvage what was left of Russia, the Soviet government decreed a most drastic war mobilization. From the very first day of war, all European Russia was placed under martial law. Thereafter, any civilian criminal was tried by a harsh army court-martial.

When war was but a few days old, all private radio sets had to be sent to government warehouses, where they stayed in storage for the duration. Many people hid their precious radios, not to listen, but to save them for postwar use. For the warehouses stacked sets in huge piles with no wrapping to keep out dampness or dirt. Penalties ranging from six months in jail to shooting were decreed for Russians who hid their radios from the state. Thus the Soviet public was sealed off from Nazi radio propaganda, and enemy spies lost their radio channels.

On the fifth day of the war, directors of factories, mines, stores, farms, and transport services were ordered to work their employees one to three hours overtime a day. Children under sixteen worked only two hours overtime a day. The same decree abolished vacations for all employees in both state enterprises and cooperatives. Most factories immediately changed from three 8-hour shifts per day to two shifts of 11 hours each, with the twelveth and twenty-fourth hours reserved for lunch.

As early as the war's second week, men from the ages of 17 to 50 were being drafted into military service. Considerable numbers of young women were also conscripted to be army nurses, communications personnel, and cooks. In frontal cities, all civilian men from 16 to 60, and women from 18 to 50, had to take turns as air raid wardens at their house or place of work. To make sure the wardens did their duty, this civil defense was headed by Local Anti-Aircraft Defense sections of the USSR police ministry.

Two weeks after war began, Stalin spoke on the public loudspeakers to his nation, ordering wholesale evacuation and ruthless earth-scorching of threatened areas:

> In case of a forced retreat, all rolling stock must be evacuated. The enemy must not be left a single locomotive, a single railway car, a single pound of grain or gallon of fuel. . . . All valuable property, including metals, grain and fuel, that cannot be withdrawn, must be destroyed without fail.

Almost as soon as Stalin finished speaking, wild defeatist rumors spread throughout Russia. Three days after Stalin's speech, a minimum punishment of two to five years in prison camp was decreed for anyone who spread false alarming rumors.

Even before Stalin spoke, the Soviet government was already evacuating Moscow. For days the city streets were littered with burnt paper, and the air was dark with smoke. Government ministries were burning their old secret files, so that no valuable information could fall into Nazi hands. Then each ministry moved inland, leaving only a skeleton staff behind. Though the Volga city of Kuibyshev later became the USSR wartime capital, most ministries did not go there. Instead they separated to various cities up and down the Volga, throughout the Urals, and even as far inland as West Siberia. When the Germans first bombed Moscow one month after the war's start, the working apparatus of the Soviet government was already gone, decentralized into a dozen or more remote cities.

Meanwhile the greatest industrial evacuation in history was under way. In or near Moscow, Leningrad, and the Ukrainian capital Kiev were three fourths of USSR munition plants, and they had to be saved. Civilian machine building factories are easily convertible to armament manufacture, and most of these were also in European USSR on the path of the German advance. So Soviet European munitions and machine building industries took to the rails, fleeing to the safe Urals and Soviet Asia. Peak factory migration came in the autumn of 1941, when the Wehrmacht attacked the Moscow region, the most heavily industrialized in Russia.

A total of 1,360 factories were evacuated eastward during the Soviet-German War. How vital these evacuated plants were to the Soviet war effort can easily be seen. When reinstalled in the East, they produced two thirds of Soviet late wartime output of shells, bombs, and mines!

When evacuation was impossible, earth-scorching prevented the Nazis from exploiting their industrial gains. Soviet sappers blew a hole in the great Dnieper dam, then second largest in the world, flooding hundreds of square miles of farmland. Water has to be constantly pumped out of the huge Donbas coal mines to keep them dry. Retreating Russians wrecked the pumps, and the mine shafts filled with water. Fires were extinguished under loaded iron and steel making furnaces, which cooled into solid masses of metal. As railways were abandoned, the last retreating train carefully removed one rail from each track. Farm tractors and trucks were absorbed by the withdrawing Soviet troops. The invading Wehrmacht lived off the land for its food, but captured Soviet industry never could be restored in time to help the Nazi war machine.

Meanwhile, riding east with the evacuated machines came 12

million people. Most were industrial workers accompanying the machines, Communist officials and their families, or the wives and children of Soviet servicemen. Refugees flooded Volga, Ural, and Asian cities in numbers almost too large to handle. In this turmoil of shifting population, factory workers began to change jobs, and evacuated plants often lost their evacuated personnel. So in December 1941, five to eight years in prison labor camp were decreed for any workers deserting a job in an armament plant, or in any factory or mine filling war industry orders.

By late 1941, all Soviet cities were living on rationed food. The size of an individual's ration depended on his importance to the war effort. Servicemen and heavy industry workers received the largest amounts. Next came light industry workers, then white collar employees, then children, and finally adult dependents. The largest rations were adequate, had they been fully received. But at first they were not. Soon one of every three people walking city streets bore facial marks of malnutrition. Old Russians became walking skeletons wasting away to wartime death.

From the early days of war, all civilians had to obtain a government permit to take a train trip, except in suburbs. Permission was rarely granted. A wife could not travel to visit her wounded soldier husband, unless he was dying. Many passenger trains were converted into mobile hospitals, hauling injured soldiers to the rear. Nonessential cargo like consumer goods and farm fertilizer was thrown off the rails. All parcel post was forbidden except packages to soldiers.

To finance the war, income taxes were doubled by a special war tax. Private bank accounts were frozen, with only small amounts allowed to be withdrawn. The public was pressured into buying more government bonds than ever before, and also into contributing immense sums to the Red Army and defense funds. One collective farmer alone gave enough money to pay for a tank.

Religion also was mobilized into the war effort. A few days after the Nazi attack, the Soviet government asked the various churches for support. Most organized religions did support the USSR war effort because of love for their native land. In return the Kremlin made considerable concessions. Religious services were again permitted in many churches, mosques, and temples, which had been closed for years. Several seminaries, monasteries, and convents were allowed to reopen. The Society of Militant Godless abruptly disbanded. For the first time in almost two decades, the Russian Orthodox Church was able to elect a Patriarch, the Orthodox chief of church. Thus the USSR countered the Nazi propaganda, which proclaimed Hitler a friend of religion and a deliverer of true believers from Communist atheism.

Soviet wartime propaganda quickly abandoned Communist dogma in favor of appeals to patriotism. Thus the army slogan "For Stalin" soon disappeared, and was replaced by "For the sacred motherland." Government censorship was eased on Soviet artists and writers, who responded by producing wartime works fervently appealing for salvation of Mother Russia. Many anti-Soviet intellectuals eagerly volunteered for front-line duty, hating Stalin but quite willing to die for their native land. A wave of patriotism swept the Soviet population into tremendous self-sacrifice, which was enhanced by the brutality of the Nazi Gestapo in the German-occupied regions of the USSR.

This total Soviet war mobilization, combining ruthless compulsion with shrewd propaganda, was masterminded by a small group of leaders who constituted the war cabinet or so-called State Defense Committee, headed by Stalin. Each committee member supervised key tasks: Molotov, foreign affairs and tank building; Malenkov, party affairs and airplane manufacture; Voroshilov (later Bulganin), armed forces; Beria, police and ammunition production; Voznesenski, economic planning and artillery output; Mikoyan, foreign trade; and Kaganovich, the railways.

The eventual fate of this brilliant committee was mostly unhappy. Voznesenski was executed in 1949 by Stalin, who himself died in 1953. Beria was executed by the post-Stalin collective leadership in 1953. Molotov, Malenkov, and Kaganovich were purged from power in 1957, Bulganin in 1958, and Voroshilov in 1960. Only Mikoyan remained an important Soviet leader long after Stalin's death.

The first great Soviet military victory came at the close of 1941 in the Battle of Moscow. Here grave errors were committed by both sides. The Germans began the offensive during the autumn rains, when progress would inevitably be slow. A large

Russian army defending the city obeyed literally the Kremlin orders not to yield an inch of Soviet soil. So the Russians held fast, only to be encircled by Nazi tank units. No Soviet troops were left between the Germans and Moscow.

The Kremlin thought that the Soviet capital was lost. Most Moscow police were thrown overnight outside the city to slow the expected German advance. All city stores abandoned rationing, so store shelves would be empty when Nazi looters arrived. Meanwhile many Moscow bureaucrats fled helter-skelter eastward in trains, trucks, and official limousines.

Muscovites awoke one morning in mid-October to find no police, no rationed stores, and a frantic official evacuation. The city panicked for three days, mobs looted stores and warehouses, and rumors spread that the Soviet government had fallen. At this moment a few German tank or parachute divisions could easily have captured the helpless USSR capital. But the poorly informed Wehrmacht delayed its advance, in order to mop up the Russian army which had been encircled.

This delay proved fatal for the Nazis. After three days Siberian troops arrived and entrenched between Moscow and the German army. Soviet soldiers hurriedly converted into police restored order in the city. Under the command of Marshal Zhukov the Siberians at first were only defensive, waiting for the weather to turn bitter cold. In early December 1941 the temperature dropped to below zero, and Zhukov counterattacked. The Germans were driven back and never again threatened Moscow.

At the time of this major victory, half of all USSR industry was out of operation, and most armament factories were inactive, moving east on railway flatcars in the industrial evacuation. But during 1942, most of the evacuated factories were reassembled and reopened in the Urals, Volga valley, and Asiatic USSR. Every trick was used to install the migrant machinery quickly. Evacuated machines were placed between the rows of original equipment in huge Eastern factories. Crude wooden sheds were jerry-built to house the incoming machines. Any buildings with wide floor-space were also used: warehouses, offices, and even schools.

All this eastern industry, new and old, made a truly tremendous conversion to armament production. Every little machine shop did its bit. Even tiny fish canneries in the remote Far East ground out shellcases. A Moscow soft drink factory made gasoline bottles for Molotov cocktails to throw at tanks. Because of total conversion, output of locomotives, railway cars, farm tractors, and farm trucks was almost zero during the whole war.

As millions of men were drafted into the army, shortage of industrial labor became acute. Yet eastern cities were swollen with unemployed evacuees. A law of early 1942 mobilized for industry all able-bodied urban men from 16 to 55, and all healthy city women from 16 to 50, who were not already employed. Sole exemptions were students, and mothers caring for small children. Persons avoiding this mobilization were sentenced to one year of forced labor in their home city.

These extreme measures produced a fantastic increase in Soviet armament output. When the Battle of Stalingrad began in the late summer of 1942, the Red Army possessed more tanks, planes, and machine guns than the invading Wehrmacht, which never again had superiority in weapons.

The six-month Battle of Stalingrad was the turning point in both the Nazi-Soviet War and the entire European phase of World War II. During the summer of 1942 the Germans started their last major offensive in Russia, driving for the Caucasus and the lower Volga River. Hitler's objective was to capture the huge Caucasian oil fields, or at least stop Caucasian oil from coming north to the Red Army via Volga tankers. The lower Volga bends furthest westward at Stalingrad (now renamed Volgograd), which also contains Russia's largest tank factory. Peculiarly shaped, the city stretches for miles in a long narrow ribbon on the west bank of the Volga.

Blocked by the Caucasus Mountains, the Wehrmacht aimed its main blow at Stalingrad. By August 1942 a Russian army of half a million men retreated into the city, defending it house by house. Despite three months of deadly assaults, the Germans could not completely capture the city ruins. Foolishly the Wehrmacht placed its weak allies—Italian, Hungarian, and Rumanian—north and south of the city to guard German flanks.

Meanwhile a huge Russian army massed across the Volga, waiting for the river to form ice thick enough to support heavy artillery, trucks, and tanks. (There was no river bridge.) In November 1942 the river froze hard. Russian forces immediately crossed the ice north and south of Stalingrad, slashed through the war-weary Axis allies, struck straight inland for 60 miles, then joined together, trapping a German army of 300,000 men.

The encircled Germans could not fight their way out of Stalingrad, and outside rescue columns failed to reach the city. About 60,000 Nazi troops were flown out of Stalingrad by the Luftwaffe. The remainder, after tremendous casualties, surrendered in February 1943.

For all practical purposes, the Nazi-Soviet War was ended. More than two years of bitter fighting was still required to drive the Germans out of Russia, through East Europe, back into capitulation at Vienna and Berlin. But after Stalingrad, the outcome was never in doubt. Russia had command of the air, and outnumbered the Wehrmacht on land in both men and machines. Deserted by one after another of its allies, Nazi Germany finally surrendered on May 8, 1945.

At the request of Britain and America, the USSR attacked Japan in August 1945 to speed the end of the War in the Pacific. The Red Army, which had defeated the mighty Wehrmacht, had little trouble subduing Japanese land forces in Manchuria, Korea, and the northern Nipponese islands. Japan, already basically defeated by the United States and horrified by American atom-bombing, surrendered one week after Russia's entry into the Pacific War.

Soviet claims that the USSR won the War in the Pacific can be taken with a grain of salt. But the Russian victory in the Nazi-Soviet War was truly stupendous, after such devastating Soviet losses in the first half-year of 1,000-mile retreat. Many reasons for USSR military success have already been described, but others merit mention:

German generals admit that Hitler was unprepared for winter war, and had foolishly planned to conquer Russia during the first six summer and autumn months. German tanks and trucks used ersatz lubricants, which froze solid when Russian thermometers zoomed far below zero. Nazi steam locomotives simply blew up, for lack of a special cold-weather valve commonplace on all Soviet railway engines. Another German loser's complaint is that the Wehrmacht simply lacked the mass manpower needed to hold the one fourth of all European USSR it occupied. In truth, many out-of-the-way peasant villages in the occupied area never saw a German soldier. Over vast 1,000-mile expanses, Nazi supply problems became immense. German artillery fired fast and furious at the start of a battle for psychological effect, then eased off to save ammunition as the battle continued. Nazi propaganda could offer nothing better to unpatriotic Soviet citizens than a life of slavery under Hitler. Instead of breaking up the unpopular collective farms, German overlords converted them into Prussian-type estates.

Then too, the Red Army used total war tactics that the Wehrmacht had never encountered. Soviet cities were converted into natural fortresses, defended to the last block and house. German troops wasted time destroying Soviet towns inch by inch. When encircled by German tank columns, Russian troops often continued fighting, sometimes fought their way out, or melted into the forests to become guerrillas. Soviet guerrillas themselves were no amateurs, but well armed groups closely coordinating their sabotage with the strategic tasks of the regular Red Army. The cute little peasant boy, whom German officers gave candy and patted on the head, was often reporting Nazi gun positions to Soviet scouts. When the Russians made their sweeping two-and-a-half-year offensive from the Volga to Berlin, little time was wasted besieging cities. Towns were simply by-passed, while Soviet troops rushed on to catch the main Nazi forces.

As shock troops, the Red Army used men whose families had been killed by the Germans. In the first days of a big attack, these shock troops did not bother taking prisoners. Early enemy capitulators were shot, so the Red Army advance would not be slowed.

Like the Russian Civil War, the Nazi-Soviet conflict ended in Pyrrhic victory. Twenty million Soviet citizens were dead—killed in battle or bombardment, perishing in Nazi prison camps, or simply wiped out by wartime malnutrition and epidemics. A combination of Russian earth-scorching, battle damage, and German planned destruction had largely devastated a USSR area as great as all the United States east of the Mississippi River. Twenty-five million Soviet citizens had lost their homes, and were residing in dugouts, caves, sheds, and every conceivable type of improvised shelter. The war destroyed or damaged more heavy industry than that possessed by either Italy or Japan. Farm war losses included one fourth of the sheep, cattle, and tractors, two fifths of the horses, and three fifths of all pigs in the Soviet Union. Over half of all rail trackage in the USSR had been damaged, and the railroads also lost one sixth of their locomotives and one fifth of their freight cars. One of every five riverships and one of every four canal barges had been sunk. Dozens of cities in the war zone were partially destoyed, while some—like Stalingrad—had nothing left but roofless, windowless, empty house walls.

The USSR fought the Nazi-Soviet War against an Axis alliance of aggressor nations. In June 1941, Germany, Finland, Hungary, Italy, and Rumania jointly invaded the USSR. The Italians and Hungarians did little fighting, and were used mostly as police troops. In contrast the Rumanians fought hard, temporarily annexing Bessarabia and the southwest Ukraine around Odessa. Finnish troops helped the Germans encircle Leningrad.

Somewhat to Kremlin surprise, the USSR quickly gained democratic allies against the Axis invasion. Britain and the United States immediately offered material aid to Russia, reasoning that Hitler was a worse enemy to Western democracy than Stalin. The aid, however, was slow in starting, and a mere 2 per cent of the total wartime supplies to Russia from Britain, Canada, and the United States arrived during 1941 in time for the Battle of Moscow.

At first during hostilities, Soviet diplomacy concentrated on winning the war. When a U.S. mission visited Moscow in July 1941 to discuss material aid, Stalin made an unsuccessful request for American troops to fight on the Russian front. By August the Kremlin had organized an All-Slav Committee, consisting of East European Communists and fellow-travelers resident in wartime Moscow, and appealing for Slavic unity against Teutonic aggression. Almost simultaneously, prominent Soviet citizens of Jewish faith formed an Anti-Fascist Committee, which asked Jews throughout the world to aid the Allied war effort against Nazi Germany.

The first Anglo-American material aid to Russia was delivered to the Soviet Arctic port of Murmansk, north of Leningrad and close to the Finnish frontier. But the sea trip around Scandinavia was very dangerous, since Allied convoys were attacked by German dive bombers, torpedo bombers, and submarines operating from bases on the north Norwegian and Finnish coasts. In search of a safer route, Britain and Russia chose Iran, where goods could be unloaded at Persian Gulf ports, then shipped on the Trans-Iranian railway north to the Caspian Sea. When Iran refused to cooperate, Britain and Russia occupied Persia in August 1941, deposed the Shah, and forced his successor to sign an Anglo-Soviet-Iranian treaty allowing Lend-Lease transport. This treaty stated that British and Russian troops would remain in Iran until the European phase of World War II had ended. The American army provided wartime crews to operate the Trans-Iranian railway.

Meanwhile Stalin was still eager for Allied troops to fight on Russian soil. In September 1941 he made an unsuccessful request for British troops to campaign on the Ukrainian front. During December the USSR concluded an alliance with the Polish government-in-exile, providing that a Polish army be formed among the million Poles whom Russia had deported inland from East Poland in 1939. This Polish army was actually formed, but its officers refused to employ Communist political commissars, which Russia insisted on including. So General Anders was permitted to evacuate the Polish force into Iran, where it sailed to the Mediterranean Sea for participation in the Anglo-American invasion of Italy.

In the spring and early summer of 1942, Soviet Foreign Minister Molotov visited Britain and America, seeking formal military alliances and an early Anglo-American invasion of German-occupied France. The latter was desperately needed by the USSR to divert some German troops from the Russian front to West Europe. Britain concluded a 20-year alliance with the USSR, but the United States refused to sign such a binding agreement. Probably to bolster Kremlin morale, both Britain and America vaguely promised that France might be invaded in 1942.

By August, British Prime Minister Churchill personally visited Moscow to explain that an early French invasion was impossible, due to lack of landing craft. Stalin was very angry, and virtually accused Churchill of treachery. The Soviet press ceased its friendly wartime attitude toward Britain and America, hinting that the Western Allies desired Germany and Russia to exhaust each other to Anglo-American advantage. Except for a brief period in 1944, when France was finally invaded, this Soviet press hostility continued for the remainder of World War II. Thus began the "cold war," which became so important in the postwar world.

After the tremendous Russian victory at Stalingrad early in 1943, Soviet diplomacy changed from winning the war to winning the postwar peace. Confident of Russian military power, Stalin no longer requested Allied troops to fight on Soviet soil. By clever diplomatic maneuvers, the Kremlin began paving the way for its postwar domination of East Europe, Mongolia, Manchuria, and North Korea.

In the spring of 1943, the Germans opened mass graves in the Katyn forest of Belorussia, and displayed the corpses of several thousand Polish army officers shot in the back of the head. These officers had been captured by the USSR in its 1939 occupation of East Poland, so the Germans blamed the mass murder on Soviet police. The horrified Polish government-in-exile at London requested an investigation by the International Red Cross, which the Germans agreed to permit so Poland and Russia would quarrel. Russia angrily broke diplomatic relations with the London Poles, and accused the latter of lack of faith in an ally, diplomatic espionage within the USSR, and obstructing the formation of a Polish army on Russian soil. All three accusations were probably true, but the real Kremlin motive for breaking relations was to free Soviet hands for communization of postwar Poland. The International Red Cross investigation was never made, but postwar Western studies indicate that the Katyn massacre was probably performed by the Russians either before or early in the Nazi-Soviet War.

Meanwhile Stalin's wartime speeches and interviews skillfully created the impression that he was no longer a revolutionary Communist but a Russian patriot. As part of this camouflage, a Soviet governmental decree of May 1943 abolished the Communist International (Comintern), which had been founded by Lenin in 1919. As the great Allied conferences met to decide the fate of the postwar world, Russia could negotiate without being accused of harboring a world revolutionary organization in Moscow.

Soon the conferences began, the most important being the

Anglo-Soviet-American summit meetings at Tehran in 1943, Yalta and Potsdam in 1945, plus the Stalin-Churchill negotiations in Moscow during 1944.

When Stalin, Churchill and U.S. President Roosevelt met in the Iranian capital city of Tehran during November-December 1943, it was obvious that the Allies were winning World War II. As is frequent among victorious allies, the Big Three leaders began to bicker. Churchill desired an Anglo-American campaign in the Balkans, to save part of East Europe from Russian military occupation. Stalin strongly opposed the British plan, demanding an Anglo-American invasion of France instead. Disputes arose on other issues such as the future of Poland.

As the conference ended, Stalin gained the most from its decisions. Russian troops were to invade and occupy Finland, Poland, Czechoslovakia, Hungary, Rumania, Bulgaria, and Yugoslavia. East Poland would be reannexed by the USSR. Britain and America agreed to concentrate their main European forces on an invasion of France, rather than the Balkans. In return, Russia consented to British occupation of Greece, and an eventual Soviet attack on Japan.

In October 1944, as the Red Army entered East Europe, Churchill flew to Moscow in a second attempt to save part of the Balkans from Soviet occupation. Stalin and Churchill struck a bargain that Bulgaria, Hungary, and Rumania would be a Soviet sphere of influence, Greece a British sphere, while Yugoslavia should be neutral territory. The bargain was realistic, since Soviet troops were already in Bulgaria, Hungary and Rumania, and British forces in Greece.

More Big Three bickering occurred in February 1945, when Roosevelt, Churchill, and Stalin again met, this time in the USSR Crimean resort of Yalta. Again Russia gained the most from the conference decisions, but made a few concessions to its Western allies. The results were as follows:

Russia agreed to join a postwar United Nations, reserving the right to a strong Soviet veto over UN operations. Stalin failed, however, to obtain membership in the UN Assembly for all 16 Soviet republics of the USSR. After lengthy debate, Britain and America allowed three Soviet members: Belorussia, the Ukraine, and the USSR itself. Thus Stalin did not obtain the huge UN voting bloc that he desired.

Trying to save East Europe from communization, the Western Allies obtained Soviet agreement for tripartite Anglo-American-Soviet commissions to supervise free elections in East European countries for the establishment of democratic national governments. Germany and Austria were to be under American-British-French-Soviet four-power occupation. Exile democratic governments and local Communists were to form coalition cabinets in Yugoslavia and Poland.

In practice the democratic elections and coalition governments later became a farce in most of East Europe, because Russian occupation troops simply put local Communists into power. Only Finland, West Germany, Austria, and Greece escaped eventual communization, the Finns because of Russian leniency, and the other three nations because of their occupation by Western Allied armies.

The greatest Western mistake at Yalta was to bribe Russia to attack Japan three months after German surrender in Europe. Anglo-American military intelligence believed that Japan would not surrender until invaded, that the Kwangtung army—Japan's best land force—was still intact in Manchuria, and that a devastated Russia did not want to enter the Pacific War. All three Western assumptions were false. Japan was already suing for peace, but didn't wish to make an unconditional surrender. The Kwangtung army had been transferred to China and the South Pacific, and replaced in Manchuria by inferior troops. Russia had rejected Japanese overtures to serve as peacemaker between America and Japan, so the Pacific War could continue until Soviet entry.

Badly misinformed, Roosevelt and Churchill agreed to pay Stalin's price for a Soviet attack on Japan. The USSR was to obtain south Sakhalin Island, the South Manchurian railway, and the Manchurian warm-water ports of Dairen and Port Arthur, all of which Tsarist Russia had lost to Japan in the Russo-Japanese War of 1904–1905. In addition, Stalin could annex Japan's Kurile Islands, which had never been Russian territory. To clarify the dubious international status of Outer Mongolia, the Mongolians were to hold a plebescite as to whether to secede from China. If the vote was for independence, Nationalist China must grant Mongolian freedom. Britain and America would convince China to sign a Sino-Soviet alliance authorizing the Mongolian plebescite, and the Russification of Manchuria's main railways and ports. In return, Stalin promised not to support Chinese Communist revolt against Chiang Kai Shek's Chinese nationalist government.

By threatening to discontinue subsidies to Nationalist China, Britain and America forced Chiang Kai Shek to conclude a Sino-Soviet alliance on Stalin's terms. Thus the West legalized Soviet Far Eastern expansion, which was unnecessary and partly at the expense of a Chinese ally. And Stalin broke his promise not to aid the Chinese Communists against the Chinese Nationalists.

After the Yalta Conference, the next Big Three meeting during May 1945 in the Berlin suburb of Potsdam was an anticlimax. Here the chief negotiators were Stalin, the new US President Truman, and Britain's newly elected Prime Minister Attlee. Supposedly temporary territorial changes in Russia's favor were made in East Europe, until a German peace treaty could be signed later. The USSR was permitted to exact heavy reparations from the defeated Axis nations: Germany, Austria, Hungary, Bulgaria, Rumania, and Finland. Stalin failed, however, to gain a Soviet trusteeship over the former Italian colony of Libya on the north African coast.

Even without Libya, devastated Russia clearly emerged as the greatest political victor of World War II. First, the USSR had gained many territorial acquisitions. Finland, surrendering in 1944, ceded to Russia the west shore of Lake Ladoga, all of the Karelian Isthmus, and the entire Finnish Arctic coast with its rich nickel mines. Estonia, Latvia, Lithuania, Bessarabia, Northern Bukovina, and East Poland were simply reannexed by the USSR. Poland was compensated by being given German Silesia and most of East Prussia, but Russia took Konigsberg, the largest East Prussian seaport. A Czech-Soviet treaty of 1945 transferred Ruthenia, with its predominantly Ukrainian population, from Czechoslovakia to the USSR. In Asia, Russia annexed satellite Tannu Tuva during 1944. The Kurile Islands and south Sakhalin were taken from defeated Japan in 1945.

Besides outright territorial annexations, Soviet armies of

occupation controlled postwar East Germany, Poland, Hungary, Rumania, Bulgaria, East Austria, the Czech uranium mines, northwest Iran, Outer Mongolia, Manchuria, and North Korea. Russian submarines were based in the Adriatic seaports of Yugoslavia and Albania, two Balkan countries ruled by Communist governments friendly to the USSR. Other Soviet subs were stationed at Finnish Porkkala, a Baltic port close to Finland's capital city of Helsinki.

In addition, during wartime the USSR had concluded long-term military alliances with Britain (1942), Czechoslovakia (1943), and France (1944). Russia was a founding father of the United Nations, was a permanent member of the UN Security Council, and in the UN General Assembly held three seats compared to the USA's one.

Such were the political results of Russian military power and Stalin's shrewd diplomacy. The question naturally arises: How much did Allied Lend-Lease contribute to Soviet military victory?

During and just after the Soviet-German war, the USA sent 11 billion dollars worth of supplies to the USSR. Britain and Canada made sizeable contributions too. The three English-speaking allies sent Russia 10,000 tanks, 10,000 pieces of artillery, 14,500 planes, hundreds of ships, over 100,000 tons of rubber, half a million tons of nonferrous metals, nearly 500,000 trucks, 2.3 million tons of food, and 3 billion dollars worth of machinery, including several complete factories. Certainly the Western Allies sent wartime Russia far more rubber and nonferrous metal than it produced. One of every three new machine tools put in operation in wartime USSR was American. In fact, American machinery largely rebuilt Ukrainian heavy industry after south European USSR was reconquered from the Germans. Half the Soviet merchant marine was sunk during the war, yet Lend-Lease ships more than replaced this heavy loss. Red Army mechanized troops rode to victory on Detroit trucks.

Enough military cloth was shipped to clothe 3 million Red Army soldiers. Lend-Lease food kept alive Soviet Arctic ports, which otherwise might have starved. America supplied the landing craft for the Red Army to invade Korea, and the fuel for the Soviet mechanized columns that conquered Manchuria.

In contrast, Allied shipments of tanks and planes to Russia amounted only to four months' USSR output of the last three years of the Nazi-Soviet War. A Free French officer, who fought alongside the Russians on the eastern front, reported that less than one tenth of Red Army equipment was Lend-Lease. A Russian general claimed that Lend-Lease equaled only 6 per cent of USSR wartime production of tanks, guns, and planes.

Russia harvested at least 200 million tons of grain during the four years of war, but received only 1 million from Lend-Lease. According to the US Department of Agriculture, American food filled no more than 5 per cent of USSR wartime food requirements.

To all this must be added Soviet greed, taking advantage of American good-will, and demanding far more supplies than could be absorbed. Americans traveling across Siberia late in the war saw unused Lend-Lease machines strewn along the whole 5,000-mile Trans-Sib railway. Four complete US oil refineries, sent to Russia at great expense, were never put into operation by Soviet engineers till the war was over.

Most Lend-Lease reached Russia in the later years of the war, when the Red Army was already winning on its own. Of the nearly 17 million tons of wartime supplies sent to the USSR by the United States, Britain, and Canada, four fifths came to Russia after the Battle of Stalingrad, the turning point in the European War. Thus the Russian claim is probably true that the USSR fought the war mostly with weapons made in Soviet factories from Soviet raw materials. On the other hand, Allied machinery and transportation supplies were very great.

The most objective estimate is that Lend-Lease was marginal assistance, coming rather late in the war. Only the Kremlin knows whether or not this marginal aid was crucial for Soviet victory. But the grand 1,400-mile Russian offensive from Stalingrad to Berlin would certainly have been much slower, had there been no Lend-Lease.

Before World War II, the United States had very few munitions factories. During the war a large American armament industry was built at great expense by the government. After the war it was decided to preserve this industry for future emergency, even though the munitions plants would be partly or wholly idle in peacetime.

At the war's end, Stalin asked for a 6 billion dollar American loan, part of which would be used to purchase the US stand-by armament industry. Russia explained that the USSR would thus relieve the USA of a white-elephant industry, unproductive in peacetime and costly to maintain. The US State Department quickly pared this monetary request down to 1 billion dollars, then dropped the matter entirely. Thus Stalin failed to buy America's munitions industry with American money. Later this stand-by armament industry proved invaluable to the United States by producing munitions for the Korean War.

Suggestions for Further Reading

Armstrong, John A., ed., *Soviet Partisans in World War II,* Madison: Wisconsin University Press, 1964.

Bialer, Seweryn, *Stalin and His Generals.* New York: Pegasus, 1969.

Churchill, Winston, *The Second World War,* Vol. I, Boston: Houghton Mifflin, 1948.

Feis, Herbert, *Churchill, Roosevelt, Stalin,* Princeton: Princeton University Press, 1957.

Gallagher, Matthew P., *The Soviet History of World War II,* New York: Praeger, 1963.

Garthoff, Raymond L., *Soviet Military Doctrine,* Glencoe: The Free Press, 1953.

Goure, Leon, and Dinerstein, Herbert S., *Moscow in Crisis,* Glencoe: The Free Press, 1955.

Herring, George C., *Aid to Russia, 1941-1946.* New York: Columbia University Press, 1972.

Krosby, H. Peter, *Finland, Germany and the Soviet Union, 1940-1941.* Madison: Wisconsin University Press, 1968.

McNeill, William H., *America, Britain and Russia, Their Cooperation ond Conflict, 1941–1946,* New York: Oxford University Press, 1954.

Neuman, William L., *Making the Peace, 1941–1945: The Diplomacy of the Wartime Conferences,* Washington: Foundation for Foreign Affairs, 1950.

Soviet War Documents, Washington: USSR Embassy, 1945.

Stalin's Correspondence with Churchill and Attlee. New York: Capricorn, 1969.

Stalin's Correspondence with Roosevelt and Truman. New York: Capricorn, 1969.

STETTINIUS, EDWARD R., *Roosevelt and the Russians,* Garden City: Doubleday, 1949.

VOZNESENSKI, NIKOLAI, *The Economy of the USSR during World War II,* New York: Macmillan, 1947.

WERTH, A., *The Year of Stalingrad,* New York: Hamilton, 1946.

WHALEY, BARTON, *Codeword Barbarossa.* Cambridge: Massachusetts Institute of Technology Press, 1973.

ZAWODNY, J. K., *Death in the Forest,* Notre Dame: Notre Dame University Press, 1962.

Chapter 8

Postwar Stalinism

"After World War II, Russia will be different. The police won't be so cruel. Stores will be full of goods at cheap prices. We'll have free elections, and maybe even be allowed to travel abroad."

The old Russian lady who made such hopeful wartime predictions to me died before the war was over. Many other Russians reasoned that Axis defeat would remove fear of war, so that Russia could disarm. Soviet industry could concentrate on producing consumer goods instead of machines.

All these illusions shared by many in the West, were shattered when Stalin made his first major postwar speech during February 1946 in an election campaign for the Supreme Soviet. He admitted that Soviet industrialization had emphasized war preparation ever since the start of the Five-Year Plans. Even collectivization of agriculture was described as preparation for war. He also gave his plan for the long-range future.

Beginning with 1946, three postwar Five-Year Plans would expand heavy industry faster than ever before. Thus by 1960, Russian heavy industry would achieve a production about equaling the 1940 output of its American competitor. In Stalin's words, a heavy industry of this size "will guarantee our fatherland against any eventualities."[1] The same speech added that this forced expansion of Soviet heavy industry to the prewar American

[1] Stalin, Joseph, *Speech at an Election Rally in the Stalin Electoral Area of Moscow,* Washington: USSR Embassy, 1946.

level "can and must be done," even if it took longer than 15 years. Like a neglected child, light industry was not even mentioned in this testament.

Soon after Stalin spoke, his words came true in the first postwar Five-Year Plan of 1946–1950. As before, the new Plan gave top priority to heavy industry, which was to be built and rebuilt before anything else. By 1950 farm crops were to increase 27 per cent over prewar 1940, light industry, 28 per cent, but heavy industry, 60 per cent. The 1950 planned quotas for output of consumer goods were woefully inadequate, amounting to but one pair of shoes, three pairs of stockings or socks, less than 1 yard of wool cloth, 3 dishes, and $1.30 worth of furniture for every person of Russia's giant population.

One of the Plan's major goals was "to assure further improvement of the USSR's capability for defense, and saturation of the Soviet Union's armed forces with the latest military equipment." Ship-building was to double its prewar size "to assure USSR construction of a strong and mighty navy." New naval bases were to be built, as well as new warships. Another Plan aim was "in the very near future to surpass scientific achievements abroad." In practice, this meant an all-out effort to produce new weapons like guided missiles, jet planes, long-range bombers, and nuclear bombs.

Though the war had damaged or destroyed the dwellings of 25 million Soviet citizens, most capital investments of the 1946–1950 Plan were assigned neither to housing nor to overall reconstruction of war-devastated south and west European USSR. For every ruble alloted to repairing war damage, two were to be spent in uninvaded regions, mostly for construction of new heavy industry in the Ural Mountains and Siberia.[2] Soviet heavy industry was retreating into interior areas, which were strategically safe and far from dangerous frontiers. In addition, most evacuated machinery remained in the eastern regions, becoming a permanent part of factories in the Volga valley, Urals, and Soviet Asia.

---

[2] *Law of the Five-Year Plan for Restoration and Development of the USSR National Economy during 1946–1950,* Leningrad: State Political Press, 1946.

Most astonishing of all features of the Fourth Five-Year Plan of 1946–1950 was its order that postwar industrial conversion from armament to civilian output should go slow. The United States, which had never been bombed or invaded, began industrial reconversion with V-E Day (May 8, 1945), and finished before the end of 1945. Russia, which suffered more war damage than any other country, deliberately planned not to reconvert till 1946. After four years of slim rations and tremendous property destruction, the USSR might have been expected to turn swords into plowshares as fast as possible. Yet Stalin wished to be militarily strong in the postwar world. Soviet tank plants did not reconvert until five months after V-E Day; mortar factories, nine months; and ammunition enterprises, almost a year. Thus the USSR created an immense stockpile of the best weapons World War II could invent.

The fruits of such militaristic planning were soon forthcoming. Soviet rockets of the V-2 type with a range of over 100 miles were being test-flown as early as 1946. In the same year new four-motored bombers and jet fighters of Soviet design flew in the Aviation Day parade at Moscow.

In September 1949 Anglo-American laboratories recorded an atomic explosion in Russia, and the Soviet Union announced that it had the atom bomb. Many Western scientists were amazed, since the Soviets had seemed to lack the uranium, physicists, and engineering skill for the complex process of producing nuclear explosives.

But the USSR had more skill and resources than the outside world knew. Uranium is far from a rare mineral in the Soviet Union, where six deposits were found as long ago as the 1920's. As for industrial skill, construction of nuclear fission plants involves much the same problems as building synthetic rubber factories, and the USSR had an artificial rubber industry second in size only to American. But what seems mainly to have escaped foreign notice was Russia's early start in both nuclear research and manufacture of atom-smashing machines.

In 1939, west European experiments proved that uranium could yield a chain reaction, unleashing power beyond the wildest dreams. Till then, the USSR had only one small cyclotron. But in 1940 Russia began building the most powerful cyclotron in

Europe. This electronic giant with a 75-ton magnet was designed by three Soviet scientists, and production was entrusted to four Leningrad factories. By late 1940 the Leningrad atom-smasher was completed, and construction of an even more powerful cyclotron commenced in Moscow. One of these two giants was installed in the Ukrainian city of Kharkov, and during 1941 fell into the hands of the invading Wehrmacht, who carefully removed it to West Germany.

Even before the Soviet-German War, Russia knew not only how to design and build cyclotrons, but what new horizons they might open. In 1940 the Soviet press published this prediction about nuclear power:

> Not only will mankind receive a new energy base, a million times larger than all bases known till now. Not only will a new "fuel" arrive to replace exhausted reserves of coal and oil, and save industry from fuel hunger. A new era of human might is commencing. . . .
>
> Man will be able to obtain any amount of energy, and direct it toward any purpose.[3]

Since Soviet postwar Five-Year Plans included the atom bomb project and in general were militaristic, the USSR became more secretive than ever before. In 1947 two new laws made many additions to the old list of state secrets, besides drastically increasing the punishment for betraying or losing confidential information. As before, secrecy blanketed the armed forces, military and industrial mobilization plans, war industry and factories filling military orders, armament inventions, defense documents, reserves of gold and foreign currency, foreign trade, industrial inventions, foreign affairs, and government codes. But the new list of secrets made it clear that local information was just as confidential as national. Even the location, size, and activity of an army local recruiting office was henceforth a state secret.

Instead of the prewar classification of inventions as open or secret, all inventions and all scientific research were now concealed. In addition, three new types of secrecy were ordered:

---

[3] Agapov, Boris, "Uranium–235," *Izvestia* (Dec. 31, 1940).

strategic stockpiling, reserves and production of nonferrous metals (including uranium), and "proposed plans" for mobilization, finance, and foreign trade.

Meanwhile the minimum penalties for betraying or losing these state secrets were raised to imprisonment from five to twenty years. Sending inventions abroad became a crime, with 10 to 15 years of prison camp as punishment. All betrayers of secrecy were thereafter to be tried by courts-martial. In extreme cases, these minimum penalties could be increased to execution by a firing squad.

Almost simultaneously, other new laws forbade Soviet citizens to marry foreigners, and even to talk to foreigners except on business. As soon as these laws were published, most Soviet citizens were afraid to talk with foreigners, who could not even meet former friends. An American fur buyer, who had lived peaceably in the USSR for many years, explained to me why he had abruptly returned to the United States:

> My life in Moscow became impossible. Every time I took a walk, five police plainclothesmen trailed me. When the crowd on the sidewalk saw those police, nobody dared walk near me. Once in a while, a former friend passed by, whispering hello from the corner of his mouth, but afraid to stop and talk. After many years of pleasant friendships in Russia, I now lived completely alone. Finally I packed my bags, and left Russia forever.

Meanwhile many Soviet citizens suspected of wartime collaboration with the German invaders were arrested, usually imprisoned, and sometimes shot. Thus an extensive purge occurred in the former German-occupied regions of the USSR, resulting in the arrest of some two million people in the Ukraine alone. This Ukrainian purge was commanded by Politburo member Khrushchev, who later became Premier after Stalin's death. At the time of these mass arrests, Khrushchev boasted in a public speech that he had purged the Ukrainian party, government, and agricultural officialdom from the top down to the village level.

Millions of Soviet citizens, who in wartime had been taken into German Europe as slave labor or prisoners of war, at the war's end were usually transported from Nazi detention camps to USSR prison camps. Actually 80 per cent of the Red Army soldiers captured by the Wehrmacht had died from Nazi mistreatment. But the 20 per cent still alive were considered by Stalin to be traitors for surrendering to the wartime enemy. Similarly the Soviet government assumed that the slave laborers might have emigrated voluntarily to wartime Germany, though most of them had actually been forced to migrate into the Third Reich.

Even the two million Red Army soldiers, who invaded East Europe at the war's end, were mistrusted by the Soviet government for fear they had been morally weakened by exposure to bourgeois life and culture. Such troops were not immediately demobilized, but were dispatched far from their homes to USSR "re-education camps," where for two years they were subjected to lectures and films about hollowness of bourgeois freedom and prosperity.

From 1946 till his death from heart disease in 1948, Politburo member Andrei Zhdanov made many speeches ordering Soviet literature and art to avoid Western influence. Party decrees merged two Leningrad literary magazines, appointed a party propaganda official as the editor of the merged publications, suppressed one motion picture and forced retakes of another, demanded that Soviet plays comprise half the repertoire of leading USSR theaters (which had been concentrating on Tsarist scripts), and commanded Soviet composers to renounce modernistic dissonance and write classical music based on Russian folk music. The extreme anti-Westernism of this propaganda campaign is revealed in the following Soviet statements at the time:

> Not all Soviet people have been freed from survivals of the old state of mind; there are backward strata among whom the capitalist survivals still have a strong say in their minds.
>
> A source for the existence and vitality of capitalist survivals in people's minds in the USSR is the existence of bourgeois states, which are endeavoring to influence the minds of the toilers of our country, and to support and enliven the survivals of reactionary bourgeois ideology. . . .
>
> At present, imperialist reaction is trying to weaken Soviet society from within by bringing various bourgeois views into our country. . . .
>
> A dangerous survival of capitalism and result of influence by

> foreign ideology is obeisance to modern bourgeois culture and ideology, obeisance which is still found among individual people.[4]

Thus, just as it was creating an empire in East Europe, the USSR tried to isolate its own people from the outside world. The Soviet postwar intellectual and ideological repression was accompanied by considerable toleration of most religions. Many seminaries, monasteries and convents were permitted to reopen. Churches were allowed to own property instead of renting it from the state. Taxes were waived on monasteries and convents. At least one large Moslem mosque was permitted to hold services in each Central Asian city. The Russian Orthodox Church even published religious books and journals, using the printing facilities of a Communist party press.

The uneasy wartime alliance between the Soviet government and many religions continued. Church leaders had to support the peace propaganda of the government, and praise its social reforms. Yet church publications openly rejected the Communist philosophy of materialism. Though never directly attacking the Soviet dictatorship, church sermons often stressed that no man was superior to God. Thus organized religion was semi-independent from the government with which it was allied. Even so, the government in 1952 bestowed a high Soviet decoration, the Red Banner of Labor, upon the Moscow patriarch of the Russian Orthodox Church.

This official toleration did not extend to religions with strong foreign connections, such as the Roman Catholic and Lutheran. For example, in Catholic Lithuania most of the bishops were arrested and more than half of the Catholic churches were forced to close. Before the war the Uniate Christians of USSR western borderlands had church services similar to those of the Russian Orthodox, but accepted the leadership of the Pope of Rome. After the war, the Soviet government forced the Uniates to acknowledge the leadership of the Moscow Patriarch of the Russian Orthodox Church.

When Israel became independent in 1948, thousands of Soviet

---

[4] Kovalyov, S., *Ideological Conflicts in Russia,* Washington: Public Affairs Press, 1948.

Jews requested permission to emigrate to Israel from the USSR. Immediately the Soviet press embarked upon an anti-Zionist campaign, which became racist and strongly anti-Semitic. Emigration to Israel was forbidden. Jews were accused of being more loyal to Israel than to the USSR. Most synagogues were closed, and many rabbis were sent to prison camp. All Yiddish-language schools, theaters, and newspapers were gradually suppressed, and the Jewish Autonomous Region in East Siberia was abolished. Many Jews were removed from high posts in the Soviet government and USSR Communist Party. Two hundred of the best Soviet Jewish writers were arrested and shot in 1949.

Meanwhile in the postwar period the Stalinist government became increasingly autocratic. Though party rules stated that a Communist Party Congress should meet every three years, none was convened until 1952—13 years after the previous congress in 1939. The highest governmental parliament, the USSR Supreme Soviet, usually met only once each year, despite the constitutional provision that it must convene twice annually. The party Central Committee, which was supposed to assemble three times a year, did not meet at all for several years. Stalin often made important decisions alone, without consulting his party Politburo.

Increasingly Stalin appeared to mistrust this Politburo, whose members were supposed to be closest associates. Politburo member Zhdanov, Stalin's chosen heir, died abruptly from heart failure in 1948 after Zhdanov's son had been publicly criticized by the Soviet press. Nikolai Voznesenski, a Politburo member and governmental vice premier, was shot in 1949. Along with him were executed the party leader of Leningrad, a secretary of the party Central Committee, and the premier of the Russian Soviet Republic.

At the nineteenth USSR Communist Party Congress in 1952, two members of the Politburo, Andreyev and Kosygin, lost their Politburo membership. The Politburo itself was renamed the party Presidium, and was enlarged from a 13-man body to a group of 25. Though 11 of the members of the old Politburo transferred to the new Presidium, they were outnumbered by the generally younger 14 new appointees. Thus Stalin was gradually weakening the power of the old Politburo members, and apparently seeking a transfer of power to younger advisors. When Stalin died in early 1953, the old Politburo members regained their former power.

Despite heavy armament, intense secrecy, cultural isolation, intellectual repression, anti-Semitism, and increasing autocracy, Stalin's postwar USSR made impressive economic progress. Soviet steel production per annum increased from about 12 million metric tons in 1945 to 35 million in 1952. After a currency reform depriving the Soviet public of nine tenths of its cash rubles in 1947, the financially deflated USSR became the first country in Europe to abandon food, clothing, and shoe rationing. From 1948 onward, annual price cuts in the cost of consumer goods slowly raised the standard of living of the Soviet people.

As early as 1949, Soviet industry and agriculture regained their prewar levels of production. By 1951, there were more retail stores than before the war. In 1952 a stupendous engineering project, the 63-mile Volga-Don canal with 20 huge locks capable of holding two steamships apiece, opened for navigation.

The foreign policy of Stalin's postwar USSR might be described as a mixture of cold war, empire building, and brinkmanship. Like most wartime alliances, the Anglo-Soviet-American alliance of World War II did not long survive after hostilities ended. At the postwar diplomatic conferences such as Potsdam in 1945, Paris in 1946, and Moscow in 1947, endless disputes arose between the USSR and its wartime Western allies, who objected to the Soviet demands for Axis territorities, enormous reparations, and total disarmament of the former Axis nations. But the chief Western complaint was against Russia's communization of East Europe.

At first the Kremlin was not sure that the Western allies would permit Russia to dominate East Europe. During 1945 and 1946 Soviet troops methodically dismantled much of East European factory machinery, which was then shipped into the USSR. So much machinery was taken that the USSR could not immediately absorb it. Broad fields around Moscow were filled with the confiscated machines for months. Similar industrial looting by Soviet troops occurred in Manchuria and North Korea.

This Soviet deindustrialization of conquered territories lasted little more than a year. By 1947, the USSR was well aware that the United States and Britain had gravely weakened their military strength by fast postwar demobilization of their armed forces. In contrast, the Soviet army was demobilized very slowly, so the USSR became the strongest military land power in the world. Of course the United States possessed the atom bomb which Russia still lacked, but the Kremlin correctly reasoned that the United States would not bomb the USSR to save an East Europe in which America was little interested.

Therefore Soviet industrial looting abruptly stopped, and the USSR began to rebuild and help expand the East European industry it had tried to destroy. A similar change of economic policy took place quickly in North Korea, but not in Manchuria until the Chinese Communists had conquered the Chinese mainland. All this reindustrialization was on the Soviet model, stressing heavy industry rather than output of consumer goods.

Certain that the United States and Britain would limit their objections to verbal protests, the USSR then established Communist governments in East Europe and North Korea. Armaments and diplomatic support were rendered to the Chinese Communists, who in 1949 gained control of the Chinese mainland. Thus in a mere five years, 1945–1949, the USSR created the largest empire in modern history, embracing one third of our globe's landspace, one third of the world's population, 12 formerly non-Communist nations (Estonia, Latvia, Lithuania, Poland, Czechoslovakia, Hungary, Rumania, Bulgaria, Yugoslavia, Albania, China, and Tibet), substantial portions of two other countries (East Germany and North Korea), plus the early Communist nations of Outer Mongolia, Tuva, and the USSR itself. The success of this empire-building was largely due to Soviet military-industrial power, clever diplomacy, and Western appeasement.

As soon as the USSR felt that its empire was reasonably secure, all Soviet satellites were required to trade mostly with Russia, and to a lesser extent with each other. Historic trade relations of the Soviet satellites were radically altered. Before World War II, East Europe exchanged goods mainly with West Europe, East European raw materials and food being traded for West European machinery and manufactures. At that time less than 10 per cent of East European trade turnover was with the USSR. Prewar

China had concentrated on sea trade with Pacific Ocean nations and Western powers. Now, regardless of capitalist trade traditions, both China and East Europe were diverted into a Communist common market. Like past empires, the colonial power—the USSR—bought cheap and sold dear, thus profiting from the satellite economies. Yet for the satellites, as in past capitalist colonies, this was not all loss and no gain. At least peace and secure markets were ensured for most of the less developed Communist nations. And in order to exploit the satellite economies, the USSR had to encourage their development so there would be more satellite goods for Russia.

The trade empire was soon bound together by military alliances, both satellite to satellite, and satellite to USSR. A Czechoslovak-Soviet alliance had already been concluded in wartime 1943. Yugoslavia and Poland signed military pacts with Russia in 1945; Mongolia in 1946; Albania in 1947; Bulgaria, Hungary, and Rumania in 1948; and China in 1950. Russia carefully trained the East European satellite armies to accept commands in the Russian language, but refused to transfer long-range bombing planes, big rockets, or nuclear bombs to the East European or Far Eastern Communist states. If questioned about this lack of military trust, the standard Soviet reply was that mighty Russia would protect all Communist countries against capitalist aggression.

At this time there was no multinational Communist military alliance, like the Warsaw Pact of the post-Stalin period. However two nonmilitary international groups were formed, one political and the second economic. During 1947 the Communist parties of the USSR, Poland, Czechoslovakia, Hungary, Rumania, Bulgaria, Yugoslavia, Italy, and France organized a Communist Information Bureau usually abbreviated as Cominform, with headquarters in the Yugoslav capital of Belgrade. France and Italy were included because their large Communist parties seemed strong enough to seize power by a coup or by parliamentary means.

The proclaimed purpose of the Cominform was to coordinate the activity of the member parties. In practice most Cominform activity consisted of anti-American propaganda, particularly against the Marshall Plan of aid to West European economic recovery. Though limited in membership to a few European parties, the Cominform issued orders to Communists throughout the world, thus operating much like the old Communist International (Comintern), which had been abolished in 1943.

In 1949 the governments of the USSR, Poland, Czechoslovakia, Hungary, Rumania, Bulgaria, and Albania organized a Council for Economic Mutual Assistance, usually abbreviated as CEMA or Comecon. CEMA, with its headquarters in Moscow, was officially proclaimed to be Communist competition to West Europe's Marshall Plan. In practice there was little real competition. CEMA largely limited its activity to exchange of techniques and technical knowledge among its member states. Despite much talk of coordinating the long-range economic plans of CEMA nations, attempts at coordination were minor. Instead each East European satellite tried to develop all branches of industry like the USSR.

Meanwhile the USSR pursued a policy of creating a series of international crises. The crises unnerved and worried the Western world, and the Kremlin thus won psychological victories.

The first major postwar crisis arose in northwest Iran, where Soviet troops were stationed during the war to expedite American Lend-Lease shipments from Persian Gulf ports through Iran to the USSR. According to the Anglo-Soviet-Iranian alliance of 1942, all Russian troops were to leave Iran six months after the end of the European phase of World War II. Instead the Soviet troops stayed until early 1946, establishing Communist-led "people's republics" in Kurdistan and Iranian Azerbaijan. Iranian troops sent to subdue the people's republics found their way blocked by Soviet troops. Iran appealed to the United Nations, which commenced its existence by debating this tense incident.

Britain strongly pressured the USSR to withdraw, and President Truman hinted that he might atom-bomb the USSR oil fields around the Caucasian city of Baku. Russia backed down, Soviet troops evacuated northwest Iran, and the two people's republics collapsed as soon as USSR military support was gone.

One crisis in early 1948 was over almost as soon as it started. In one day, the Communist minority within the Czechoslovak coalition government seized complete control of Czechoslovakia in a bloodless coup d'etat. Caught by surprise and faced with a *fait accompli,* the Western powers made ineffectual protests. A

Soviet veto blocked the United Nations from investigating the coup.

The major crisis of 1948, however, was the Soviet blockade of the roads, railroads, and inland waterways connecting West Germany with West Berlin. The USSR claimed that the blockade was retaliation against the West German currency devaluation, which introduced new marks into West Berlin much higher in value than the Communist currency of East Berlin. Since transit within Berlin was unrestricted before the blockade, West Berliners using the new currency had been able to shop very cheaply in East Berlin, thus upsetting the latter's economy.

Quickly it became apparent that the USSR was trying to starve West Berlin into submission, so that French, British, and American troops would be forced to leave and turn West Berlin over to Communist control. Since West Berlin normally depended on food and fuel from West Germany, the Kremlin apparently expected that the blockade would achieve fast political results. Russia even offered to feed the West Berliners, if they would pay for the provisions with East German marks.

The Western allies decided not to use force to reopen the railways, waterways, and roads into West Berlin. Instead the American and British air forces undertook a massive air lift of food and coal to the beleagured city. The air shipments of this "Operation Vittles" rose from 250 tons on the first day to an average of 3,500 tons daily by late 1948. By early 1949 the airlift was actually bringing more food into West Berlin than the pre-blockade trains. Obviously the Kremlin had badly underestimated the power of Western air transport, and was afraid to attack the cargo planes for fear of outright war. (At this time Russia did not have the atomic bomb, so war would have been suicidal against American nuclear arms.)

Since West Berlin did not starve and refused to submit to Communist control, the blockade became embarrassing to the Kremlin. Furthermore, the West German counter-blockade threw East Germany into economic difficulties. Early in 1949 Stalin announced the Berlin blockade would be lifted if the Western allies would stop the West German counter-blockade and postpone the formation of an independent West German government. Secret negotiations at the United Nations resulted in a Soviet-

Western agreement to remove both blockades in May 1949. But France, Britain, and the United States refused to delay formation of a sovereign West German government. Oddly enough the question of West German currency, which had been the original Soviet excuse for the Berlin blockade, was not raised by the USSR in the final blockade-lifting negotiations.

Because of the Berlin blockade, the United States proclaimed the "Truman Embargo" on shipments of strategic machinery and strategic raw materials into the Soviet orbit of nations. America's Western allies soon joined this embargo, as also did West Germany and Japan. The Berlin crisis induced America, Canada, and most of West Europe to form the North Atlantic Treaty Organization (NATO)—a military alliance against the USSR. Still another result was the Schuman Plan, setting up an international authority governing the coal and steel production of France, West Germany, Italy, Belgium, Holland, and Luxembourg. The remarkable success of this customs union soon convinced the same six nations to form the European Common Market, whose prosperity dimmed the prospects for Communist revolution in West Europe.

Blocked by NATO from further adventures in Europe, the USSR then turned eastward for its next major crisis, the Korean War. Both Russia and Red China wished to control a Korea rich in minerals and ricelands, and strategically located like a dagger pointing at the heart of Japan. At the close of World War II, Korea was supposed to become a free nation under a five-year trusteeship by the USSR, United States, Britain, and Nationalist China. In practice Soviet troops occupied and satellized North Korea, thus preventing Korean unification. Meanwhile America rebuilt South Korea, and helped it establish a constitutional government.

The USSR trained and equipped a mechanized North Korean army, many of whose officers and technicians were Russified Koreans born and raised in the Soviet Union. (The USSR contains about 360,000 Koreans, mostly residing in Central Asia.) The North Korean army had heavier weapons than the armed forces of South Korea and was twice as large, though South Korea had a much greater civilian population.

At the end of 1949 Liu Shao-Chi, a member of the Politburo

of the Chinese Communist Party, in a speech to a Peking conference of Asiatic trade unions, gave the following instructions to Asian Communists: form revolutionary armies, and fight the West wherever possible. During February 1950 the USSR and Communist China signed a 30-year military alliance. North Korean leaders began to make public speeches threatening to unify Korea by force. In May a National Assembly, allegedly representing all of Korea, met in North Korea and proclaimed Korean unification. Less than a month later in June 1950, Communist North Korea invaded the pro-American South, thus starting a four-year war. It is unknown whether North Korea itself, or China, or Russia first proposed this military operation. However all three Communist nations certainly conspired to commence hostilities.

As the war began, Russia requested the United States not to intervene, and tried to block anti-Communist action by the United Nations. But American troops immediately aided South Korea, the United Nations condemned North Korean aggression, and eventually several member-countries of the UN sent small military units to aid the South Korean and American armies. Russia stayed officially neutral, but sent large arms shipments to the North Koreans.

At first South Korea was almost conquered. Then the combined American-South Korean-United Nations forces swept northward deep into Communist Korean territory. Still Russia did not intervene, but a huge Chinese Communist army entered the war on the North Korean side. The UN forces were driven back to the North Korea-South Korea border, where the military situation stabilized. Major military operations continued until mid-1951, when at Russia's suggestion the two sides commenced truce negotiations. But the truce talks deadlocked in bitter arguments, so military skirmishes continued two more years until an armistice was finally arranged in 1953 after Stalin's death.

Thus the war ended in stalemate, its main achievement being the devastation of Korea, which remained a divided nation. On the Communist side, North Korea had to be rebuilt almost from the ground up, using large-scale Russian and Red Chinese economic aid. Communist China was heavily in debt to Russia for the enormous armament shipments sent to the Chinese on credit during the war. Russia itself had to delay starting its Fifth Five-Year Plan of 1951–1955, because of the unexpected increase in armament production required by the Korean War. Yet one great Communist moral victory had been won: In land fighting, Chinese military power had proved equal to the highly mechanized forces of the United States.

Meanwhile during the postwar Stalinist regime, the Kremlin was confronted with an unpleasant surprise: the rise of national Communism within the Soviet orbit of nations. Yugoslavia was a Soviet satellite where the USSR did not maintain troops immediately after World War II. The Kremlin presumed that the Yugoslav Communist Party was completely loyal to the USSR, and that the Yugoslav Red Army (which had fought guerrilla warfare against Nazi Germany and Fascist Italy) was sufficient to control the country. In turn, Yugoslavia appeared to be the most Stalinist of all East European satellites, and violently anti-Western. Nevertheless Moscow and Belgrade began a quarrel which erupted openly only three years after World War II.

On June 28, 1948, evidently on Moscow orders, the Cominform issued a statement denouncing Marshal Tito's leadership of the Yugoslav Communist Party. This criticism accused Tito of excessive nationalism, underestimation of Soviet military specialists in Yugoslavia, surveillance over USSR economic specialists there, propaganda against the Soviet Union, purge and arrest of two prominent Yugoslav Communists because of their friendliness toward the USSR, refusal to act on Cominform criticism, and making concessions to capitalist states. The Cominform concluded by threatening that Tito could repent and reform, or be removed from power by the Yugoslav Communist Party.

Tito made a public reply immediately, repudiating all the Cominform accusations. He stressed that Yugoslavia had received little material aid from the USSR. Tito further emphasized the heavy guerrilla fighting done by the Yugoslav Communist army during World War II. Meanwhile Yugoslavia called unsuccessfully for a Balkan federation of Bulgaria, Albania, and Yugoslavia.

The USSR and its East European satellites then stopped all trade and aid to Yugoslavia, trying to weaken the latter by economic blockade. In 1949 the USSR denounced its 1945 treaty of alliance with Yugoslavia, withdrew the Soviet ambassador from

Belgrade, expelled the Yugoslav ambassador from Moscow, and publicly ridiculed Yugoslavia's attitude toward the Soviet Union as a "puppy barking at an elephant."

The puppy retaliated by closing the Yugoslav frontier in 1949 to the Greek Communist army, which had been fighting the pro-Western Greek government for three years. Deprived of Yugoslav material aid, the Greek Communists soon suffered heavy military reverses, and began retreating into Bulgaria and Albania. Thus Tito helped end the Greek civil war in favor of the West.

Meanwhile there was evidence of strong sympathy for Yugoslavia among Communist leaders of many east European nations. On Moscow orders, these pro-Titoists were demoted, imprisoned, and often executed. Among the victims was Wladyslaw Gomulka, a Polish vice-premier, who was first demoted, then imprisoned. (Gomulka survived to become a leader of Polish semi-independence in post-Stalin 1956.) Less fortunate were Bulgarian vice-premier Traicho Kostov, Albanian vice-premier Koci Xoxe, and Hungarian foreign minister Laszlo Rajk, all of whom were executed. The attraction to Titoism spread also to rank-and-file members of the East European Communist parties. During 1949 alone, the Czechoslovak Communist Party expelled 100,000 disloyal members, and the Hungarian party, 200,000.

At first during the Soviet-Yugoslav dispute, Tito stoutly proclaimed that he was not breaking with the Soviet orbit to join the West. Yet inevitably, the Communist economic blockade of Yugoslavia drove the latter into Western trade. Almost immediately after the break, Yugoslavia shipped its nonferrous metals out to the West as a sort of hard currency paying for desperately needed imports. By 1950 Tito accepted American economic aid, and by 1951, US armament shipments. In 1953 Yugoslavia concluded a military alliance with Greece and Turkey, both of whom were already members of NATO. Economically and militarily, Tito slowly joined the West, though he continued to proclaim himself a devout Communist and international neutralist.

An almost comic result of the Soviet-Yugoslav dispute was the hurried transfer of Cominform headquarters in 1948 from Belgrade to the Rumanian capital of Bucharest.

Perhaps because of fear that Communist China might become

Titoist, the USSR in 1952 returned to China the Chinese Eastern and South Manchurian railways with all their subsidiary property, as well as the Manchurian port of Dairen.

During 1952, the last year before Stalin's death, the USSR toyed with two new foreign policies which became keystones of post-Stalin foreign affairs. During the spring of 1952, an international economic conference was held in Moscow, at which Soviet spokesmen made an offer of 2.5–3.75 billion dollars worth of trade with countries outside the Soviet orbit. Of course, these offers were primarily an attempt to break the Truman Embargo against shipment of Western strategic machinery and raw materials into the USSR. More significant, however, was Soviet talk of a "Stalin Plan" to render technical aid to underdeveloped nations of the free world. The USSR thus hinted at opposing the US Point Four program by vast Soviet material aid, which began in 1954 after Stalin's death.

Late in 1952 Premier Stalin also offered to settle all outstanding differences with Italy and France, if the two latter countries would withdraw from NATO. Both the Italian and French ambassadors in Moscow considered the offers so important that they immediately flew home to consult their governments. At the time there was no positive result, since France and Italy refused to withdraw from the NATO alliance. Yet clearly, Russia was exploring a new tactic of wooing certain Western nations, instead of merely threatening them by creating international crises. Walter Lippmann, the famous American political columnist, was sufficiently impressed to predict that Stalin's cold war was changing to "cold peace."

After Stalin's death in early 1953, cold peace became official Soviet policy, at least for the two years of collective leadership under the premiership of Georgi Malenkov. It was a logical development, since Stalin's Iranian, Berlin, and Korean crises had failed to gain territory for Communism. Worse than that, from the Communist viewpoint, was the Western reaction creating NATO, the European Common Market, the Truman Embargo, and US Point Four.

After Stalin's death, his successors eventually vilified him. Yet they followed his deathbed foreign policy. And they inherited and had at their disposal the great military-industrial power which Stalin had created within the USSR. Also inherited was Titoism, which neither Stalin nor his successors could fully suppress.

Suggestions for Further Reading

ADAMS, ARTHUR E., *Stalin and His Times*. New York: Holt, Rinehart and Winston, 1972.

BELOFF, MAX, *Soviet Policy in the Far East, 1944–1951*, New York: Oxford University Press, 1953.

DEDIJER, VLADIMIR, *The Battle Stalin Lost*. New York: Viking, 1971.

DRAGNICH, ALEX N., *Tito's Promised Land*, Trenton: Rutgers University Press, 1954.

JASNY, NAUM, *Soviet Industrialization, 1928–1952*, Chicago: Chicago University Press, 1961.

KOCHAN, LIONEL, ed., *The Jews in Soviet Russia Since 1917*. New York: Oxford University Press, 1972.

KHRUSHCHEV, NIKITA, *Khrushchev Remembers*. Boston: Little, Brown, 1970.

LAQUEUR, W. Z., *The Soviet Union and the Middle East*, New York: Praeger, 1959.

RIGBY, T. H., *Stalin*, Englewood Cliffs: Prentice-Hall, 1966.

SCHWARTZ, HARRY, *The Red Phoenix*, New York: Praeger, 1961.

SETON-WATSON, HUGH, *From Lenin to Malenkov, the History of World Communism*, New York: Praeger, 1953.

SHULMAN, MARSHALL D., *Stalin's Foreign Policy Reappraised*, Cambridge: Harvard University Press, 1963.

SPINKA, MATHEW, *The Church in Soviet Russia*, New York: Oxford University Press, 1956.

VON RAUCH, GEORG, *A History of Soviet Russia*, New York: Praeger, 1965.

WITTLIN, THADDEUS, *Commissar: The Life and Death of Lavrenty Pavlovich Beria*. New York: Macmillan, 1972.

WOLFE, BERTRAM D., *Khrushchev and Stalin's Ghost*, New York: Praeger, 1956.

Chapter 9

The Khrushchev Era

As 1953 began, unusual events occurred within the Kremlin. The commander of the Kremlin guard was removed and replaced by another general. Fifteen longtime Kremlin doctors were suddenly arrested on charges that they had assassinated and were planning to assassinate high Soviet leaders. According to Khrushchev, Stalin had become suspicious of all old party Presidium members and was actually preparing to oust them from power.

Then fortuitously for the old Presidium members, Joseph Stalin died of a cerebral hemorrhage on March 5, 1953. The Georgian dictator who had ruled the USSR for 25 years died at the age of 73. He was pronounced dead by a group of new Kremlin doctors who had replaced those in prison. Shortly after his death, the old Kremlin doctors were exonerated and released, except for two who had died from prison torture.

The old Presidium members then set up a "collective leadership" which apparently feared an immediate upheaval. The Soviet press described Stalin's death as a "crisis" and appealed to the population for "high political vigilance, irreconcilability, and stalwartness in the struggle against internal and external foes." Obviously feeling insecure, the new ruling group feared primarily the dissatisfaction of the Soviet people, second the military power of the West, and finally, a possible revolt by a Soviet satellite nation. All this was openly revealed in the USSR press.

De-Stalinization began about two weeks after Stalin's death. The Georgian dictator was given a magnificent state funeral, after which his body was preserved and put on display in Lenin's tomb on Moscow's Red Square. But almost all mention of Stalin soon disappeared from the Soviet press. Even the new regime's new summary history of the USSR Communist Party barely noticed him. Quotations cited from the Communist past to support collective leadership policies were usually taken from Lenin, not Stalin.

Concession after concession was made to appease the Soviet masses. Children, the aged, and mild offenders were released from Soviet prison camps. State purchase prices were raised for farm produce, and taxes in kind and cash were lowered on the private gardens of rural residents. Promises were made that the 1955 plan for production of consumer goods would be fulfilled a year in advance.

As after Lenin's death, the collective leaders almost immediately began struggling for supreme power. The post-Stalin leaders first made sure that newcomers would not challenge their authority. Two thirds of the Communist Party Presidium were removed, the Supreme Soviet Presidium received a new president and secretary, and about half of the Council of Ministers were demoted or removed by consolidation of ministries. This reorganization concentrated total power in the hands of the old Party Presidium members, who were then safe to quarrel among themselves.

Georgi Malenkov, Stalin's chosen heir, made the first bid for supreme power by succeeding Stalin both as Premier and chief secretary of the USSR Communist Party. The collective leadership quickly forced him to relinquish the top party secretaryship to Nikita Khrushchev. Lavrenti Beria, longtime head of USSR police, was next to move too strongly in the race for power. In July 1953 he was arrested, expelled from the Communist Party, stripped of his governmental vice-premiership and police ministership, and charged with treason. During December he was executed, after allegedly confessing that he had sought total power, spied for foreign countries, tried to restore capitalism in the USSR, blocked farm reforms, and aroused racial friction among various Soviet nationalities. It is inconceivable that Beria was a capitalist spy or desired to restore capitalism, though the other accusations against him were more realistic. For several years after his death, the police were drastically purged so no police chief could again challenge party Presidium authority.

The next showdown for power was between Premier Malenkov and party secretary Khrushchev. In February 1955 the collective leadership forced Malenkov to relinquish his premiership to Marshal Nikolai Bulganin. Malenkov's letter of resignation, which he did not read, apologized for his agricultural mismanagement and his inexperience in economics and local political work. Actually Malenkov's apology seemed even more unreal than Beria's confession. Malenkov had much past experience in local political work as a student leader in Moscow colleges, and supervised the entire Soviet aircraft industry during World War II. Khrushchev, not Malenkov, appears to have been responsible for Soviet farm difficulties after Stalin's death. Aside from struggle for power, the main quarrel between Malenkov and the collective leadership appeared to be over economic priorities. Malenkov desired fast expansion of output of consumer goods, and his consumer propaganda excited and attracted the Soviet masses to his support. Though Malenkov did little to produce more consumer goods, his popularity apparently worried the collective leaders, who in purging him reaffirmed the Stalinist priority for heavy industry over light industry and agriculture.

Malenkov was demoted to a vice-premier and minister of electric power stations (a heavy industry ministry). No less than 27 cabinet ministers, 6 supreme court judges, and several provincial party leaders were dismissed to remove his supporters from positions of power. The collective leadership continued, now dominated by Bulganin and Khrushchev.

Within a year after Malenkov's demotion, Bulganin and Khrushchev were already copying his consumer program and promising a more abundant Soviet life. The pressures from the Soviet populace, which had forced Malenkov into making alluring promises, were now being felt by Bulganin and Khrushchev. Like Malenkov, they did little to make consumer abundance come true. But at least the lowest wage-scales and pensions were raised, farm taxes were reduced, and more short-term offenders were released from prison camps.

It's an old political trick, not unknown in America, to glorify yourself in a new post by criticizing your predecessor. This is exactly what Khrushchev did in 1956 at the Twentieth Congress of the USSR Communist Party. His public and private speeches at the congress described the dead Stalin as one of the greatest criminals in Russian history. The public speeches appeared in the Soviet press, and copies of the private talk were circulated to local organizations of Communist parties throughout the Soviet orbit of nations.

Khrushchev said Stalin was actually a sadist, coward, megalomaniac, paranoid, even a fool. In the great purges of the 1930's, the Georgian dictator executed 70 per cent of Russia's leading Communists, after extracting false confessions from them by torture. On the eve of World War II, he neglected to mobilize USSR industry for war, and weakened the Red Army by purging its loyal officer corps. Just before Hitler invaded Russia, Stalin ignored all warnings of the imminent danger, and when invasion was launched became hysterical, fleeing from Moscow. Later, trying to direct military operations, his amateurish mistakes caused needless Soviet casualties. When peace came, a militarily inept and cowardly Stalin assumed full credit for all Soviet victories, jealously demoting the Red Army marshals who had actually won the war. Then he unnecessarily angered foreign governments, particularly Yugoslavia and Red China.

The entire Soviet orbit was stunned by Khrushchev's denunciation of Stalin. Within a few months, open intellectual unrest had arisen in the USSR, Poland achieved a Titoist semi-independence, and Hungary plunged into all-out revolution. Temporarily Khrushchev softened his attacks on Stalin, but de-Stalinization continued.

In many respects Marxism is a materialistic religion, with its own god Marx, and his prophets Engels, Lenin, and Stalin. Throughout human history, no other organized religion has condemned its past prophet or high priest as a criminal, though many past church leaders have been cruel or corrupt. Normally religious congregations prefer to ignore any infamy in the history of their particular church.

Khrushchev could easily have ignored any misdeeds of Stalin. Why did he run the risk of shattering the Marxist faith of millions of Communists both in the Soviet orbit and throughout the world?

Perhaps Khrushchev hated and feared the Georgian dictator and took revenge. But there were several sound reasons for this desecration of the dead: Stalin in disgrace was a scapegoat who could be blamed for the difficulties of Soviet life. For several years after 1956, almost everything wrong in the Soviet system was officially described as inherited from the Stalinist past, whose ills required much time to cure.

De-Stalinization also assured USSR officials, industrialists, scientists, artists, and writers that they would not be punished for trying new methods which worked out badly. There would be freedom of experimentation by creative people, who in Stalin's time were afraid to take chances.

A de-Stalinized USSR could make friends with foreign governments which Stalin had antagonized. De-Stalinization also encouraged optimism among the Soviet masses by promising more legality, less police terror, and a better standard of living.

Of all the collective leaders, only Anastas Mikoyan strongly supported Khrushchev in the 1956 condemnation of Stalin. During the winter of 1956–1957, after de-Stalinization had caused more and more upheavals within and without the USSR, it was obvious that Khrushchev was in danger of being purged by his colleagues.

When in trouble, Khrushchev's technique was to overwhelm his opponents with a startling new idea. In early 1957, he proposed de-centralization of Soviet industrial management, abolishing most USSR industrial ministries and replacing them with over 100 regional economic councils. Central economic planning would be retained, but actual industrial administration would be in the hands of regional governments. Khrushchev explained that the world's second largest industry could no longer be governed by remote control from a Moscow bureaucracy. Aside from economic logic, the proposed industrial decentralization had political implications. The Moscow economic bureaucracy contained many powerful supporters of Khrushchev's enemies. Conversely, most regional party and governmental leaders would welcome a respite from arbitrary control by the Moscow industrial bureaucracy.

By July 1957 an alliance had been formed between the Malenkov liberals and Molotov conservatives in the Communist Party Presidium, attracting even some post-Stalin appointees who were considered protégés of Khrushchev. While Khrushchev was on a good-will tour in Finland, the alliance voted him out of the party presidium and his party secretaryship. Upon returning to the USSR, Khrushchev appealed for support of the party's Central Committee, which consists mainly of provincial leaders. After a lengthy stormy meeting, the Central Committee restored Khrushchev to power.

Khrushchev's opponents were officially labeled as an "anti-party group," which had opposed his agricultural experiments, foreign policy, de-Stalinization, and industrial decentralization. All six members of the anti-party group were expelled from the Communist Party Presidium, deprived of their high governmental posts, and demoted to minor positions. Thus Malenkov lost his vice-premiership and ministry of electric power stations, and was exiled to Central Asia to manage a power station. Molotov was deprived of his vice-premiership and ministry of state control, and sent first to Outer Mongolia as ambassador, then to Austria as a Soviet representative on the International Atomic Energy Agency.

By the autumn of 1957 a new struggle developed within the Communist Party Presidium, this time between Marshal Zhukov and Khrushchev, who again emerged victorious. Zhukov was dismissed as Defense Minister, and expelled from membership in both the Presidium and Central Committee of the USSR Communist Party. In his speech accepting Central Committee expulsion, Zhukov recalled that he had been expelled from that committee once before, by Stalin in 1946.

Zhukov was not labeled a member of the anti-party group, but was officially accused of trying to liquidate Communist Party control over the USSR armed forces, encouraging idolatry of himself, establishing personal dictatorship over the army, and being adventurous in both internal and foreign policy.

Next to fall was Marshal Nikolai Bulganin, who, like Zhukov, had helped Khrushchev seize supreme power. In 1958 he was dismissed as USSR Premier, expelled from the Communist Party Presidium, and demoted first to chairman of the USSR State Bank, then to head of a regional economic council in the North Caucasus. Soon the Soviet press accused him of being the leader of the Malenkov-Molotov anti-party group.

Khrushchev replaced Bulganin as USSR Premier. As Premier and first secretary of the party's Central Committee, Khrushchev now held the same key posts of power as the late Joseph Stalin. Thus six years after Stalin's death, the USSR again lived under one-man rule.

More protégés of Khrushchev were purged in 1960: USSR party secretary Aleksei Kirichenko; Nikolai Belyayev, first party secretary of the Kazakh Soviet Republic; and Yekaterina Furtseva, a USSR party secretary and the first woman to join the party Presidium. All three were removed from the party Presidium to which they had been appointed by Khrushchev. The reasons for their dismissal were never stated. Kirichenko and Belyayev were given minor party posts in south European USSR, then disappeared. Furtseva, a longtime associate of Khrushchev, continued to be USSR Minister of Culture.

Somewhat different was the fate of Marshal Kliment Voroshilov, a Politburo member since the late 1920's and President of the USSR since Stalin's death. In 1960 he resigned from the party Presidium and was replaced as USSR President by a Khrushchev protégé, Leonid Brezhnev. Soon Voroshilov was accused of being a member of the 1957 anti-party group. However, Voroshilov became a member of the Supreme Soviet Presidium, which he had formerly headed as USSR president. Of the entire anti-party group, only Voroshilov retained a high governmental post.

The anticlimax of the collective leadership struggle came in 1961 at the twenty-second Congress of the USSR Communist Party. Khrushchev not only condemned Stalin, but publicly revealed how members of the anti-party group aided Stalin in the great purges of the 1930's. Upon Khrushchev's suggestion, Stalin's corpse was removed from Lenin's mausoleum and buried in an earthen grave near the Kremlin wall. Bulganin, Voroshilov, and two others of the anti-party group were expelled from the Central Committee of the USSR Communist Party. Molotov lost his post as Soviet representative to the International Atomic Energy Agency.

During 1961–1962, all places and enterprises named after Stalin and members of the anti-party group were given new names. Hundreds of Soviet towns, districts, factories, and schools were therefore given new titles. Stalingrad became Volgograd, Ukrainian Stalino, Donetsk; Siberian Stalinsk, Novokuznetsk; and Mount Stalin (the highest peak in the USSR), Mount Communism. In 1961, a Central Asian mountain was renamed Mount Khrushchev.

As yet the Soviet government has failed to devise any orderly system of succession from one top leader to the next. After Lenin died in 1924 and Stalin in 1953, a struggle for power occurred. A collective leadership was set up to rule Russia, but the collective leaders quarreled, and one finally emerged as the victor. In both cases the struggle for power lasted about five or six years. And in both struggles, the victor was a relatively obscure man with middle-of-the-road policies at the time, not a liberal Bukharin or Malenkov, nor an extremist Trotsky or Molotov. Both victors removed their rivals from power, then purged some of the subleaders who had contributed to the victory. As time went on, both victors accused more and more people of opposing them in the past struggle for power. All this is a ruthless drive for authority against both enemies and friends. Thus it is uncertain if Bulganin and Voroshilov really belonged to the 1957 antiparty group. Perhaps they were falsely accused, so they could be gracefully discarded. Maybe Kirichenko, Belyayev, and Furtseva demanded too many favors for supporting Khrushchev during the 1957 showdown, and thus also had to be removed. Zhukov's purge is more understandable, since he was apparently building up his own dictatorship in the armed forces.

Despite the palace quarrels for the throne after Stalin's death, most of Stalin's internal policies were continued without major change. As violently as Khrushchev criticized Stalin, he still praised the Georgian dictator's basic economic practices. Thus according to Khrushchev, Stalin was correct in rejecting "cotton-dress industrialization" and in emphasizing heavy war-potential industry at the expense of consumer goods. The collectivization of Russia's peasantry was also justified. Khrushchev explained that both heavy industry and collective farms are necessary for Russia to be a great military power.

The post-Stalin leaders have spared no effort to increase direct and indirect Soviet armament. Particularly impressive have been the post-Stalin achievements in science. All scientific research is planned, and every year the plans are modernized and revised. There are no 8-hour workdays or weekend rests. It's not unusual for a Soviet laboratory to be open 24 hours a day, every day of the week, all year long.

Like USSR industry, Soviet science concentrates on building up the war potential of the Communist state. Many laboratories operate directly under the management of defense industry and the armed forces. A chain of police laboratories does research on the most secret weapons. Ordinary industrial and college laboratories are compelled to work on defense projects too.

Not long after Stalin's death in 1953, Russia exploded its first hydrogen bomb. The world's first earth satellite was launched by the USSR in 1957, lifted into space by a rocket with a speed of 15,500 miles per hour. During the same year Russia's atomic city of Dubno near Moscow opened a 10-billion electronvolt synchrophasotron, which at the time was the largest atom-smashing machine in the world. Dubno illustrates how Communist talent has been concentrated to make a fast scientific breakthrough. Top atomic scientists from Russia, East Germany, Czechoslovakia, and Poland work there as a team.

In 1958 the largest hydroelectric power station in the world started operating at Kuibyshev on the Volga River, with a generating capacity of 2.3 million kilowatts. In comparison, the greatest American station produces only 1.9 million kilowatts. By 1963 both were dwarfed by the Bratsk power station of 4.2 million kilowatts, completed on the Angara River in east Siberia.

Russia opened its first atomic power station of commercial size in 1958, trailing Britain by two years and America by a few months. All three nations are building large chains of atomic power stations, but the American and British plants will range in size from 100,000 to 300,000 kilowatts. Meanwhile, each USSR atomic power station when fully completed will have a production capacity of 400,000 to 600,000 kilowatts.

Other Soviet scientific victories include the world's largest passenger airplane (1957), the world's first atomic-powered surface ship (the icebreaker "Lenin," 1959), the world's first rockets to reach and closely photograph the moon (1959), orbiting the world's first man in space (1961), exploding a 50-megaton hydrogen bomb (the world's largest at the time, 1961), orbiting two men in space a few miles apart (1962), and repeating this unprecedented feat with a man and woman (1963). Clearly

Russia could no longer be described as a giant with feet of clay.

During the Khrushchev era, the USSR began building an atom-smasher of 50-billion electronvolts, larger than any under construction or operating in the West.

This race for scientific supremacy was very costly, especially when combined with large-scale armament and fast expansion of heavy industry. For this reason, Khrushchev was unable to fulfill his oft-promised fast rise in the Soviet standard of living. When Stalin died in 1953, USSR living standards were below those of 1928. By 1963 there was considerable improvement, but food and housing remained below 1928 levels.

No political freedom resulted from Stalin's death, but there was more personal liberty. Police terror was curbed, and arbitrary arrests of the innocent largely ceased. The prison camp population was reduced by two thirds. Racial equality was restored to several North Caucasus nationalities persecuted by Stalin. Artists, writers, scientists, and scholars were permitted to be more truthful, critical, and experimental. There was much more Soviet contact with foreigners due to cultural exchange, the post-Stalin influx of foreign tourists into the USSR, and travel by large numbers of Russian tourists in Communist East Europe.

However, in some respects the Khrushchev regime was harsher than the Stalinist past. Economic criminals such as speculators and embezzlers were severely punished and often executed. When Stalin died, Soviet law codes provided death sentences only for treason, espionage, and sabotage. Under Khrushchev, death sentences were awarded for many more crimes: premeditated murder, assassination of a Soviet official, membership in an anti-Soviet organization, banditism, embezzling, speculation, counterfeiting, brutality by prisoners toward other prison inmates, bribery, assault on a policeman, and rape. In addition to the regular police, army patrols began to preserve order in many Soviet cities.

At first the post-Stalin regime was lenient toward organized religion. During 1954, when Malenkov was still Premier, the Central Committee of the USSR Communist Party issued a decree forbidding local governments to persecute or ridicule clergymen and church congregations. In the same year, the Jewish Autonomous Region was recreated in East Siberia, signifying the end of the post-World War II Stalinist persecution of the

Jews. Throughout the USSR, devout believers repaired and reopened churches, mosques, temples, and synagogues which had been closed for many years.

Soon after Khrushchev achieved supreme power in 1957, religious persecution began again. The first targets were the Jews, who were subjected to a quota system allowing less than 2 per cent of government bureaucrats and college students to be Jewish. On various pretenses, synagogues were closed and rabbis were arrested. In some localities small pogroms occurred, unchecked and unpunished by the local police. The Jews did not suffer alone. Small Protestant sects such as the Pentacostals, Shakers, and Jehovah's Witnesses were also severely repressed.

By the early 1960's, the official persecution spread to all religions. Priests, ministers, mullahs, and clergy of all faiths were arrested and imprisoned on alleged charges of immorality, speculation, and anti-Sovietism. Many churches, mosques, temples, monasteries, and shrines hitherto tolerated were forced to close. Thus Russia returned to the religious persecutions of the 1930's, after two decades of partial tolerance during the Stalinist 1940's and early 1950's, and the collective-leadership respite of 1953–1957.

Industrial planning in the post-Stalin era may be described as confused. In 1953, Premier Malenkov pledged that the 1955 plan for output of consumer goods would be fulfilled in 1954. By late 1954 the Soviet press ignored this promise, which was not fulfilled. The Sixth Five-Year Plan was adopted in 1956 as the economic program for 1956–1960, then cancelled in 1957 because its production goals were unrealistically high. During 1958 the USSR economy had no long-range plan, and the factories and farms—left to their own devices—continued to follow the Sixth Five-Year Plan which had been abolished. A Seven-Year Plan for 1959–1965 was then published, including a program for modernizing heavy industry by concentrating on chemical production rather than metallurgy or machinebuilding. Plastics were to substitute for various metals, and synthetic fibre would provide clothing for the Soviet people. The chemical program remained a dead letter, only to be revived in 1964.

Meanwhile in 1957 most USSR industrial ministries were abolished, and their factories and mines were placed under the jurisdiction of more than 100 newly created regional economic councils. After a year the industrial ministries began to be re-created, and by 1963 there were as many such ministries as in 1957. The 100 regional economic councils became too independent, and were consolidated into some 40 economic regions under strict centralized control. Despite this managerial reorganization, Soviet heavy industry grew at an impressive rate after Stalin's death. The USSR in 1952 produced 35 million metric tons of steel, and in 1963, 80 million.

Post-Stalin agricultural planning largely consisted of experiments that ended in failure. In 1954 an entire year's output of tractors along with 150,000 Soviet citizens (mostly urbanites) were dispatched into the semi-desert pasturelands along the northern edge of the great Central Asian desert in an attempt to grow huge quantities of grain on these marginal lands, which usually had not been farmed because of the constant danger of drought. No provision was made for irrigation of these so-called "new lands," nor for crop rotation to ensure continued fertility of the soil. About 100 million acres of grain were planted in the new lands, which suffered droughts in 1955, 1957, 1960, and 1963. After 1958 the grain crops there consistantly declined. By 1964 Khrushchev admitted the bankruptcy of the new lands, and predicted that they would soon be reconverted into pastures.

Another dramatic agricultural undertaking began in 1955 when corn acreage was tremendously expanded throughout the USSR. Though corn has a higher yield per acre than other grains, most of the Soviet Union is too dry and too cold for maize to ripen fully. By the early 1960's, 80 million acres were under corn, which was proving to be unproductive. Khrushchev, who had introduced corn on such a large scale, finally in 1964 advised farms to change to more sensible types of grain.

In 1962, while his new lands and corn were failing, Khrushchev condemned the crop rotation system which had existed in the USSR since the 1930's. The system allowed one fourth of all arable land to lie under fallow or hay, a practice which the premier considered wasteful. He therefore ordered that millions of acres of grassland and fallow should be sown in 1962–1963 with corn, sugar beets, beans, and peas. The President of the Soviet Academy of Agricultural Science resigned rather than approve this scheme, which would deplete soil fertility throughout the USSR.

All these unsound experiments contributed to a disastrous crop failure in 1963, when a severe winter, a late spring, a dry summer, and early fall reduced the grain harvest by 20 per cent. The USSR, which had exported 7,800,000 metric tons of grain in 1962, was forced to import 11,000,000 tons during the 1963–1964 winter. Millions of livestock were slaughtered for lack of feed, including two fifths of all hogs.

This economic failure severely damaged the reputation of Premier Khrushchev, who had assumed personal control over Soviet agriculture ever since Stalin's death. The Soviet public grumbled about bread shortages, and underdeveloped nations became suspicious of farm technical aid from the USSR. Abandoning further experiments in agriculture, Khrushchev in 1964 ordered a crash program for fast expansion of output of chemical fertilizer, which had previously been in short supply. Thus he returned to the Stalinist concept he had formerly condemned: Higher yields per acre are more important than expanding the sown acreage.

Soviet foreign policy after Stalin's death was a mixture of great successes and grave failures. When Stalin died in early 1953, at first the collective leadership changed from cold war to "cold peace," thus adopting an idea which the Georgian dictator was considering just before his death. During 1953 and 1954 Premier Malenkov re-established diplomatic relations with Israel, normalized relations with Yugoslavia by exchanging ambassadors, helped arrange armistices for the Korean conflict and Indochinese civil war, and secured USSR admission into two specialized agencies of the United Nations: UNESCO and the International Labor Organization. Apparently the Kremlin desired to remain aloof from the West, while achieving some relaxation of East-West tensions.

At the beginning, no special Soviet consideration was displayed toward the Communist satellite nations. When East German workers rioted in June 1953 for better food and more pay, USSR tanks suppressed the riots, despite protests from the United States, Britain, France, and West Germany. The Soviet Union refused an American offer to distribute food to the hungry East Germans, and harassed those East Germans who visited West Berlin to obtain such food.

Nevertheless, the East German riots frightened the Kremlin, which began making concessions to the satellites. East Germany was freed from paying its remaining reparations to the USSR; all East German postwar debts to Russia were cancelled; Soviet occupation expenses in East Germany were reduced to 5 per cent of the East German budget, and East Germany was given a Soviet credit equivalent to $121,000,000.

Also after the East German uprising, North Korea was awarded a Soviet credit equaling $250,000,000 for reconstruction of war damage, and Communist China obtained a Soviet loan of $230,000,000 for industrial expansion. Other concessions to the satellites included the withdrawal of Soviet troops from Port Arthur in Manchuria, the granting of sovereignty to East Germany, and the sale of Soviet-owned enterprises in North Korea, Bulgaria, Hungary, Rumania, and Communist China to the governments of those countries.

After USSR Premier Malenkov was forced to resign during February 1955, Soviet foreign policy became much more active. In April 1955, the USSR unilaterally annulled the Anglo-Soviet alliance of 1942 and the Soviet-French alliance of 1944 because Britain and France had permitted West Germany to rearm and to join NATO. Almost immediately a 20-year military alliance was formed between the USSR, Albania, Bulgaria, Czechoslovakia, East Germany, Hungary, Poland, and Rumania to counteract West German rearmament. Soon called the Warsaw Pact, this alliance included a joint military command with headquarters in Moscow.

With satellite East Europe united militarily, the USSR set forth to gain friends in the West. Austria was granted a peace treaty which converted it into a permanently neutral nation. Yugoslavia received offers of Soviet economic, technical, and scientific aid. Russia established diplomatic relations with West Germany, despite West German rearmament. The Soviet-Finnish alliance of 1948 was extended until 1975, and the Soviet naval base at Porkkala on Finnish soil was returned to Finland. On Soviet and British initiative, an inconclusive summit conference of President Eisenhower, Premier Bulganin, British Prime Minister Eden, and French Premier Faure was held at Geneva, Switzerland, in July 1955.

These Soviet concessions in Europe soon proved to be an attempt to keep the West quiet while the USSR wooed neutralist underdeveloped nations, seeking to detach them permanently from the West. Technical aid from the Soviet Union had already started to India in 1954, and was extended to Afghanistan, Burma, and Egypt in 1955. Camouflaged as Czechoslovak munitions, large shipments of Soviet arms were reaching Egypt by late 1955. USSR credits worth $100,000,000 were granted to Afghanistan in 1955, while in 1956 Yugoslavia received $84,000,000 and Indonesia, $100,000,000. Also in 1956, for the first time since 1945, diplomatic relations were established between the USSR and Japan. Related to these Soviet overtures toward Asia and Africa was the Soviet abolition of the Communist Information Bureau (Cominform) in 1956, ending an organization which had openly given revolutionary orders to Communist parties throughout the world. Rid of the Cominform, the USSR could pose as an unselfish power offering unconditional aid to weak underdeveloped nations.

At the USSR Communist Party Congress in February 1956, Khrushchev and other Soviet leaders proclaimed the ideological bases of their post-Malenkov foreign policy: Communist world revolution could be achieved peaceably, without a third world war or even civil wars. In the West, socialists should ally with Communists to bring about Communism by parliamentary means. Meanwhile the USSR would aid colonies and underdeveloped nations to achieve political and economic freedom from domination by the great Western powers. Soviet satellites need not imitate USSR internal policies, but could socialize in accord with their national peculiarities. By allowing Soviet satellites some internal independence, the USSR attempted to quiet satellite discontent and attract underdeveloped nations into the Soviet orbit.

Accompanying the announcement of this foreign policy were the party congress speeches violently denouncing Stalin. This strong de-Stalinization disturbed the entire international Communist movement. Many non-Russian Communist leaders objected to the degradation of Stalin, or accepted it very reluctantly.

In the Soviet satellites of eastern Europe, de-Stalinization contributed to the already great unrest against Russian domination.

By October 1956 a new Communist government in Poland demanded Polish semi-independence. Khrushchev and other Soviet leaders hurriedly visited Poland, unsuccessfully attempting to curb Polish liberalism. A bargain was struck that Poland would remain in the Soviet orbit, but could manage its own internal affairs. Poland immediately restored private stores, broke up many collective farms, and granted some cultural freedom.

Excited by events in Poland, Hungary hurled itself into outright rebellion against Soviet rule. At first the USSR wavered, again sending Soviet leaders to make a personal investigation. Then Soviet tanks suppressed the Hungarian rebels.

Fortunately for the USSR, the world was distracted from the Hungarian revolution by the simultaneous Anglo-French-Israel invasion of Egypt. Immediately the USSR threatened to attack Britain and France with hydrogen bombs unless the invasion were stopped. Soviet appeals were made both to the United Nations and United States to restore peace in the Near East. When the invasion of Egypt ceased, the USSR assumed full credit for ending this undeclared war, although American pressure was probably more important for the cessation of hostilities.

Meanwhile Russia's bargain with Poland and reconquest of Hungary disillusioned the most important of all Soviet satellites: Communist China. As long as Premier Stalin had ruled the USSR, China had supported USSR foreign policy, while maintaining some independence in internal affairs. Until 1956, China also cooperated with Stalin's successors. But China did not approve Khrushchev's peaceful coexistence with the West and de-Stalinization. China aided Poland in achieving semi-independence, but was horrified by the Hungarian revolution. Thereafter China decided its future could not be entrusted to Khrushchev. China began to pursue a semi-independent foreign policy in 1957. To placate China, the USSR offered to teach Chinese industry the difficult techniques of producing nuclear bombs.

Starting in 1957 the USSR became tougher in relations with the West, perhaps because the West failed to aid the Hungarian revolution or because the Soviet Union was superior to the United States in long-range rockets. Repeatedly the USSR threatened to drop hydrogen bombs on NATO countries if the latter attacked the Soviet Union. Often the threat listed the small number of bombs which would be sufficient to devastate the NATO country. Angered in 1958 by a liberal new Yugoslav Communist program, the USSR suspended credits of $285,000,000 previously assigned to help expand Yugoslav industry. During the same year the entrance of British troops into Jordan and American troops into Lebanon brought forth a wave of official Soviet protests. In 1958, 1959, 1961, and 1963, the USSR created international crises in an attempt to force French, British, and American troops out of West Berlin. Soviet pressures on West Berlin included demands for the city to be demilitarized and neutralized, the construction of a wall around West Berlin to block normal traffic from the city into Communist East Berlin, and roadblocks delaying Allied military convoys traveling between West Berlin and West Germany. Despite this firm stance, the USSR was unwilling to risk a nuclear war. In 1958 for example, the USSR at first supported Communist China's demand that American troops leave Formosa, and declared that an attack on Red China would be considered an attack on the Soviet Union. But when the United States rejected a violent Soviet diplomatic note about Taiwan, the USSR made no further demands.

Despite the Soviet policy of forcing crises to the brink of war, Soviet Premier Khrushchev requested and obtained summit meetings with President Eisenhower in 1959 at Camp David, with leaders of the French-British-American alliance at Paris in 1960, and with President Kennedy at Vienna in 1961. The Camp David and Vienna conversations were inconclusive, and the Paris conference was cancelled by Khrushchev when the U.S. government refused to apologize for flying U-2 reconnaissance planes over the USSR.

Meanwhile the USSR consistently pursued its policy of wooing underdeveloped nations and aiding colonial revolution. Long-term credits at low interest for economic development included the ruble equivalent of $30,000,000 to Ceylon, $100,000,000 to Egypt, and $100,000,000 to Argentina in 1958; $100,000,000 to Ethiopia and $137,000,000 to Iraq in 1959. By 1964 this technical aid program had pledged credits worth $3,300,000,000, not counting armament shipments amounting to an additional $2,000,-

000,000. Altogether the USSR was building 500 factories and other economic enterprises in 25 underdeveloped nations of Asia, Africa, and Latin America. Two thirds of the Soviet economic aid was concentrated on five strategically located countries: Egypt, Afghanistan, India, Indonesia, and Cuba.

Other methods of aiding underdeveloped nations were also used by the USSR. Soviet trade with such nations grew ten times from about $200,000,000 in 1956 to some $2,100,000,000 in 1963. Recipients of Soviet armament included Egypt, India, Indonesia, Algeria, the Congo, and Cuba. Diplomatic maneuvers by the USSR obstructed Western attempts to end the civil wars in Laos and South Vietnam, while Soviet arms were supplied to Laotian and Vietnamese Communist guerrillas.

Soviet attempts to gain influence in underdeveloped nations did not always progress smoothly. During 1960 the USSR developed close relations with Premier Patrice Lumumba's government in the Republic of the Congo. The USSR promised to aid the Congo against Western aggression, and sent sugar, milk, wheat, arms, and technical and military advisors by air to the Congolese capital. Then Lumumba was overthrown by an army coup, and the Soviet Union found itself in the embarrassing position of having supported the losing side. The USSR ceased its aid, was forced to withdraw its advisors, and severed diplomatic relations with the Congo.

Later the USSR managed to establish diplomatic relations with the new Congo government, but made the mistake of supporting a provincial rebellion against the Congolese capital. As a result, in 1963 the Congo expelled the entire staff of the Soviet embassy.

In contrast, the USSR was extremely successful in making friends with Cuba, which became the first Communist foothold in Latin America. When Cuban Premier Castro appealed for Soviet aid in 1960, the USSR immediately gave Cuba a $100,-000,000 credit for purchasing Soviet machinery and promised to buy 5 million tons of Cuban sugar over a period of five years. Large numbers of Russian technical and military advisors swarmed into Cuba, building new factories and establishing Soviet rocket and air bases against the United States.

When the US Navy blockaded Cuba in the autumn of 1962, the USSR offered to withdraw its intermediate missiles from

Cuba if the United States would cease the blockade and pledge not to invade Cuban territory. The United States accepted these proposals on condition that Soviet jet bombers also be withdrawn from Cuban soil. More than 40 intermediate missiles (with ranges of 1,000 to 2,000 miles) and over 40 jet bombers were shipped back from Cuba to the USSR. Since Cuba refused to permit United Nations inspection of these shipments, it was uncertain if all Russian bombers and rockets had been removed.

Undaunted by this setback, the USSR kept Soviet troops in Cuba, established submarine bases there, and sent economic supplies to Cuba at a rate of $1,000,000 per day. The USSR claimed that its bargaining with the United States in 1962 had saved Cuba from invasion.

Such claims made little impression on Communist China, which blamed the USSR both for adventurously placing rockets and bombers in Cuba, and cowardly withdrawing them when confronted by US pressure. This Chinese criticism could have been expected, because Moscow-Peking relations had deteriorated badly after 1958. Just as Premier Khrushchev was embarking on a good-will tour to America in 1959, Chinese Communist troops attacked Indian frontier posts along the Tibetan border. Annoyed by this affront to Khrushchev, the USSR urged India and China to settle the frontier dispute peaceably, and suspended Soviet aid to Chinese nuclear armament. Skirmishes along the Sino-Soviet border began in 1960 between troops of the two nations, and by 1962 had increased to 5,000 incidents per year. Meanwhile in 1961, when the USSR broke trade, aid, and diplomatic relations with Albania, an East European satellite, Communist China immediately came to Albania's rescue. At the time Albania had a harvest failure, and was dependent on Soviet grain shipments, which were suspended. China saved Albania from famine by sending Canadian wheat to Albanian ports. The USSR retaliated against China by terminating most Soviet technical aid to Peking. Soviet technicians withdrew from China, even taking with them the blueprints for half-completed Chinese factories. By 1963, Soviet-Chinese annual trade had decreased to one third of the 1960 level. China in 1964 openly urged the formation of leftist anti-Russian Communist parties throughout the world, condemned the USSR for exploiting the Moslems of Soviet Central

Asia, and appealed to the black, brown, brunette, and yellow peoples of Asia, Africa and Latin America to unite against all white nations (including Russia).

In turn, the USSR accused China of Trotskyite extremism, and wooed the socialist parties of the Western capitalist countries. Possibly to free its hands for a showdown with China, the USSR in 1963 concluded three significant treaties with the United States: a pact establishing direct radio-telephone communication between the Kremlin and the White House, another providing for Soviet-American cooperation in space research, and a third outlawing above-ground nuclear tests. This last treaty was signed by Britain and most other Western, underdeveloped and Communist nations, but not by France, Albania, or Red China.

The Khrushchev era wrought great changes in the USSR. Stalin worship was destroyed, despite later attempts to credit the Georgian dictator with some achievements. Though Russia remained a one-party dictatorship, Khrushchev permitted some freedom of discussion in the press, literature, and at public meetings. Hence Soviet society began to produce a healthy diversity of ideas, much more conducive to progress than the rigid Stalinist dogmas.

Many of Khrushchev's managerial, industrial, and agricultural experiments were unsuccessful. But he set a precedent that the Soviet system was not an iron mold impossible to alter. Thus post-Khrushchev organizational changes became easy.

With both its successes and failures, Khrushchev's foreign policy attracted worldwide attention. Personal diplomacy, increased foreign trade, technical aid, tourism, cultural exchange, and space ships made Russia a truly international power.

Stalin industrialized Russia, but ruled it like a medieval nation. Khrushchev ended Soviet medievalism.

Suggestions for Further Reading

BRUMBERG, ABRAHAM, *Russia under Khrushchev,* New York: Praeger, 1962.

BRZEZINSKI, ZBIGNIEW K., *The Soviet Bloc: Unity and Conflict,* Cambridge: Harvard University Press, 1967.

FAINSOD, MERLE, *How Russia is Ruled,* 2nd ed., Cambridge: Harvard University Press, 1963.

GITTINGS, JOHN, *Survey of the Sino-Soviet Dispute.* New York: Oxford University Press, 1971.

HAHN, WERNER G., *The Politics of Soviet Agriculture, 1960-1970.* Baltimore: Johns Hopkins University Press, 1972.

JORAVSKY, DAVID, *The Lysenko Affair.* Cambridge: Harvard University Press, 1970.

KHRUSHCHEV, NIKITA, *Khrushchev Speaks,* Ann Arbor: University of Michigan Press, 1963.

KHRUSHCHEV, NIKITA, *Khrushchev Remembers.* Boston: Little, Brown, 1970.

LEONHARD, WOLFGANG, *The Kremlin since Stalin,* New York: Praeger, 1962.

LINDEN, CARL A., *Khrushchev and the Soviet Leadership, 1957–1964,* Baltimore: Johns Hopkins University Press, 1966.

LOWENTHAL, RICHARD, *World Communism: The Disintegration of a Secular Faith,* New York: Oxford University Press, 1964.

NUTTER, WARREN, *The Growth of Industrial Production in the Soviet Union,* Princeton: Princeton University Press, 1962.

RUBINSTEIN, ALVIN Z., *The Foreign Policy of the Soviet Union.* New York: Random House, 1972.

RUSH, MYRON, *Political Succession in the USSR,* New York: Columbia University Press, 1965.

ZIMMERMAN, WILLIAM, *Soviet Perspectives on International Relations, 1956-1967.* Princeton: Princeton University Press, 1969.

Chapter 10

The Brezhnev Regime

In October 1964, for the first time in Soviet history, a supreme leader—who had held power for a lengthy period—was dethroned before his death. In a secret meeting, the Central Committee of the Communist Party ousted Nikita Khrushchev from the party presidium and from his post of first party secretary. The next day, the Supreme Soviet Presidium removed him from the positions of USSR Premier and Commander-in-Chief of the Soviet armed forces. Khrushchev had been a member of the party Politburo (later presidium) since 1939, a party Central Committee secretary since 1949, first party secretary since 1953, and Soviet Premier since 1958. From 1957 to 1964, he had obviously been the chief ruler of the Soviet Union.

Khrushchev's overthrow was the work of a small Moscow group of other leaders, operating in the greatest secrecy. They had not only worked closely with Khrushchev when he ruled Russia, but were to all appearances his friends.

How could Khrushchev be removed so easily? Though popular abroad, he was disliked in his own country. Without mentioning him by name, the Soviet press has accused Khrushchev (after his fall) of promoting unworkable projects, of placing members of his family in important public offices, of making key decisions on the spur of the moment without consulting his colleagues, and of promoting hero worship of himself.

In private conversations, Soviet officials list more grievances. Khrushchev's mismanagement of the Soviet economy had not only slowed industrial growth, but forced Russia into the humiliating position of importing grain from capitalist countries. He had antagonized the army officer corps by neglecting conventional weapons in favor of nuclear rockets, when Soviet rocket production was in its infancy. By creating or aggravating international crises, he risked war with the better-armed United States. During the two final years of Khrushchev's era of power, he reverted to Stalinism by widespread purging. Thousands of Soviet citizens were sent to prison camp for minor offenses, and no official was safe from Khrushchev's wrath. For example, a college boy was sentenced to a year's imprisonment for refusing to work during summer vacation. And every regional tour of Russia by Khrushchev resulted in demotion of local agricultural bureaucrats. To save themselves from purge, Khrushchev's party presidium had to purge Khrushchev.

Traveling too much, making clever speeches both inside and outside of Russia, Khrushchev had to entrust the daily management of the USSR to his friends, who quietly, easily, and calmly removed him. The removal was not an admitted crisis, as when Stalin died. No tanks ringed the central squares of Moscow. Khrushchev's successors were certain of their own popular support.

Khrushchev was neither executed nor imprisoned, but was retired on a pension. He was succeeded by a collective leadership headed by Leonid I. Brezhnev and Aleksei N. Kosygin. Brezhnev was a Khrushchev protégé, who started his political career as a Ukrainian provincial leader. Kosygin, a skilled economist, had risen through the industrial hierarchy to become Stalin's expert on light industry. Both new leaders were college graduates, whereas Khrushchev never completed high school. About a decade younger than Khrushchev, Brezhnev and Kosygin were children during the Bolshevik Revolution, and joined the Communist Party years thereafter. Thus, for the first time in Soviet history, a postrevolutionary generation of rulers assumed command.

Brezhnev became the party first secretary—a title changed to "secretary-general" as in the days of Lenin and Stalin. Kosygin replaced Khrushchev as USSR premier. Both new rulers were members of the party presidium, which resumed its old name of "Politburo." Though allowing some rehabilitation of Stalin's image and continuing Khrushchev's foreign policy, the new Soviet regime could be called neither Stalinist nor Khrushchevian. Gone were the threatening gestures toward the West, and impolite remarks by Kremlin leaders. Kosygin and Brezhnev might best be described as a managerial team, quietly trying to solve Soviet domestic and international problems.

By the late 1970's this businesslike post-Khrushchev regime, led by colorless leaders, had ruled Russia longer than either Lenin or Khrushchev. And for the first time since Lenin, both top leaders were college graduates, Brezhnev having majored in steel and armament engineering while Kosygin held a degree in textile manufacturing.

A changeover of government in the USSR in the past was usually accompanied by widespread purging. When Khrushchev fell, the purge was small. Only a few prominent men lost their posts at first, mostly in ideology and propaganda. The twenty-third USSR Communist Party Congress in 1966, in choosing a new Central Committee, re-elected more Central Committeemen than at any recent party congress. Also in 1966, a newly elected Supreme Soviet appointed the same cabinet ministers as before.

Nevertheless, there was some subtle purging. The new regime reunited the industrial and agricultural party organizations, which had been formed at the provincial level by Khrushchev. All the 40 regional economic councils created by Khrushchev were abolished, on the grounds that they fostered local favoritism and blocked the standardization of machinery parts. The new government also discontinued Khrushchev's Supreme Economic Council, the Soviet Economic Council, and inter-regional economic councils such as those in Central Asia, the Caucasus, and the Baltic states. In place of regional, inter-regional and national economic councils, the government created 30 new industrial USSR ministries, of which seven were for production of munitions. Khrushchev's decentralization of industrial management in 1957 was completely reversed, and the Soviet economy was once again controlled from Moscow, as it had been in the time of Stalin. These party and economic reorganizations provided an opportunity for quietly demoting officials who were unsympathetic to the post-Khrushchev regime. Yet the shift of officials from one post to another was more like a game of musical chairs than a brutal Stalinist purge.

The post-Khrushchev regime tackled Russia's urgent agricultural problems, which had been aggravated rather than eased by Khrushchev's attempt to farm 100 million acres of marginal land. A series of major decrees were issued for the purpose of raising farm income so that peasants would perform better work. Collective-farm income taxes were cut in half. Debts of the poorer collective farms to the state were cancelled. The government assumed all costs for soil improvement. Government purchase prices for collective farm produce were raised from 36 per cent to 50 per cent for grains, and from 20 per cent to 100 per cent for livestock. Prices of consumer goods in rural stores were reduced to the price level in city stores. Collective farmers were allowed to set their own prices on produce they grew in their private gardens and sold at city markets. Many markets closed by Khrushchev were reopened, while existing markets were expanded. In a few months, food market trade increased by 100 per cent.

Rates charged by state power stations for electricity were lowered for both state and collective farms. Collective and state farms also paid from 10 per cent to 50 per cent less for tires, machinery, electrical equipment, tractor parts, autos, tractors, and trucks purchased from the state. In 1966, the government recommended that collective farms pay guaranteed monthly wages to their members at the same rate of pay as on state farms. Previously, collective farmers had been paid according to the size of the harvest, while state farmers always had guaranteed wages. This reform doubled the income of collective farmers, whose pay in the 1970's rose even higher. Livestock herdsmen on state farms also gained salary increases, and in 1971 the minimum pensions for collective farmers were raised. Efforts were also made to improve rural schools.

These measures improved the lot of the peasants, and resulted in higher crop yields per acre. But poor mechanization still created huge harvest losses, especially during bad weather. Drought and extreme cold caused crop slumps in 1965, 1969, 1971, 1972, 1974 and 1975, requiring billions of dollars in grain imports.

The unsuccessful agricultural reforms were paralleled

by the industrial changes decreed by the new Soviet regime in 1965. Premier Kosygin explained that, since increasing capital investments had not stopped the slowdown of USSR industrial growth, more drastic steps would be taken.

First, according to the premier's order, factories and mines would no longer be judged efficient if they merely fulfilled production plans. Instead, they were to be rated by how much of the finished product was sold. Thus, for the first time since the NEP, quality of output became more important than quantity. No longer, for example, could an auto factory manufacture cars without starters, then claim it had fulfilled its production plan.

Second, Soviet industry would be required mostly to pay its own way. Previously, new plants had been built and old factories expanded at the expense of the state. Henceforth any money granted for plant expansion was to be a loan, not a gift, and had to be paid back. If a factory should lose money in operating and needed a state subsidy, the latter would be offered not as a grant but as a loan. To repay these loans, factories would be allowed to retain more of their profits instead of paying a profit tax of 80 per cent.

Third, an industrial manager would no longer receive from Moscow a table of organization ordering him to hire exactly so many engineers, foremen, and workers. Instead, the manager was told how much he could spend on wages. Within this framework, he could hire as many engineers, foremen, and workers as he needed. They are paid whatever wages the manager can afford. The first result of this reform was some unemployment, because the average manager dismissed his incompetent personnel, then gave the highest possible salaries to the remaining skilled staff.

This major industrial reorganization has been largely sabotaged by the USSR industrial bureaucracy. Plant plan fulfillment is still often judged by quantity not quality of output. Factory profits continue to be overtaxed. And enterprise managers are constantly hampered by excessive orders from above. The result has been a rate of industrial growth slower than during the Khrushchev period.

Due to industrial and farm problems, the Brezhnev regime has slowed down the rate of planned economic growth. Rather than set goals that might be impossible or difficult to achieve, the post-Khrushchev leaders have adopted a more moderate and feasible program. This slowdown is clearly depicted by Table 2, which compares planning production for 1970 and 1980 by former Premier Khrushchev with the plans adopted by the more cautious Brezhnev regime.

Table 2. *Planned Industrial and Farm Production for 1970 and 1980 (in million metric tons unless otherwise specified)*

Products	Khrushchev's 1970 Plan	Brezhnev's 1970 Plan
Steel	145	124-129
Petroleum	390	345-355
Coal	686-700	665-675
Electricity (bil. kw hr)	900-1000	830-850
Textiles (bil. sq. meters)	13.6	9.5-9.8
Shoes (million pairs)	825	610-630
Grain	230	175-180
Milk	135	83-85
Cotton	8	5.6-6.0
Potatoes	140	100
Meat	25	11
Products	**Khrushchev's 1980 Plan**	**Brezhnev's 1980 Plan**
Steel	250	160-170
Electricity (bil kw hr)	2700-3000	1340-1380
Grain	260	215-220
Milk	185.1	94-96
Meat	34.8	15-15.6

Source: *Pravda,* 1961, 1966, 1975.

According to these statistics, Brezhnev set lower economic goals than Khrushchev for both 1970 and 1980. The agricultural production slowdown was generally greater than the industrial. Thus Brezhnev's planned output of grain, meat, and milk for 1980 is less than Khrushchev's plan for 1970. In general, Brezhnev's cautious economic planning and slow economic growth have provided only modest improvement in the inadequate Soviet standard of living.

Yet even the slow industrial growth should not be underestimated. By the late 1970's, Soviet industry was seven times larger than at the end of World War II. The USSR today outproduces the United States in such basic items as oil, steel, coal, cement, and machine tools. From these basic industries Russia has manufactured more than half of the world's submarines and tanks, and the majority of world medium missiles and medium bombers.

In ideology the Brezhnev regime has been harsh toward Russian writers who criticize the Soviet system. Many dissident intellectuals have been incarcerated in prisons, prison labor camps, or mental hospitals. Others have been permanently exiled abroad, such as the Nobel prize-winning author, Aleksandr I. Solzhenitsyn.

As early as 1966, the Brezhnev regime displayed its intolerance of dissent when a Soviet court sentenced Andrei D. Sinyavsky and Yuli M. Daniel to seven and five years' imprisonment, respectively, for publishing anti-Soviet books in the West. Sinyavsky wrote for Western audiences under the pseudonym of Abram Tertz, and Daniel used the pen name of Nikolai Arzhak. The two writers claimed that their foreign books attacked Stalin's Russia, not the post-Stalin USSR. They maintained that they did not necessarily share the anti-Soviet thoughts of their fictional characters. The Kremlin refused to moderate the prison sentences despite protests from other Soviet authors, Western intellectuals, and even Western Communist parties.

The Brezhnev regime has apparently been more tolerant toward religion than the Khrushchev government. Few of the clergy have been arrested or imprisoned. Religious congregations remain constant in size. The Orthodox, Moslem, and Baptist faiths operated thousands of houses of worship, had a few seminaries for training clergy, and even published church literature.

After a lapse of several years, Jews in the Soviet Union were permitted to bake matzo (unleavened bread) in state bakeries for the Passover holidays. However, articles attacking Israel and Judaism continued to appear in the Soviet press, only 62 synagogues remained open throughout the USSR (for 3,000,000 Jews), and the Jewish theological seminary in Moscow was not permitted to hold classes. Less than two per cent of USSR college students are permitted to be Jewish. Yet for the sake of detente with the West, Brezhnev has allowed over 100,000 Soviet Jews to emigrate abroad.

Brezhnev, who once served as chief political officer of the Soviet navy, has greatly expanded USSR maritime activity. By the late 1970's the Soviet merchant marine was nine times larger than under Stalin, and had become the fifth largest commercial fleet in the world, already competing with Western shipping in Atlantic and Pacific Ocean trade. Quietly the Brezhnev regime has also acquired one third of the world's passenger ships. One third of the world's fishing vessels now belong to the USSR, which accounts for one tenth of all the world's fish catch.

Despite great expansion of shipping and fishing, Brezhnev's USSR has been plagued by perpetual store shortages. The Soviet press still complains about the scarcity of simple goods like clothing, shoes, dishes, kitchen utensils, furniture, medicine, eye-glasses, paper and even bottles. Unlike heavy industry, light industry is still weak and undersized.

For the first time in Soviet history, the Five-Year Plan of 1971-1975 called for faster expansion of light, consumer-goods industry than heavy war-potential industry. During 1971 this actually occurred. Then as US-USSR detente in 1972 limited the mutual number of certain superweapons such as ICBM's, submarine missiles and nuclear submarines, the Soviet emphasis returned to heavy industry. By 1972, the USSR armed forces had also increased by 1,000,000 men over the 1970 level.

As Brezhnev's heavy industry expanded, Russia's armament greatly increased. When the Brezhnev regime began in 1964, the USSR possessed only 200 intercontinental rockets, 120 submarine-based missiles, and about a dozen nuclear-powered submarines. The "missile gap" was Soviet, not American. But by the late 1970's the USSR armed forces had eight times as many intercontinental rockets as in 1964, six times as many submarine missiles, and about ten times as many nuclear submarines. In all three of these superweapons, Russia now holds numerical superiority over the United States. Table 3 compares Soviet and

American strength in important types of armament, according to the best Western estimates:

Table 3. *Comparison of the Armament of the United States and the USSR*

Item	United States	USSR
Intercontinental rockets	1,054	1,590
Medium-range rockets	0	700
Intercontinental bombers	330	210
Aircraft carriers	13	2
Submarine-based missiles	656	700
Tanks	8,500	34,500
Nuclear warheads	7,600	3,500
Tactical atomic weapons	6,800	3,500

Source: U.S. Department of Defense, 1977.

Comparison of overall Soviet and American strength in armament is difficult, because each side is preparing for a somewhat different type of war. Russia needs many tanks for possible land offensives against West Europe or China. America plans for land defensive war, using tactical atomic weapons to stop Soviet tanks. On the sea, Russia is strong under water, but weak on the surface, because the Soviet navy intends to harass the enemy rather than control the seas. Russian medium rockets exist to threaten Europe and China. Though the USSR now has more intercontinental and submarine missiles, the USA has twice as many hydrogen-bomb warheads. Most Western experts consider that Soviet and American armed strength is roughly equal.

The Brezhnev regime has largely avoided brinkmanship in foreign relations, obviously desiring to avoid any risk of a major war. Besides wooing the underdeveloped nations of Asia and Africa, the Soviet Union sought closer ties with certain anti-Communist powers—France, Turkey, Japan, and others—who wished to assert more independence from American policy. The Soviet intent was to break up the anti-Communist military alliances to which these countries belonged.

The first Soviet success in Europe during the Brezhnev era was establishment of close relations with France. When French

President Charles de Gaulle visited the USSR during 1966, he was the first foreign statesman ever permitted to witness the launching of a Soviet space rocket. As a result of de Gaulle's visit, France and Russia agreed to install direct radio-telegraph communication (a hot-line) between the Kremlin and French governmental headquarters, to conduct periodic political discussions on a regular basis, to expand scientific and cultural exchange, and to cooperate on space research.

While visiting Italy during 1967, USSR President Podgorny had an audience with Pope Paul VI. This was the first conversation between a pope and a USSR chief-of-state in all of Soviet history. Thus the post-Khrushchev Soviet regime, though officially atheist, was willing to negotiate with a powerful Christian church.

An old Russian enemy, Turkey, was converted into a friend by large Soviet technical aid, and by support of Turkish claims in the Cyprus crisis. Similarly, Iran was soothed by Soviet construction of an Iranian steel mill, which in turn helped build a pipeline now sending Iranian natural gas into the USSR.

However, the greatest diplomatic achievement of the post-Khrushchev USSR was its encirclement of Communist China. This was accomplished by establishing or strengthening Soviet friendship with most of the nations possessing common frontiers with China. During 1966, Soviet Premier Kosygin arranged an armistice between India and Pakistan, thus preventing China from profiting from an Indian-Pakistani undeclared war. In the same year, the USSR and Mongolia concluded a new 20-year military alliance, obviously aimed against China. Meanwhile Japan and the USSR established the first foreign airline to fly over Siberia (Moscow-Tokyo), and concluded a commercial agreement providing for joint Japanese-Soviet economic development of East Siberia. By skillful Soviet maneuvering, North Korea swung over to the Soviet side. Immense Soviet aid to wartime North Vietnam, and to all Vietnam after the South surrendered, induced the Vietnamese Communists to be neutral in the Sino-Soviet split.

As might be expected from Russia's encirclement of China, Soviet-Chinese relations continued to deteriorate.

Chinese fear of the USSR greatly increased in 1968, when Soviet troops invaded Communist Czechoslovakia to suppress the political liberalization begun by the Czech government.

Early in 1968, Alexander Dubcek became top leader in Czechoslovakia, and under public pressure instituted a free press, free speech, freedom of organization, milder police, and impartial courts. After much hesitation and many warnings, the USSR invaded Czechoslovakia during the summer, with small accompanying invasions by Polish, East German, Hungarian, and Bulgarian troops. Czechoslovakia did not resist, its liberalization was stopped, Dubcek was slowly demoted into oblivion, and a Soviet military occupation force remained permanently in Czechoslovakia.

The reaction of several Communist countries was swift, fearful, and angry. Rumania created a home defense corps, and anounced that it would resist any Soviet invasion. Yugoslavia also said that it would defend itself, and partially mobilized its army. Albania increased its defense budget, and withdrew from the Warsaw Pact military alliance. China intensified civilian military training, and offered to defend Rumania against Soviet invasion. All four countries condemned Russia's newly announced "Brezhnev doctrine," which claimed that the USSR could intervene by arms in any Communist country where internal changes threatened socialism.

Then in 1969 Soviet and Chinese border troops battled over the ownership of Damanski Island in the Ussuri frontier river, and over a mountain on the Central Asian boundary. On Soviet initiative, Russo-Chinese negotiations began to define the precise border, and have lasted years without result.

The bitter Sino-Soviet dispute resulted in the loss of control of the world Communist movement by both the Soviet Union and Communist China. As the two giant Communist nations openly quarreled, small Communist countries found themselves wooed by both sides and were able to practice an unprecedented degree of independence. Communist parties in non-Communist countries found themselves in the same unusual situation, which resulted in each party having the freedom to set its own policies.

Most of the world's newly decentralized Communist parties supported the Soviet Union against Communist China. China's effort in recent years to unite Asian, African, and Latin American Communists under Peking leadership failed, probably because the

Maoist appeal for immediate violent revolution seemed impractical to the radicals of underdeveloped nations.

As in the Khrushchev era, the post-Khrushchev regime tried to establish friendship with the new African nations. A large Soviet program of cultural and educational exchange attempted to influence African governmental leaders, rebel leaders, army officers, trade unions, and youth organizations. In diplomacy the USSR supported the grouping of African nations into regional associations, opposed nationalistic African socialism, and condemned the white-dominated government of Rhodesia.

In the 1970's the USSR supplied arms to the local guerrillas fighting to free Portugal's African colonies. When the colonies were given independence, Russia armed the pro-Soviet Angolan government against pro-Western Angolan rebel groups.

By the late 1970's the Soviet Government openly boasted that it was financing and arming African guerrillas who were fighting to overthrow the white regimes in Rhodesia and South Africa. A small Soviet naval fleet had also started operating in the Indian Ocean, using port facilities in such friendly nations as Somalia, Iraq, and South Yemen.

In the Near East, the USSR displayed hostility toward Israel, refusing to trade even before the Arab-Israel war of 1967. When this conflict broke out, Russia severed diplomatic relations with Israel, offered military and economic aid to the Arab nations, and asked the UN to make Israel return captured territory to Egypt, Jordan, and Syria. However, no Soviet troops were sent to assist the Arab armies.

During the 1973 Arab-Israeli war, the USSR airlifted large quantities of armament to both Egypt and Syria. After the war ended in stalemate, Russia replaced the Arab war losses of military equipment.

Soviet-Egyptian relations, however, were already deteriorating before the 1973 Near Eastern war. In 1972 Egypt sent home most of the 20,000 Soviet military advisors who had been stationed on Egyptian territory. After the war, in 1976, Egypt unilaterally renounced the 1971 Soviet-Egyptian Treaty of Friendship, because the USSR had refused to reschedule the large Egyptian debt owed to Russia, and also to supply spare parts for Soviet armament already sent to Egypt.

Soviet-American relations in the post-Khrushchev era were marred by many incidents. American cultural exchange groups encountered difficulties while touring the USSR. Some American tourists were arrested in Russia, and given prison sentences or large fines for minor offenses. Both the United States and the USSR occasionally expelled each other's diplomats for alleged espionage or subversion. American correspondents were repeatedly expelled from Russia for being too friendly with Soviet dissident intellectuals. Militant American Jewish organizations frequently protested against USSR mistreatment of Soviet Jews by harassing Russian performers, and by bombing or strafing Soviet diplomatic and commercial offices in the USA.

Despite this tension, Soviet-American relations slowly improved by concluding a long series of treaties which attempted to reduce the danger of nuclear war. In 1967 the United States, Britain, and Russia concluded a treaty banning the use of outer space for military purposes, and forbidding weapons of mass destruction to be installed on the moon or other celestial bodies. During 1968 the same three nuclear powers signed an atomic non-proliferation pact, inviting all nations to become signatories. Any nonatomic nation, which signed, agreed never to purchase or produce nuclear weapons, in exchange for US-USSR protection from any nuclear attack.

Then in 1971 the USSR, Britain, and the USA adopted an agreement banning the emplacement of weapons of mass destruction on the seabed of seas and oceans. In the same year America and Russia agreed to outlaw biological weapons, and to destroy their stockpiles of germs and poisons intended for military use. Also in 1971 a USSR-US-Britain-France treaty provided for unimpeded traffic between West Germany and West Berlin, which would remain under American-British-French military occupation, and which would not be legally part of West Germany.

The 1972 visit of US President Nixon to Moscow resulted in three important arms-limitation treaties between Russia and America. The first created rules to prevent air and naval incidents on and over the open seas. The second limited each country to 200 antiballistic missiles (ABM's) apiece. A third agreement restricted each country to its current number of intercontinental rockets, submarine-based missiles, and nuclear-powered missile-firing submarines either in operation or being built. Secretary-General Brezhnev's visit to the United States in 1973 produced an additional pact, in which both countries pledged not to start nuclear war against each other. President Nixon's second journey to Moscow in 1974 resulted in agreements limiting the USA and USSR to 100 antiballistic missiles apiece, and restricting underground test-explosions of nuclear weapons to 150 kilotons in explosive power. Later in 1974 US President Ford during his visit to Siberia concluded a pact limiting the USA and USSR each to a total of 2,400 intercontinental rockets, submarine-based missiles, and intercontinental bombers, with 1,320 of the missiles permitted to have multiple hydrogen-bomb warheads (MIRV's). Further US-USSR pacts in 1976 restricted underground nuclear explosions for peaceful purposes to 150 kilotons, and created a code warning signal to inform each other about accidents which might be interpreted as the start of nuclear war. Meanwhile in 1975 Russia, almost all European nations, Canada, and the United States concluded the Helsinki agreement, which recognized as inviolable all frontiers of all signatory countries, who also promised to promote more economic cooperation, cultural exchange, and freedom of information among each other. All of these "peace pacts," together with greatly expanded scientific cooperation and a tenfold increase in Soviet-American trade, are officially described as US-USSR "detente."

Yet these pacts present many problems: Some are unverifiable, like the seabed, biological, and space disarmament agreements. The treaties limiting superweapons numerically do not prevent improvement of weapon quality. Not even numerical limits exist for small missiles capable of carrying hydrogen bombs. Still the Brezhnev regime, unlike Stalin and Khrushchev, has been willing to make a small start in arms limitation, thereby lessening the chances for outbreak of nuclear war.

Thus the Brezhnev regime has provided great industrial growth, vast armament expansion, farm failure, harsh suppression of dissidents, and very shrewd diplomacy.

Suggestions for Further Reading

BREZHNEV, LEONID, *On the Policy of the Soviet Union and the International Situation.* Garden City: Doubleday, 1973.

DALLIN, ALEXANDER, and LARSON, THOMAS, *Soviet Politics Since Khrushchev.* Englewood Cliffs: Prentice-Hall, 1968.

FELKER, JERE LEAKE, *Soviet Economic Controversies,* Cambridge: Massachusetts Institute of Technology, 1967.

GEHLEN, MICHAEL P., *The Politics of Coexistence: Soviet Methods and Motives,* Bloomington: Indiana University Press, 1967.

HAYWARD, MAX, ed., *On Trial,* New York: Harper, 1966.

HORELICK, ARNOLD L., and RUSH, MYRON, *Strategic Power and Soviet Foreign Policy,* Chicago: Chicago University Press, 1966.

HUTCHINGS, RAYMOND, *Soviet Economic Development.* New York: Harper and Row, 1971.

KATZ, ABRAHAM, *The Politics of Economic Reform in the Soviet Union.* New York: Praeger, 1972.

POLMAR, NORMAN, *Soviet Naval Power.* New York: Crane Russak, 1974.

REDDAWAY, PETER, ed., *Uncensored Russia: Protest and Dissent in the Soviet Union.* New York: American Heritage, 1972.

SHULMAN, MARSHALL D., *Beyond the Cold War,* New Haven: Yale University Press, 1966.

WESSON, ROBERT G., *The Soviet State: An Aging Revolution.* New York: Wiley, 1972.

ZARTMAN, I. WILLIAM, ed., *Czechoslovakia, Intervention and Impact.* New York: New York University Press, 1970.

Part II

Government

Since the USSR is a one-party state, our discussion of government begins with a description of the Communist Party in Chapter 11. Propaganda is one of the most important party functions, and is therefore analyzed in detail in Chapter 12. Chapter 13 describes the formal government, which parallels but is subordinate to the party structure. Minority races and nationalities are a Soviet problem discussed in Chapter 14. At times in Soviet history, the secret police have challenged the supremacy of the party, and their role is treated in Chapter 15. Extremely important to Soviet political control is the widespread use of organized recreation to channel the USSR population into activities helpful to the Soviet state, and this organizational theme is discussed in Chapter 16.

Chapter 11

The Communist Party

Not everyone can join the Communist Party of the Soviet Union. Belief in Marxism-Leninism, or even expert knowledge of this ideology, is not sufficient for admission. The party desires its new members to be proven administrators rather than ideologists, for Marxism-Leninism can be learned after a person joins the party.

An applicant must be at least 18 years old, and must obtain character references from three party members who have been Communists for five or more years, and who have been co-workers of the applicant for at least one year. Applicants between the ages of 18 and 23 must previously have been a member of the Komsomol (Communist youth organization). A recommendation of a district Komsomol committee can be substituted for the recommendation of one Communist Party member. In practice most Komsomol members are not permitted to apply for party membership until they are 28, the age when they can no longer remain in the Komsomol. All sponsors are held responsible for the accuracy of their recommendations. Thus a Communist Party member can be expelled from the party if he has recommended an applicant who later proves undesirable.

The application and references are submitted to a primary (lowest) party organization, whose decision must be approved by a city or district party headquarters. Party and police officials examine the applicant's school and employment records for any evidence of disloyalty to the Soviet regime. The applicant must answer a long and detailed biographical questionnaire. Discovery of the slightest political taint, such as a mother who attends church, may result in rejection.

If the applicant is cleared by this investigation, he is accepted as a party candidate. The candidacy period lasts one or more years during which the candidate pays party dues, attends meetings of his primary party organization, and learns the party program, statutes, and tactics by attending party nightschools. Meanwhile the candidate is required to pass a rigorous achievement test in his particular profession.

Thus a candidate who is a young engineer is often transferred into a factory workshop lagging behind its production plan. He takes charge of this workshop, which he must bring up to plan during his candidacy period. A schoolteacher will probably be assigned to a school plagued by poor scholarship. An agronomist might be appointed chairman of a backward collective farm. City or district party officials arrange these transfers, which state enterprises, cooperatives, or collective farms must accept. But whatever difficult task the candidate is assigned, he must produce good results.

The party also consumes much of the candidate's spare time outside of working hours. He spends many evenings at party meetings and party schools. He must assist current party campaigns, which may range from collection of scrap metal to arousing mass anger against a hostile state. Possibly he may be required to become a verbal propagandist lecturing to housewives, workers, or peasants. Senior party members audit these lectures, which must be made interesting and convincing. The successful candidate undergoes a second loyalty check, and finally becomes a party member.

Because of the difficult candidacy tests, many Soviet citizens make no attempt to join the party. On a trip through Russia, I asked many college students if they intended to join the Communist Party. Most replied that they were not interested in becoming Communists. A few said they would try, then usually complained: "Perhaps the party will not accept me."

Since the Bolshevik Revolution of 1917, there have been only three brief periods in Soviet history when the party was relatively easy to join. The first was during the Russian Civil War of 1918–1920. The second was the Lenin Enrollment after Lenin's death in 1924, and was Stalin's method of adding 200,000 of his supporters to the party so he could more easily compete against other Politburo members to become the new top leader. During World War II several million soldiers were taken quickly into the party, partly as a reward for heroism but mainly to put them under party discipline before the war ended. Stalin correctly foresaw that these heroes might demand Soviet political and economic liberalization after the war. In a speech at the 1952 USSR party congress, Khrushchev admitted that these war heroes had been a troublesome element within the party during the first postwar years.

After each period of fast party recruitment, there usually is a party purge to weed out undesirables who joined the party without sufficient investigation. Lenin purged the party after the Civil War. Stalin conducted a purge immediately following the Lenin Enrollment, and then a much more drastic purge in the 1930's. After World War II there was no mass expulsion from the party, but recruiting slowed for several years while the war heroes were brought under full party control.

During all of Soviet history a tiny minority of select people have been urged to join the party without undergoing aptitude tests. These are people who are already famous and who would add luster to the party. Opera singers, premier ballerinas, movie stars, and top scientists encounter few difficulties during party candidacy. For example, the first Soviet astronauts, Gagarin and Titov, were taken into the party soon after their spaceships circled the world.

Ever since the Bolshevik Revolution of 1917, each Soviet leader has endeavored to keep the party small. Lenin, Stalin, Khrushchev, and Brezhnev all preferred a small, capable, loyal party to a large amorphous group. Nevertheless, the party has consistently tended to grow. The sole political party legalized by the USSR Constitution is the Communist Party of the Soviet Union. Articles 6 and 99 of this constitution grant this party the right to nominate candidates in all governmental elections, to lead all state organizations, and also to lead all public organizations (like the trade unions and Komsomol) which share the power of nominating governmental officials for election. Even in the West a powerful political party attracts supporters who desire to join the winning team. This attraction is much more alluring when the political party is supreme in a one-party state.

The growth of Communist party membership in Soviet Russia and the USSR is outlined in Table 4:

Table 4. *Number of Communist Party Members and Candidates*

Year	Number
1917 (March)	40,000
1917 (November)	240,000
1918	270,000
1920	612,000
1921	732,000
1922	532,000
1923	386,000
1924	736,000
1925	643,000
1927	887,000
1930	1,261,000
1934	1,874,000
1939	2,477,000
1940	3,400,000
1941	3,876,000
1944	5,000,000
1946	6,000,000
1950	6,000,000
1952	6,882,145
1956	7,215,505
1958	8,239,131
1960	8,708,000
1961	9,716,000
1962	10,866,000
1966	12,471,079
1971	14,455,321
1977	15,900,000

Source: Stalin, Joseph, *History of the Communist Party of the Soviet Union,* (English translation), Moscow: Foreign Languages Publishing House, 1939.
Pravda, Moscow: 1938-1976.

A party member has many duties. He must accept the party program, obey party orders, and work in a party organization.

Moreover he is ordered to study Marxism-Leninism constantly, put party policies and decisions into practice, obey labor laws, continually improve his technical training, and explain party policy and decisions to the masses. He must fulfill decrees of the Communist Party "quickly and exactly." As punishment for nonfulfillment the party may warn him privately or publicly, remove him from responsible party or government work, or expel him from party membership. The highest party punishment for an individual is expulsion from party membership with the offender's crime reported to the state police or government courts.

A former party member has reported the following reasons why various people were expelled from his college party organization during a routine party purge: being married in a church wedding, refusing to divorce a spouse arrested on political charges, former association with Ukrainian nationalists, former association with a disloyal party group, criticizing harsh governmental measures against the peasantry, and being the son of a private artisan.

The USSR Communist Party claims to be a party of the proletariat. At the time of the Bolshevik Revolution in 1917 the majority of party members were industrial workers, although the party leaders were intellectuals like lawyer Lenin, journalist Trotsky, and former divinity student Stalin. During the 1920's and early 1930's the majority of new party members were workers and peasants, with the former considerably outnumbering the latter. However, in the late 1930's the recruiting policy changed, and the majority of new members came from the "intelligentsia" —a Soviet term embracing white-collar workers, true intellectuals, and the entire middle and upper class. This change became permanent, despite periodic campaigns to reproletarianize the party membership. Table 5 illustrates this change.

From the Russian Civil War to the present, the majority of party members regardless of origin soon became administrators in all levels of government, public organizations, and the party itself. As early as 1919, 61 per cent of all party members held administrative positions. By 1922 this percentage had risen to 66 per cent, and today it is estimated at 68 per cent or more. Origin must not be confused with occupation. For example, Khrushchev was born in a peasant family, and as a youth was an industrial

Table 5. *Origin of Communist Party Members by Class*

Year	Workers	Peasants	Intelligentsia
		in per cent of annual totals	
1917	60	8	32
1921	41	28	31
1929	61	22	17
1932	65	27	8
1956	32	17	51
1960	34	18	48
1966	38	16	46
1976	42	14	44

Source: Fainsod, Merle, *How Russia is Ruled,* Cambridge: Harvard University Press, 1963.

Schapiro, Leonard, *The Communist Party of the Soviet Union,* New York: Random House, 1960

Pravda, Moscow: 1961-1976.

worker. By origin he was therefore classified as a peasant or worker. But soon after joining the party he became an army officer (during the Russian civil war), then a party official, and finally Premier of the USSR. By 1960 one fourth of all full party members were officials in the Communist Party alone, not counting those who were army officers, economic managers (from foremen to ministers), government bureaucrats, and national, regional, and local leaders of mass organizations. Hence the party is basically an administrative elite controlling positions of power throughout the USSR.

Because of this administrative power, the USSR Communist Party has been described by Djilas (a former Yugoslav Communist leader) as a "new class." However, this class is not unified. In private conversations Soviet diplomats divide the party into three competing groups: the military, the economists, and the party politicians. An example of the first group was Marshal Zhukov, the greatest Soviet general of World War II, whose entire life was spent in military affairs. An extremely successful economist is Aleksei Kosygin, a textile engineer who rose through many high economic positions before becoming Premier of the USSR. Lenin, Stalin, and Khrushchev all came to power as party politicians. Thus far the politicians have dominated the Communist Party, but economists have been influential since the Five-Year Plans began in 1928. The political power of the military was weak until after Stalin's death, when the army helped Khrushchev to become top leader. Later the military marshals cooperated with the party Presidium in forcing Khrushchev into retirement. Khrushchev was succeeded by two top leaders: Kosygin the economist, and Brezhnev the politician. Hence all three party groups are important, and will continue to be so in the Soviet future.

Aside from occupational groupings, the party is and always has been predominantly male, urban, and Russian. Thus in 1976, the party membership was approximately 77 percent male, 86 per cent urban, and 61 per cent Russian.

Soviet refugees divide party members into three groups by character: believers, draftees, and opportunists. The believers are fervent Marxists, and in refugee opinion, comprise no more than 10 per cent of party membership. Draftees are the party majority, joining mainly to seek better jobs for themselves and better living conditions for their families. Opportunists are described as seeking only wealth and power, rising in rank by purging party and nonparty competitors.

Regardless of whether a party member be a politician, economist, military man, believer, draftee, or opportunist, his personal future depends largely on the stability of the Soviet regime. Therefore he works hard to contribute to Soviet success. If he desires changes in the USSR governmental or economic system, he is usually reformist rather than revolutionary.

The lowest party groups are the primary organizations, which can be formed at any place of work where three or more party members are employed. Primary organizations exist in the majority of large factories and mines, most state and collective farms, the majority of military units, and in many offices, schools, colleges, cultural institutions, construction sites, railway junctions, airports, and ships. Any large place of work usually has the three party members required for formation of a primary organization, even though these party members may comprise only the administrative staff.

Today there are some 390,000 primary party organizations in the USSR, of which about 39 per cent are in economic enterprises. The remainder are in offices, cultural institutions, and military units.

A primary party organization ranges in size from the minimum three members to a society of several thousand people. In a large place of work there may be two levels of primary organizations. Thus a university may have primary organizations in each of its colleges, all united under a second primary organization for the university as a whole. However, most primary organizations are small, averaging around 40 members apiece. A tiny primary organization has only one official, a part-time secretary. Larger organizations have a full-time secretary, assisted by a bureau or committee. Legally these officials are elected by a meeting of the primary organization's membership. But the party statutes state that these primary officers must be confirmed in office by the district or city party organization. Hence in practice, the primary officials are appointed from above.

The party statutes also grant to primary organizations the power of control in economic enterprises of all types (including state and collective farms), all cultural, scientific and other non-economic enterprises, and all government offices including cabinet ministries. Usually this control is exerted by the primary party secretary, or so-called "partsec." In a state factory, the partsec watches the governmental director to see that he does no wrong. But if the director makes mistakes, the secretary can veto a managerial order. In extreme cases the partsec takes over management until the factory again runs smoothly.

If the factory still performs poorly, a party organizer ("partorg") may be sent from Moscow to replace the partsec. Like the secretary, the organizer has the power to veto or replace the factory manager. Originally these organizers were thus named because they organized new primary organizations in new places of work. Today they are professional trouble-shooters dispatched from Moscow to solve problems which ordinary partsecs have failed to overcome. Whenever such organizers appear in an industry, this is an indication that the industry is either performing poorly or under intense pressure. Almost the entire aircraft industry of the USSR was operated by party organizers during the Nazi-Soviet War of 1941–1945.

In the same war, large armament plants other than aircraft

were usually managed by party secretaries rather than government directors. The directors were still there, but became assistants to the partsecs. At the war's end the party secretaries clung to their managerial power, which was relinquished only when Moscow ordered them to return to watchdog status.

Party organizers appear to operate mainly in industry, while regular primary party secretaries normally watch and exert veto power over schools, colleges, theaters, museums, publishing houses, hospitals, government offices, and other non-economic enterprises. For example, during a visit to a college student camp it was obvious to me that the partsec was the real boss of the resort. The camp director was busy all day long arranging meals, organizing group activities, and the like. Meanwhile the partsec strolled around, observing. But the moment any slight social or political disorder emerged, the party secretary took command, while the director sat silent.

This system of local party watch over governmental, economic, and cultural officials began during the Russian Civil War of 1918–1920, when the Communist Party contained few experienced administrators in any line of work. To obtain efficiency, former Tsarist officials, experts, engineers, and even aristocrats had to be employed as managers or directors in Soviet enterprises. But these bourgeoisie were not trusted, so a party secretary or organizer had to be present. Today, from the Western viewpoint, this party watchdog system would seem to be outmoded. By now most of the old Tsarist managers are dead or retired. In their place is a new managerial class, educated under Soviet rule and usually members of the Communist Party. Today in a Soviet factory, a Communist partsec is supervising another Communist, the plant director. Yet the Kremlin refuses to abandon this party control, despite the obvious disadvantages of dual management. Apparently the party leaders are willing to sacrifice efficiency to maintain control over all aspects of Soviet life.

One group that has already aided, and can possibly restrain, the party dictatorship are the top officers of the USSR armed forces. Each Soviet political leader has feared the army officers, and has used the same system of party control to limit military power. As early as 1918, Lenin created the "political commissars" to watch the Red Army. A commissar was a party official attached to each important commanding officer. The commissar watched the officer, and had the power to countermand his orders if the officer seemed treasonable. By 1919 the commissars were made responsible to a newly formed organization entitled the "Army Political Administration." At first this office was controlled by the Revolutionary War Council, a mixed party-governmental group supervising the Red Army. After a few years the Army Political Administration became a section of Communist Party headquarters, and has remained there ever since. Today it is called the Main Political Administration of the Soviet Army and Navy.

Commissars were needed during the Russian Civil War of 1918–1920, when the Red Army had few Communist officers and was forced to employ many officers of dubious loyalty from the former Tsarist army. Among these non-Communist officers were three fifths of the former Tsarist general staff. Both Soviet publications and Russian émigré literature have long tried to conceal a military fact: The Russian Civil War was won by a Red Army largely led by Tsarist officers.

The commissar's power of veto resulted in a system of dual command which was inefficient and even dangerous. Regular army officers resented the veto and asked to have it abolished. In 1925 the commissars were deprived of the veto, but remained in the armed forces as party watchdogs and political officers. After an alleged attempt of several army marshals to assassinate Stalin in 1937, the veto power was restored. It was again removed in 1940 after the Red Army had performed badly during the Soviet-Finnish winter war. Hitler's great victories early in the Nazi-Soviet war resulted in restoration of the veto in 1941. The veto was permanently abolished in 1942, shortly before the Battle of Stalingrad. This last abolition was motivated by two main reasons: to avoid dual command, and to replace the huge losses among combat officers by converting many commissars into troop commanders. A commissar who became a commander was replaced by a party official entitled "Zampolit" (assistant for political work). This new designation for political officers is still used.

Today most officers of the Soviet armed forces are either Communist party members or belong to the Komsomol. Even most of the enlisted men are in the Komsomol. Thus, as in civilian life, the Zampolit is a Communist watching Communists. The original purpose of the commissar system is long outmoded, but the Zampolits remain to safeguard against army revolt. Zampolits are attached to every unit of the armed forces down to the company level, and are responsible to the Main Political Administration which appoints them. Before assuming office, they are trained in the Lenin Military-Political Academy, which teaches both political skills and some combat knowledge. Even without the veto, the Zampolit still possesses great power.

Take the example of a company Zampolit. He is second in command in his company, and takes charge if the commander is killed, captured, or wounded. He is a member of the commander's staff, and attends all staff meetings. One of the Zampolit's assistants heads the Communist Party organization in the company. Another heads the company's Komsomol organization. Both of these assistants are appointed by and responsible to the Zampolit. The Zampolit and his assistants give approximately two hours of political instruction a day to the soldiers. By lectures and supervised reading, the Zampolit personally indoctrinates the company officers in political matters. Assistants of the Zampolit manage the company recreation hall, library, movie projector, and nonmilitary adult-education school. Thus the Zampolit might be described as the chief propagandist and educator of his military unit.

Examples of films used by Zampolits in their political work fell into US Army hands during the Korean War of 1950–1953, when Soviet military movies were captured from the North Korean forces. One lengthy movie consisted entirely of old US newsreels portraying breadlines, beggars, slums, and race riots in American cities. Such films try to arouse anti-American sentiment among Soviet military personnel.

The Zampolit and his assistants serve as party spies on the officers and enlisted men of the military unit. Periodically the Zampolit sends confidential reports about the company to the Main Political Administration. When the company commander is due for promotion, he usually is not promoted if the Zampolit's reports about him have been unfavorable.

The party organs of the USSR are outlined in Table 6:

Table 6. *The Communist Party Hierarchy*

Area	Legislature	Rump Legislature	Bureau	Secretariat	Courts
USSR	Congress	Central Committee	Politburo	Central Committee Secretariat	Control Committee
Republic	Congress	Committee	Bureau	Secretariat	Commission
Region	Conference	Committee	Bureau	Secretariat	Commission
District	Conference	Committee	Bureau	Secretaries	—
City	Conference	Committee	Bureau	Secretaries	—
City ward	Conference	Committee	Bureau	Secretaries	—
Place of work	Meeting	(Committee)	(Bureau)	Secretary	—

Source: Speeches at the 25th Congress of the USSR Communist Party, *Pravda*, February and March, 1976.

As can be seen from Table 6, the party is on a territorial basis, with a USSR organization and then one for each Soviet republic. Within a republic, each region has its party organization. A region is divided into districts, which are roughly the size of American counties. Subordinate to district party organizations are the party organs of small cities. However, a large city is considered equivalent to a district in importance, and therefore is directly under regional party control. Besides its own party organization, a large city may have party organizations in each of its wards. There are no village party organizations. Primary party organizations in the countryside are under direct district control.

Each party organ above the primary party organization has about the same appearance: a legislature, rump legislature (committee), bureau, and secretariat (or secretaries). Alongside is the party court system: the USSR Party Control Committee, with its republic and regional control commissions. Below the USSR level the bureau actually is an office assisting the secretaries, who function as the party executives.

Every 2-3 years the primary organizations elect delegates to the party conferences of city wards, small cities, and districts. City ward conferences elect the delegates to the conference of their large city. Small city conferences elect their representatives to their district conference, whose rural delegates come directly from primary organizations.

Normally the city ward, city, or district conference meets only once every two or three years, quickly delegating its authority to a committee it elects. The committee then elects the party bureau and secretaries. The secretaries must be approved by the regional or republic party committee, and thus actually are appointed from above.

The party conferences of districts and large cities choose the delegates to the regional conferences, which meet every 2-3 years. A regional conference elects its committee, which chooses the regional party bureau and secretaries. Regional secretaries must be approved by the party committee of their republic. Republic congresses meet every five years, are elected by regional conferences, and similarly choose committees which select the republic bureaus and secretaries. The USSR Central Committee must approve republic secretaries.

The USSR party congress, the highest party legislature, meets ordinarily once every five years. Its delegates are elected by the republic congresses. The USSR congress elects the party Central Committee, which in turn chooses the USSR secretaries, the Politburo, and the Party Control Committee.

In theory USSR or republic party conferences can be convened between meetings of the USSR or republic party congresses. Such conferences do not possess the elective powers of the congresses. In practice such conferences are rare, the last USSR conference having been in 1941.

The party committee at each level of the hierarchy determines the representation to its congress or conference. Thus a city committee establishes how many delegates can come from each city ward or primary organization to a city conference. And the Central Committee decides the representation of republics in the USSR congress. Actually in recent decades the representation in party legislatures has been based on party (not total) population of a given area. A city with many party members will therefore have more delegates in a regional party conference than a large rural district with few party members.

To summarize, each party legislature elects the legislative body above, ensuring a chain of indirect elections easier to control than direct elections. At each level, the party legislature meets infrequently, and then only for a short time. The legislature delegates its authority to a committee it elects. But these committees also are not in constant session. The party committees of districts, cities, and city wards meet once every three months, and of regions and republics, every four months. The USSR Central Committee convenes regularly just twice a year. In the interim between meetings the committees delegate their authority to the bureaus and secretaries. The committees between conferences or congresses can remove and replace committee members, bureau personnel, and secretaries.

The intent of all this elaborate procedure is to ensure party discipline. The party legislatures consist largely of high, medium, and low party officials. Yet each party legislature is required to delegate its authority first to its committee, which in turn surrenders power to a small bureau and a few secretaries. For example, the USSR party congress of nearly 5,000 members yields its authority to a Central Committee of over 420 persons, who transfer power to some 10 secretaries and 20 Politburo members. From top to bottom the USSR Communist Party is actually managed by a few thousand men—the bureau members and secretaries.

The weakness of party legislatures was displayed in the Stalin era, when no USSR party congress met for 13 years (1939–1952). After Stalin's death, party congresses began to meet regularly, and Khrushchev criticized Stalin for ignoring party legislatures so long. Then in 1957 after the 1956 Hungarian Revolution, many USSR party members demanded true election of party secretaries rather than appointment from above. This attempt at party democracy was publicly quelled by Khrushchev, with admonitions that Lenin himself had preferred appointment to election. The speeches of Brezhnev, Khrushchev's successor, have stressed party discipline rather than party democracy.

Of the bodies elected by the Central Committee, the Control Committee enforces party discipline. It appoints "control commissions" in every Soviet republic and region. The committee and its commissions try party members for violating party rules and edicts, government laws, and "party morality." Those found guilty are given the party punishments already described. Anyone expelled from the party can also appeal to the control apparatus for reinstatement.

"Party morality" means good behavior. The control committee and commissions often apprehend and try party members for social offenses like drunkenness, immorality, nepotism, or abuse of power.

More important, however, is the Secretariat of the party's Central Committee. Originally formed during 1918 as a party archive and mail center, the Secretariat quickly grew into a huge organization with many thousands of employees. Being the communications center of the party, the Secretariat receives all reports, suggestions, and complaints from local party organizations, and decides which data is sufficiently important to be forwarded to party leaders. Conversely, the orders of the party leaders are transmitted through the Secretariat to local party organizations. A very great power, dating from the Russian Civil War of 1918–1920, is patronage—the Secretariat's right to appoint minor party officials.

From 1922 until his death in 1953, Stalin was party secretary-general, and thus chief of the USSR party secretariat. After his death Khrushchev became first secretary, a title different in name but with the same party power. After Khrushchev was forced into retirement, Brezhnev became first secretary and in 1966 resumed the old title of secretary-general.

The Secretariat may be roughly described as the chief executive of the party. Like government ministries, its departments are frequently merged, split, or reorganized. Often these changes are not announced, so the precise table of organization is difficult to ascertain. At present the Secretariat appears to have the following departments: heavy industry, light and food industries, construction, transport and communications, agriculture, trade and public services, planning and finance, cooperatives, party organizational work, trade union and Komsomol, military (Main Political Administration of the Soviet Army and Navy), administrative organs (controlling the governmental police and courts), science and education, culture, propaganda and agitation, foreign cadres, international affairs, affairs of the parties of the socialist bloc (relations with the Soviet orbit), and affairs of the Communist parties of nonsocialist countries (the successor to the former Communist International).

Each department of the Secretariat serves as a watchdog over its field of competence. Thus the heavy industry section watches the performance of government industrialists through the eyes and ears of the primary party secretaries in factories and mines. The agricultural section observes collective and state farm managers through primary party secretaries on the farms.

But the Secretariat is much more than a party watchdog over the government. Each department of the Secretariat keeps dossiers on all outstanding personnel, party and nonparty, in its field of competence. At times the Secretariat has even had a "Cadres Department," where this personnel work was centralized. However, at present this activity is spread throughout the Secretariat.

If a person displays ability in his work and has a reliable political record, the Secretariat arranges for his promotion. If he is poorly educated and needs more schooling to handle a higher job, the Secretariat makes arrangements for his free education with pay in either the governmental or party school system. Many a Soviet man started his career as a factory worker with perhaps no more than a grade-school education. He displayed great ability, was promoted, then sent to school maintaining his full pay, and through successive promotions and additional schooling finally is appointed to the party Secretariat or government Council of Ministers. An outstanding example was Khrushchev, who started his career in the early 1920's as a machinist in a Ukrainian coal mine. After rising from a local party propagandist to assistant chief of party propaganda in the Ukraine, he was given additional education at a party college for industrial management. From college he became a Moscow party leader, then party leader of the Ukraine, and finally (1957–1964) top leader of the USSR.

This personnel system is one of the greatest explanations for Soviet success in industrialization, armament, and science. The personnel records of the Secretariat are more thorough and complete than those in any large business company of the capitalist world. Soviet talent is constantly uncovered, trained, promoted,

Commuter crowd in railway station.

Group of Central Asians visiting Moscow, and apparently impressed.

Monument to achievement of hydroelectric power station (Volgograd).

Monument which reads "Glory to the Builders of Communism" (Volgograd).

Building left most intact after Battle of Stalingrad during World War II (Volgograd).

Wall dividing East and West Berlin (Germany).

Statue of St. Vladimir overlooking Dnieper River (Kiev).

Portrait of Lenin done in floral arrangement on the embankment beside the street (Kiev).

Peasant house (outside Kiev).

The Winter Palace in Leningrad, scene of the overthrow of the Provisional Government by the Bolsheviks in 1917.

and concentrated on tasks to which the party leadership gives priority. Conversely the personnel power of the Secretariat prevents persons of dubious political loyalty from attaining high governmental positions.

The departments of the Secretariat also draft much governmental legislation. For example, in 1958 the Secretariat issued proposals that the Soviet educational system be reorganized, and in 1959 the USSR government passed a law adopting these party proposals. The majority of important government decrees are issued jointly with the party, being entitled "from the USSR Council of Ministers and Central Committee" or "from the Supreme Soviet Presidium and Central Committee." Actually these are decrees not of the Central Committee but of the party Secretariat. Sometimes the Secretariat issues a decree which never becomes government law, yet is binding on the entire country. This occurred during the winter of 1959–1960 when a series of party decrees ordered governmental industry to conserve electric power, iron, steel, and strategic nonferrous metals.

It is easy to understand how control of the USSR party Secretariat has been the road to power for Soviet leaders Stalin, Khrushchev, and Brezhnev. But despite its tremendous authority the Secretariat is basically an executive fulfilling orders from the highest party body: the Politburo, which during 1952–1966 was called the Central Committee Presidium.

In 1917 shortly before the Bolshevik Revolution the first Politburo was formed by Lenin to draft proposals for consideration by the Central Committee and party Congress. After the revolution the first Politburo was disbanded on the grounds that it was no longer needed. But it was re-established in 1919, and has existed ever since. By the late 1920's the Politburo had become the true party legislature, whose decisions were simply adopted by the Central Committee and party Congress. The Congress became a mere forum for Politburo speeches, while the Central Committee turned into an assembly of high public and party officials meeting occasionally to be briefed by Politburo members. After Stalin's death the Central Committee regained some power, because it had to resolve disputes among Politburo members for party leadership. The Central Committee in 1957 placed Khrushchev in power, and in 1964 removed him. In the periods between leadership disputes, however, the Central Committee appears to have little authority.

Except for short periods of collective leadership, the USSR has mostly lived under one-man rule. But the top leader needs a board of advisors, and the Politburo fills this need. In American terms it might be defined as a "brain trust." All major decisions of foreign and internal policy are made in the Politburo, though the details may be worked out by the party Secretariat or by governmental organizations like the Supreme Soviet Presidium, Council of Ministers, and individual ministries.

Politburo decisions are secret and unannounced. If the average Soviet citizen learns about them, he knows only from actions taken by the government or hints in the Soviet press. For example, the 1953 Politburo decision to purge police minister Beria was not publicly known until after Beria's arrest.

Lenin's original Politburo had only seven members, all of whom were revolutionary leaders. Under Stalin the Politburo usually consisted of about a dozen men, mostly former regional leaders but including some economic administrators. Since Stalin's death, the Politburo has enlarged to about twenty members and candidate members, with much the same occupational composition as in the Stalin era. Politburo membership rises and falls slightly each year in conformity with annual promotions, deaths, and expulsions. At times, police chiefs like the present Yuri Andropov have been members. Under Stalin, the army was represented by political officers; but two real combat commanders, Zhukov and Grechko, served on the Politburo in the post-Stalin period. Today Dmitri Ustinov, a war industry administrator, is both Minister of Defense and a Politburo member. While on the Politburo, Trotsky and Molotov served as Foreign Ministers, but the first professional diplomat to achieve Politburo status was Andrei Gromyko in the 1970's.

Since the early years of Soviet power, one member of the Politburo has always headed the Supreme Soviet Presidium of the Soviet government. Similarly the premier, some vice-premiers, and a few ministers of the Council of Ministers are chosen from the Politburo. The secretary-general and several assistant secretaries of the party Secretariat also are Politburo members. Other members of the Politburo are regional party or governmental leaders, or heads of mass organizations like the trade unions. By dual jobholding at the pinnacles of power, the Politburo ensures its control over the entire nation. Among present Politburo members, Brezhnev is party Secretary-General, Kosygin is Premier, and Brezhnev, as chairman of the Supreme Soviet Presidium, is president of the USSR.

Without the Communist Party, the Soviet regime could not exist in its present form. Each USSR leader has insisted on a one-party state. Thus Brezhnev said at the twenty-third Congress of the Communist Party:

> The Soviet people view the party as their leader, director and organizer of all victories. . . . The policy of the party—both foreign and internal—is the only correct policy, and the road along which the party leads the Soviet people is the only true Leninist road.

Suggestions for Further Reading

Barghoorn, Frederick C., *Politics in the USSR.* Boston: Little, Brown, 1972.

Conyngham, William J., *Industrial Management in the Soviet Union: The Role of the C.P.S.U. in Industrial Decision-Making, 1917-1970.* Stanford: Hoover Institution Press, 1973.

Fainsod, Merle, *How Russia is Ruled.* Cambridge: Harvard University Press, 1963.

Hough, Jerry F., *The Soviet Prefects.* Cambridge: Harvard University Press, 1969.

Kolkowicz, Roman, *The Soviet Military and the Communist Party.* Princeton: Princeton University Press, 1967.

Meissner, Boris, *The Communist Party of the USSR,* New York: Praeger, 1956.

Reshetar, John S., *A Concise History of the Communist Party of the Soviet Union,* New York: Praeger, 1960.

Schapiro, Leonard, *The Communist Party of the Soviet Union.* New York: Random House, 1970.

Chapter 12

The Power of Propaganda

In a Soviet lecture-hall sat a man who wished he wasn't there. The year was 1943, the occasion a war-bond drive, and the man, a petty black-marketeer anxious to keep his ill-gotten gains. The bond saleslady could easily have made the meeting a formality, since the audience either had to pledge money or publicly be labeled unpatriotic. But the lecturer spurned the use of compulsion. Instead her speech was a fervent patriotic appeal that entranced the listeners. At its conclusion the black-marketeer burst into tears and emotionally subscribed 2,000 rubles, a sum beyond even his illegal means. For weeks thereafter he mourned this rash moment of generosity.

This incident, which I witnessed, illustrates an important phase of Soviet political life. In the West a popular misconception is that the USSR is ruled by force alone. Of course compulsion is ever present in the Soviet Union, in the form of police, army, and courts. But the Politburo controls Russia with a combination of force and propaganda. The 1917 Bolshevik Revolution was largely achieved by propaganda, Lenin then having little force at his disposal. In the three years thereafter, almost all of former Tsarist Russia was conquered by Communist armed forces possessing less military equipment than the small Rumanian army.

Current examples of propaganda effort appear in the elections every four years to the chief governmental legislature, the USSR Supreme Soviet. For each elective office the ballots list only one candidate, the person approved by the Communist Party. Although voting results are never in doubt, from three to six million verbal propagandists lecture during the election campaign in villages, factories, offices, schools, and apartment houses throughout the USSR, urging the public to vote for the one and only choice.

Stalin, who relied heavily on police authority, nevertheless stated:

> There is hardly need to dwell on the cardinal importance of propaganda. If our propaganda should go lame, our entire state would inevitably languish.
>
> The Communist Party must convince the masses that its policy is correct. Before commencing decisive political actions, the party must ensure itself the support of the majority of the masses, or at least their benevolent neutrality.
>
> In its foreign policy the Soviet Union relies on the moral support of the working people of all countries. A task of the Communist Party in foreign policy is to strengthen international bonds of friendship with the working people of all countries.[1]

These statements by Stalin concisely summarize the main aims of Soviet propaganda. These aims were formulated originally by Lenin, and have remained essentially unchanged ever since.

Freedom of speech is guaranteed to Russian citizens by Article 50 of the USSR Constitution. However the Soviet criminal law code warns:

> Agitation or propaganda, conducted for the purpose of subverting or weakening Soviet power, or the commission of individual especially dangerous state crimes, the dissemination for the same purpose of slanderous falsehoods injurious to the Soviet governmental and social structure, as well as distribution or preparation or preservation for this purpose of literature of such content:
>
> is punished by deprivation of freedom for a period from six months to seven years and with exile for a period from two to five years, or without exile, or by exile for a period from two to five years.

---

[1] Stalin, Joseph V., *Problems of Leninism* (English translation), Moscow, 1945.

Report to the 18th Congress of the Communist Party of the Soviet Union, March 10, 1939 (English translation), Moscow, 1939.

> The same acts, committed by a person previously sentenced for especially dangerous state crimes, as well as such acts committed in time of war:
>
> are punished by deprivation of freedom for a period from three to ten years and with exile for a period from two to five years, or without exile.[2]

Appeals to overthrow the government are considered treasonable in all countries. But the Soviet definition, in which propaganda weakening the government is a crime, can encompass the slightest criticism of the Communist system. The sentence of "deprivation of freedom" usually means confinement to a prison or corrective labor camp, while "exile" is banishment from one's home to remote regions of the USSR.

Soviet official propaganda originates not in the government but in the Communist Party. There has never been a governmental Ministry of Propaganda. Within the Secretariat of the USSR Communist Party is the Propaganda and Agitation Department, which a former chief has described as "a powerful apparatus centralizing all work of written and verbal propaganda." This propaganda center was first formed as early as 1920 under the name of Agitation and Propaganda Department. In 1930 it was divided into the Department for Agitation and Mass Campaigns, and the Department for Culture and Propaganda. By 1934 the two divisions were reunited into a Department of Culture and Propaganda of Leninism. This in 1939 became the Directorate of Propaganda and Agitation, and then in 1948 the Department of Propaganda and Agitation. Regardless of name changes, Soviet officials usually refer to this propaganda center as "Agitprop," the official abbreviation for its first title.

According to the statutes of the USSR Communist Party, Agitprop controls the party press, publication of propagandist and agitational literature, organization of printed and verbal propaganda of Marxism-Leninism, the ideological content of propagandist work, selection and distribution of propagandists, political training and retraining of party members, and organization of

---

[2] *Criminal Code of the RSFSR,* Moscow: Juridical Literature Press, 1966, Article 70, p. 32.

mass political agitation. In addition, Agitprop supervises propaganda work of the schools, literature, the arts, and even science.

To cope with these many duties, Agitprop has a huge central office with several thousand employees. This office has various departments which are periodically reshuffled in interoffice reorganizations. A recent breakdown listed the following departments: party propaganda, press, rural newspapers, rural propaganda, current events, lectures, lecturer group, agitation, movies, drama, art, literature, radio and television, school, and science. A college (for propagandists) and a research institute are attached to Agitprop.

Although Agitprop is a party organization, it exerts unquestioned authority over the entire apparatus of the Soviet government. Agitprop often publicly criticizes the propaganda mistakes of governmental organs, up to and including USSR cabinet ministries. Recent targets of such criticism include the newspaper of an economic ministry, the head of a chain of publishing houses, a professor of literature, several historians, a university, many poets and authors, and numerous avant-garde artists. The government office or official, teacher, writer or artist usually promises to reform.

In the West the staffs of governmental information agencies like the Voice of America or BBC often are largely composed of professional journalists. In contrast, the top men in Agitprop are intellectuals and often have been professors. Chiefs, assistant chiefs, and departmental heads of Agitprop have written and published serious books on such topics as Aristotle, history of philosophy, military history, socialist literature of the nineteenth century, and scientific atheism.

Agitprop does not confine its work to the Soviet press and radio, but utilizes all means of influencing human thought. Thus an Agitprop magazine stated:

> The Bolshevik Party guides the activity of all governmental and social organizations in the field of ideology. The press, propaganda, agitation, science, the movies, literature, art, the radio, museums, libraries, and other cultural and educational institutions are all means for political education of the masses.

Agitprop controls these many propaganda channels primarily through lower organizations of the Communist Party. The republic, regional, city, and district party organizations each have a propaganda office subordinate to Agitprop in Moscow. Since Communist parties outside the USSR are generally organized on the Russian model and sometimes look to Moscow for spiritual guidance, Agitprop has at its disposal not only a Soviet but also a worldwide party propaganda apparatus located wherever pro-Moscow Communists are found.

At home Agitprop also relies on the support of large public organizations. In *Communist,* a magazine for Soviet officials, an Agitprop executive has boasted:

> An important role in the Communist training of people is played by the Young Communist League, the trade unions and other social organizations, which under the direction of the Communist Party conduct great work to change all workers into active builders of Communism.

The vast majority of USSR industrial and white-collar workers are trade union members, and a large percentage of Soviet youths are in the Young Communist League. Attempts of Communists outside Russia to infiltrate and control labor unions and youth movements are at least partly inspired by propaganda considerations.

Newspapers and magazines are considered by Agitprop to be "the strongest means for Bolshevik agitation among the masses." Agitprop controls, primarily through the lower party apparatus, the approximately 8,000 newspapers and 6,600 magazines in the USSR. The statutes of the USSR Communist Party provide that each party organization, large or small, controls its press organs and appoints their editors. This rule is more inclusive than it seems, since most regional and local newspapers are official joint organs of both the government and party at the particular level. Many ministerial newspapers, professional magazines, and periodicals of mass societies are also party outlets, representing not only the ministry, profession, or society but the party groups within them. The nonparty press of the USSR is small, and usually artistic, governmental, or scientific. In practice their editors also usually obey Agitprop. Thus when two Leningrad artistic magazines once published pro-Western and pessimistic literature, Agitprop closed one of the magazines and appointed a new chief editor for the other.

The importance of other means of propaganda can be summarized in the following official statements, which have remained virtually the same throughout Soviet history.

> Radio is a very important weapon for propaganda and agitation, and for Communist training of people.
>
> Our motion pictures help the Communist Party train workers in the spirit of socialism, organize the masses in struggle for socialism, and increase their ability for political fighting.
>
> Soviet schools are a very important weapon for Communist training of youth, and are transmitters of the principles of Communism.
>
> The most important duty of Soviet art is to participate actively in the Communist training of Soviet people.
>
> Soviet literature is one of the most important weapons for political education of the masses, and arms people with the ideals of Communism. In its development Soviet literature has been carefully guided by the Bolshevik party.

Most Soviet poets and novelists are members of a small select professional society called the Union of Soviet Writers. The statutes of this society frankly proclaim:

> The aims of the Union of Soviet Writers are to train the masses in a spirit of socialism, and to participate in the international revolutionary movement by making literature reflect the struggle of toilers in capitalist and colonial countries.

The means of Soviet propaganda other than the press are usually controlled directly or indirectly by governmental committees or ministries, of which the most important today is the USSR Ministry of Culture. These governmental organizations simply fulfill Agitprop orders. Recently a Soviet radio correspondent in New York City was asked by an American to explain Agitprop. Officially the correspondent was a representative of a governmental radio station in Moscow. But he replied: "Agitprop is my boss."

A very important governmental organization subordinate to Agitprop is TASS (Telegraph Agency of the Soviet Union), which since 1972 has been a Soviet cabinet ministry. Except for a few foreign correspondents of USSR newspapers, magazines, radio, and the Novosti publishing society, TASS does the distribution of foreign news within the USSR. TASS does not inundate Russia with foreign news, but only releases enough daily to fill one or two pages of the standard four- or six-sheet Soviet newspaper. Every day the identical foreign news appears in all USSR papers from the authoritative *Pravda* down to the local press of Siberia or Central Asia. TASS selects foreign news items which reflect the current propaganda of Agitprop. Many world events remain unknown to the average Soviet citizen because TASS does not report them. Political editing is also constantly practiced by TASS. By cutting certain words, phrases, or sentences from a neutral or even anti-Soviet foreign speech or article, the work appears in the USSR press as virtual praise of Communism. Outstanding Western anti-Soviet statesmen, who were thus deliberately misinterpreted by the USSR press, include the late Winston Churchill, Herbert Hoover, and Senator Taft. TASS also sends abroad carefully selected USSR news, which is much larger in volume than the foreign information released to the Soviet people.

A second crucial governmental auxiliary of Agitprop is Glavlit (Chief Administration for Literature and Publications), which was first formed in the late 1920's. During Stalin's rule no overall Glavlit existed, but a Glavlit office was located in the Education Ministry of each Soviet republic of the USSR. By 1958 Glavlit was centralized as an organization subordinate to the USSR Council of Ministers. Glavlit is the chief Soviet censor, operating by the following rules:

> Glavlit is formed to accomplish all types of political and ideological control over publications, manuscripts, photographs, pictures, etc. planned to be printed or distributed, as well as over radio broadcasts, lectures and exhibits. . . .
>
> Pre-publication control is accomplished by Glavlit through its agents at publishing houses, editorial offices of periodicals, printing establishments, radio stations, telegraph agencies, customs houses, main postoffices, etc. . . .
>
> All periodical and non-periodical publications as well as all small printed matter, regardless of publisher, must be inspected by organs of Glavlit. . . .
>
> If office forms, account books, order forms, notebooks, mail

> wrappers, postcards, tickets or checkbooks contain slogans or instructions for use, they are not exempt from inspection by Glavlit organs. . . .
>
> Glavlit issues permission for the opening of new publishing houses, for the starting of new magazines and newspapers, and permits and forbids import and export of literature from and to abroad.

A third governmental organization linked closely to Agitprop is Glavrepertoire (Chief Administration for Control over Performances and Repertoires). Formed shortly after Glavlit and like it, Glavrepertoire was for many years a group of offices located in republic Education Ministries. After World War II it was centralized, and now is a branch of the USSR Ministry of Culture. Regardless of administrative shuffles, Glavrepertoire continues to operate under the following rules, which were originally issued by the ministries of Education, Police, and Justice:

> Not one dramatic, choreographic, circus, vaudeville or musical work, or movie or phonograph record, can be issued for public use, display, production or distribution without previous permission from Glavrepertoire. . . .
>
> Organizations, institutions or persons, which propose to present any type of public performance, must not later than five days before the performance, send to the control organs a detailed program of the proposed show, listing the play, music or concert piece. . . .
>
> All existing theatrical enterprises, both permanent and temporary, must register at Glavrepertoire or its local organs. . . .
>
> The opening of new theatrical enterprises such as touring troupes, concert organizations and groups, as well as stationary organizations, is allowed only by permission from Glavrepertoire or its local organs. . . .
>
> All theatrical enterprises and organizations, as well as the Phonograph Record Trust, must send to Glavrepertoire or its local organs their repertoire plans and the plan for producing phonograph records within time limits set by Glavrepertoire or its local organs. . . .

For the Soviet censors, control over radio listening is a problem. No law has ever forbidden Soviet citizens to hear foreign broadcasts, although the press preaches that such listening is useless and disloyal. As far as possible, mechanical means are used to isolate Soviet citizens from foreign radio programs. It is cheaper in the USSR for a family to purchase a radio loudspeaker rather than a receiving set. The loudspeaker is wired to a central receiving set operated by local governmental authorities, who tune in the receiving network only to Soviet programs. Such wired loudspeakers are also located in various public places such as city squares, parks, and amusement centers. At present the USSR has about 50 million wired loudspeakers compared to 60 million actual receiving sets. There also are 65 million television sets.

In addition, noise machines are ringed around large cities like Moscow to intercept and jam foreign radio broadcasts from any direction. This jamming network existed as early as the 1930's, and was augmented at the end of World War II by the transfer of many Nazi noise machines from East Germany into the USSR. Altogether the USSR today has about 300 jamming stations, which can be mobilized against an undesirable foreign radio program in a few minutes by centralized control from Moscow. In practice the jamming network is expensive to operate, and therefore is used only occasionally, in particular during international crises.

On a recent trip through Russia, many Soviet citizens told me that they listened to the Voice of America, but preferred the news broadcasts of the British Broadcasting System (BBC). I heard this even in Central Asia, which is quite remote from British and American transmitters in western Europe. The Voice of America, BBC, and Radio Liberty (an official American organization) all receive letters from Soviet citizens both praising and attacking their programs. Because of the vast distances within the USSR, most Soviet private radio receiving sets must be shortwave, in order to hear long-distance USSR broadcasts. By beaming short-wave transmissions into Russia from many stations in various countries, the Voice of America, BBC, and Radio Liberty can penetrate.

These foreign radio broadcasts normally surmount Soviet censorship. A few years ago the Voice of America even forced a USSR radio program off the air. At the time a Moscow radio station had a weekly question-and-answer period, broadcast in shortwave to the USSR. One question asked: What is a "People's Democracy" (the Communist title for a Soviet satellite)? The answer was rather vague. The next day the Voice of America broadcast its definition, whose essence was summarized in the first sentence: "A People's Democracy is a land surrounded by barbed wire and armed sentries, which one cannot leave if he wants." On the following day Moscow radio made the mistake of declaring: "The definition of a People's Democracy you heard yesterday from the Voice of America is untrue." The Voice countered by stating: "The Moscow radio is displeased with our definition of a People's Democracy. Perhaps you did not hear our definition, and wonder why Moscow radio is displeased. So we will repeat our definition in full." Next week the Moscow question-and-answer program disappeared, and was replaced by concert music.

Since Stalin's death, large numbers of foreign tourists have been admitted into the USSR, much like tourism during the 1930's. Not long after the first foreigners of the post-Stalin era arrived, the Soviet press began warning the USSR public not to accept tourist views about politics, economics, literature, and art.

The main themes of Soviet propaganda are apparently devised by the Politburo. These themes in rough outline are sent to Agitprop, which adds the necessary details and supplies the logical proof. Then Agitprop releases the embellished themes as detailed instructions to the Soviet press, news agencies, radio, television stations, schools, theaters, publishing houses, museums, and other propaganda media. These instructions are either tactical propaganda (sometimes called "agitation") or strategic propaganda.

Tactical propaganda tries to justify the Communist interpretation of current events and to explain the alleged correctness of current Soviet policy. Since current events can change rapidly and Soviet policies often suddenly reverse, tactical propaganda mainly uses fast means of mass communication like newspapers, radio, television, and the 3,000,000 to 6,000,000 verbal lecturers. A typical difficult case for tactical propaganda was the conclusion of the Nazi-Soviet nonaggression pact in 1939, dividing east Europe between the two signatories. For the previous six years Agitprop had violently criticized German Fascism as the "death-throe of capitalism." So Agitprop justified the pact mainly by two arguments: The USSR wished to have peaceful relations and trade with all nations, regardless of differences in ideology. Second, the pact kept Russia from being immediately embroiled in World War II (which started soon after this Nazi-Soviet treaty was signed).

Strategic propaganda attempts to instill absolute loyalty to the Soviet regime, so that the USSR masses will work hard for Communism and even be ready to die in battle against capitalism. This endeavor for loyalty is a long-time effort little affected by current events or USSR policy reversals. Thus strategic propaganda is disseminated not only by newspaper, radio, television, and lectures, but also by magazines, books, placards, schools, theaters, arts, museums, music, and even parades. Strategic propaganda mainly glorifies the USSR and friendly Communist countries, while exposing the seamy side of capitalist life. Not since the late 1920's has the USSR published accurate statistics on the Soviet suicide rate, death rate, prevalence of disease, and amount of crime. Domestic accidents and natural disasters are rarely reported in the Soviet press, though the USSR has had many train wrecks, spring floods, and earthquakes. Agitprop constantly stresses optimism. Recently several USSR publishing houses tried to sell songs with melancholy words. Agitprop stopped the sale, and compelled the music publishers to change the lyrics into words of happiness.

A grave problem for strategic propaganda is the low USSR standard of living, of which the Soviet people are fully aware. So Agitprop rarely claims that Communist living conditions are better than capitalist. Instead capitalism is pictured as declining and decadent, while the Soviet Union is ever progressing. Anything unfavorable to Western capitalism is published, such as suicide rates, divorce rates, prevalence of disease, amount of crime, strikes, accidents, natural disasters, stockmarket declines, rise of unemployment, and so on. The Soviet reader receives the impression that the capitalist world is bedeviled by troubles which do not exist in the USSR.

Meanwhile every example of Soviet progress is published, from the opening of a tiny power station on a collective farm to the explosion of a 50-megaton hydrogen bomb. This desire to display progress results in deliberate inaccuracies by Soviet statistical compendiums, which juggle figures to prove that both Tsarist Russia and early Soviet Russia were worse economically than they actually were. By this device the USSR planned industrialization after 1928 is made to appear faster and greater than it really was. Similarly in the political sphere the de-Stalinization campaign by Khrushchev blamed Stalin for some crimes he did not commit, in order to magnify political progress in Khrushchevian Russia.

As much as possible Agitprop bases its propaganda on the truth or half-truths, so that the propaganda will be difficult to refute. An example of true propaganda was the Soviet slogan of World War II: "The Red Army has lost battles but has never lost a war." To date this statement is true, and also assures Soviet citizens not to be alarmed by temporary military reverses.

Partly true is the Soviet explanation that the wall built by Communists around west Berlin in 1961 was erected to stop Western spies and agents from entering East Germany. Until the wall was constructed, thousands of west Berliners commuted daily into east Berlin to work or shop, and western undercover agents were undoubtedly among them. But the obvious main reason for the wall was to prevent the flight of masses of people from Communist East Germany into the democratic West. Millions of East Germans had previously escaped through Berlin, and the runaways included a high percentage of East German intellectuals and youth.

However, if complete falsehoods are necessary, Agitprop will issue deliberate untruths, which are justified by the official Soviet slogan: "Truth is anything that aids the cause of Communism." Such an intentional lie was apparently the Communist accusation that US bombers dropped germ bombs on North Korea during the Korean war of 1950–1953. Wartime sanitary conditions were bad in North Korea, caused many needless deaths, had to be explained, and were therefore blamed upon the American enemy. This untruth was generally not believed in Western countries. But several people were killed in Tehran by Iranian rioters protesting American germ warfare. Thus a falsehood can achieve results, even if accepted only by a minority of people.

How successful has Agitprop been in winning the loyalty of the Soviet people and moral support from foreigners? By its vast size alone, the Communist propaganda apparatus is bound to achieve some success.

Yet half a million Soviet citizens, who had been captured by the Germans during World War II, refused to return to the USSR at the war's end. A high percentage of these nonreturnees were intelligentsia—a Soviet class which has always resented governmental thought control.

Throughout Soviet history, some writers have been clever enough to fool the censors and publish subtly anti-Soviet books. In the 1920's when censorship was mild, Zoshchenko wrote many short stories satirizing Communist life. One described how a factory tried to save money in winter by turning off the heat in the washrooms, whose waterpipes promptly burst and required expensive repairs. During the 1930's many intellectuals were executed in the great purge. One was a writer whose book implied that Stalin had murdered a Politburo rival. Many Jewish writers were executed in the first years after World War II.

After Stalin's death, though censorship laws remained unchanged, the censors were confused by de-Stalinization and the Kremlin tolerated more individualistic writing. Soviet writers were quick to take advantage of this thaw. In 1956 Russia's most outspoken literary magazine published the novel *Not by Bread Alone,* in which a poor non-Communist schoolteacher is finally rewarded for his invention, that Communist industrialists first rejected and then tried to steal. The chief villain was a factory director who looked, acted, and talked much like Khrushchev, the party first secretary at the time. Boris Pasternak received the Nobel Prize in 1958 for his novel *Doctor Zhivago.* This book was never published in Russia, but Pasternak sent a poorly censored copy to an Italian Communist publisher who printed it abroad.

By the 1960's much critical literature was appearing in Soviet Russia with such themes as the horrors of war, the poverty of collective farms, abuse of power by Soviet officials, the cruelty of prison camps, and the injustice of Stalin's purges. The Kremlin was often annoyed by these writings, at times silencing or even arresting authors who stressed Soviet faults. Brezhnev, Khrushchev's successor, stated his own views very strongly:

> We are unchangeably guided by the principle of the party feeling of art, and of the class approach toward the evaluation of everything done in the field of culture. . . .
>
> The party will always support art and literature which

> strengthens faith in our ideals, and will conduct an implacable struggle against all manifestations of alien ideology. . . .
>
> Unfortunately one also meets such journeymen of art who, instead of helping our people, make it their specialty to blacken our system and to slander our heroic people. . . . It is fully understandable that the Soviet people cannot overlook the shameful activity of such persons. It will give them their just deserts.[3]

From the 1930's to the present Agitprop publicly complains each year that its propaganda is not fully successful. These complaints have stressed much the same themes for three decades.

Such complaints often take the form of party decrees, criticizing Soviet propaganda work for ineffectiveness and ordering drastic improvement. According to the decrees, the following anti-Marxist attitudes are widespread among the Soviet population: love of private property, admiration for Western culture, nationalism among minorities, belief in religion, disinterest in politics, scorn for manual labor, waste of public property, bureaucracy, bribery, black-marketing, drunkenness, hooliganism, bourgeois ideology, revision of Marxism, and right-wing socialism.

In the 1970's the Soviet government seemed worried by an increasing tendency of educated Soviet youths and college students to become infatuated with pure science. Such youths were officially criticized for preferring science to Marxism and scorning volunteer manual work. Other charges leveled at them included hero-worship of scientists, love of nonpolitical science fiction, pacifism toward atomic war, and belief that an unknown power created the world.

Only Agitprop and the Soviet police probably know the true mood of the USSR people. Russian-speaking visitors find that Soviet officials usually talk the party line, while ordinary persons display considerable originality of thought. On a recent trip through Russia the author discovered that many Russians disliked the deposed Khrushchev, and accepted the Brezhnev-Kosygin leadership as dull but progressive. But such conversations, even from a hundred people in widely scattered cities, cannot be assumed to reflect the viewpoint of a vast nation.

---

3 *Materials of the 23rd Congress of the Communist Party of the Soviet Union,* p. 68.

The most scholarly attempt to ascertain Soviet public opinion thus far has been made by Harvard University, which carefully interviewed over 2,700 Soviet refugees who left the USSR during and after World War II. The results were as follows:

Most of the refugees thought in socialist terms, with little desire for the USSR to return to complete capitalism. They praised the Soviet welfare state for its free medical care, tuition-free education, and state pensions. Their belief was strong that the peaceful USSR was threatened by war from the capitalist West. The majority desired state ownership of transport and heavy industry in Russia to be permanent.

The refugees were definitely republican, with no desire to restore a Tsar, even as a constitutional monarch. But the refugees seemed politically immature, lacking any plan for a better type of government than the Communist. Instead they wanted the civil liberties of the Soviet Constitution to be actually enforced, so Russians would enjoy real freedom of speech, freedom of assembly, privacy of correspondence, and protection from arbitrary arrest.

In economics almost all refugees complained about the low Soviet standard of living, even though some had held good jobs and lived rather well. Both urbanites and peasants agreed that USSR agriculture would not be productive until the collective farms are abolished. The majority of refugees desired Russia to return to a NEP economy of state-owned large enterprises, private small business, and little private farms.

The greatest political complaints were against the Soviet secret police and the Communist Party, both of which the refugees desired to destroy and even punish. In refugee opinion, police officials were torturers while party members were tough bosses. Hatred for the party and police was practical rather than ideological, for the refugees seemed little interested either in denouncing or approving Marxism-Leninism. Nor was much distinction drawn between Soviet leaders, Lenin being considered almost as harmful to Russia as Stalin.

Many refugees were patriots loyal to Mother Russia, which they said without Communists could be a great nation. They were also proud of Soviet achievements in industry, science, education, and military power. But their loyalty to native country was emotionally profound, while loyalty to the Soviet regime was respect for strength. When German early military victories in the Nazi-Soviet war undermined this respect, many willingly defected from the USSR.

The Harvard survey is now largely out-of-date. The refugees interviewed were the generation of World War II, with memories only of harsh Stalinism. Since then a new generation has matured during the milder regimes of Khrushchev and Brezhnev. Concepts of World War II may not hold true today. Russian-speaking Americans who have visited the USSR contradict each other on the moods of the Soviet people interviewed. Some Soviet citizens appear eager to discuss politics, while others simply withdraw into a seemingly nonpolitical existence.

We can conclude that the West does not really know what presentday Russians think. Yet certain facts are clear: Agitprop admits it has partially failed. The Soviet nation has a diversity of thought. This diversity does not please the Kremlin, but in the long run may strengthen rather than weaken Russian national character.

Suggestions for Further Reading

Alexandrova, Vera, *A History of Soviet Literature,* New York: Doubleday, 1963.

Current Digest of the Soviet Press, New York: Columbia University, 1948–

Graham, Loren R., *Science and Philosophy in the Soviet Union.* New York: Knopf, 1972.

Heen, Nancy Whittier, *Politics and History in the Soviet Union.* Cambridge: Massachusetts Institute of Technology Press, 1971.

Hollander, Gayle Durham, *Soviet Political Indoctrination: Developments in Mass Media and Propaganda Since Stalin.* New York: Praeger, 1972.

Hopkins, Mark W., *Mass Media in the Soviet Union.* New York: Pegasus, 1969.

Kruglak, Theodore E., *The Two Faces of TASS,* Minneapolis: Minnesota University Press. 1966.

Mickiewicz, Ellen P., *Soviet Political Schools.* New Haven: Yale University Press, 1967.

Wolfe, Bertram D., *Khrushchev and Stalin's Ghost,* New York: Praeger, 1956.

Chapter 13

Government and Law

When Lenin seized power in Russia in November 1917, he was soon confronted by an honestly elected parliament, the Constituent Assembly, whose election had been arranged by the Russian Provisional Government that Lenin had overthrown. The Assembly met in January 1918, and only one fourth of the deputies were members of Lenin's Bolshevik Party. When the Assembly refused to accept Lenin's extreme socialist program, he dissolved this legislature by force. Thereafter Lenin openly admitted that he ruled by dictatorship:

> The revolutionary dictatorship of the proletariat is power won and maintained by the violence of the proletariat against the bourgeoisie, power that is unrestricted by any laws.[1]

To maintain a pretense of democracy, Lenin converted the workers' soviets into state parliaments. Soviets had been formed spontaneously before the Bolshevik Revolution as workers' strike committees. Each factory usually formed a soviet, and representatives from factory soviets organized a city soviet. On the eve of the Bolshevik Revolution, an all-Russian (national) soviet had been formed. The Bolsheviks gained control of the major soviets just before Lenin's seizure of power.

The Soviet Russian Constitution of 1918 formalized these soviets into parliaments. Thereafter soviets existed for each level

---

[1] Lenin, V. I., *Proletariat Revolution and Renegade Kautsky*, 1918.

of government: village (actually township for several villages), city, district (roughly corresponding to an American county), region, and nation. At first only the village and city soviets were elected directly by the population. These soviets elected the district soviets which chose the regional soviets, that in turn elected the All-Russian Soviet. Only peasants and workers could vote. Members of the former upper classes, priests, former Tsarist officials, and businessmen were deprived of the franchise. Because city workers were more pro-Communist than the peasants, one urban proletarian vote was rated equal to five peasant votes in the village and city elections.

This election system applied at first to the Russian Soviet Republic. In 1924 the Russian Republic forced the Ukrainian, Belorussian, and Caucasian Republics to unite into the Union of Soviet Socialist Republics (USSR). A new USSR constitution maintained the same electoral system as previously in the Russian Republic. However a USSR Soviet was added at the top of the pyramid of soviets. Meanwhile, during the Russian Civil War of 1918–1920, the practice had arisen that all soviet deputies had either to be Communists or belong to no other party.

A new Soviet Constitution was issued in 1936, allowing all USSR citizens to vote except insane persons and certain categories of criminals. The weighting of popular votes in favor of the urban worker was abandoned, and all votes were made equal. Indirect soviet elections were also abolished, and since then all soviets have been directly elected. Today the legal age for voting is 18, and to be elected to office a Soviet citizen must also be 18. These age limits were set by a new 1977 Constitution.

Only the Communist Party or public organizations controlled by the party are permitted to nominate candidates. The candidate does not need to be a Communist Party member, but must publicly accept and support the party's program. Since the average election district contains several public organizations, at first several candidates are usually nominated for the same soviet seat. After this, the leading Communist Party official of the district selects only one of the nominees to be placed on the ballot. Hence when the voter goes to the polls on election day, he finds only one name on the ballot for each Soviet seat open for election.

With such careful selection of candidates, a nominee is rarely withdrawn from the ballot after being placed upon it. Occasionally a candidate misbehaves politically during the election campaign. Then the Communist Party withdraws his name from the ballot and nominates another person. In each USSR Supreme Soviet election, one or more such withdrawals usually occur.

When election day arrives, Communist Party members go from door to door, urging citizens to go out to vote. If a Soviet citizen does not vote, the police will record this fact in his dossier. So the average Soviet citizen goes to the polls. There his name is checked on the precinct list of voters. Then he is handed a paper ballot, containing the name of only one candidate for each post. To vote "yes," the voter simply folds the ballot and drops it into the election box.

A booth is provided where a voter in supposed secrecy can cross out the candidate's name, which is the only legal procedure for voting "no." But the governmental election commission has just checked the voter's name on the list of voters, and knows his identity. If he disappears into the booth, this probably means he is voting "no." The average voter does not enter the booth, but merely folds the ballot and drops it into the box, registering an automatic "yes." Yet in each election to the USSR Supreme Soviet thus far, several hundred thousand Soviet citizens have voted "no."

If the majority of voters in an election district have crossed out the candidate's name, the candidate is not elected. The Communist Party then nominates another candidate, and a by-election is conducted. Thus far in Soviet history, several candidates have usually been defeated in each election to the USSR Supreme Soviet.

At present the lowest tier of elected soviets is the village (township) soviet in rural areas, and the city ward in cities. Next highest is the district soviet in the countryside, and the city soviet in urban centers. (After a city attains a population of 50,000, it is released from district control, and is directly subordinate to the regional government.) Above the city and district level are a variety of regional soviets. The most common are simply called regional (oblast), and territorial (krai). If a minority nationality inhabits the particular region, this area and its soviet may be entitled autonomous republic, autonomous region, or national area. Still higher are the soviets of the 15 Soviet republics comprising the USSR. All of these soviets are unicameral. All are elected for 2½-year terms, except in the autonomous and Soviet republics where the term is five years.

The highest soviet today is the Supreme Soviet of the USSR, consisting of two houses equal in power and elected for a five-year term. One house is the Soviet of the Union, with one deputy for about 300,000 inhabitants of the USSR. The Soviet of the Union, with 767 members, represents the population. The other house is the Soviet of Nationalities, with 32 deputies from each of the 15 Soviet republics, 11 from each of the 20 autonomous republics, 5 from each of the 8 autonomous regions, and 1 from each of the 10 national areas. The Soviet of Nationalities, with 750 members, represents the major nationalities. Each house also has several deputies representing the Soviet troops stationed inside the USSR and abroad in the Soviet satellites.

Though Lenin originally created this system of Soviets, he had little faith in them. Thus he announced:

> The class which took political power in its hands did so knowing that it took this power alone. This is contained in the concept of dictatorship of the proletariat. This concept has meaning only when a single class knows that it alone is taking political power in its hands and does not deceive itself or others with talk about "popular, elected" government "sanctified by the whole people."
>
> Soviet socialist democracy is not contradictory to individual management and dictatorship in any way. . . . The will of a class may sometimes be carried out by a dictator, who at times may do more alone and who is frequently more necessary.[2]

However, Lenin realized that even an unfairly elected high soviet might quarrel with the Communist leaders, if the soviet actually exerted its constitutional powers. There was a precedent in the four Dumas (lower house of Tsarist parliament) serving from 1906 to 1917. Each Duma was unfairly elected, so that upper classes would be overrepresented. Despite pseudo-election, and

---

[2] Lenin, V. I., *Speech to the Ninth Congress of the Russian Communist Party,* March 31, 1920.

Also see *Ibid., Speech at a Transport Workers' Congress,* March 27, 1921.

although possessing very little legal power, each Duma opposed Tsarist autocracy.

Therefore Lenin established a system in which each soviet rarely convened, and then only for a few days. During the interim, its powers were delegated to small committees, which acted in the name of the soviet with all of its power.

Lenin's parliamentary practices have been continued by his successors. Today the USSR Supreme Soviet delegates its immense constitutional power to the Supreme Soviet Presidium and the Council of Ministers (cabinet). The soviets of Soviet republics and autonomous republics also delegate their authority to presidiums and councils of ministers. Below this level instead of two committees, there is only one for each soviet: an executive committee which combines the functions of presidium and council. Accordingly the soviets of regions, territories, autonomous regions, national areas, districts, cities, city wards, and villages delegate their power to "executive committees."

Thus the soviets are deprived of their legal power. Instead of being governed by a network of parliaments, the USSR is ruled by a network of small committees. Let us see how this operates in practice:

The Soviet Constitution divides the legislative power of the USSR central government among three bodies: the Supreme Soviet, the Supreme Soviet Presidium, and the Council of Ministers. If both houses of the Supreme Soviet pass a bill by majority vote, the bill becomes law. The Supreme Soviet also has the constitutional power to amend the USSR Constitution, in which case, however, a two-thirds vote of each house is required.

The Supreme Soviet Presidium is elected for five years by the Supreme Soviet, when the latter commences its five-year term. During the five years, however, the Supreme Soviet can appoint and dismiss Presidium members if the necessity arises. Article 121 of the USSR Constitution gives the Presidium the power to issue decrees.

Members of the USSR Council of Ministers are appointed and dismissed by the Supreme Soviet when the latter is in session. At other times the Supreme Soviet Presidium makes the cabinet appointments and dismissals. Article 132 of the USSR Constitution gives the Council of Ministers the right to issue "decisions and orders on the basis and in pursuance of the laws of the USSR." Article 132 adds that "decisions and orders of the USSR Council of Ministers are binding throughout the territory of the USSR."

Most of the laws of the USSR are published not in the relatively brief law codes, but in the annual *Collection of Laws,* which corresponds roughly to the United States Statutes at Large. An examination of the USSR *Collection of Laws* reveals that in an average recent year, the Supreme Soviet passed about five to ten laws of its own. Aside from issuing medals, decorations, and citations, which seems to be the main business of the Supreme Soviet Presidium, this Presidium issues about forty laws of importance during a year. Meanwhile some 200 or more important laws are proclaimed by the Council of Ministers, which thus is the main legislature of the Soviet government.

The Supreme Soviet has an impressive legislative procedure. Constitutionally the Soviet must meet twice a year, and can be convened by itself or its Presidium into special additional sessions. Each house of the Supreme Soviet has standing committees for foreign affairs, legislative proposals, planning, industry, agriculture, transport, trade, construction, welfare, education, youth affairs, consumer goods, and ecology. These committees function. They meet shortly before each session of the Supreme Soviet, and help draft the proposed legislation which the Soviet will consider. A Council of Elders (a large joint-committee of the older members of both houses of the Supreme Soviet) meets just before a Supreme Soviet session, decides matters of high policy, and recommends that the Supreme Soviet accept the Council's decisions.

This complex procedure might be meaningful if the Supreme Soviet stayed in session long enough to be effective. But on the average, each of the two annual sessions of the Supreme Soviet does not last more than one week apiece. In 1953 just after Stalin's death, one set a record of meeting only one day. In such short periods the Supreme Soviet can handle only a small volume of business. During the brief sessions there is no real debate. The Supreme Soviet Presidium presents a list of edicts it has issued, and the Supreme Soviet automatically approves them. One or more members of the Council of Ministers present new draft laws. At times there is no discussion. Sometimes a few speakers approve the draft, but suggest minor changes. The Minister makes a final speech, accepting some suggested amendments and rejecting others. Then a unanimous vote approves the draft, which becomes law.

The Supreme Soviet is important not as a parliament, but as a forum for important policy statements by high Soviet leaders. For example, Premier Khrushchev revealed at a Supreme Soviet meeting in 1960 that the USSR had shot down an American U-2 reconnaissance plane. Since Supreme Soviet meetings are attended by foreign diplomats and newspapermen, the policy is thus announced to the entire world.

The Supreme Soviet does not even convene on set dates of the year. Sessions are called by the Supreme Soviet Presidium. During periods of great crisis, the Supreme Soviet is often prevented from taking any action because it is simply not convened until the crisis has passed. For example, the Supreme Soviet was not in session when Khrushchev was ousted from power in 1964, nor when the USSR army invaded Czechoslovakia in 1968.

Compared to the 1,517 members of the Supreme Soviet, the Supreme Soviet Presidium is a small body of 39 men. Fifteen of the members are ex-officio, by virtue of being the presidents of the presidiums of the 15 Soviet republics. The Supreme Soviet elects 22 other members, plus the President and Secretary of the Supreme Soviet Presidium.

Meetings of the full 39-man membership of the Supreme Soviet Presidium are probably rare. According to the Soviet press, the presidents of the presidiums of the Soviet republics spend most of their time in the capitals of their republics rather than in Moscow. Thus the decrees of the Supreme Soviet Presidium are probably issued by a rump membership of about 24 men.

Most of the decrees of the Supreme Soviet Presidium issue decorations or citations to individuals, groups, or organizations which have aided the Communist cause. However, some decrees are of national importance. In particular, the Presidium has the constitutional authority to ratify and denounce treaties and to declare war and peace. Thus the Presidium is very active in the formal aspects of foreign affairs. For example, in 1975 the Presidium made the formal announcement renouncing the 1972 trade agreement between the United States and USSR.

The Council of Ministers, which issues most decrees of importance, has a nominal membership of about 105 men. These include a premier, some 11 vice-premiers, about 80 ministers or heads of organizations of ministerial rank, and 15 ex-officio members. The latter are the premiers of the councils of ministers of the 15 Soviet republics.

Like the Supreme Soviet Presidium, the full membership of the Council of Ministers probably rarely meets. The premiers of the Soviet republics are usually outside Moscow in their republic capitals. Thus decrees of the Council of Ministers are probably issued by a rump membership of about 90 persons. When necessary, the USSR Premier and Vice-Premiers meet alone as an inner cabinet, with the power also of issuing decrees.

The decrees of the Council of Ministers and Supreme Soviet Presidium are the day-by-day law governing the USSR. These decrees are particularly numerous in the fields of economic planning, finance, police control, and defense. Yet the average Soviet citizen has little knowledge of these decrees, since only those of utmost importance are published in the daily press. Most others appear in the *Collection of Laws,* a periodical of limited circulation read mainly by officials who must enforce the decrees. Some decrees are secret, are not published at the time of issuance, but are simply sent to the officials who must enforce them. For example, on December 1, 1934, the Presidium circulated the following secret decree:

> Investigative agencies are directed to speed up the cases of those accused of the preparation or execution of acts of terror.
>
> Judicial organs are directed not to delay the execution of death sentences pertaining to crimes of this category in order to consider the possibility of pardon. . . .
>
> The organs of the Commissariat of Internal Affairs are directed to execute the death sentences against criminals of the above-mentioned category immediately after the passage of sentences.[3]

At their levels of operation the councils of ministers and presidiums of the Soviet and autonomous republics, and the

[3] Khrushchev, N. S., *Special Report to the 20th Congress of the Communist Party of the Soviet Union,* February 24–25, 1956.

executive committees of the autonomous regions, regions, territories, national areas, districts, cities, city wards, and villages have similar decree powers to those of the USSR Supreme Soviet Presidium and Council of Ministers. These lesser councils of ministers, presidiums, and executive committees are elected by their soviets.

The hierarchy of all Soviets and their committees is outlined in Table 7:

Table 7. *Committee Structure of Soviet Government*

Soviets	Committees	
USSR	Council of Ministers	Presidium
Soviet republic	Council of Ministers	Presidium
Autonomous republic	Council of Ministers	Presidium
Autonomous region	Executive committee	
Region	Executive committee	
Territory	Executive committee	
National area	Executive committee	
District	Executive committee	
City	Executive committee	
City ward	Executive committee	
Village	Executive committee	

Source: *Pravda,* 1976.

Since power is constitutionally centered in the USSR government, governmental committees below the USSR level function mainly as executives fulfilling USSR orders. Hence the lower committees issue edicts only on minor matters. For example, a village executive committee is largely occupied in ensuring good agricultural work by the surrounding collective and state farms. City governments mainly deal with such problems as housing, public utilities, residence permits, local industry, sanitation, and traffic regulation.

Important legislation largely originates from the USSR Council of Ministers and Supreme Soviet Presidium. However, according to the Soviet Constitution, both of these top committees are also the chief centers of executive power in the USSR. Articles 119 and 120 of the Constitution give the following executive powers to the Supreme Soviet Presidium: convening the sessions of the Supreme Soviet; ordering elections for a new Supreme Soviet; appointment and dismissal of members of the Council of Ministers, high military officers, diplomats, and other important government officials; granting of pardons; ordering of partial or general mobilization; proclamation of martial law either in a locality or throughout the USSR; and accrediting foreign diplomatic representatives to the USSR. Other executive powers are granted to the Presidium by Soviet law. For example, a person may not renounce his Soviet citizenship without Presidium approval.

Thus the executive work of the Supreme Soviet Presidium is mainly of a formal nature. Soviet scholars describe the Presidium as a "collective president," and the president of the Presidium as the official chief of state. However, this presidency is not of the strong American type, but of the weak formal nature like the presidents of Italy, West Germany, or Switzerland.

Many of the Presidium's executive decisions are not announced. The Presidium usually publishes the appointments and dismissals of Soviet ambassadors and cabinet ministers. The announcement, however, is sometimes made after the event has occurred, and often the new post of a dismissed person is not indicated. Changes in the high command of the Soviet armed forces are rarely announced, and can be learned only weeks or months afterward by incidental data appearing in the Soviet press.

The Supreme Soviet Presidium almost never publicizes its proclamations of partial mobilization or regional martial law, except in the particular region concerned. For example, in 1956 Georgian students organized political demonstrations against the new policy of de-Stalinization. For several days the Georgian Soviet Republic was under martial law while police troops suppressed student unrest. But no announcement was made about this regional martial law to the remainder of the USSR or the outside world. The first indications of trouble occurred when both Soviet and foreign tourists were forbidden to enter Georgia. Later, after the martial law ended, the truth became known from Georgian newspapers.

The Supreme Soviet Presidium has changed little in form since its inception in the first years of Soviet rule, except to increase its membership in proportion to the increase in the number of Soviet republics. In contrast, the Council of Ministers, until 1946 called the Council of People's Commissars, has undergone constant structural changes, with ministries and organizations of ministerial rank being formed, abolished, merged, split, or renamed almost every year.

In general, the tendency has been for the number of cabinet ministries to increase along with the growth of Soviet industry, so that a ministry or organization of similar rank exists for each major branch of industry. There have been three attempts, one under Stalin and two under his successors, to reduce the size of the Council of Ministers to a smaller and more efficient body. All three attempts failed, and the number of ministries or similar organizations soon regained the prereduction total.

The Soviet Constitution describes the USSR Council of Ministers as the highest executive of the Soviet government, and lists the Council's executive powers as follows: coordination and direction of the work of the USSR ministries and organizations of ministerial rank; national economic planning; preparation of the USSR budget (which is a combined budget including all republic, regional, and local budgets); direction of the monetary and credit systems; control of all police; conduct of foreign relations; organization and direction of the armed forces; and the right to set up special committees or offices for economic matters, cultural affairs, or defense.

The foregoing constitutional powers of the Council of Ministers are more concrete and practical than the formal powers of the Supreme Soviet Presidium. And in practice, the Council of Ministers has the task of the day-by-day management of the USSR. A mere listing of the Council's ministries and organizations of ministerial rank indicates the immense scope of the Council's executive authority. These ministries are shown in Table 8.

In addition to this large number of offices of ministerial rank, the Council of Ministers directly controls a number of offices without ministerial rank. These offices have the same authority in their fields as a ministry, but the head of the office does not attend meetings of the Council of Ministers as a cabinet member. Such nonministerial offices are constantly being created and abolished, often without public announcement, so their exact number

Table 8. *Ministries of the USSR Council of Ministers*

	Industrial	
Electrification	Machine tool making	
Oil mining	Precision machinebuilding	
Oil refining	Automobile industry	
Gas industry	Agricultural machinebuilding	
Coal mining	Light industry machinebuilding	
Ferrous metallurgy	Wood industry	
Nonferrous metallurgy	Building materials industry	
Chemical industry	Light industry	
Heavy machinebuilding	Food industry	
Electrical engineering	Meat and dairy industry	
Chemical machinebuilding	Aircraft industry	
Transport construction	Defense industry	
Civilian construction	Radio industry	
Special construction	Electronics industry	
Medium machinebuilding	Shipbuilding	
Medical industry	Civil engineering	
Paper industry	Construction of oil and gas works	
Machinebuilding	Industrial construction	
Livestock machinebuilding	Rural construction	
General machinebuilding	Heavy industry construction	
Communications equipment	Electrical equipment	
	Other economic	
Agriculture	Internal trade	
Food procurement	Technical supply	
Farm machinery supply	Foreign trade	
Fishing	Foreign economic relations	
Forestry	State planning	
Finance	State construction	
State bank	Science	
Labor and pay	Geology	
Standards	Railways	
Inventions	Merchant marine	
Prices	Communications	
Statistics	Air transport	
Land reclamation		
	Political	
Higher education	Education	Public health
Justice	Technical education	People's Control
Television and radio	Culture	State Security
Cinematography	Internal affairs	Defense
TASS news agency	Publishing	Foreign affairs

Source: *Pravda,* 1974-1976.

and titles vary. Among them are the Committee for Physical Culture and Sport, the Council for Religions, the Administration for Foreign Tourism, and the Chief Administration for the Northern Sea Route.

In many respects the Soviet government and economy might be compared to a vast corporation, dwarfing in size the largest trusts and cartels of the capitalist world. Day-by-day management of this giant Soviet corporation is entrusted to the Council of Ministers of the USSR. The extreme importance of the USSR Council of Ministers is proven by the fact that top Soviet leaders have served as Premier: Lenin from 1917 to his death in 1924, Stalin from 1941 until his death in 1953, Khrushchev from 1958 till his removal in 1964, and Kosygin since 1964.

When the Bolsheviks first seized power in Russia, they believed the Marxist precept that law codes and a formal network of courts were bourgeois institutions unnecessary in a socialist state. Therefore, during the Russian Civil War no Soviet law code was compiled, and no elaborate court structure was established. Emergency decrees issued by the government and Communist Party served as laws. Civil disputes and ordinary criminals were tried by so-called People's Courts, which were simply groups of workers led by Communist Party members. More serious cases were processed by Revolutionary Tribunals set up by local governmental authorities. Meanwhile the Cheka police established their own tribunals to sentence anti-Communists and important criminals. Cheka courts were notorious for their cruelty, often sentencing people to death if there were mere suspicion that the defendant was anti-Soviet.

When internal peace came in 1921, and the New Economic Policy of mixed capitalism and socialism was established, the Soviet government realized that a formal law system was needed to ensure orderly administration. Communist lawyers compiled criminal, criminal procedural, civil, and civil procedural law codes for the Russian Soviet Republic. Other Soviet republics in the 1920's adopted copies of these codes, with slight variations from republic to republic to adjust to varying local conditions. From the 1920's to the 1950's many amendments were added to these republic codes to conform to changing circumstances. Such amendments were particularly numerous in the early 1930's to provide a legal background for economic planning, industrialization, and the collectivization of agriculture.

Meanwhile no law code for the entire USSR has yet been issued, though drafting of such a code began before the death of Stalin. As the republic law codes were adopted in the 1920's, a formal system of civil-criminal courts was established, and this system was further elaborated from the 1930's to the present. Today the regular court system consists of the People's, City, Regional (including territorial, autonomous republic, autonomous region, and national area courts), Soviet Republic, and the USSR Supreme Court.

The People's Court is the lowest, and is the court of original trial of ordinary civil and criminal cases. There is no jury. A panel of one judge and two assessors makes the decisions. The judge is elected for a five-year term by the voters of the court district. To assist him, 50 to 75 assessors are similarly elected for 2½-year terms, and in pairs serve ten days with the judge, somewhat like jurors in America. The judge, however, is a full-time court employee and with his superior knowledge and experience usually dominates the inexperienced assessors, who in theory could outvote him.

The judges and assessors of the city, regional, republic, and supreme courts are elected for five-year terms by the governmental soviet at the same level. Thus a republic court is elected by a republic soviet. These higher courts have more judges and fewer assessors, and the latter serve longer periods. Sometimes more than three judicial officials sit in judgment. In these higher courts, assessors serve only on cases of original jurisdiction. A case appealed from a lower court is tried by a panel consisting entirely of professional judges.

The city, regional, and republic courts have original jurisdiction on high-cost civil suits and for grave crimes. The USSR Supreme Court is normally a court of appeal, but has original jurisdiction over political crimes of national importance. For example, in 1953 former police minister Beria was sentenced to death for treason in a trial before the USSR Supreme Court.

Paralleling the system of courts is the network of procurators, or state attorneys. They are centralized under the USSR Procurator-General, who is elected for five years by the USSR Supreme Soviet. He appoints, or approves the appointment of, all lower procurators, who are independent from the republic, regional, or local governments of the court district in which they work. These procurators have the power of arrest, detention, and investigation, and serve as state attorneys in the courts.

By Western standards, the court system of the USSR is unfair to the individual citizen. Both the judges and assessors are elected in one-slate elections, in which all candidates must be approved by Communist Party officials. The law codes assert that the state is supreme over the individual, and all judges must make their decisions accordingly. There is no right of habeas corpus, and virtually no bail. A Soviet citizen can be arrested and held legally in prison for nine months, while his case is being investigated and before he is brought to trial. During investigation of his case, a defendant cannot see a defense attorney. Both are not shown the state evidence against the defendant until the day before his trial.

The defense attorney can only be hired from a lawyers' collegium, existing in every Soviet city. If the defendant can afford it, he pays for this lawyer. If not, the collegium furnishes him one without cost, since the collegium is subsidized by the state. The defense attorney is actually a state employee, who is ordered by law to keep the interests of the state uppermost in his practice. At times the defense attorney accuses the defendant in court instead of protecting him.

The trial itself has peculiarities by American standards. The judge can act like a prosecutor, questioning the defendant and witnesses. A judge can also refuse to hear witnesses, or he may order additional witnesses to be brought into court. Judges and assessors are ordered by the Soviet government to enforce the letter of the law, and not to use their own discretion. The USSR Supreme Court constantly instructs the lower courts whether to apply heavy or light penalties for various types of crimes. Furthermore, the defendant is presumed guilty until he proves his innocence.

If a defendant proves himself not guilty in a lower court, this may not end the case. For 16 years after the alleged crime, a higher court may reopen the case at its own discretion, retry the defendant, and reverse the decision of the lower court.

In practice the courts issue quick, rough, but just decisions on ordinary criminals, or in civil suits between two individuals of approximately equal rank. But an individual can rarely win a suit against a government enterprise or organization.

A political criminal is usually doomed to imprisonment before his trial begins. Most serious political cases are not tried in the regular civil-criminal courts. Instead, they are tried in the courts-martial, which exist in each military district, army group, corps, and division. These military courts usually operate in secret, and can impose death sentences on civilians convicted for treason, espionage, assassination of a Soviet official, sabotage, membership in an anti-Soviet organization, flight abroad, banditry, or premeditated murder. Assisting such courts is the network of military procurators appointed by the Chief Military Procurator of the USSR, who is subordinate to the Chief Procurator of the USSR.

Formerly most of the political criminals were tried by the police "Special Boards," which were officially abolished in 1953. However, the police troops probably still have their own courts-martial. Soviet press reports about the work of the USSR State Security Committee (political police ministry) indicate that the Committee may still have some power to process political criminals without going through the regular civil-criminal courts.

During the Khrushchev era the court system was enlarged by the formation of an extensive network of Comrades' Courts. These are formed in neighborhoods, places of work, schools, summer camps, and the like by the local people electing the panel of judges. A Comrades' Court has no formal procurator, and anyone from the neighborhood can attend and speak up. Petty cases are tried here, such as drunkenness, loafing, public misbehavior, prostitution, minor theft, or household quarrels. Any Soviet citizen can make a complaint to a Comrades' Court, which then decides whether to take action. The court usually warns offenders, or subjects them to public ridicule. However, a Comrades' Court has the power to exile a parasite from his or her home city or village for several years. A parasite is defined as a person who refuses to work, or who lives on income from such illegal activities as begging, gambling, black-marketing, or prostitution.

Apparently the Comrades' Courts have been successful. Today

the USSR has 200,000 of these informal courts, which try one fifth of all criminal cases in the Soviet Union.

Another network of special courts is economic. This is the hierarchy of arbitration boards headed by a USSR arbitration office, with branches in every region and some large cities. These commercial courts judge violations of contracts between state enterprises and organizations buying and selling from each other. Such violations (failure to deliver goods, late delivery, failure to pay for deliveries, delivery of substandard goods) are so numerous that these special courts were devised to settle such disputes. There is even a court to arbitrate disputes between the Soviet government and foreign companies over foreign trade. In general, the arbitration courts are primarily interested not in who is technically right or wrong, but who is responsible for slowing the flow of goods throughout the USSR. Whoever slows the freight traffic is considered guilty.

Superior to these civil-criminal, military, and arbitration courts, and supervising all of them, is the USSR Supreme Court with approximately 50 judges and assessors. This supreme judicial body is divided into three collegia: civil, criminal, and military. The military collegium is the highest court martial in the USSR, and in the 1930's and 1950's held the show or secret trials condemning leaders to death on charges of alleged treason. The Supreme Court is a judicial body with great prestige. However, it has no power of judicial review and is not independent.

The hierarchy of Soviet courts and procurators is shown in Table 9:

Table 9. *The Soviet Judicial Structure*

	USSR Supreme Court	
Regular Courts	*Military Courts*	*Arbitration Courts*
Soviet republic	Military district	USSR
Regional	Army group	Foreign trade
City	Corps	Regional
People's	Division	City
Comrades'		

Table 9 (*cont.*)

	USSR Chief Procurator
Civilian Procurators	*Military Procurators*
Soviet republic	USSR Chief Military Procurator
Regional	Military district
District	Army group
City	Corps
	Division

In 1958 during the Khrushchev era the Soviet government issued new "Principles of Criminal Legislation in the USSR" and "Principles of Criminal Procedure of the USSR." Similar principles for civil law were published in 1961. Thereafter, all the Soviet republics adopted new law codes based on these USSR principles.

The new republic criminal codes are milder than the old codes they superseded. By inference, "analogy" is abolished. This was a procedure used since 1917 whereby a mild crime (or even an action not legally defined as a crime) could be judged by a court as analogous to a serious crime. The criminal could receive the same severe sentence for the analogous crime as for the serious one.

Other features of the new republic codes are that future laws, which make an act punishable or increase the penalty, shall no longer have retroactive force. The minimum age for criminal responsibility of children is raised from 12 to 14. The maximum prison sentence is reduced from the former 25 years to 15. Sentences for many specific crimes have also been decreased.

Yet the new republic criminal codes are still much harsher than the laws of Western democracies. And law codes are meaningless as protection to a citizen, unless a government sincerely honors them. In Western democracies the governments are fairly honest in enforcing laws. But many legal rights have been issued to Soviet citizens in the past, and have been temporary or have remained a dead letter. Time will tell if the new Soviet republic codes will bring greater legal protection to the average USSR citizen.

Suggestions for Further Reading

BERMAN, HAROLD J., ed., *Soviet Criminal Law and Procedure*. Cambridge: Harvard University Press, 1972.

CONNOR, WALTER D., *Deviance in Soviet Society: Crime, Delinquency and Alcoholism*. New York: Columbia University Press, 1972.

CORNELL, RICHARD, ed., *The Soviet Political System*. Englewood Cliffs: Prentice-Hall, 1970.

FLERON, FREDERIC J., ed., *Communist Studies and the Social Sciences*. Chicago: Rand McNally, 1969.

HAYWARD, MAX, ed., *On Trial*, New York: Harper, 1966.

MORGAN, GLENN G., *Soviet Administrative Legality: The Role of the Attorney General's Office*, Stanford: Stanford University Press, 1962.

MOTE, MAX E., *Soviet Local and Republic Elections*, Stanford: Stanford University Press, 1966.

OSBORN, ROBERT J., *The Evolution of Soviet Politics*. Homewood: Dorsey, 1974.

RESHETAR, JOHN S., *The Soviet Polity*. New York: Dodd, Mead, 1971.

Chapter 14

The Racial Federation

One of the problems of the Soviet government is that it rules the most multi-national country in the world. The USSR contains a total of 177 nationalities, speaking 80 different languages. Of course, most of these nationalities are very small. But about 20 nationalities number more than a million apiece.

According to the latest USSR census, only 54 per cent of the 257.9 million people in the Soviet Union are Great Russians. The average Great Russian is a blue-eyed blond with a round face and soft features. The next largest nationality is the Ukrainian, which composes 17 per cent of the Soviet population. Most Ukrainians are tall, brunette, and strongly built. Four per cent of the population consists of Belorussians, who are blonds very similar in appearance to the Great Russians.

In ancient times the Russians, Belorussians, and Ukrainians were all one Indo-European nationality living in Russia's western borderlands. During the Middle Ages the Great Russians moved to the large northern forests, which gave them some protection from incessant invasions by Mongoloid tribes from Asia. The Belorussians sought similar protection in the vast marshlands along the Polish border. But the Ukrainians remained on the southern treeless steppes, and were conquered by wave after wave of invaders. Through the centuries the Russians, Ukrainians, and Belorussians developed different languages and cultures. Together these three East Slavic nationalities constitute 75 per cent of the Soviet population.

Another 9 per cent of the population consists of a variety of Caucasian nationalities. Many live in the western borderlands, such as the Indo-European Moldavians, Poles, Latvians, and Lithuanians. Large numbers of Jews fleeing German persecution immigrated into the same area during the Middle Ages. During the eighteenth century Empress Catherine the Great invited many Germans to settle in Russia, mostly in the Volga valley. In the Caucasus Mountains live the two unique nationalities of Armenians and Georgians, who may be descendants of the ancient Hittites. Though highly cultured, the Armenians and Georgians are proud, fierce, and not easy to control.

Added to the East Slavs, all these nationalities constitute 84 per cent of the Soviet population belonging to the category of Caucasian race. The remaining 16 per cent is Mongoloid and is divided into three major groups:

1. The Eskimo-type tribes, who inhabit the Soviet Arctic, are of Finnish stock. Those in East Siberia have many customs in common with the American Indians. Apparently the Indians migrated in prehistoric times from Siberia into Alaska, then drifted south throughout the western hemisphere.

2. A much larger and more important group than the Soviet Finns are the USSR Mongols—twentieth-century descendants of the medieval hordes of Genghis Khan. They are scattered through a broad belt of territory stretching from the Volga valley thousands of miles across north Central Asia into East Siberia.

3. The third large Mongoloid group is the Turks, who live mainly in the Caucasus and south Central Asia. The Mongols look much like the Chinese. In contrast, the Turks are darker in color but possess European features. These Mongoloid nationalities usually bear ancient Oriental names such as the Mongol Tatars, Kazaks, and Kalmyks, or the Turkish Uzbeks, Turkmens, and Kirgiz.

One might presume that Russia, like America, would be a "melting pot" of many nations. In practice, interracial marriage occurs somewhat in Soviet cities, but is almost unknown in the countryside. Most nationalities live in their ancestral homelands, cling to ancestral traditions, and regard other nationalities as inferior foreigners. Marriage is even uncommon between Russians and Ukrainians, though both were originally one nationality.

During the last century of Tsarist rule, the Russian imperial government pursued a policy of Russification of national minorities. For example, the Ukraine was forbidden for about one hundred years to construct buildings in Ukrainian architectural style. Most national minorities suffered varying degrees of Tsarist Russian oppression, ranging from the relatively liberal treatment of the Germans and Finns to extreme brutality against Poles and Jews.

The vast majority of rank-and-file members in Lenin's prerevolutionary Bolshevik party were Russians. A number of Bolshevik leaders were from national minorities, such as Lenin who was Mongol-German, Stalin who was Georgian, and Kamenev, Zinoviev, and Trotsky who were Jewish. But such men were highly Russified and did not support the anti-Russian sentiments of their own nationalities. Under such circumstances, national minorities could easily consider Bolshevism as a Russian rather than socialist movement. For example, the Ukrainian Bolshevik party first consisted almost entirely of Russians who were residing in the Ukraine.

Therefore, before the Bolshevik Revolution, Lenin asked Stalin to draft a socialist racial program which would appeal to Russia's national minorities. Stalin was given the assignment because he was a member of a national minority and had spent his youth in the multinational Caucasus. At the time both Bolshevik leaders opposed the creation of a federal Communist state based on racial areas. It was believed that a racial federation would simply accentuate ethnic differences.

Stalin's plan was embodied in the "Declaration of Nationalities" issued by the Soviet government during its second week of power. The Declaration promised complete equality to all nationalities in Russia and granted cultural autonomy to each. It also stated that any national minority could secede from Russia if the minority so desired.

The Soviet government thought that no national minority would secede, since the Bolshevik offer of complete equality and cultural autonomy was so generous. In fact, however, a wave of racial secessions occurred during 1918–1920. Finland, Estonia, Latvia, Lithuania, Poland, Belorussia, the Ukraine, Georgia, Armenia, Azerbaidzhan, and all Central Asia attempted to secede on an ethnic basis. Politically Lenin and Stalin opposed such secession, because socialism would be confined only to the Russian-inhabited areas of Russia. Economically the Russian domain is a unit. If such vast regions as the Ukraine with its grain, coal, and iron, the Caucasus with its oil, and Central Asia with its cotton were lost, Soviet Russia would have been economically crippled.

Therefore the Red Army was ordered to reconquer the seceding nationalities by force. Finland, Estonia, Latvia, Lithuania, and Poland managed to defend their freedom and achieved independence. Belorussia, the Ukraine, Georgia, Armenia, Azerbaidzhan, and Central Asia were reconquered by 1920 and brought under Communist rule.

During 1918–1920, Lenin and Stalin made an agonizing reappraisal of their racial policy. When major seceding nationalities were reconquered, Soviet Republics were created for them. The title of "republic" eased the humiliation of being reconquered. Thus the Ukraine became the Ukrainian Soviet Socialist Republic, and Belorussia, the Belorussian Soviet Socialist Republic. Georgia, Armenia, and Azerbaidzhan were combined into the Trans-Caucasian Soviet Socialist Republic. These three republics were then linked to the Russian Soviet Federated Socialist Republic by close military and economic alliances. Lenin and Stalin thus formed the racial confederation they had previously condemned.

After a Georgian independence movement was crushed by the Red Army in 1921, Lenin and Stalin decided that the confederation of four Soviet republics was too loose. So from 1922 to 1924, the four were united into a federation—the Union of Soviet Socialist Republics (USSR). Nationalities of lesser importance than the Russians, Ukrainians, Belorussians, and Caucasians were also honored by giving their regions the status of autonomous soviet socialist republic (ASSR), autonomous region (AR), or national area (NA). These lesser racial units were always part of one or another of the Soviet socialist republics (SSR's).

During the late 1920's and mid-1930's, several national minorities were elevated to Soviet republic status. Central Asia, which originally was an autonomous republic within the Russian SFSR, eventually was divided into five Soviet republics: Kazakhstan (Mongol), Tadzhikistan (Iranian), and Kirgizia, Turkmenia, and Uzbekistan (all Turkish). The Trans-Caucasian Soviet Republic was split into three Soviet republics: Armenia, Georgia, and Azerbaidzhan.

In 1940 the USSR annexed Bessarabia, Estonia, Latvia, Lithuania, and parts of Finland. Southern Bessarabia was incorporated in the Ukraine, but the remainder was merged with the former Moldavian autonomous republic to form the Moldavian SSR. Estonia, Latvia, and Lithuania also became Soviet republics. The Karelian autonomous republic and the former Finnish territories were combined into the Karelo-Finnish Soviet Socialist Republic, which after the death of Stalin was converted into the Karelian autonomous republic of the Russian SFSR.

As a result of all these territorial alterations, the USSR today has 15 Soviet republics, whose areas and 1974 populations are shown in Table 10:

Table 10. *Areas and Populations of the Soviet Republics of the USSR*

Soviet Republic	Area (sq. mi.)	Population (1974 est.)
Russian SFSR	6,600,000	132,913,000
Ukrainian SSR	240,000	48,521,000
Kazakh SSR	1,050,000	13,978,000
Uzbek SSR	156,000	13,289,000
Belorussian SSR	80,000	9,268,000
Azerbaidzhan SSR	33,000	5,514,000
Georgian SSR	30,000	4,878,000
Moldavian SSR	13,000	3,764,000
Tadzhik SSR	55,000	3,283,000
Lithuanian SSR	25,000	3,262,000
Kirgiz SSR	77,000	3,219,000
Armenian SSR	12,000	2,728,000
Latvian SSR	25,000	2,454,000
Turkmen SSR	187,000	2,430,000
Estonian SSR	17,000	1,418,000
Total	8,600,000	250,919,000

Source: *Yearbook of the Great Soviet Encyclopedia,* Moscow, 1975.

At present the USSR also contains 20 autonomous republics, 8 autonomous regions, and 10 national areas. These minor racial areas, and the Soviet republics in which they are located, are listed in Table 11:

Table 11. *Racial Administrative Areas of the USSR*

Soviet Republic	Autonomous Republic	Autonomous Region	National Area
Russian	Bashkir	Adygei	Agin-Buriat
	Buriat	Gorno-Altai	Komi-Perm
	Dagestan	Jewish	Koriak
	Kabardino-Balkar	Karachaevo-Cherkess	Nenets
	Kalmyk	Khakass	Taimyr
	Karelian		Ust-Orda-Buriat
	Komi		Khanty-Mansi
	Mari		Chukot
	Mordva		Evenki
	North Oset		Yamalo-Nenets
	Tatar		
	Udmurt		
	Checheno-Ingush		
	Chuvash		
	Yakutsk		
	Tuva		
Uzbek	Kara-Kalpak		
Georgian	Abkhaz	South Oset	
	Adzhar		
Azerbaidzhan	Nakhichevan	Nagorno-Karabakh	
Tadzhik		Gorno-Badakhshan	

There is no set rule determining whether a Soviet nationality receives the status of Soviet republic, autonomous republic, autonomous region, or national area. Density of an ethnic group in a single area, location, historic background, and political loyalty all appear to be pertinent factors. Sheer size alone does not automatically entitle a nationality to a Soviet republic. The Tatars are the fifth largest ethnic group in the USSR but have no Soviet republic. Instead they are dispersed in several autonomous republics. The Estonians, with a Soviet republic, are outnumbered by the Finnish Mordvians, who have a mere autonomous republic. Such inconsistencies are found throughout the USSR.

Nationalities can be a minority in their home area, yet receive the status of Soviet republic, autonomous republic, autonomous region, or national area. Russians outnumber Kazaks in the population of the Kazakh Soviet Republic. Jews constitute only one tenth of the population of the Jewish Autonomous Region.

What does the status of Soviet republic, autonomous republic, autonomous region, or national area mean? In theory each Soviet republic is autonomous in both government and culture. In practice the political autonomy is virtually nonexistent. In fact, a Soviet republic has less authority than a state of the USA. New York State, and even New York City, can levy and collect some of its own taxes. No Soviet republic has this power. Instead it depends for funds on subsidies from the USSR central budget.

Careful examination of the USSR Constitution reveals much of the pattern of Soviet power. Article 72 provides for centralization of power in the USSR federal government, which is given authority over war and peace, admission of new republics into the USSR, defense, foreign trade, all police, economic planning, all taxation, all banks, much of industry and agriculture, all transport and telecommunications, money and credit, all insurance, all borrowing and granting of loans, land, minerals, waters, forests, education, public health, statistics, labor, courts and law codes, citizenship, marriage and family law, and amnesty. The Constitution indicates that the USSR is not a true federation, since the central government legally assumes all important governmental powers, leaving nothing of consequence to the competence of the 15 Soviet republics. Actually a republic government is a regional agency carrying out orders issued from Moscow. In turn the lesser racial units (autonomous republic, autonomous region and national area) simply fulfill Soviet republic orders.

Each of the four types of racial areas has the right to use its own language as its official language. To some extent, the native culture is also encouraged. In the Ukrainian Soviet Republic, for example, buildings can be designed in Ukrainian architectural style (Mazeppa baroque), newspapers and books are published in the Ukrainian language, and theaters produce plays, ballets, and operas on Ukrainian themes. Ukrainian folk dances, music, painting, and sculpture are fostered.

But this cultural autonomy is limited. Much of the old and new Ukrainian literature is forbidden to be published, because it demands freedom of the Ukraine from Russian rule. Ultranationalistic books, plays, operas, dances, music, and graphic art are suppressed in all non-Russian republics. The national anthem of Armenia, a musical appeal for Armenian liberty, cannot be sung publicly within the USSR.

Article 71 of the USSR Constitution gives each Soviet republic the right to secede from the USSR, but the autonomous republics, autonomous regions, and national areas have no such constitutional right. In practice no Soviet republic has been permitted to secede since the USSR was formed in 1922. During the Soviet-German War of 1941–1945, the Soviet republics of Estonia, Latvia, Lithuania, and the Ukraine all separately rebelled against Soviet rule. Late in the war the Red Army reconquered all four seceding republics, and reannexed them to the USSR.

Stalin, who was the Soviet official mainly responsible for formulating the racial policy of the USSR, justified the lack of freedom for racial minorities in his official history of the USSR Communist Party, which for many years was a textbook studied in all Soviet high schools and colleges. Today new revised editions of this textbook have been published, which however leave the following racial philosophy unchanged:

> The right of nations freely to secede must not be confused with the expediency of secession of a given nationality at a given moment. The party of the proletariat must decide the latter question quite independently in each particular case. . . .
>
> The party of the proletariat resolutely rejects what is known as "national cultural autonomy," under which education, etc., is removed from the competence of the state and placed within the competence of some kind of national diets. National cultural autonomy artificially divides the workers living in one locality, and even workers in the same industrial enterprise according to their various "national cultures." . . .
>
> The interests of the working class demand that the workers of all the nationalities of Russia should have common proletarian

> organizations: political, trade union, educational institutions of the cooperatives, and so forth. Only such common organizations of the workers of the various nationalities will make it possible for the proletariat to wage a successful struggle against international capital and bourgeois nationalism.[1]

Racial minorities are promoted, demoted, or punished according to their loyalty to the Soviet regime. In the early years of Soviet power, many Chinese and Koreans lived in the Soviet Far East. Mostly these were immigrants migrating northward in search of better living conditions and higher wages. Today their descendants reside in Soviet Central Asia, to which both nationalities were deported during the late 1930's. The official excuse for this deportation was that the Japanese militarists, who then controlled Korea and Manchuria, might use the Chinese and Koreans as spies and saboteurs. Thus far neither the Chinese nor the Koreans have ever been permitted to have a racial administrative region, though the Koreans today number more than 300,000 persons.

Five autonomous republics and one autonomous region in the lower Volga valley, north Caucasus, and Crimean peninsula were abolished during the Soviet-German war of 1941–1945 because their nationalities allegedly collaborated with the invading Germans. Their populations were sent inland to Central Asia and Siberia. After Stalin's death, four of these minor racial areas were restored, and the native populations were invited to return. But two autonomous republics, the Volga German and Crimean Tatar, have not been reconstituted and their former populations remain deportees.

The Jewish Autonomous Region was created in East Siberia during the 1930's, abolished in the 1940's after the Nazi-Soviet War, then restored in the 1950's following the death of Stalin.

These are some of the examples of punishment by nationality in past Soviet history. Quite often some racial minorities were favored or punished. The punishment was not always announced in Soviet publications available to Western readers. But a new

---

1 Stalin, Joseph, *History of the Communist Party of the Soviet Union, Short Course,* Moscow: Foreign Languages Publishing House, 1939, pp. 190–191.

USSR official map will reveal that a former autonomous republic, autonomous region, or national area was missing.

The Soviet press complains frequently about anti-Russian sentiments among the racial minorities of the USSR. The majority of complaints are against intellectuals, students, and artists; but occasionally even government and Communist Party officials are implicated.

On a lengthy tour through various Soviet republics, a Western traveler may catch glimpses of this anti-Russianism. For example, on a recent tour of the USSR, I found that most people in Ukrainian cities speak Russian. But even Intourist guides explained that the peasants in the countryside usually refuse to speak anything but Ukrainian. If addressed in Russian, the peasants understand but reply in their own language.

During the same tour I visited Soviet Central Asia. There most cities have a mixed population of Russians and natives. In the streets, parks, and restaurants, the Russians and Asians rarely mix. Groups of Russians stroll down streets, followed by groups of Asians. In the hotel dining rooms one table is filled with Russians, another with Asians, and so forth throughout the hall. Few married couples are seen who cross the color line between Russian and Central Asian.

A Russian in the Kazakh Soviet Republic remarked tersely: "We Russians get along very well with the Kazakh city intellectuals, but the Kazakh peasants hate us. They regard us as foreign conquerors." Later as my Intourist guide and I walked through a park, we passed a group of Kazakh men on a park bench. We heard one aged Kazak complain: "Our Kazakh nation has been suffering under Russian rule for an entire century." The guide pretended not to hear, and hurried me away.

Many Soviet army and police troops are visible in and around Central Asian cities. Most of these troops are Russian, Ukrainian, or other Soviet Europeans. Even the white-coated, black-trousered, and brown-booted police patrolmen on the streets are mainly Europeans. Of course, the Central Asians are conscripted into the Soviet armed forces. But most serve their military duty in Siberia or European USSR. Few are stationed in their homeland of Central Asia, where they might be tempted to start or join Asian revolt.

In the 1930's the USSR armed forces contained some troop divisions organized by nationality. During the Soviet-German War a number of these divisions turned traitor and joined the invading German army. This changing of sides was particularly prevalent among divisions from Central Asia and the Caucasus. Today the Soviet army contains no divisions entirely composed of a national minority. Soldiers of minority race are scattered through predominantly Russian troop units.

Obviously if the national minorities of the USSR cannot be trusted as racial troop units within the Soviet armed forces, the anti-Russian sentiments of USSR minority races are very real. What is the cause of such racial hatred?

Perhaps one explanation is the domination of the huge Russian republic over all other Soviet republics of the USSR. The Russian Republic extends over all Siberia and four fifths of European USSR. This republic alone contains four fifths of the area, three fifths of the farmland, and two thirds of the industry of the entire Soviet Union. The five Soviet republics of Central Asia have only 7 per cent of all Soviet industry, the three Caucasian republics, 3 per cent, and the five republics in the western frontier areas, about 6 per cent. Great Russians compose four fifths of the population of the Russian Soviet Republic.

Another reason for anti-Russianism in the USSR may be the job discrimination in favor of Great Russians. Apparently in high-level employment the Russians come first, then other Caucasian nationalities, with the Mongoloid peoples trailing far behind.

Let us examine Soviet job-holding, with particular reference to Asians. Several hundred marshals, generals, and admirals govern the regular armed forces, 4.4 million strong, into which all Soviet nationalities are conscripted. According to data in the Soviet press, almost none of these top military men are Asians. The majority are Russians, plus a substantial number of Ukrainians and Poles. The remainder are mainly Armenians, Georgians, and other Europeans. Turks and Mongols are drafted into the armed forces, but it's almost impossible for them to rise to high military rank.

Among civilian officials, factory directors are very important. Of the 200,000 managers of factories and mines in the Soviet Union today, the vast majority are Russian. A large minority is

Ukrainian. Persons from other Caucasian nationalities compose most of the remainder. Hardly any are Asian.

Much the same racial imbalance prevails in the top organs of the Soviet leadership. There are many Asians in the USSR Supreme Soviet, which theoretically is the highest government parliament. But in practice this legislature is a largely ceremonial body. The real center of Soviet government is the USSR Council of Ministers (cabinet), which is both chief legislature and chief executive. During the first three decades of Soviet history no Asian was permitted to join this cabinet. The first Oriental was admitted shortly before Stalin's death, and was soon dismissed. Today there are several Asians, most of whom however are ex-officio members who apparently do not regularly attend cabinet meetings.

No Asian was permitted to become a member of the Politburo or party Presidium until Stalin died, 36 years after the Communist seizure of power. Today three Asians have been recruited into the Politburo, most of whose 20-odd members are Russians and other Europeans.

The president and premier of each Soviet republic in Central Asia are Asians, but their chief assistants are usually Russians. The same system prevails at the regional level. This is much like the Tsarist era, when each Turkic prince was supposedly assisted but was actually governed by a Russian advisor.

In the non-Russian republics of the USSR, much of the technical work is performed by Russians. The huge Ukrainian industry, which produces about one fifth of all Soviet industrial output, is largely managed and staffed by Russian engineers and workers. There are large Russian colonies in Ukrainian cities, while the surrounding countryside is almost entirely Ukrainian. Many Russians or other Soviet Europeans have been imported into Central Asia as teachers, lawyers, doctors, engineers, and factory managers. Intourist once gave me a guidebook for Tashkent, the capital of the Uzbek Soviet Republic in Central Asia. The producers of this book are listed as: a Ukrainian chief editor; Russian and Ukrainian technical editors; and Russian and Jewish photographers. Only one Uzbek, a photographer, appears in the long credit list at the back of the guidebook.

Russian colonization of the non-Russian Soviet Republics of

the USSR by now is very great. At least half the population of Tashkent is Russian, according to Intourist guides. According to the latest Soviet census, the Kazakh Soviet Republic in northern Central Asia contains more Russians than Kazaks, while the Kirgiz are outnumbered in their Soviet republic by non-Kirgiz nationalities. Soviet press reports indicate Kazakh and Kirgiz resentment against being minorities in their homelands. Even in the Ukrainian Soviet Republic about one sixth of the population is Russian.

The Tsars, particularly in their last 100 years of power, tried to Russify their empire's national minorities under the slogan: "one language (Russian), one religion (Russian Orthodox), and one Tsar." In the 1920's early Soviet Russia maintained tight political control over the national minorities but avoided strong Russification. Since the mid-1930's, however the Soviet government has actively pursued Russification along with socialization. Today all national minorities in the USSR are forced to learn the Russian language. Again there is one religion—Communism, and one Tsar—the Communist leadership.

The present Russification assumes many forms, some of which are quite subtle. Histories of racial minorities must describe past conquest by Tsarist Russia as being advantageous to the minority race, which thus obtained the benefits of Russian superior culture and civilization. Soviet Russian literature is widely translated into the minority languages. Grade and high schools in the minority regions are divided into those where the teaching is in Russian, and others where most courses are taught in the native language. But colleges and universities throughout the USSR teach almost entirely in Russian. So if a Ukrainian, Georgian, Mongol, or Turkish child hopes to enter college, he usually attends the Russian-language grade and high schools.

Involuntarily the racial minorities of the USSR harm their own chances for autonomy or independence by their stubborn national pride. The national minorities usually dislike each other, and have never united against either Tsarist or Soviet Russian rule. For example, the world-famous novel *And Quiet Flows the Don* by Soviet author Mikhail A. Sholokhov vividly describes the gangfights between the Don Cossacks, who are a mixed nationality originally formed by refugees from Tsarist Russia, and the Ukrainian peasants moving into Don Cossack territory.

In addition, each national minority is usually divided within itself. Perhaps the majority are anti-Russian, but a minority join forces with the Soviet Russians. There is considerable truth in the old Soviet joke that the Red Army is loyally led by many marshals who are Ukrainians and Poles. At present Politburo member Kunayev is a Mongol, Vice-President Mazurov is Belorussian, while the aged Politburo member Pelshe is Latvian. Such examples have occurred throughout Soviet history.

An interesting group are the minority-nationality people who are anti-Communist but pro-Russian. Usually these are professors, engineers, artists, or other intellectuals. While living and traveling in the USSR I have encountered Germans who were anti-German, Ukrainians who insisted they were Russians, Armenians with no racial consciousness, and Jews who ridiculed Israel. Yet these same people would speak against the Soviet regime.

Especially dangerous for the Kremlin are the minority leaders who are devout Communists, but wish their homeland to become autonomous or independent. The Soviet government has purged these "national Communists" again and again in all non-Russian Soviet republics. Particularly widespread purges of national Communists occurred in the late 1920's, the early and late 1930's, after World War II, and following Stalin's death.

Complicating an already complex picture, the first three top Soviet leaders came from Russia's minorities. Lenin had a Volga German mother and a father who was either a Mongol Kalmyk or possessed mixed Russian-Kalmyk blood. Stalin was Georgian. Khrushchev apparently was a Russified Ukrainian, whose original family name—before Russification—was "Khrush." Yet all three were as pro-Russian as a Great Russian.

The Brezhnev regime has consistently fulfilled and confirmed the nationality policy of Russification of minorities, as set forth in the 20-year Communist Party Program adopted in the Krushchev period. This program states:

> The boundaries between the constituent republics of the USSR are increasingly losing their former significance. . . .
>
> An international culture common to all the Soviet nations is developing. . . .

The Russian language has, in effect, become the common medium of intercourse and cooperation between all the peoples of the USSR. . . .

The liquidation of manifestations of nationalism is in the interests of all nations and nationalities of the USSR. Every Soviet republic can continue to flourish and strengthen only in the great family of fraternal Socialist nations of the USSR.

Suggestions for Further Reading

ALLWORTH, EDWARD, *Central Asia: A Century of Russian Rule,* New York: Columbia University Press, 1966.

ARMSTRONG, JOHN A., *Ukrainian Nationalism, 1939–1945,* New York: Columbia University Press, 1955.

GOLDHAGEN, ERICH, ed., *Ethnic Minorities in the Soviet Union.* New York: Praeger, 1968.

KOREY, WILLIAM, *The Soviet Cage: Anti-Semitism in Russia.* New York: Viking, 1973.

LANG, D. M., *A Modern History of Soviet Georgia,* New York: Grove, 1962.

RESHETAR, JOHN S., *The Ukrainian Revolution, 1917–1920,* Princeton: Princeton University Press, 1952.

SULLIVANT, ROBERT S., *Soviet Politics and the Ukraine,* New York: Columbia University Press, 1963.

TARULIS, ALBERTAS, *Soviet Policy Toward the Baltic States.* Notre Dame: Notre Dame University Press, 1959.

VAKAR, NICHOLAS P., *Belorussia,* Cambridge: Harvard University Press, 1956.

VARDYS, V. STANLEY, ed., *Lithuania under the Soviets,* New York: Praeger, 1965.

WHEELER, GEOFFREY, *Racial Problems in Soviet Muslim Asia,* New York: Oxford University Press, 1960.

Chapter 15

The Secret Police

When Lenin first seized power in 1917, he opposed the formation of a secret police, since he considered it to be one of the worst features of Tsarist autocracy. However on December 20, 1917, the new Soviet government soon organized its own secret police, the so-called Cheka (Extraordinary Commission to Combat Counter-Revolution), which originally was intended to be a palace guard to protect Soviet leaders. During the Russian Civil War of 1918–1920, the palace guard expanded to become a huge organization suppressing the many cases of treason behind the Red Army lines. Once the Red Army had occupied an enemy city, the Cheka would enter to arrest, imprison, or execute all real or potential leaders of anti-Communist resistance. At this time the Cheka was officially proclaimed to be a temporary wartime institution.

Despite Soviet official promises, the Cheka continued to exist after the civil war. The excuse for its continuation was that Soviet Russia was surrounded by a ring of hostile capitalist states, which encouraged espionage and sabotage in all walks of Soviet life. In 1922 the Cheka was renamed as GPU (State Political Administration), and in 1923 as OGPU (General State Political Administration) when Soviet Russia forced other Soviet republics to form the USSR. During 1934 at the start of the great Stalinist purges, the OGPU was elevated to ministerial rank and renamed as NKVD (People's Commissarist for Internal Affairs). On the eve of the Soviet-German War the NKVD was divided into two Commissariats: Internal Affairs (NKVD), and State Security (NKGB). When war began the Commissariats were abruptly merged, only to be split again after the war ended, and renamed as MVD (Ministry of Internal Affairs) and MGB (Ministry of State Security). After Stalin's death in 1953 the two ministries merged again under the name of MVD, but this ministry was divided anew in 1954 into MVD and KGB (Committee for State Security). During 1960 the USSR MVD was abolished, but MVD ministries continued at the Soviet republic level. In 1962 these republic MVD's were renamed as MOOP's (Ministries for Defense of Public Order), then in 1966 recentralized under a USSR MOOP, with all MOOP's resuming the name of MVD in 1968.

The precise division of authority between the KGB and MVD is not fully publicized by the Soviet government. Like other branches of Soviet administration the police ministries are constantly being reorganized, and various functions may be shifted back and forth between them. We must therefore rely mainly for information on Soviet police officials who defect to the West, and their data is up-to-date only at the time of their defection. Thus the following description of the police ministries must be considered approximate:

The ordinary police, called the militia, are part of MVD. Most of the militia work is nonpolitical such as directing traffic, patrolling streets and highways, and apprehending ordinary criminals. However, the militia becomes semipolitical by also controlling the internal passport system of the USSR. From the age of 16, the average urban Soviet citizen must possess an internal passport listing his or her full name, age, race, residence, occupation, and place of employment. (Collective farmers have similar identity papers which are membership cards in a collective farm.) The militia issues the city passports, and punishes those who lose them. In order to reside in a city, a Soviet citizen's passport must be registered with the nearest office of the local militia. Even if a Soviet citizen merely visits a city overnight, the militia is supposed to check his passport. Thus the MVD militia keep a continuous record of the whereabouts of most urbanites in the USSR.

If a Russian house catches on fire, police firemen come to the rescue, since the fire departments of the USSR are operated by

MVD. In the past other unusual functions were also conducted by the police, apparently because of its efficiency. Before World War II the police maintained USSR highways, and from the war till 1961 the MVD was in charge of civil defense.

Throughout the USSR one sees police guards standing with their guns at the gate of every big factory, warehouse, and construction site. These are the MVD industrial police. They and their families receive the same educational, housing, and tax benefits as members of the Soviet regular army. But along with army benefits comes military punishment. If a factory guard falls asleep on duty, or leaves his post unguarded, he receives the same punishment as an army sentry. Sometimes the industrial police are armed with revolvers, but often they carry rifles and bayonets. At night they may patrol with huge dogs who can scent an unseen intruder.

Inside the first factory I visited during a trip through Russia, was an office whose door was made of unusually thick wood, padded around the edges with heavy felt. Over this door hung the sign "Secret Section." This was an office of the MVD economic police, who are stationed inside every large factory, mine, warehouse, or other nonagricultural economic enterprise in the USSR. In contrast to the industrial police who are watchmen for the yard and outside walls, the economic police protect an economic enterprise from inside sabotage. This particular plant I visited was a famous candy factory, many of whose chocolates were sold to the Soviet army and to special stores for high officials. Hence the economic police are there to prevent poisoning of the candy.

MVD also operates the vast network of prison labor camps which exist throughout the USSR. There now are seven types of prison camps, which since Stalin's death have been entitled corrective-labor colonies. Three kinds of penal colonies exist for youths. For boys there are two types of colonies, one mild and the other severe. Girls are imprisoned in a third type of camp. Adults of both sexes are imprisoned in four additional types of colonies: colonies of general regime for mild criminals with short sentences, colonies of strong regime for criminals with medium sentences, colonies with strict regime for hardened criminals who have been previously imprisoned, and colonies of special regime for dangerous repeater criminals.

MVD also operates the Soviet prisons, which are mainly used to hold persons under investigation or those awaiting trial. Once a criminal has been sentenced, he or she is usually sent to a corrective-labor colony. Some court sentences provide that part of the imprisonment be spent in a prison and part in a colony. Occasionally a person misbehaving in a colony is transferred into a prison.

Apparently the majority of prisoners in the corrective-labor colonies are political criminals. Most of these are probably in the colonies with strong, strict, or special regimes, since political offenders normally receive longer sentences than ordinary criminals. The colonies with special regimes are considered death camps, and are usually located in the Arctic, Central Asian desert, or some other area with a drastic climate. For example, a Soviet refugee has described to me how he spent seven years in Central Asian prison camps. He was among 300 prisoners who were sent into the mountains near Tashkent to dig mines at Angren. Because of the altitude, the climate was frigid. When they first arrived there were no barracks, only a snowy field. They had to build the camp themselves, with almost no tools. In one year 294 of the original prisoners were dead. The survivors were the camp tailor, shoemaker, storekeeper, chauffeur, and cooks. My informant was the camp tailor, and only this light work saved his life.

Corrective-labor colonies are the most unpleasant aspects of Soviet scenery. During a recent trip through the USSR I saw several, usually in city outskirts. Outside Moscow there was a large colony surrounded by a high stone wall topped with barbed-wire stanchions slanting inward. Guards with rifles were posted in several high wooden watchtowers, which rose far above the walls. I had a good look at some prisoners who had been brought outside to repair the camp wall. They were middle-aged men dressed no worse than a peasant. But their arms and legs moved slowly and awkwardly as if they were old men. Obviously they were tired and lacked spirit.

Many colonies treat the prisoners like coolies. Regardless of his previous occupation or state of health, the prisoner is often required to perform hard physical labor. Professors, artists, and office clerks cut down trees, mine coal, and drain swamps. Many have no strength for such work, and die from exhaustion. The Soviet press has recently complained that intellectual skills are thus wasted, and that prisoners are forced to perform heavy work beyond their strength.

Prison labor does considerable mining, timbering, farming, and even operates some factories. But the main task of the corrective-labor colonies appears to be construction of airfields, railways, mines, factories, and canals. Because MVD often rents out prison labor to various economic ministries and organizations, MVD is partially self-supporting.

The prison colony population of the USSR was small during the 1920's, but rose into the millions in the early 1930's when many peasants were imprisoned for resisting collectivization of agriculture. When the peasants ended their sentences, their places were taken by victims of the great purge of the late 1930's. As they left the camps, in came suspected collaborators with the enemy and prisoners-of-war during World War II. Postwar purges under Stalin maintained a high prison camp population.

However, the prison camp population has never been constant, but rises and falls with purges and amnesties. The latter have occurred after the great purge of the late 1930's, at the end of World War II, and for several years following Stalin's death in 1953. The prisoners released by amnesty often cannot return home, but must remain as exiles in the area of their former prison camp. Usually the amnestees are ordinary criminals rather than political prisoners. Prison labor numbered about 6,000,000 men and women at the time of Stalin's death. Soviet jurists claim that this figure has now been reduced to about 2,000,000. In comparison, some 200,000 criminals are in all types of prisons in the USA.

Besides operating prison camps throughout the USSR, MVD also has railway police troops which guard all Soviet rail lines. Take a railway trip anywhere in the USSR, and you will see these railway police. The sentries are dressed in army uniforms but wear a distinctive red hat-band. Cross even a medium-size trestle, and on one bank or the other of the creek is the sentry box. Out in front of the box is the policeman with his rifle and bayonet. On a large river bridge there may be two, three, or even half a dozen police scattered in sentry boxes all the way across. These police also protect railway junctions, yards, freight depots, and large stations.

Not part of MVD but under its jurisdiction are the volunteer police, an innovation of the Khrushchev era which became permanent. Today there are 5,500,000 of these volunteers, who in the evening patrol streets, squares, parks, summer camps, and places of entertainment to prevent disorder. Unpaid, unarmed, dressed in civilian clothes but wearing a distinctive armband, they can arrest drunks, prostitutes, hooligans, pickpockets, and other minor criminals, then turning them over to the MVD. militia or a comrade's court. Though sometimes exceeding their authority, and sometimes behaving with brutality, the volunteer police have contributed greatly to public safety.

The MVD republic ministries cooperate closely under the leadership of MVD of the USSR. Taken together the MVD ministries constitute an enormous organization, believed to number about 2,000,000 police plus 2,000,000 prison colony laborers, not counting the 5,500,000 volunteer police. Yet defectors from the Soviet police consider the KGB more important, though it is much smaller than MVD.

Cross the border by train into the USSR and a green-hatted officer examines your luggage, while his subordinates look between the railway car wheels. These are KGB border police troops, for the Kremlin does not trust the regular army to patrol its frontiers. Regular army personnel might be too lenient, while the border police are trained to be severe. So police troops maintain the Iron Curtain, using wolf dogs on land, airplanes in the sky, and small patrol boats on sea, river and lake frontiers.

In any Soviet city one may occasionally see marching columns of soldiers with blue uniforms and scarlet hatbands. These are the KGB security troops. Small armies of these security police are stationed near every major Soviet city to suppress local riots or revolts. They are armed with machine guns, light artillery, tanks, and even light bombers.

Aside from these two police armies, KGB has many other functions:

The KGB political guards protect and spy upon high Soviet officials to make sure that officialdom does not misbehave. Inside all large USSR offices, cultural institutions, and schools, the KGB

Political Police guard against sabotage and subversion, much as MVD's economic police watch industrial and commercial enterprises. An extensive system of KGB laboratories invents and develops new military and police weapons, like cigarette cases and fountain pens that shoot poisoned darts. The Soviet atom bomb and space rocket were probably first developed by police laboratories, which then turned these military inventions over to industrial ministries for large-scale production. Another KGB section attempts to decipher the coded cablegrams sent and received by foreign embassies located in Moscow. This codebreaking is fairly efficient, creating many difficulties for the embassies. The KGB special political police investigate cases of high treason, and are probably responsible for the execution of former Soviet leaders such as Bukharin in 1938 and Beria in 1953.

The KGB also has a network of police agents throughout the Soviet armed forces. These police officers wear army uniforms, and are part of the staff of each military commander down to the battalion level. The present name of these army police is Counter-Intelligence. In wartime they had a more appropriate title: Death to Spies.

Every precaution against army revolt is taken by police counter-intelligence. Army soldiers and officers are forbidden to carry their guns when off duty. After practicing with firearms, servicemen must immediately return them to camp arsenals guarded by police. When Soviet leaders review the big Moscow military parades on Red Square, the troops march with guns but no ammunition. Long beforehand every soldier has been searched, and all ammunition put under police lock and key at army camps.

The same disarmament is applied to the air force, just in case an aviator might feel disposed to drop a bomb on the Politburo taking the salute on Red Square. A Soviet military pilot told me that such a feat would be almost impossible. Parade crews are chosen long in advance, after passing a severe police security check. The day before the big air parade, a police officer crawls into all corners of each plane, removing anything loose that might drop out. Then all airplane doors are sealed, and not reopened until just before take-off.

The KGB foreign police is a fascinating operation, a worldwide spy ring stealing Western military and scientific secrets. Thus far agents of this police have either been caught, or have hurriedly defected to the USSR, from the US State Department, Atomic Energy Commission, and National Security Agency, and the British Foreign Office, United Kingdom Atomic Energy Authority and Defense Ministry. In addition, a number of high-placed Soviet agents have been arrested in other Western countries such as West Germany and Sweden. The foreign police also sometimes kidnap troublesome Soviet refugees, an example being the abduction of five USSR runaway sailors from Greater New York in 1955. Such kidnappings occur frequently in west European seaports, with the victims being shanghaied back to the USSR. Rare, but occasional, are political murders of outstanding Soviet refugees. The assassination of Leon Trotsky in Mexico during 1940 is an example. His murderer was a Spanish Communist who intrigued his way into the Trotsky household.

Meanwhile the KGB foreign counter-intelligence watches foreign diplomats, newsmen, students, and businessmen residing in the USSR. These same police spy on foreign tourists traveling through the Soviet Union. Yet the KGB operates so stealthily that the average foreign visitor does not realize he is being watched. Often the tourist's hotel room is wired with microphones. While he is out of the hotel room, very plainly dressed people—who could easily pass for charwomen—search his suitcases. There is a large ventilating grille in many hotel bedrooms. If the tourist would bother to aim a flashlight into it, he would see a superb camera, ready to record any indiscretion. Many visiting politicians have been trapped by these cameras, and then been subjected to political blackmail.

The fact that the KGB and MVD are separate organizations does not mean that they conflict. In most Soviet cities the local representatives of KGB and MVD share the same central office and prisons. KGB officials often order arrests, which are then performed by the more numerous MVD police.

A number of Soviet books have described the philosophy and methods of the USSR police. According to these publications the police does not judge enemies of the state but "strikes" them. Conclusive detailed proof is not always gathered before making arrests, because there are too many cases. The police assert that they execute very few people, but will kill groups of people in an emergency without delaying to investigate, in order to stop riots which might cause greater bloodshed if not instantly checked. The more common punishment is confinement in prison labor camps, where offenders are isolated from society and perform work useful to the state. It is claimed that only Communist Party members of strong will are chosen as secret police officials, yet many of them develop nervous disorders because of the strain of security work with its almost unlimited power. The police does not rely on its own personnel alone, but teaches and encourages all Soviet citizens to report anything they consider suspicious. Thus the secret police has unpaid assistance from "millions of eyes and millions of ears." Asserting that spies and saboteurs can appear in every segment of Soviet society as long as capitalist states exist, the police argues that it must therefore have police agents everywhere in the USSR—in government offices, factories, farms, the railways, schools, and armed forces.[2]

The Soviet police openly admit that they conduct their operations to create "terror" (public fear of the police). Arrests are often made at night, persons under interrogation are deprived of normal sleep, and prisoners are subjected to mental tortures such as sharing a pitchblack cell with snakes and rats. The purpose of such terror is to compel Soviet citizens to speak cautiously and behave correctly even when no police are present to observe them.

Intourist guides report on foreign tourists to the Soviet police. After the tourist leaves town, the guide writes a character description. Yet I have seen several guides show abject fear of the police.

Such a case occurred during a recent trip through Russia. I revisited one provincial city where I had spent some time during World War II. In wartime several local people had befriended me, and I wanted to see them again. The local telephone book was no help, since it mainly listed the addresses of government offices and state enterprises. So I asked my Intourist guide, a young woman and fervent Communist, to show me the police informa-

---

[2] Latsis, Martin, *Two Years of Battle on the Internal Front,* Moscow, 1920.
Mikoyan, Anastas, *CHEKA-OGPU-NKVD,* Moscow, 1938.
Vyshinsky, Andrei, *The Law of the Soviet State,* New York: Macmillan, 1948.

tion bureau operated by MVD where my friends' addresses might be on file. Small address booths were scattered throughout the city, but in a great burst of efficiency the guide took me to the regional police headquarters. This was a huge stone building, four stories high and filling an entire city block. The front contained police offices and interrogation rooms. The back was a large prison with its tiny windows heavily barred.

As we drove up, our Intourist chauffeur looked nervous and growled: "Why in the devil are we coming here?"

My guide explained that this police headquarters had the largest address bureau in town, and ushered me inside. The bureau was a small windowless room off the main corridor of the building. I wrote out the names of my friends and gave them to a policewoman, who immediately disappeared to search the files.

While waiting for an answer, I examined the posters on the room walls. One was a placard containing eight small paintings of police heroism. Two were paintings of border guards catching American spies. Suddenly the guide said in a strained voice: "Are you looking at pictures of police firemen? Oh, how silly of me! Of course they are not firemen. But at a distance they looked like firemen, firemen, firemen."

She was babbling incoherently, and her face was drawn and white. It was not the spy-catching pictures that frightened her. She was terrified to spend five minutes in a windowless police room. Only after we left the building and returned to our car, did she regain her composure.

An obvious purpose of the ever-present police is to prevent revolt in the Soviet Union. For revolution is almost impossible in the USSR. To overthrow the government, a Soviet citizen must form a huge organization at least a million strong, armed with tanks, planes, and artillery. Suppose he tries to do this. He may recruit one hundred people. At this point the police usually get wind of the plot. Perhaps a jealous neighbor has reported something suspicious, Maybe a police agent has been recruited into the revolutionary group. For the main work of the police is endless watching, everywhere.

So the police catch the conspiracy, just as it starts. Most of the rebels may be released. But they are warned that thereafter the police will watch them day and night. The ringleaders are arrested and sentenced to many years in prison camps. Chances are that they will perish in camp and never return.

Police power is always greatest during a major purge. Purges have occurred throughout Soviet history, but the most thorough was during Stalin's dictatorship in the late 1930's. Millions of loyal Soviet citizens were demoted, dismissed, arrested, imprisoned, or killed.

The millions of victims of Soviet purges have at least one consolation: The police themselves are occasionally purged by the Communist Party, which is even stronger than the police. At times the police become so powerful that they threaten the supremacy of Communist Party dictatorship. Then the police purgers must be purged.

The fall of a police chief is not unusual, for a police career is one of the most hazardous of Soviet professions. A Soviet refugee in America, by profession a shoemaker, has told me his experiences in USSR prison camps. While in camp he repaired the shoes of the guards, who became his friends. They cynically remarked:

> You are in prison camp today. Tomorrow we guards may be imprisoned too. So we eat well, drink heavily, and live a life of pleasure, knowing that it may soon end.

During the six decades of Soviet history, three police ministers have been executed thus far. Very many assistant ministers have died before firing squads. When each police minister or assistant minister is liquidated, many lesser sleuths are killed or imprisoned. Lenin curbed the police in the early 1920's, Stalin at the end of the 1930's, and Stalin's successors for three years in the 1950's. After each major purge of police, there has been a thaw allowing more personal (but not political) freedom.

Besides need to purge a too powerful police, there is another reason for Soviet thaws. An extended period of repression creates fear of initiative, which blocks Soviet military, industrial, scientific, and educational progress. In turn, an extended thaw permits USSR intellectuals to criticize the Soviet regime, thus starting an artistic revolt which might endanger Communist rule. (The Hungarian rebellion of 1956 began in precisely this form.) Therefore neither purges nor thaws have so far been permanent.

Of course, purges and thaws may occur simultaneously, and have coexisted. During a widespread purge, certain groups or regions may suffer lightly. Conversely, some groups or regions may be oppressed during a thaw. For example, the Ukraine was so thoroughly purged during the early 1930's that it was not greatly affected by the mass purge of the late 1930's. During persecutions of various religions, the Baptists have survived rather easily.

Nevertheless, thus far, Soviet history has alternated between periods of repression and periods of thaw. During periods of purge and repression there are mass arrests of whole groups of the population, particularly members of the intelligentsia, the bureaucracy, the army officer corps, the peasantry, the various national minorities. Thaws are usually marked by a loosening of censorship, amnesties for many inmates of prison camps, and less ruthless police activity.

Generally speaking, the Russian Civil War of 1918–1920 was a period of repression when real or presumed anti-Communists suffered mass execution. This wartime terror was followed by the thaw of the New Economic Policy during the 1920's, when art and literature flourished. Then came two periods of repression: the collectivization of agriculture during 1929–1933, and the great Stalinist purge of 1934–1938. These grim years were succeeded by a thaw which continued throughout the Soviet-German war of 1941–1945, and artistic life revived. After the war there was another repression until Stalin's death in 1953.

Stalin's successors instituted another thaw. Under Malenkov the police lost one of its greatest powers when most police courts were abolished. Mass purging was officially condemned in 1956 and 1961, as it had been previously condemned in 1922 and 1939.

But Premier Khrushchev instituted another period of repression during 1963–1964, apparently in an attempt to retain power. After his ouster, the Brezhnev-Kosygin regime created a new thaw.

The police appear to be indispensable in maintaining the Communist dictatorship. After each past thaw, the police have always regained at least part of their power. It is quite possible that there will be another purge or period of repression in the Soviet future.

Suggestions for Further Reading

CONQUEST, ROBERT, *Religion in the USSR*. New York: Praeger, 1968.

DERIABIN, PETER, *The Secret World,* New York: Doubleday, 1959.

DERIABIN, PETER, *Watchdogs of Terror: Russian Bodyguards from the Tsars to the Commissars*. New Rochelle: Arlington House, 1972.

KAZNACHEEV, ALEKSANDR, *Inside a Soviet Embassy,* Philadelphia: Lippincott, 1962.

LEVYTSKY, BORIS, *The Uses of Terror: The Soviet Secret Police, 1917-1970*. New York: Coward-McCann, 1972.

LEWIS, DAVID, *Sexpionage: The Exploitation of Sex by Soviet Intelligence*. New York: Harcourt, Brace, Jovanovich, 1976.

MEDVEDEV, ZHORES A., *The Medvedev Papers*. New York: St. Martins, 1971.

MOORE, BARRINGTON, *Terror and Progress USSR,* Cambridge: Harvard University Press, 1954.

ORR, CHARLES A., *Stalin's Slave Camps,* Boston: Beacon Press, 1952.

PETROV, VLADIMIR and EVDOKIA, *Empire of Fear,* New York: Praeger, 1957.

WOLIN, SIMON, *The Soviet Secret Police,* New York: Praeger, 1956.

Chapter 16

An Organized People

The Soviet regime has held power for six decades partly because socially the USSR is well organized. Employment alone unites the Soviet public in mass organizations like collective and state farms, handicraft and consumer cooperatives, government bureaucracy, the armed forces, police armies, and police. Though such organizations exist primarily for economic or administrative work, they also provide some propaganda, care and entertainment for their employees.

More important politically are the huge public societies such as the trade unions, defense, and sport clubs. Youth is organized too in the Komsomol (Young Communist League) for persons of high school and college age, and Pioneers, and the Octobrists for younger children. Almost every man, woman, and school-age child in the Soviet Union is a member of one or more of these mass societies, which are easy to join. There are considerable advantages in joining. A member of the Komsomol is given preference over a nonmember in being admitted to college. Joining a trade union increases a worker's pension benefits.

Lenin started these Soviet societies, describing them as "Transmission belts" between the motor (the Communist Party) and the nonparty masses (the obedient machine). Since Communist Party members have never numbered more than 6 per cent of the vast Soviet population, there always is the political problem of holding the nonparty masses under tight party rule. Of course, shrewd propaganda and a strong police are a great help, and *Pravda* has even described the army, police, and propaganda as three pillars of the Soviet State. But Lenin felt the necessity of forming huge nationwide societies, which would unite and control vast blocs of non-Communist citizens, thus augmenting and making easier the persuasion and coercion exercised by propaganda, army, and police.

Altogether the USSR has dozens of transmission-belt societies. Some, like the Partisans of Peace and the women's society, are large but relatively inactive except in promoting Soviet foreign policy at nongovernmental international conferences. Others, such as the unions of writers, artists, or musicians, are small but important because of their highly skilled membership. These unusual unions commission intellectuals to produce new books, musical compositions, or works of art; issue monetary advances to support the creator until the work is done; then partly decide whether the work should be displayed, published, or performed. Expulsion from such a union prevents the member from publicly disseminating any new works in the USSR, as happened in 1969 to Soviet author Aleksandr I. Solzhenitsyn after publication abroad of several of his writings criticizing the USSR regime.

The transmission belts are not always permanent. Sometimes new organizations are created, and old societies abolished. The atheist society, created in 1925 to conduct antireligious propaganda, was abolished during 1941 when Premier Stalin needed church moral support for the war against Hitler. During 1947 the 25-year-old MOPR (International Organization to Aid Revolutionary Fighters) was disbanded, while the USSR established a new belt—the All-Union Society for Dissemination of Political and Scientific Knowledge. The former assisted Communist revolutions abroad, while the latter is an association of about 2,500,000 professors and intellectuals who by lectures and exhibits propagandize politics, science and atheism among workers and peasants.

Among the various transmission belts, two are considered most important by the Kremlin. These are the trade unions, and the trio of youth societies united around the Komsomol. A special section of the Communist Party secretariat watches both of these mass societies, which have existed since the early years of the Soviet regime.

Legally or illegally, a few labor unions were formed in Tsarist

Russia before 1917. After the March 1917 abdication of the Tsar, unions greatly increased in both variety and membership. During the Russian Civil War of 1918–1920, these unions supported Lenin and strongly aided the Communist battle of assembly lines. However, when civil war ended in Red victory, the trade unions tried to take over the Soviet government. Labor union leaders argued that Soviet Russia was a workers' state, and therefore should be ruled by workingmen's unions. Lenin opposed this viewpoint, since he did not wish political power to pass out of the hands of the Communist Party. The trade union endeavor was defeated, and thereafter organized labor ceased to be an independent political force. However, during the NEP the unions bargained with state enterprise over wages and work-hours, and until 1927 even led strikes against oppressive directors of government industry.

During 1929 the trade unions again came into conflict with the Soviet government. The unions demanded free collective bargaining, which their employer (the Soviet government) opposed on the grounds that excessive worker demands might slow the pace of industrialization and give organized labor unfair advantages over the remainder of the population. The governmental attitude prevailed, and Mikhail Tomski—the old Bolshevik who had spearheaded the opposition—was dismissed from leadership of the trade unions. Several years later, he committed suicide.

After 1929, USSR trade unions became much like the oldtime company unions in capitalist countries, with the Soviet government as the company. Soviet unions are all linked together on a regional and industrial basis, the supreme authority being the USSR Central Council of Trade Unions (AUCCTU), which is usually headed by a member of the Communist Party Politburo. Naturally with such a leadership, the unions discourage strikes and accept without protest the wages and work-hours imposed by the government.

At present virtually all Soviet governmental employees join the trade unions, which are open to anyone on salary from the state. Even students working during their summer vacations and all specialists and machinery operators on collective farms can be unionists. As Soviet industry has expanded, so has trade union membership, as shown in Table 12.

Table 12. *Growth of Trade Union Membership in the USSR*

Year	Number of trade union members
1917	1,500,000
1920	4,300,000
1926	9,500,000
1928	11,000,000
1930	13,000,000
1933	17,100,000
1939	25,000,000
1948	27,000,000
1954	40,000,000
1958	50,000,000
1960	55,000,000
1962	63,000,000
1964	68,000,000
1966	80,000,000
1974	103,000,000
1977	113,500,000

Source: *Great Soviet Encyclopedia,* post-World War II edition. *Small Soviet Encyclopedia,* post-World War II edition, *Pravda,* 1948-1976.

The Soviet trade unions constitute the largest national bloc of organized labor in our world. Though these unions propagandize workers to speed up and produce more goods, the considerable union benefits attract a giant membership. For example, a worker's retirement pension doubles if he has been unionized. The government turns over state social insurance to the trade unions, which issue relief payments to the sick, the disabled, and women on maternity leave. Naturally a worker is wise to join the organization which pays his social insurance. At state enterprises the union committees perform safety and sanitary inspection, help prepare data for the award of old-age pensions, and try to ensure good service at the enterprise restaurant and store. Workers can bring their complaints to the union committee, which also organizes periodic "production meetings" where labor openly criticizes technical inefficiencies of management. Such meetings cannot attack governmental planning or policy, but still serve as a safety-valve where angry workers can let off steam. Unions also maintain more than 3,000 sanatoria for sick civil servants, and several thousand rest homes where workers and their families can spend summer vacations at low cost. A rest home is a hostel or small hotel, usually located in the countryside near the city where union members work.

Of vast importance are the clubhouses which unions maintain at every large state enterprise. For example, at a big factory the club has a bar, snackbar, and small dancehall, where unionists and their guests can relax more cheaply than in a public cafe or restaurant. Often there is a crude theater, for famous actors, singers, and musicians to provide entertainment at low cost to the union audience. (Soviet stage artists are required to perform such club service in addition to their regular work.) Professors and intellectuals also guest-lecture on politics, science, atheism, and so on from the same clubhouse platform. The club even operates "study circles" on art, literature, theater, music, ballet, and technical subjects, all taught by professional instructors drawn from institutions throughout the city.

Perhaps a worker loves music and aspires to become a musician. The club circle gives him an opportunity to learn music, tests him in musical contests with other clubs, and may even launch him on an artistic career. Even if the worker displays little talent, he has fun.

Thus the union club provides relaxation and release from the routine of daily life. Remember that "home" in a Soviet city is usually one or two crowded rooms, in comparison with which the clubhouse is a spacious paradise. A middle-aged Russian clerk expressed this feeling very clearly in conversation with me:

> For seven years I worked at a mine office in the Donets coal basin. The mining town was dirty and uninteresting. My office work was dull, and my shabby room was a tiny place only for sleep. All day long I merely existed until 7 P.M., when I went to the theater circle of the mine union club. Learning to act each evening from 7 to 11, I really lived.

Much of the social life of Soviet urbanites takes place in such clubs, which foreigners rarely visit. A club also provides some unusual care and protection for its members. Should a trade unionist be hospitalized by illness or accident, the trade union committee arranges that union members visit the hospital ward to cheer him up. Such kindness makes a strong impression on peasants who have just migrated into the city, leaving friends and relatives behind in a rural village.

Similarly, if a trade unionist commits a minor nonpolitical crime, like brawling while drunk, the trade union committee of his enterprise often obtains his release from jail. The offender is placed on probation under the collective guardianship of his union local, which tries to keep him out of further trouble.

Thus the unions and their clubs offer members entertainment, culture, escape from reality, communal friendship, and real assistance when in need. For the sake of these benefits, a unionist surrenders his political and economic independence.

Second oldest of the Soviet transmission belts is the Young Communist League, usually abbreviated as Komsomol. Founded by Premier Lenin in 1918, the Komsomol recruits male and female youths between the ages of 14 and 28, and today contains the majority of Soviet young people in this age bracket. The Komsomol is the chief society for high school and college students, provides a common organization for young workers and collective farmers, and is extremely important in the armed forces where most enlisted men and many junior officers are of Komsomol age. Growth of the Komsomol society is depicted in Table 13. Noteworthy are the small membership of the 1920's, rapid expansion in the 1930's, and the temporary decline in members during the Soviet-German War when millions of Komsomol soldiers died in battle.

Ever since the Komsomol was established, its main task has been the Communist indoctrination of Soviet youth. Thus Brezhnev, the Secretary-General of the USSR Communist Party, recently urged all Komsomol members:

> to be persistent in the study of Communism, to enrich their minds with all wealth of mankind's knowledge, to acquire an integral Marxist-Leninist world outlook, to use their education, knowledge and upbringing in productive work, to consolidate Communist morality.

Brezhnev also set forth Komsomol future goals:

Table 13. *Growth of Membership in the USSR Young Communist League*

Year	Number of Komsomol members
1918	22,000
1920	400,000
1924	700,000
1928	2,000,000
1931	3,000,000
1936	4,000,000
1939	9,000,000
1940	15,000,000
1949	9,000,000
1950	12,000,000
1955	18,800,000
1962	19,400,000
1966	23,000,000
1974	34,000,000
1976	35,000,000

Source: *Pravda*, 1949-1976.
Towster, Julian, *Political Power in the USSR*, New York: Oxford University Press, 1948.

to take a still more active part in creative work and socialist emulation, to use their work for the maximum good of society, to fight for the new and progressive, to care for people's property, to take a firm stand against waste and extravagance, to strengthen labour and production discipline;

to prepare not only for work but also for the defense of the country, to acquire military skills, always to be on the alert and guard the achievements of the October Revolution, to strengthen capability of the country and the might of the Soviet Army and Navy.

to . . . work towards making every young person an active builder of the new society.[1]

Local Komsomol organizations are formed in schools, military units, and various places of work. Like the trade unions, the Komsomol has clubs providing entertainment and culture for all members. But Komsomol activities are not entirely for pleasure, since members are repeatedly mobilized for work on crash eco-

[1] *USSR—Questions and Answers*, Moscow: Progress Publishers, 1975, pp. 148-149.

nomic programs. In the late 1970's at least 200,000 Komsomol members were building river dams, hydroelectric power stations, lumber mills, railways, oil and gas wells, and other projects in Siberia. Every summer many Komsomol college students spend their school vacations laboring on collective and state farms. Supposedly all this work is voluntary, but should a youth refuse to volunteer, he later may be barred from good jobs or admission to the Communist Party.

Communist Party control over the Komsomol is direct, since local, regional, and national leaders of the Komsomol are Communist Party members. Such leaders are allowed to exceed the Komsomol age limit of 28, and are often men and women in their thirties. They are members of both the Komsomol and the Communist Party, though such dual membership is prohibited for rank-and-file Komsomol members.

All Komsomol organizations are also ordered to be subordinate to the Communist Party organization at the same level. Th subordination is facilitated by the fact that the Komsomol has the same structure as the party, both possessing primary, city ward, city, district, regional, republic, and USSR units. At a place of work where the Communist Party primary organization is small, joint meetings are often held of the party and Komsomol units so that the party primary secretary can operate a larger group.

The Komsomol is intended to be a training ground for future Communist Party members, and the best Komsomol youths are encouraged to try to join the party. Legally a Komsomol member could transfer to the party at the age of 18. In practice a promising youth is usually kept in the Komsomol till the age of 28, then recruited into the party. In recent years, however, one third of new party members have been older people not transferring directly from the Komsomol.

Among other duties the Komsomol has the task of leading the Pioneers, who are boys and girls from the ages of 10 to 14. A common sight in Soviet youth camps is the ceremony where the Komsomol leader shouts:

> Are you ready to defend the cause of Communism?

And the Pioneers' high-pitched voices chorus back:

We are ready! Always ready!

Almost all Soviet children in middle and upper classes of grade school join the Pioneer society, which was started by Lenin in 1922. The immense growth of this society since its inception is depicted in Table 14:

Table 14. *Growth of Membership in the USSR Pioneer Society*

Year	Number of Pioneers
1922	4,000
1923	5,000
1925	1,000,000
1930	3,300,000
1934	7,000,000
1939	11,000,000
1949	13,000,000
1952	19,000,000
1964	19,000,000
1977	25,000,000

Pioneers are organized in squads of 10 members, with four squads constituting a brigade. In charge of each brigade is a Komsomol member, who receives his instructions from a special department of local Komsomol headquarters.

The Pioneer clubs in cities and summer camps in the countryside are very impressive. The main club in each town is called a Pioneer Palace, and is often housed in an old Tsarist mansion. Like an adult club, the Pioneer Palace has study circles for chorus, ballet, painting, sculpture, music, and even a little acting. Pioneer troupes frequently stage public performances of folk singing and dancing. The best art work may be displayed in the Palace museum. Also there are gamerooms for chess, table tennis, and volleyball, and a hall for ceremonies and political lectures. Sometimes the Palace is surrounded by a Pioneer park, which has facilities for outdoor games, a swimming pool, and possibly even a children's railway operated by Pioneer crews endlessly tooting the engine whistle.

A Pioneer summer camp has much the same outdoor games,

plus tents, barracks, and mess-halls where the children perform most of the housekeeping. On a parade ground the Pioneers practice marching in German-style goosestep. Occasionally the camp may have its own radio studio, from which the children broadcast news, recorded music and amateur entertainment over the camp loudspeakers. Such camps are not free, but the fee per child is not too expensive for many parents.

Though most Pioneer activities might be described as constructive play, the children sometimes undertake useful work like helping the Komsomol clean litter or collect scrap metal. On summer hikes the Pioneer brigades are encouraged to seek unusual rocks, and have actually discovered some new mineral deposits. In frontier zones the children are trained to watch for foreign spies and warn the police about suspicious strangers. Both Pioneer work and fun are always accompanied by Communist indoctrination.

Least successful of the Soviet youth organizations is the Octobrist society for boys and girls from age of 7 to 10. Founded in 1925, the society has grown from 274,000 members in 1926 to about 12,000,000 today. Octobrists are organized in groups of 25 children, each group being attached to a Pioneer brigade led by a member of the Komsomol. The name of Octobrist honors the 1917 Bolshevik Revolution, which occurred in the month of October according to the incorrect Tsarist calendar.

Theoretically all children in the lower classes of grade school are Octobrists. In practice these children are too young for most Pioneer indoctrination and activities. So the little Octobrists learn to march, wave red flags, and sing patriotic songs, but not much else. The society is loosely organized and lacks its own clubs. After 1940 the Octobrists were almost disbanded until 1957, when a Communist Party decree ordered the revival of Octobrist groups attached to Pioneer brigades.

The trade unions and youth organizations are primarily political, using welfare, entertainment, and propaganda to achieve their goals. These societies also conduct some paramilitary training. In addition, several other transmission belts train the Soviet people—men, women, and children—for fast effective action in future war. Many millions of ordinary civilians are thus being taught military skills, as was done in Nazi Germany.

Soviet Russia has had universal military conscription ever since 1918. Today the healthiest half of young Soviet males spend some time in the armed forces. Army and air force conscripts serve two years, naval draftees for three years and college graduates for only one year. If the conscripts are school dropouts when drafted, the armed forces have courses to complete a serviceman's grade or high school education. The conscripts may also be taught mechanized-war skills, which help them become factory, farm or transport machine-operators after demobilization back into civilian life.

Because of this school and technical training, the Communist indoctrination of servicemen, plus the existence of army and navy clubs, the Soviet government considers its armed forces to be a transmission belt, even though troop units are governmental rather than public organizations. Six decades of this conscription have by now produced an armed forces active reserve of about 16 million trained men. For all able-bodied ex-servicemen in the USSR are forced to join the military active reserve, where they are required to remain until attaining the age of 48. The 16 million active reservists have little chance to get out of shape, since they are kept fit every summer by refresher maneuvers.

Just in case, practice mobilizations of these reservists are held every few months. Each reservist carries a card telling him when and where to appear when M-Day comes. When mobilization practice is announced, all reservists rush to their recruiting stations. The roll is called to see if all are present, then they are sent home. So perfect are these mobilization plans that the whole 16 million can be called to colors in just one month.

Military training is also encouraged for almost all Soviet citizens: old, young, male, female, weak as well as strong. Even the world's largest army cannot train an entire nation, so the army has turned for help to civilian transmission belts. Of the latter the network of sport societies is very important.

Organized sport began in Soviet Russia in 1920, and throughout the next decade developed rather slowly. During the 1930's athletic associations expanded quickly under the supervision of a national sport committee attached to the USSR Council of Ministers. Growth of organized sport since then is depicted in Table 15:

Table 15. *Increase in Membership of USSR Sport Clubs*

Year	Number of organized athletes
1938	10,000,000
1955	16,000,000
1956	17,500,000
1959	20,000,000
1963	32,800,000
1967	35,000,000
1976	54,000,000

Soviet sport clubs are operated by the trade unions, schools, Komsomol, and armed forces. All clubs are controlled by the USSR sport committee, which heavily stresses the military nature of athletic training. All athletes are encouraged to pass the Ready for Labor and Defense (GTO) test, which was invented in 1931 by the Komsomol and redefined in 1934, 1939, 1946, 1959 and 1972. Today there are seven types of GTO tests, divided by age and sex: both sexes 10-13, 14-15, and 16-18; women 19-34 and 35-55; and men 19-39 and 40-60.

All seven tests are semi-militarized decathlons. At present a GTO test usually includes sprinting, cross-country running, high jump or broad jump, ball throwing, swimming, gymnastics, skiing or bike riding, hand grenade throwing, map reading, and rifle shooting. In adult tests the swimming may be either while wearing clothes or carrying a weapon. Sometimes the shooting is done from horseback or during the cross-country run.

Sport clubs are ordered to concentrate on Ready for Labor and Defense, and they obey. According to the Soviet press, 90 million living USSR citizens have passed the defense tests. The pressure to pass is very great, for an athlete is told that it's humiliating and unmanly to fail. Organized sport thus provides a vast pool of semitrained manpower which the armed forces can recruit in case of war.

GTO tests can be taken but are not demanded from grade school pupils, who may attempt the militarized decathlon from age 10. But high school and college students are pressured to try the defense test, which is somewhat simplified for youths from 14 to 18. And all school athletics stress the skills needed to pass. From the fifth grade up, physical culture is a compulsory course in all Soviet schools until graduation from college. It is not merely playing games but a real course with set hours, tests, and marks. And school physical training is extremely tough. For a final examination an eighth-grade girl is often required to make a running jump from a springboard, land with her hands on the coach's shoulders, then straighten out, heels in air, perfectly balanced. How many American eighth-graders could perform this difficult trick?

Besides compulsory athletics, Soviet civilian schools provide real military training. At the very start, childish minds are molded to love war. When a 7-year-old commences first grade, he learns the alphabet from readers with stories like this:

> Little Gregory's brother is a tankist. He writes to Gregory: "Study, don't be lazy."
>
> Gregory also wants to be a tankist. He will beat the enemy strongly. Gregory drew a tank and wrote: "Here is a tank. What a tank! It smashes trees and bushes, walls and poles."

From grade four through high school, military training is compulsory. At first the 10-year-olds learn marching and how to save their lives during atomic airraids. As they grow older, they study rifle and machine-gun shooting, donning a gasmask fast, first aid, and atomic radiation survival. In high school, junior and senior boys must now take 138 hours of basic infantry training before graduating. If a high-school dropout, the boy still studies the 138 hours at his factory, office or farm village. Either at school or place of work, reserve or retired military officers are the teachers. If not drafted into the armed forces at age 18, the able-bodied high-school dropout, or high-school graduate not entering college is automatically enlisted in the armed forces reserve as soon as he completes the 138 hours of combat classes.

When they reach college, most Soviet girls are exempt from further military training. But the equivalent of ROTC is compulsory for almost all male college students. The USSR borrowed the idea of ROTC from the United States. Few college boys in

Russia escape this training, even if they are weak, sick, or wear glasses.

This military education is no mere one-semester course, but three to four hours a week for all four or five years of college. If their military marks are good, seniors graduate as reserve officers, who serve only one year of armed forces' conscription. Should a student fail college military training, after graduation he is drafted into the army infantry to spend two years as a private. Naturally most students try hard to pass ROTC and become properly paid lieutenants rather than earn a tenth as much by being humble privates doomed to crawl through battlefield mud.

All these military courses in Soviet civilian schools and colleges are taught by regular or reserve army officers. But their salaries are paid by the educational or economic ministry operating the school. Thus a vast military training expense is hidden in the educational ledger of the national budget.

Though the schools are officially regarded as a transmission belt, by strict definition they are government cultural institutions. But there are two mass public societies which are not governmental, and which specialize in war preparation even more than the state schools. One of these societies has a predominantly female membership and is the Soviet Red Cross.

Tsarist Russia had Red Cross units, which continued after the Bolshevik Revolution for each of the Soviet republics. In Moslem areas of the USSR these humanitarian organizations took the Islamic name of Red Crescent. During 1925 all republic societies joined together in a national Union of Red Cross and Red Crescent, usually abbreviated as Red Cross. Growth of this transmission belt is shown in Table 16. Noteworthy is the tremendous expansion during World War II and in the post-war atomic age.

In all countries the Red Cross primarily exists to aid war wounded. Though providing disaster relief both at home and abroad, the Soviet Red Cross mainly trains women to be wartime nurses. They must pass tests in first aid for casualties of nuclear war. The Red Cross operates clinics among the USSR armed forces, and maintains first aid units near cities which could be future air raid targets. One of the most successful innovations

Table 16. *Growth of the Soviet Red Cross and Red Crescent*

Year	Membership
1935	7,000,000
1941	7,900,000
1946	14,200,000
1957	24,000,000
1962	45,000,000
1967	56,000,000
1976	95,000,000

of the USSR Red Cross has been airplane ambulances, which proved invaluable during the Soviet-German War.

Of all mass Soviet organizations, however, the most important militarily is DOSAAF—the Voluntary Society to Aid the Army, Air Force and Naval Fleet. A military aid society was founded in Soviet Russia as early as 1920. Soon other civil defense organizations arose, and in 1927 they all united into one mass society entitled Osoaviakhim. Renamed DOSAAF after World War II, the society temporarily split into army, navy, and air associations, which quickly reunited into one organization. This society expanded very fast in the early 1930's and again after World War II, as depicted in Table 17:

Table 17. *Growth of the DOSAAF Defense Society*

Year	Membership
1927	2,000,000
1930	5,100,000
1931	9,100,000
1933	12,000,000
1940	13,000,000
1954	20,000,000
1964	40,000,000
1977	80,000,000

In the Western World there is nothing like DOSAAF. Picture a militia, home guard, and civil defense rolled into one. Almost unknown outside Russia, DOSAAF has branches in virtually every Soviet factory and in most offices, colleges, state and collective farms. The society is almost a branch of the USSR armed forces. The president is a general or marshal from the army or air force, while reserve army officers are the teachers. These instructors and their families receive the same housing, school, and tax privileges as regular army officers.

No Soviet citizen has trouble joining this defense organization. DOSAAF welcomes anyone, male or female, from the age of 14 onward. Army reservists often enroll in DOSAAF to keep in fighting trim. Boys yet to be conscripted are taught to shoot, scout, fight with bayonets, attack at night, camouflage, and dig themselves in. Why should any boy submit to this workout? The answer is that a DOSAAF trainee more easily rises to noncommissioned officer rank during military service. Roughly half of all new conscripts drafted into the Soviet army have already received DOSAAF training.

DOSAAF has its own marksmanship medal. To win it, one must be both a crack shot, and expert at his or her civilian job. By now, millions of Soviet civilians are wearing these badges of distinction. For the young and strong, however, sharpshooting is the DOSAAF kindergarten. Many members are required to endure the most rugged and realistic infantry training. In midwinter they maneuver all day long in subzero temperatures. And DOSAAF trains more than infantrymen. One million members are being trained as truck drivers, and another million are learning to operate tanks. Other large groups study rocket artillery.

If a Russian radio-ham wishes to build and operate his private broadcasting set, he must join DOSAAF. About a million members are radio-hams or receive DOSAAF instruction in radar or Geiger counters. DOSAAF has long tried to install a radio transmitter on every collective and state farm, so the villages could remain in contact if Soviet cities were devastated by nuclear war.

Nor are naval skills forgotten. Each year DOSAAF trains about 100,000 men and women to row, sail, and steer small boats. Swimming, navigation, and naval signaling are taught by DOSAAF too. Much lifeguard work on beaches is done by its members.

In today's air age, DOSAAF takes great pains to make the Soviet population air-minded. The society founded the first amateur flying club in the USSR in the early 1920's. Today there are hundreds of these clubs throughout the country. They are training at least a hundred thousand DOSAAF members to become glider pilots. Superior glider pilots are also taught to loft light motored planes. The majority of USSR airline and air force pilots first learned to fly in these clubs, and so did some Soviet astronauts. The late Yuri Gagarin, after being the world's first man in space, boasted: "I was, am, and always will be a member of DOSAAF." Yet the average club is no more than a mown grass field and a row of tiny planes.

In future wars, casualties in the air force will be very high, and air crew replacements must be ready. The Soviet Union has gone a long way in solving this replacement problem.

The Red Army was the first in the world to train paratroops. As early as the 1930's, DOSAAF cooperated by staging mass amateur jumps from planes. Today perhaps a hundred thousand DOSAAF civilians are parachuting, and some of them hold world records. Kremlin leaders boast that the USSR is the world's only nation where parachuting is a mass sport.

More than half of DOSAAF's huge membership are women, or men too old and weak for combat training. Almost all these noncombatants receive intense instruction for the humble yet vital profession of airraid warden. DOSAAF has a test for nuclear devastation, combining all the arts a skilled airraid warden must know. The DOSAAF present goal is to organize "self-defense groups" of wardens in every factory, office, and apartment house. Each such group contains teams of amateur watchmen, medical assistants, firemen, deradiation personnel, and rescue workers.

Just before Stalin's death, the aged premier made a public request that DOSAAF double its already large membership. Though Stalin's successors criticized many of his internal policies, his defense request was fulfilled. As early as 1957, DOSAAF had twice as many members as in 1953.

The immense extent of the organization of the Soviet public in mass societies is depicted in Table 18. Combined membership of the major transmission belts exceeds the total population of the USSR. No better proof can be offered of the widespread dual

Table 18. *Membership in Mass Soviet Societies and USSR Total Population (1976)*

Mass Society	Society Membership	Total Population
Octobrists	12,000,000	
Pioneers	25,000,000	
Komsomol	35,000,000	
Trade Unions	113,500,000	
Organized Sport	54,000,000	
Red Cross	95,000,000	
DOSAAF	80,000,000	
	414,500,000	257,900,000

or even triple membership of Soviet citizens in political or paramilitary societies.

In theory any of the adult transmission belts might become a center for mass opposition against the Soviet regime. Since the 1920's, however, the Communist Party has managed to keep mass societies under control by several methods. As already indicated, party control of the youth organizations is direct.

The national, regional, and important local officials of all adult transmission belts are also Communist party members. At the regional and local levels, no official heads more than one society. Thus no local tyrant can accumulate power by controlling several belts.

In addition, party control is also exerted through so-called "party groups." If there are at least three party members attending a local, regional, or national meeting of a transmission belt, these Communists are obliged to form a party group to induce the society to follow Kremlin policy.

Suppose several dozen city women join together to form a local branch of the Soviet Red Cross. Among these volunteer nurses are several women Communists, numbering three or more. They immediately meet separately, organize a party group within the Red Cross unit, and elect a party group secretary. The latter is never the same person as the head of the Red Cross unit, who is probably also a Communist. Before each meeting of the Red Cross unit, the party group convenes to receive instructions from its secretary on party strategy. At the Red Cross assembly the party group acts and votes as a unit to influence the meeting to follow the party line. Unlike a primary party secretary in a place of work, a party group secretary lacks the power of veto over transmission belt officials. But the group secretary reports any wrongdoings to the city party secretariat, which also constantly instructs the group how to operate in the interests of the party. More than 235,000 party groups are watching transmission belts at present throughout the USSR.

Thus at the local and regional levels, each public society is led by Communists who are watched by party group secretaries. But at the USSR level, all the transmission belts are pulled together under tightly interlocked leadership. Some belt leaders are members of the Communist Party Politburo, while the others are usually in the party Central Committee. And all mass societies are supervised by the USSR party secretariat.

If a Soviet citizen feels rebellious, there is not much he can do. For no individual can fight an interlocking network of powerful organizations. Thus the transmission belts are bulwarks of Soviet power.

Suggestions for Further Reading

Brown, Emily Clark, *Soviet Trade Unions and Labor Relations,* Cambridge: Harvard University Press, 1966.

Kassof, Allen, *The Soviet Youth Program: Regimentation and Rebellion,* Cambridge: Harvard University Press, 1965.

Lane, David, *Politics and Society in the USSR.* New York: Random House, 1971.

Madison, Bernice Q., *Social Welfare in the Soviet Union.* Stanford: Stanford University Press, 1968.

Morton, Henry W., *Soviet Sport, Mirror of Soviet Society,* New York: Collier Books, 1963.

Osborn, Robert J., *Soviet Social Policies: Welfare, Equality and Community.* Homewood: Dorsey, 1970.

Sokolovsky, Marshal Vasili D., *Military Strategy, Soviet Doctrine and Concepts,* New York: Praeger, 1963.

Sorlin, Pierre, *The Soviet People and Their Society.* New York: Praeger, 1969.

Part III

Economic Power

Starting with an economy devastated by World War I and the Russian Civil War, the Soviet Union not only recovered but built the second largest industry in the world. The basis of Soviet world strength today rests on industrial might. Thus careful examination of the Soviet economy is of both political and military importance. The following chapters discuss the success and weakness of economic planning, which has made Russia powerful without providing a high standard of living. Subordination of the entire Soviet economy to heavy industry is explained in Chapter 17. Agriculture is a perennial weakness, and the sociological and economic causes are described in detail in Chapter 18. Relatively unknown in the West is the careful peacetime mobilization of the Soviet economy for future war described in Chapter 19. The economic chapters conclude with Chapter 20, an evaluation of the Soviet standard of living, which is modest for a nation possessing great industrial power.

Chapter 17

The Planned Economy

Perhaps the most distinctive feature of the Soviet economy is the attempt to replace private profit by national economic planning. Like many other Soviet methods, economic planning was not immediately introduced after the Bolshevik Revolution of 1917, but developed slowly by trial and error over a long period.

Karl Marx, the creator of Communist ideology, wrote that in the early stages of Communism the workers' government should own all land, and control all credit, banking, transportation, telecommunications, industry, and agriculture. However, he did not foresee the need for extensive economic planning in a socialist state, and wrote little concerning such plans.

In contrast, Lenin realized that any attempt at national socialism would be meaningless without a planning agency to develop and coordinate the various branches of Russia's economy. The Russian Civil War of 1918–1920, however, prevented any early endeavors at systematic economic planning. The wartime Soviet government and its several mobilization agencies simply improvised economic measures to gain military victory.

In 1920, when victory in the Civil War was near, Lenin formed Goelro (State Commission for Electrification), the first economic planning agency of the Soviet government. Goelro compiled a plan for construction of about 30 large electric-power stations and expansion of certain other basic industries. The electric power program was slowly fulfilled during the 1920's, but the rest of the plan remained a dead letter.

During 1921 the State Planning Commission (Gosplan) was organized and absorbed Goelro. Gosplan had the rank of a cabinet ministry with the power to supervise other economic ministries. Throughout most of the 1920's Gosplan was ineffective, largely confining its work to industrial-agricultural forecasts which proved incorrect. In this period, however, Gosplan established a large network of regional planning offices as well as planning units in the central and branch offices of economic ministries.

These regional and functional planning offices proved invaluable when troubles abroad in 1927 stimulated the Soviet government to prepare the First Five-Year Plan of 1928–1932. Thereafter Gosplan became extremely active in managing the entire Soviet economy, compiling and enforcing plans with the aid of its subordinate regional and ministerial planning network. After the First Five-Year Plan came the Second (1933–1937), the Third (1938-1942) interrupted by the Nazi-Soviet War, Fourth (1946-1950), Fifth (1951-1955), Sixth (1956-60), Seventh (1961-1965), Eighth (1966-1970), Ninth (1971-1975), and Tenth (1976-1980). Originally only a few Five-Year Plans were officially promised, but in actuality they have become permanent Soviet practice.

In addition to these plans, Gosplan has drafted Fifteen-Year Plans before and after the Soviet-German War, and Twenty-Year Plans after the death of Stalin. These are vague long-range programs into which the Five-Year Plans are fitted.

In theory an adopted Five-Year Plan is a complete blueprint for economic development, encompassing all industry, agriculture, transport, trade, housing, labor, and taxation of the USSR. Education is also planned to provide the proper number of skilled workers and engineers for industrial expansion. Gosplan even plans scientific research, and orders artists to propagandize the plan goals. An adopted Five-Year plan is "law," and Soviet officials can be imprisoned for not fulfilling it.

The preparation of a proposed Five-Year Plan requires approximately one year. First, the Politburo orders the plan, and lists its overall objectives which thus far have been armament and fast industrial growth. Gosplan then queries its regional and ministerial suboffices as to how each region and economic ministry can fulfill the plan goals. These suboffices in turn query their subdivisions right down to the farm and factory level. The basic working units of the economy, such as factories, farms, and stores, send their proposals back up the planning chain of command. From these low-level proposals the regional and ministerial planners compile regional and ministerial plans. Gosplan makes the final overall coordination of the regional and ministerial plans, thus producing a plan for the entire USSR.

Naturally during this planning procedure, the proposals of the lower planners are often altered, amended, or even vetoed by the higher planning bodies. Attached to Gosplan is the Central Statistical Administration, which collects all important statistical information in the USSR. Sometimes local officials make false statistical reports of economic performance to this administration in order to display success. But during the planning process, for safety's sake the same officials will set their production goals very low. By cross-checking various statistics Gosplan can often detect this cheating and underplanning, and make the necessary corrections in the plan. However, the value of consulting the planning network is that long-range plans are more realistic than if compiled by Gosplan alone.

Despite these painstaking procedures, thus far every Five-Year Plan in Soviet history has been unevenly fulfilled. Agriculture, light industry, retail trade, transport, and housing construction have consistently fallen behind plan. Various branches of heavy industry have often overfulfilled their plans. Experience has proved that even the most careful planning cannot accurately chart the course of the nation's economy five unknown years in advance. Many unexpected events can arise during a plan period to throw the program out of gear.

For example, drought occurs every few years in the major grain-growing regions of the USSR: the Ukraine, North Caucasus, Volga valley, Western Siberia, and north Central Asia. In 1975, drought struck all five of these granaries. There are no Soviet plans against unforeseen drought. A severe drought in the midst of a Five-Year Plan upsets the planned programs for crop production, food processing industry, retail food sales, food exports, and the sales tax collected on foodstuffs.

Likewise an unusually severe winter will snarl highway and rail transport, which cannot deliver on time the raw materials and fuel required by factories. Thus an unplanned winter industrial slump occurs.

A war scare may require unexpected increases in armament output in the midst of a long-range plan. Other production must be reduced in order to shift labor, materials, and factories to munitions manufacture.

Most modern industries are closely intermeshed, relying on each other for raw materials, semimanufactures, and spare parts. No amount of planning has been able to guarantee that each interlocking industry will have equally efficient labor and management. An industry with good personnel overfulfills its plan, while its industrial partner falls behind. For example, during the late 1930's, the machinebuilding industry outstripped both of its suppliers—mining and metallurgy. The machinebuilding industry had to operate at partial capacity because the mines and smelters provided insufficient metal and fuel. Today the reverse occurs. Mining and metallurgy have outstripped machinebuilding, so the USSR ships its excess metal and fuel to the machinebuilding industries of East Europe.

A new industrial invention may also upset parts of a long-range plan. Even though science is planned, the results are very unpredictable. Years of experimentation may end overnight in sudden success. The Five-Year Plan of 1956–1960 called for the construction of medium-size atomic power stations. But early during this plan, Soviet scientists discovered how to design large stations, and the atomic power program had to be revised.

In addition, a Soviet satellite may attempt to revolt against Communist rule, quarrel bitterly with the USSR, or secede from the Soviet orbit of nations. Since World War II, each USSR economic plan provides for exploitation of the Soviet satellites. Thus hostility, revolt, or secession by a satellite reduces or even eliminates some planned profits of USSR exploitation.

Besides these faults, Gosplan at times simply misplans. During a guided tour of Russia I chanced upon such a blunder from the top. In Tashkent, the largest city of Soviet Central Asia, Intourist took me to an important factory—the only plant in the USSR producing cotton-picking machines. This factory had 4,000 workers and occupied a compound about the size of a large city block. The factory chief engineer served as our guide. This engineer was taciturn, almost surly, and seemed unhappy about escorting a foreign visitor.

Finally he explained the situation into which his factory had fallen. For 20 years this plant had manufactured large cotton-picking machines, which harvested two rows of cotton bushes at a time on the fields. He showed me one of these machines on the factory grounds. It was as big as a medium-sized American truck. In front there were two funnels about six feet apart, which picked the cotton off the bushes by suction. The remainder of the machine consisted of its motor and a large storage bin for the cotton. He said the machine could pick about an acre of cotton per hour.

But Gosplan in Moscow decided that more cotton could be grown if the bushes were planted closer together. As a result the cotton-picking machines produced by this factory for 20 years became obsolete overnight, being too wide to pass through the new cotton-field rows. Gosplan had not notified the factory in advance about this major agricultural decision. Caught unawares, the factory was now undertaking the one-year retooling required to manufacture new cotton-pickers which could operate between narrow rows of cotton. Though the factory engineer did not say so, most of that year's cotton crop would have to be picked slowly by hand.

Articles published later in the Soviet press admitted that the entire cotton crop of that year had to be harvested by hand labor. There was a shortage of cotton for textile mills; and clothing manufacture declined.

Long ago Gosplan realized that long-range economic plans are unrealistic. As early as the 1930's, Gosplan augmented its Five-Year Plans with One-Year Plans, which try to adjust the difficulties arising during the five-year period. Besides planning, Gosplan has become an economic general staff, watching plan fulfillment, coordinating economic regions day by day, and making adjustments midway in the plans to cope with unexpected unbalances, disproportions, and bottlenecks.

The hierarchy of planning organizations today is depicted in Table 19. Most industry, all agriculture, and the majority of construction are controlled by USSR ministries, which in turn are responsible to USSR Gosplan. In many cases, such as agri-

Table 19. *The Planning Chain of Command*

USSR State Planning Committee (Gosplan)		
Republic Planning Committee	USSR Ministry	USSR Ministry
Regional Government	Republic Ministry	
District Government	Association	Association
City Government		
Enterprise	Enterprise	Enterprise

culture, the USSR ministry issues its orders through subordinate ministries of the Soviet republics. For some industries or economic activities, such as atomic bomb production, there is a USSR ministry but no republic ministries. However, in such instances the USSR ministry is still subordinate to Gosplan. Most ministries, either USSR or republic, contain subdivisions which are usually entitled administrations, firms, trusts, or associations. Today the most common name is "production association."

At times, particularly after Stalin's death, other USSR cabinet organizations have been established to relieve Gosplan of some planning. There have been committees for current planning, which are usually temporary, and are soon absorbed by Gosplan.

Soviet economic planning would be much simpler if all economic enterprises were owned and operated by the state, and if all labor were government employees. Such "statism" has been the goal since the 1930's, but has never been achieved. In some cases, such as agriculture, popular resistance has prevented complete ownership by the state. In other instances, such as rural stores, the state has been unwilling to assume a burdensome economic function. The USSR economy today is a mixture of state enterprise, cooperatives, and private business.

The state owns all land, mineral deposits, forests, and waters in the USSR. State enterprise includes all banks, most industry, the railways, shipping, airlines, telecommunications, the postal system, insurance, public utilities, most hospitals and schools, most theaters and other cultural institutions, most city stores, the majority of urban housing, the state farms, and rural repair stations for farm machinery. Obviously most state enterprise is urban, and the average city worker is a government employee. However, 52% of arable land is tilled by state farms.

The cooperatives exist mainly in rural regions. By far the most important are the collective farms, which till 48% of all arable land in the USSR. Most rural stores are operated by consumer cooperatives owned by peasant shareholders in the villages. The consumer cooperatives also engage in wholesale trade and operate some small industries. Many Soviet fish are caught by fishing collective farms, and the majority of fur-bearing wild animals are trapped by hunting collectives. At least half of rural workers are employees of some cooperative.

However, a few cooperatives exist in the cities. Handicraft cooperatives, often employing housewives who can't leave home, still produce a considerable share of Soviet clothing, crockery, kitchen utensils, and musical instruments. The coop provides the raw materials and markets the finished product, paying its members according to the amount of goods they produce. Special invalid cooperatives, subsidized by the state, provide light productive work for cripples. A cripple gains the satisfaction of feeling useful and makes some contribution to Soviet society. Cooperatives also provide many urban services such as tailoring, window washing, laundering, shoe repair, and piano tuning.

Of course, all cooperatives operate under state regulation. In addition, Soviet laws discriminate against cooperatives in favor of state enterprise. For example, cooperatives of all types, collective, consumer or handicraft, are taxed much higher than state enterprises. During the Khrushchev era many collective farms were converted into state farms, and some handicraft cooperatives were forcibly changed into state enterprise. However, despite discrimination and enforced nationalization, the cooperatives today remain a vast and important sector of the economy. At least one seventh of all Soviet workers are still employed by cooperatives.

Private business survives in the USSR in three main forms: the peasant market, the private garden, and illegal black-marketing. All rural and suburban residents are permitted to have large private gardens, which are as big as a half-acre for a farm family. Altogether these gardens hold only 3 per cent of the farmlands, but produce 61 per cent of all USSR potatoes, 33 per cent of all Soviet meat, 33 per cent of all milk, plus 43% of eggs. Since the gardens are allowed a limited amount of livestock, they also raise one fifth of all Soviet sheep and hogs, besides one third of all cows. Garden produce can be sold at the peasant markets in the cities at uncontrolled prices, which usually are one quarter to one half above prices in urban state stores. These markets account for about one twelfth of all food trade, because they sell a greater variety of fresh food than the state stores. At times during both the Stalin and Khrushchev eras, the Soviet government has attempted to curb the prosperous garden and market business. But each time the government has retreated when confronted by passive popular resistance. For the gardens are a big source of cash income to the gardeners, while the markets are important to urban diets.

There are no statistics on black-marketing, which is large-scale and centers around the city markets, where Soviet citizens illegally buy goods not for use but for resale at a profit. Such speculation is severely punished by Soviet law, with death sentences meted out to major offenders. Yet constant court trials of speculators prove that this illegal private business is widespread. Some cases are fantastic in scope, as when a group of local officials in Central Asia converted a small state factory into their private enterprise producing scarce textiles for high-priced sale on the black market.

Gosplan has the power to compel most state enterprises and cooperatives to submit to planning. However, state plans can only estimate the probable future performance of the private gardens, and peasant markets. Black-marketing is completely unplanned, except that Gosplan sets low wages for crews of trains and ships, knowing that trainmen and sailors will purchase available goods in one city and resell at a profit in another city where such goods are scarce.

Despite all the imperfections of economic planning, Gosplan's management of Soviet economy has made the USSR the second greatest industrial power in the world, yielding only to the United States. In 1928, when the First Five-Year Plan began, the Soviet Union held the same rank in world industry as Tsarist Russia in 1913—fifth, following the United States, Germany, Britain, and France. Today the USSR has left Germany, Britain, and France far behind.

This fast rise of Soviet industry has not been accompanied by an equivalent rise in the standard of living. The Soviet economy is one of scarcity, with officially admitted shortages of clothing, shoes, furniture, and housing. Instead of constructing factories to make sweaters, socks, and shoes, the Five-Year Plans specialized in heavy industry turning out steel, heavy chemicals, machine tools, armament, and other wares the average person can never use. Light industry, maker of consumer goods, grows only enough to outpace slightly the one to two million yearly growth of Russia's already huge population.

Soviet heavy industry does not produce many refrigerators, vacuum cleaners, and other durable consumer goods, as heavy industry does in America. As fast as Soviet heavy industry expands, it builds more heavy industry. A large part of Soviet industry is also working on armament. The Soviet public pays the heaviest taxes in the world both to build this heavy industry, then sometimes subsidize it after it's built.

Soviet planning turned the usual process of industrialization upside-down. Outside the Iron Curtain, most countries industrialize by building light industry first, since light industry factories can be very small and don't need expensive equipment. For example, the basic machinery of a garment mill comprises sewing machines, not much larger than those used by housewives. But a steel mill needs giant furnaces, each weighing many tons. The funds needed to start are much smaller for light industry than for the mines, smelters, chemical plants, and machinebuilding factories of heavy industry. Then too, consumer goods are bought quickly by the public, finding a ready market, so light industry soon pays its own way. Heavy industry makes small profits, and may have to be subsidized for years after the start.

But the USSR chose to sacrifice everything else to build expensive heavy industry. In his 1946 election campaign speech, Stalin explained that the Communist USSR could easily have built light industry first, just like capitalist countries. But, he added, a large modern war cannot be won by army skill and bravery alone. The army must have huge quantities of up-to-date armament. In turn, the USSR needs quantities of metal to make munitions, much machinery for arms factories, and fuel to keep the factories and railways going. All these are provided by heavy industry. So, said Stalin, in deciding how to industrialize:

> The Communist Party knew that a war was looming. Our country could not be defended without heavy industry. The development of heavy industry had to be undertaken as soon as possible. To be behind with this would mean to lose out. The Party remembered Lenin's words: without heavy industry, it would be impossible to uphold our country's independence. Without it, the Soviet order might perish.[1]

Khrushchev said much the same, but in different words:

> We had to do without a great many things. We imposed restrictions in food and clothing upon ourselves, in the production of mass consumer goods, and used every saved ruble for building factories, combines, the heavy industry, the erection of power stations. We made great haste with these efforts, for we knew if we did not create—in the historically shortest period—our own powerful industry and our own mechanized great agriculture and train our own qualified cadres, or if we remained behind in the development of science and techniques, the imperialists would stifle us, they would destroy this country in which the workers and peasants—the toiling people—had for the first time assumed power. We have won the race against time.[2]

Brezhnev speaks much more calmly:

> The Party's policy of ensuring the priority development of socialist industry, and principally its basis, heavy industry, has turned our country into a mighty power.

Since 1928 all branches of the Soviet economy have been forced to sacrifice in order to supply labor, materials and machines to build up a huge heavy industry. During the Stalin, Malenkov, and Khrushchev eras as well as part of the Brezhnev period, the Five-Year Plans spent more money on heavy industry

---

[1] Stalin, Joseph V., *Text of a Speech at an Election Rally in Stalin Electoral Area, Moscow, February 9, 1946,* Washington: The Soviet Embassy, 1946.

[2] Khrushchev, N. S., *Speech to the East German Party Congress,* Berlin: 1958.

than on light industry, transport, and agriculture taken together. The following table compares the distribution of capital investments in typical Five-Year Plans of Stalin, Khrushchev, and Brezhnev. Noteworthy are the decline of investments in housing and public facilities under Brezhnev and the rise of funds for agriculture.

Table 20. *Distribution of Capital Investments by Percent of Total in Various Five-Year Plans*

Item	Stalin 1933-1937	Khrushchev 1961-1965	Brezhnev 1971-1975
Heavy industry	43	34	40
Housing & public facilities	17	35	23
Agriculture	13	16	22
Communications	19	10	10
Light industry	8	5	5
	100%	100%	100%

When the First Five-Year Plan began in 1928, about 40 per cent of USSR industry was heavy, and 60 per cent was light. Today approximately 74 per cent of Soviet industry is heavy, and only 26 per cent is light. No other nation in the world has such a preponderance of heavy industry over consumer goods production. Most capitalist nations have more light industry than heavy. Highly industrialized countries like West Germany, Britain, and the United States divide their industry roughly 50 per cent each way.

Thus the record of Sovet economic planning is a mixture of success and failure. It has not provided the population with a high standard of living, because this has never been its goal. While Soviet sputniks circle the earth, the average peasant still lives in a one or two-room hut, heats his home with charcoal or wood, draws his water from a well, and tills his big garden with hand tools. Large sections of many Soviet cities lack running water and sewers.

The strength of heavy industry, and weakness of light industry, are revealed in Table 21, which compares these industries with their American counterparts.

Table 21. *US–USSR Comparative Industrial Production*

Heavy Industry	USSR (1975)	US (1975)
Million Metric Tons		
Coal	701	584
Petroleum	491	410
Steel	141	110
Billion Kilowatt-Hours		
Electricity	1,038	1,950
Billion Cubic Meters		
Natural gas	289	570
Consumer Goods		
Millions		
Passenger automobiles	1.2	6.7
Television receiving sets	7	10.6
Million Metric Tons		
Plastics	2.8	8.2

Source: *Moscow News,* 1976. *Americana Annual,* 1976. *Statistical Abstract of the United States,* 1976.

From the Communist viewpoint, economic planning has built a USSR heavy industry which threatens capitalist world supremacy. Therefore Soviet emphasis on heavy industry is not likely to be abandoned.

Suggestions for Further Reading

Ames, Edward, *Soviet Economic Processes,* Homewood: Irwin, 1965.

Bergson, Abram, *The Economics of Soviet Planning.* New Haven: Yale University Press, 1967.

Campbell, Robert, *Soviet Economic Power,* Boston: Houghton Mifflin. 1966.

Cohn, Stanley H., *Economic Development in the Soviet Union.* Lexington: Lexington Books, 1970.

Felker, Jere Leake, *Soviet Economic Controversies,* Cambridge: Massachusetts Institute of Technology, 1967.

NOVE, ALEC, *An Economic History of the USSR*. Baltimore: Penguin, 1972.

NOVE, ALEC, *The Soviet Economy,* New York: Praeger, 1966.

NUTTER, WARREN, *The Growth of Industrial Production in the Soviet Union,* Princeton: Princeton University Press, 1962.

PRYDE, PHILIP R., *Conservation in the Soviet Union*. New York: Cambridge University Press, 1972.

SPULBER, NICOLAS, *The Soviet Economy,* New York: Norton, 1962.

Chapter 18

The Farm Problem

The collective farm is an accident of Soviet history. It represents an awkward compromise between the government and the peasants. The government would prefer a state farm, which is owned and operated by the state just like a factory. The manager of a state farm is a government appointee, and the farmhands are paid fixed salaries. Today 52 per cent of all Soviet crop acreage is on state farms.

The collective farm is an agricultural cooperative operating under heavy state control. Peasants form a collective by pooling most of their land and livestock. If a person desires to leave the collective, he cannot withdraw his land or any communal livestock. He can only take away his household goods, tools, and private livestock. Even his house reverts to the collective, which reassigns it to another family.

A collective has its own parliament—a general meeting of the adult farmers. In theory the meeting elects the farm president and board of directors for three-year terms. In practice the Communist Party usually forces the collectives to elect trusted Communists. At present most collective farm presidents are actually appointed by the regional or district party secretary.

The difference between state farms and collective farms is partly financial. A state farmer receives his fixed governmental salary whether the harvest is good or bad. Collective farmers share the money and excess produce accumulated by their collective farm. A collective farmer has a fixed minimum pay, which increases with a good harvest.

The government prefers a state farm because the farmers are under more direct state control than in a collective. But peasants like to see their income rise with a good harvest and don't like the state farm's fixed salary. When the harvest is abundant, an efficient collective farmer receives a higher wage than a state farmer. Peasants also prefer the slightly freer life on a collective. Thus far peasant attitudes have deterred the government from converting all collectives into state farms. Government economizing on agriculture also tends to preserve the collectives. If a state farm suffers a crop failure, the government must subsidize the farm because it is a state enterprise. At present at least some state farms receive government subsidies each year. But if a collective harvest fails, the government will only grant loans, which the collective farm must eventually repay.

According to Stalin, both state and collective farms were originally introduced more because of practical reasons than a desire to bring socialism to the village. Thus Stalin explained:

> In order to do away with our backwardness in agriculture and to provide the country with greater quantities of marketable grain, cotton, and so forth, it was essential to pass from small-scale peasant farming to large-scale farming, for only large-scale farming can make use of new machinery, apply all the achievements of agronomical science and yield greater quantities of marketable produce.
>
> There are, however, two kinds of large farms—capitalist and collective. The Communist Party could not adopt the capitalist path of development of agriculture, and not as a matter of principle alone but also because it implies too prolonged a development and involves preliminary ruination of the peasants and their transformation into farm hands. Therefore, the Communist Party took the path of collectivization of agriculture, the path of creating large-scale farms by uniting peasant farms into collective farms.[1]

The main clue to the governmental desire for collectivization lies in Stalin's remarks about "marketable" produce, particularly

---

[1] Stalin, Joseph, *Speech at a Meeting of Voters of the Stalin Electoral Area of Moscow, February 9, 1946,* Washington: USSR Embassy, 1946.

marketable grain. For grain has always been the largest Soviet crop, and bread is the basic Russian food. Marketable grain does not mean the entire grain crop. In an agricultural country like Russia, about three fifths of the cereals harvest never leaves the farms, but is consumed there in seed, food, or fodder. The surplus production above and beyond the farmer's own needs is marketable—moving off the farms to feed the cities. Though this may seem a routine economic process, the availability or dearth of marketable grain has often decided the fate of modern Russia.

In the years immediately preceding the Bolshevik Revolution, about half the farmland of Tsarist Russia was in great estates, and half was tilled by small private farms. The marketable grain came mainly from the estates, since the average peasant farm was too small to raise much surplus. In 1913, Tsardom's last year of peace, 21.6 million tons of grain were sold by the estates and farms to feed the cities and army. Then during 1914–1917 came the crop decline and railroad breakdown of World War I, and less than 6 million tons of cereals left the farms each year. Russia's city populations ran short of bread, began to hunger, revolted, and overthrew the Tsarist government. "Bread for the cities" became an appealing slogan of the Bolsheviks and greatly eased their seizure of power.

The peasants supported the Bolshevik Revolution, because Lenin promised to divide estate land among the small peasant farms. During the revolution the peasants carved up the estates and added this land to their tiny plots. A few estates were seized by the Soviet government, and converted into model state or collective farms. But basically the revolution changed agriculture from a mixture of estates and small farms into a countryside of tiny homesteads. During the Russian Civil War of 1918–1920 the Soviet government tried to force these little farms to sell all of their marketable produce to the state at a low fixed price, to feed the city populace cheaply. But the peasants resented the low government price, hoarded food, then sold it to urbanites at a high price on the black market. Meanwhile the Civil War caused an even worse collapse of farms and railways, and the annual amount of grain leaving the farmlands shrank to less than 4 million tons. Had the Soviet government not pacified the peasants in 1921 by restoring some private trade in food, the Bolsheviks might have suffered the fate of the Tsars.

The NEP reform of 1921 provided that the government would purchase about half the marketable grain at a low fixed price, while the other half could be sold by the peasants on the open market without price restrictions. Agriculture slowly revived, and by 1927 the total cereals harvest was nearly nine tenths of 1913 production. Yet the 1927 amount of marketable grain was only 10.3 million tons—less than half the normal Tsarist quantity. Moscow, Leningrad, and other large cities had to reintroduce bread rationing, which had not existed since the Russian Civil War.

Part of the trouble was the absence of large farms. Also the number of small farms constantly increased as parents died and divided their farmsteads among their children. But total agricultural acreage did not increase, so peasant farms became smaller as the farms multiplied. The smaller the farm, the less the marketable surplus. Again the peasants hoarded grain from government requisitions in order to sell at a higher price on the open market. A huge illegal vodka industry arose in the villages. Peasants distilled home-brew from grain and sold this vodka at a huge profit. To fool the state inspector, farmers often hid grain in holes deep underground. Even the vast Soviet bureaucracy lacked the manpower for a thorough search of 26 million small private farms.

With the start of the Five-Year Plans in 1928, the Russian peasants were forced into collective and state farms not just as a socialist experiment, but to provide adequate food for city dwellers. Need for the cities was especially acute, as they were bound to grow along with Five-Year Plan industrialization. The large collective and state farms could use machinery and thus grow bigger crops than the tiny private farms. Fewer farmers would be needed, and the surplus peasants could move to the cities and work in the growing industries. The farmers would be under stronger political control and would no longer be able to hide food. And since the average peasant lived poorly, it was assumed that the peasantry would welcome collectivization.

This logical collectivization plan ignored one vital factor: peasant psychology. The basically urban Communist planners did not understand that the main aim of every peasant in the world is to own his own farm.

In 1929 a million gun-toting Communists marched out to the villages with the class-war slogan: "Rely on the poor peasant, ally with the middle peasant, down with the kulak!" And the tragedy of errors began. Poor peasants were generally inefficient farmers; yet they became the main laborers on the new collective farms. Meanwhile the kulak, who had made his dwarf farm pay, was officially branded as a capitalist. He lost his hut, livestock, and land to the collective but was forbidden at first to join it. Naturally the kulaks fought against collectivization. Even the poor and middle peasants, who had little to lose, had to be forced into collective farms at gun point.

For several years in the early 1930's, undeclared civil war raged in the villages. Stalin later confessed to Churchill that fighting Hitler was easier than socializing the stubborn Russian peasants. When it was over, most of the peasants were collectivized. But crops had declined by one third, and half of Russia's farm animals were missing. The peasants had slaughtered many livestock instead of surrendering them to collective farms. Five million kulaks were dead or deported to prison camps, while many others fled into the cities, never to return to farming. Food rationing had to continue in Soviet cities until 1935, when crops and livestock herds began slowly to recover.

During this violent collectivization. the Soviet government was compelled to make some concessions to the peasantry. State farms did not perform well, and many were converted into collective farms. At first the collectives themselves were largely "communes," in which the peasants were forced to pool all their land and livestock. The commune soon gave way to the present type of "collective farm," in which each peasant family is allowed to retain its hut, a large private garden, and some private livestock. The collective farm contains what amounts to tiny private farms, and is a Soviet governmental retreat from the commune. The peasant open market also reopened in the cities, where peasants could market their garden produce, at whatever price the traffic would bear.

Yet the Kremlin gained what it wanted. Twenty-six million small private farms were forced into 250,000 huge agricultural collectives. Each collective farm had to store its harvest in a central yard over which the government could easily post armed guards, because only one farm existed where there had been one hundred before. The government seized a lion's share of the crop at its own cheap price.

Soviet farm guards have done an efficient job. Once collectivization began, grain requisitions from the farms tended to increase from year to year, regardless of good or bad harvests. For example, the 1932 grain harvest slumped, because of a combination of drought and peasant sabotage. Yet grain shipments off the farms were 19.8 million tons, almost twice as much as in 1927. The result was farm famine in two breadbaskets: the North Caucasus and the Ukraine. A Russian friend of mine visited the Ukraine during this famine. In city hotels there was food. But outside the cities he saw peasants walk slowly along the road, suddenly slump, then crumple silently to the ground, dead.

In 1947, after World War II, drought and heavy government requisitions again caused a farm famine in the Ukraine. Though less severe than the famine of 1932, it caused some peasant deaths from starvation. But the increase in marketable grain continued, so that today as much as 90 million tons of grain leave the farms in a bumper-crop year.

From the late 1930's until the early 1950's, the organizational pattern of Soviet agriculture remained much the same. About nine tenths of the farmland was held by collective farms, and one tenth by state farms. (In both cases, these statistics include the large private gardens of the state and collective farmers.) With slight variations from year to year, the number of collective and state farms did not change. In the original collectivization, each peasant village became the nucleus of a collective farm. Small collectives predominated in the northern wooded steppe where villages were tiny, and large collectives in the southern treeless steppes where villages were big. The state farms at first lost money, so there was no incentive to increase their number. Many state farms became experimental agricultural units, testing new seed and breeding new types of livestock. Others specialized in providing vegetables and livestock products to nearby cities.

In 1949–1950 great organizational changes began, largely sponsored by Khrushchev. The number of collective farms was sharply reduced by merging adjacent collectives. The average collective today contains several peasant villages. At first, however, the acreage balance between collective and state farms did not change.

After Stalin's death in 1953, Khrushchev began to create many new state farms on marginal land, which had never been tilled or had not been farmed for years. Later he started converting many inefficient collectives into state farms. The outstanding organizational fact of recent years is the decline of collective sown areas, accompanied by a tremendous increase in the acreage of state farms. This shift is depicted in Table 22:

Table 22. *State Farms Versus Collective Farms*

Year	Number of collectives	Number of state farms	Percent of total sown area in collectives	Percent of total sown area in state farms
1932	211,000	4,337	87	13
1938	242,400	3,992	90	10
1940	236,900	4,159	91	9
1953	93,300	4,857	90	10
1958	69,100	6,002	76	24
1960	44,900	7,375	65	35
1961	41,300	8,270	58	42
1967	36,000	12,000	50	50
1977	28,000	19,636	48	52

Source: Baykov, Alexander, *The Development of the Soviet Economic System,* New York: Macmillan, 1947, pp. 327–333.
Pravda, 1953-1977.

The Soviet countryside today is therefore a landscape of giant farms. In the United States, a country with enormously productive agriculture, the average farm is about 387 acres tilled by one or two farmers. The average Soviet collective farm has 8,450 acres and 540 workers. State farms are even larger. At present the average state farm operates about 14,900 acres and employs about 570 fulltime permanent workers. Though other Communist countries try to copy USSR agriculture, and despite the predominance of large estates in some underdeveloped countries of the capitalist world, apparently no nation on earth has as much large-scale farming as the Soviet Union.

Even though approximate, these statistics reveal some peculiarities of Soviet agriculture besides large-scale farming. The average collective has 22 times the acreage of the average American private farm, yet employs as many as 540 farmers. In brief, a Soviet collective farm is overstaffed. This is almost unavoidable in a collective, which cannot refuse to employ any resident able-bodied male or female who is willing to work on the collective fields. In contrast, an average state farm is understaffed, because its permanent personnel includes just enough hired employees to maintain the farm during slack seasons of agricultural work. When the busy seasons of spring sowing and fall harvesting occur, a collective farm does not need much outside help. But a state farm is compelled to recruit large numbers of part-time workers, who often are urbanites unskilled in agriculture.

The state dictates to each collective farm what crops shall be sown, how much each farmer must work, and how each farmer is paid. Thus the governmental Ministry of Agriculture has surveyed each collective farm and measured its land. Then the ministry arbitrarily decides how much grain, vegetables, fruit, industrial crops, and livestock a farm of that size should raise if weather conditions were perfect. Naturally in these calculations, regions are specialized by climate and soil, so that in Estonia the collectives concentrate on dairy farming, in the Ukraine on grain, sunflowers, and sugar beets, and in Central Asia on cotton, rice, fruit, and silk.

Then the Ministry of Agriculture decrees that a large portion of these planned crops must be sold to the state at a government-fixed price. Since Stalin's death these prices have been raised, but they still barely cover the cost of farm production.

It is up to the collective farm to raise big enough crops to meet the government levies. If bad weather or harvesting losses reduce the total crop below the ministry's estimates, the government usually requisitions as much as if the harvest were good. In exceptional cases, such as a severe drought, the government will postpone part of the deliveries until better years.

Thus the government buys farm food very cheaply, then sells it to city people at a high price, and pockets the middleman's profit. This profit is used for various state expenses, but largely for industrialization.

To use grain again as an example, in recent years the government has requisitioned about 40 per cent of the total grain crop from the state and collective farms. By law, another 35 per cent is set aside for state and collective farm needs, such as seed, fodder, food for pensioners, and an emergency reserve. The remaining 25 per cent is distributed as pay in kind to collective and state farmers, who thus consume only one quarter of the crop they raise. (The state and collective farmers together with their families still constitute about one third of the total Soviet population.) On collective farms the food allotments are apportioned to the peasants on a piecework basis. The more they have worked on the collective fields, the more food they receive.

Of the money a collective farm receives from forced sale of agricultural produce to the state, one fourth is taken by the government in taxes. The land is taxed, and so are the crops raised on this ground. Another one fourth of the collective money must by law be set aside in reserve funds for farmer pensions, farm emergencies, and general farm improvement. The remaining half is distributed on a piecework basis as money pay to the collective farmers. Thus on a collective, the peasant actually receives only two of every four rubles that the collective farm has earned.

State farms do not pay the high money taxes levied on collective farms, yet the state farmer earns little more than a collective farmer. One reason is that the government purchase prices for forced sale of produce to the state are lower to state farms than to collectives. The state farm also assigns larger sums than a collective for general farm improvement.

Largely as a result of the low government prices for farm produce, the monetary pay of both state and collective farmers is below urban salary levels. Farm pay has consistently increased since Stalin's death, but is still inadequate. During the Khrushchev era, the few published statistics indicated that the majority of collective farmers earned the ruble equivalent of only 33 dollars per month. Premier Khrushchev stated that some collective farmers received 55 dollars monthly, and some state farmers, 44 dollars.

After Khrushchev's retirement, rural wages greatly improved. According to the Soviet press, a state farmer now receives 148 dollars monthly. The average collective farmer earns monthly wages of approximately 120 dollars, which can rise higher if the harvest is good. Still these monthly earnings are below the average urban monthly salary of 201 dollars.

Of course, a collective or state farmer pays no rent for his hut, and obtains most of his food from his garden and pay in kind. Nevertheless by Western standards, his money wage is low, leaving him constantly short of cash.

The peasants dislike their low cash wages; and according to the Soviet press, they migrate into the cities at the rate of two million people per year. In the cities rent and food are no longer free, so the peasant migrant at first may live worse than on the state or collective farm. But the city has on-the-job training, night schools, and adult education schools, all of which provide an ambitious migrant the opportunity to rise.

Intourist guides dislike showing state or collective farms to Western tourists. Peasant life is so poor that guides will invent every plausible excuse not to visit the countryside. "The roads are impassable." "It's harvest time, and we can't interrupt the peasants' work." "Too many tourists have visited our collectives, and the farm presidents are complaining." None the less, a persistent tourist can sometimes arrange a rural visit.

It is worthwhile for a tourist to insist on a rural trip outside the city he is visiting, for the sight of even a showplace collective or state farm quickly reveals what is wrong with socialist agriculture.

The average farm settlement consists of rows of huts stretching along both sides of a highway or main village street. A few huts may be on side streets, but most of the village has the appearance of a long narrow ribbon. The style of the huts varies according to the region. In the northern wooded steppe the huts are log cabins, with beautifully decorated windows. Ukrainian villages consist of white-walled adobe huts with thatched roofs, while Central Asian hamlets have mud huts with roofs of sod. Some village huts appear quite sturdy, while others are in disrepair. Hunks of thatch may hang down from a thatched roof. Some huts have rickety walls, which lean at seemingly dangerous angles. A torrential rain will make holes in the walls of a mud hut. The larger villages may contain a little stone church, sometimes open but often closed and boarded up.

The peasant's private livestock may be quartered in the back of the hut. Or there can be one or more small sheds for livestock and storage of fodder. Often the hut and sheds circle or semicircle a small dirt courtyard. Stretching a hundred yards or more behind each hut is the private garden, to which each farm family is entitled. These gardens are quite large, averaging about 1.3 acres on a collective, and about three fourths of an acre on a state farm. Beyond the gardens are the communal fields encircling the village.

A collective or state farm usually has no silos and no large barns. After harvesting, hay and grain are simply stacked out in the open air in a central yard, exposed to wind and rain. The only barns normally are long low sheds for communal livestock. As a rule there are no garages for the farm machinery, which is parked all winter long in an open field. Thus harvest losses and machinery deterioration from bad weather are very great.

Both communal and private livestock look much thinner than in America. Horses appear almost too thin for effective use. Cows are about medium weight. A Soviet pig is about half the weight of an American hog of similar age. Proper feeding of livestock is very difficult during the long Russian winter, which in most areas lasts about six months of each year.

In large villages one sometimes sees a big school building, two or three stories high and two or three hundred feet long, dominating the skyline and looking almost out of place among the huts. No better proof could be found of the great Soviet emphasis on education. Occasionally this is a boarding school which serves two or more collectives, and where farm children study and live during weekdays at no charge or at low cost. I asked one collective farm president why a boarding school was necessary for farm children who grow up in private huts and have plenty of space to play outdoors. The president's frank reply reflected village life:

> Both the father and mother in each farm family work all day long in the fields, leaving no one at home to take care of the children. And our collective farmers are too poor to raise their children properly.

Peasant life has improved very little since the collectivization of the 1930's. The Kremlin assigns small sums of government money for betterment of rural living conditions. Each peasant family still lives in its small hut. Though the USSR mines more coal than the United States, hardly any of this fuel reaches the villages. Instead, the hut stove is fed with charcoal or wood. All household life revolves around this huge, old-fashioned stove. It cooks the food, furnishes heat, and on cold winter nights becomes a warm but hard bed where the whole family sleeps. The ice box is simply a deep hole in the ground. There is no running water, so the housewife has to make frequent trips with pails to the outside pump. Of course, sewers are also non-existent. The hut has no cellar, and drafts blow through the loose floorboards in winter.

One sight in the farm villages is startling. The majority of adults are women. In European USSR some collective and state farms appear to have 50 women for every one man. The balance between sexes is less uneven in Central Asia and Siberia, yet even there the women outnumber the men. One cause is the widespread migration of peasant youths off the farms into the cities. A second reason is the great loss of male lives during the Soviet-German war. The Soviet government has never published full statistics on these losses, but does admit that there were 20 million war deaths. Some of these casualties were women but the vast majority were men. And the Red Army recruited most of its wartime infantry from the peasantry, who therefore suffered the heaviest male losses.

Today, according to official Soviet statistics, 60 per cent of the state and collective farmers are women. War and collectivization have actually caused the peasant labor force to deteriorate. Strong as Russian peasant women are, they are not as husky or efficient as male farmers. In the precollectivization 1920's Soviet crop production depended primarily on male workers, but now the harvests are mainly gathered by women. To make matters worse, the male minority on the farms usually manage to become the administrators and foremen, avoiding hard physical labor. According to the Soviet press, very few state or collective farms have female managers or presidents. A common scene on communal vegetable fields is a group of women weeding with hand tools or bare hands. Nearby stands the foreman—a man, loafing, with his hands in his pockets.

One might ask: Are not presentday state and collective farms highly mechanized, whereas NEP Russia was a land of sickles and wooden plows? There has been considerable mechanization of farm work since collectivization. But the tasks turned over to machines were those mostly done before by horses, not by men. Tractor power has replaced horse power. Chores such as milking, watering and feeding livestock, weeding, sorting seed, stacking the sheaves, and even threshing are still largely done by hand labor.

According to the Soviet press, two thirds of the potato harvest and one half of the cotton crop are still harvested by hand labor. Soviet state and collective farms operate only half as many tractors as American agriculture.

Another sight surprising to the tourist is the large number of weeds in the communal fields of both state and collective farms. Most grain fields are not properly cleaned before sowing, and tall green weeds grow sporadically among the yellow ripening grain. Almost everywhere one sees the same poorly weeded fields. Even Soviet newsreels sent abroad reveal this basic fault.

Weeds are so commonplace on communal fields that the farm officials take them for granted. Many a time I have stood on the edge of a grain field with a collective farm president. He would point to the mixture of wheat and weeds, and boast: "There is my fine grain." Other communal crops are weedy too. For example, in Central Asia one can see vineyards with almost more weeds than grape vines. Long tentacles of weeds twine all over the wooden trellises, surrounding and choking the vines. The Soviet press frequently complains about the large number of weeds on state and collective fields.

But there is another side to the story of Soviet farming. Almost every collective and state farm displays colorful proof that Soviet peasants can still work efficiently if private profit is involved. Stretching for miles around each village are the weedy—and sometimes sparse—communal fields. Yet around every peasant hut is the lush private garden bursting with greenery. To utilize each inch of soil, even the front lawn is planted with vegetables. Here not a single weed can usually be seen. The ground between the plants is as clean as if swept with a broom. Peasants earn as much money from these gardens as from their state or collective farm wages.

The intensive farming of the private gardens is revealed in Table 23:

Table 23. *Productivity of Private Gardens*

Item	Garden Ownership as Per Cent of USSR Total
All crop acreage	3
Cattle	21
Cows	33
Pigs	21
Sheep and goats	20
	Garden Production as Per Cent of USSR Total
Potatoes	61
Meat	33
Milk	33
Eggs	43

Source: Various Soviet agricultural publications, 1976. *Moscow News*, 1977.

Obviously the peasant gardeners cannot consume all this immense production, particularly when some of their food comes from pay in kind issued by state and collective farms.

The excess garden produce is sold by collective and state farmers, and other rural residents, in the cities at the so-called "collective-farm markets." Every Soviet city contains one or more of these peasant markets, which are located in vacant lots, city squares, or large high-roofed buildings provided by the municipality. The peasants pay a small tax to use the market, which the city government supervises with police and sanitary inspectors.

The name of collective farm market is derived from a state regulation permitting collective farms to sell excess collective produce at these markets. In practice this is seldom done. If a collective has excess produce (after fulfilling state requisitions and storing reserves for communal needs), the excess is usually added to the peasants' pay in kind. Then the peasants will individually market the excess, rather than the collective.

Since Stalin's death, the government has encouraged the consumer cooperatives to buy up peasant garden produce and bring it to the city markets for sale. But this attempt to set up a middleman for garden trade has largely failed. The consumer cooperatives are too busy with their normal duty of operating rural stores, and do not wish to assume extra workloads. And the peasants do not desire to divide their market profit with the cooperatives.

About half a million peasants a day trek from the farms into the city markets to sell their garden produce. Carrying huge baskets of food, the half million peasants crowd into state and collective farm trucks, ride into the cities almost every morning, and do not return to the farms until late afternoon. The Soviet press frequently complains about the farm labor loss and misuse of communal trucks due to this daily peasant commuting.

Of course, the Kremlin predicts that both the gardens and markets are temporary and will eventually be abolished. Khrushchev actually tried to eliminate the collective farmers' gardens after Stalin's death. The peasants responded with passive but massive resistance. So Khrushchev retreated, reversed himself, and reduced taxes on the private gardens he had planned to abolish.

Soviet agriculture is a mixture of large inefficient farms and extremely productive gardens. The government's problem is to increase the efficiency of collective and state farms. After Stalin's death, Khrushchev attempted some agricultural reforms. Government prices were raised for food requisitioned by the state from collective farms. Taxes on collective farms were reduced. Collective farm money income therefore almost doubled. Hundreds of thousands of college students were forced to work on the state and collective farms each summer, thus increasing the farm labor pool.

In the past, Russia planted little Indian corn, because this crop requires a hot moist climate. Most of the USSR is cool even in summer and has little summer rainfall. But Khrushchev, hoping that Russia could duplicate America's huge crops of corn, ordered it to be planted on 50 million acres. Corn has a high yield in America, but in Russia has been an indifferent success.

Another major experiment after Stalin's death was an even more dangerous gamble. About 100 million acres of dry pasture-land in north Central Asia, the lower Volga valley, and Siberia were plowed up and sown to grain. These were Khrushchev's "new lands" or "virgin soil." Such lands are good black earth and very fertile, but they receive little rainfall and suffer constantly from drought. No large-scale irrigation was undertaken in the new lands, because the Kremlin believed this would be too expensive. Little scientific crop rotation was employed, since grain was planted year after year.

Oddly enough, the new lands are not really new. This is the area in which many state farms were created during the early 1930's, when agriculture was first collectivized. Like the Khrushchev experiment, the state farms used no crop rotation and failed to develop irrigation. The lack of crop rotation exhausted the soil, and drought repeatedly ruined the crop. By the mid-1930's, many of the state farms had failed, and the land was converted back into pasture.

History repeated itself. For several years before Khrushchev's enforced retirement, the grain harvest steadily declined in north Central Asia and West Siberia, the two largest concentrations of new lands.

Since the mid-1930's most state and collective farms in the USSR followed a five-field crop rotation, which replaced the primitive three-field rotation used in Tsarist and NEP Russia. The five-field system provided that one fourth of all arable land should lie each year under fallow or grass, to restore fertility of the soil. But in 1962, Premier Khrushchev condemned the five-field rotation, and ordered millions of acres of grassland and fallow to be planted with corn, sugar beets, beans, and peas to be used for animal feed. Khrushchev predicted that soon all fallow and grassland would be sown to such crops.

The danger in this experiment was the shortage of chemical fertilizer in the USSR. Even today, fertilizer production is adequate only for fields under industrial crops like cotton, sugar beets, and sunflowers. Khrushchev's plans to expand fertilizer output were grossly underfulfilled. The pre-Khrushchev fallow and grasslands restored the fertility of the soil each year in the absence of sufficient fertilizer. Had Khrushchev's plan continued, the sowing of fallow and grasslands would have resulted in soil depletion throughout the USSR. When Khrushchev was ousted from power, the sowing of fallow and grasslands was discontinued.

Of course, the USSR is not starving. There has been no Soviet famine since 1947. With today's total Soviet sown acreage of more than 500 million acres, the USSR ranks among China, India, and the United States as one of the largest food producers in the world. For years the Soviet Union has outproduced the United States in wheat, wool, potatoes, flax, hemp, sugar beets, and sunflowers.

The USSR does not have the overpopulation problem of China or India. But Soviet agriculture does not grow enough crops to give the average Russian a good diet. And the population is increasing without an equal growth in farm output.

To an American or West European, the present Soviet diet is monotonous, dull, and reminiscent of wartime rations. There is too much bread and potatoes, and too little meat, butter, sugar, and fruit. Milk is usually drunk only by children. Even the Soviet press complains about periodic shortages of tea, sugar, and livestock products in provincial cities. In tourist hotels about half the items listed on the dining-room menu are unobtainable. The large amount of starch in the diet gives most Soviet citizens a stocky appearance, but insufficient protein and vitamins have stunted their growth. The average Russian is shorter than the average American.

Table 24 compares livestock herds and output of basic foods in the USSR and United States.

According to both the Soviet press and USSR officials I have interviewed, a major reason for the forced retirement of Premier Khrushchev was the failure of his agricultural experiments. His successors have reduced the USSR acreage under corn, and have converted some of the new lands back into pasture. Large-scale irrigation projects are now under way, so future crops will not be greatly harmed by drought. All Khrushchevian restrictions on private gardens and collective farm markets have been removed. As already indicated, the Brezhnev-Kosygin regime also introduced a large number of administrative and financial reforms, which have resulted in roughly tripling the pay of the average collective farmer.

Table 24. *Comparison of Agriculture in the US and USSR*

No. of livestock	USSR (1976)	US (1975)
Millions		
Cattle	111.0	140.1
Hogs	57.8	81.8
Farm Production		
Million metric tons		
Grain	223.8	273.0
Potatoes	85.0	14.5
Meat	14.7	16.7
Billions		
Eggs	32.9	64.3

Source: Statistical Reporting Service, U.S. Department of Agriculture. *Moscow News,* 1977.

The past history of Soviet agriculture has been depressing. Even the many agricultural improvements attempted by the Brezhnev regime have not ensured consistently good harvests, with the result that the USSR has become a large importer of American, Canadian, and Australian grain. Poor mechanization and poor labor are grave handicaps for socialized farming.

Suggestions for Further Reading

BELOV, FEDOR, *The History of a Collective Farm,* New York: Praeger, 1955.

DOBROVOLSKY, ALEXANDER, *Economic Administration and Labor Productivity on a Soviet State Farm,* New York: Columbia University Press, 1954.

GOLDMAN, MARSHALL I., *Soviet Marketing: Distribution in a Controlled Society,* New York: The Free Press, 1963.

HAHN, WERNER G., *The Politics of Soviet Agriculture, 1960-1970.* Baltimore: Johns Hopkins University Press, 1972.

JASNY, NAUM, *The Socialized Agriculture of the USSR,* Stanford: Stanford University Press, 1949.

KABYSH, S. S., ***Results of the March Plenum of the Central Committee of the USSR Communist Party,*** **Munich: Institute for the Study of the USSR, 1962.**

STUART, ROBERT C., *The Collective Farm in Soviet Agriculture*. Lexington: Lexington Books, 1972.

VOLIN, LAZAR, *A Century of Russian Agriculture*. Cambridge: Harvard University Press, 1970.

WALSTON, LORD, *Agriculture Under Communism*. New York: Capricorn, 1973.

Chapter 19

Militarized Industry

A British diplomat once visited a poverty-stricken Russian village. One peasant woman succinctly put him in his place. He had sarcastically asked: "What kind of country is this? You don't even have shoes."

Quickly came the reply: "Yes, I have no shoes. But we have the finest tanks in the world!"

The peasant woman was not far from wrong. Soviet tanks may not be the finest, but Russia has more of them than any other country. The Soviet Armed Forces also lead the world in number of submarines, submarine-based missiles, and intercontinental rockets. Table 25 gives some comparative data.

Table 25. *Some Comparative Equipment of USSR and US Armed Forces (1977)*

Item	USSR	United States
Tanks	34,500	8,500
Submarine-based missiles	700	658
Intercontinental missiles	1,590	1,054

Source: US Department of Defense.

Building these tank, submarine, and missile forces, plus a large stockpile of land weapons and nuclear bombs, has been a task of Soviet industry for many years. The most careful Western estimates, based on Soviet official statistics, conclude that about one fifth of all Soviet industrial production since the late 1940's has been armament. Other Soviet factories work night and day, producing the many items from coal to conveyors required to support armament manufacture.

Refugee factory managers estimate that roughly half of all Soviet industry works directly or indirectly for defense, There is nothing new in this economic policy. It started in the mid-1920's, when War Minister Mikhail Frunze induced the USSR Congress of Soviets to pass a momentous law:

> Past experience in the imperialist World War and our Civil War have shown with full clarity that modern war is waged not by armed forces alone, but by the entire country, and requires strain by all production forces of a state. Under these circumstances, our country's defense preparation requires not only military training of the widest strata of the population, but a development of industry and agriculture which, without violating the normal growth of production forces, would simultaneously create a firm foundation for defense needs. . . .
>
> The USSR Congress authorizes its government to take all measures necessary to improve national defense ability by:
>
> Appropriate expansion of war industry, and an organization of all the Soviet Union's other state industry that even in peacetime would satisfy wartime needs. . . .
>
> These planned measures cannot be accomplished by the efforts of the War Office alone. Hence the Congress obliges all Commissariats (ministries) of the USSR and of the Soviet republics to take a very active part in conducting them. . . .[1]

Mikhail Frunze, the man who militarized Russia, was unusual among early Communist leaders. In a political party of professional pacifists who hated war and all army traditions, he took the pains to train himself thoroughly in modern military science long before the Bolshevik Revolution of 1917. Naturally he was in great demand as a Red Army leader during the Russian Civil War, when almost all other Soviet commanders were unskilled Bolshevik guerrillas or mistrusted former Tsarist officers. Today he is considered even by professional military men outside Russia

---

[1] *Collection of Laws and Edicts of the USSR Government, Vol. I.*, No. 35, June 6, 1925.

as having been the greatest general—Red or White—in that war. Russia's highest army school has long been named the "Frunze Military Academy," the Moscow equivalent of America's Command and General Staff College for high-ranking officers.

In January 1921, two months after the Russian Civil War, with Russia still in the depths of economic depression, both government and people war-weary, and intense effort needed merely to stay alive, Frunze published an article demanding total Soviet militarization. He analyzed peacetime war preparations in leading capitalist countries, and concluded that each was developing a consistent pattern of preparedness embracing not their armies alone, but certain civilian institutions too. In turn, he advised Soviet Russia to abandon its practice of preparedness embracing the army alone, and to concentrate on economic mobilization.

In 1924 Lenin died, Stalin seized control of the Communist Party machine, and Frunze was promoted from Commander of Soviet armies in the Ukraine to Assistant War and Navy Minister under Trotsky. Early the next year Trotsky was accused of gross incompetence and dismissed as Minister, and Frunze took his place. Frunze was War Minister barely nine months, then died during a cancer operation. But just before his premature death at the age of 40, Frunze had the satisfaction of seeing his total militarization plan made Soviet law.

The law of June 1925 ordering total mobilization was a turning point in Soviet history. In the late 1920's and entire 1930's, Soviet bureaucracy, industry, and daily life were remolded slowly but surely to fit Frunze's mobilization pattern. Through the years other laws amplified the original 1925 decree. Each Five-, Seven- or One-year Plan contained sections on economic mobilization. These peacetime preparedness measures greatly aided the USSR in winning the Soviet-German War of 1941–1945, and the same preparedness continues today with some improvements learned in wartime. Despite press censorship, Soviet economic and military journals give a considerable explanation of this preparedness, whose known features are as follows.

First, the USSR has greatly emphasized its heavy industry, as shown in Table 26. Regardless of changes in Soviet leadership, this emphasis has been consistent.

The second major feature of Soviet economic preparedness has

Table 26. *Share in All Soviet Industrial Production of Heavy Industry and Light Industry*

Regime	Year	Heavy Industry (in per cents)	Light Industry
Tsardom	1914	33	67
Lenin	1921	31	69
Stalin	1928	40	60
	1940	61	39
	1950	69	31
Khrushchev	1955	71	29
	1961	73	27
Brezhnev	1970	73	27
	1975	74	26
	1980 Plan	74	26

Source: Various Soviet publications, 1966-1976.

been the location of much heavy industry in the interior, far from dangerous frontiers. From the viewpoint of military security, Tsarist Russia's industry was wretchedly located. Half of all industrial output was concentrated in the capital city of St. Petersburg and the so-called Central Industrial Region stretching from Moscow to the middle Volga. One fourth of all Tsarist industry was split between the Ukraine and the Urals—the two main areas of coal mining and steel smelting. The fifth and final concentration of industry was in the Caucasian city of Baku, where most of Tsarist oil was extracted. Russian geographers have long defined the eastern regions (or East) of Russia as being Siberia, Central Asia, the Urals, and even European territory east of the Volga. In Tsarist days the Russian East possessed almost no industry except in the Urals. Huge Siberia contained a mere 2 per cent of all Russian industry, and Central Asia had even less. This was the industrial map of Tsardom at the time of the 1917 Bolshevik Revolution. The first ten years of Soviet rule made no major change.

But, from their start in 1928, the Five-Year Plans began to build new factories in new places. Though smokestacks multiplied in old European industrial districts like Leningrad, Moscow, and the Ukraine, a substantial part of the factory and mine construction was diverted to the Russian East, as shown in Table 27.

Table 27. *Growth of the Share of the USSR East in Soviet Industrial Output*

Year	Coal Mining	Steel Smelting	Petroleum Production
	(in per cents)		
1913	12	21	3
1928	19	22	2
1933	26	22	3
1940	36	31	7
1965	49	41	12
1970	51	41	25
1973	52	43	37

Source: Raymond, Ellsworth L., *Soviet Preparation for Total War,* (microfilmed doctoral dissertation), Ann Arbor: Michigan University, 1952, pp. 98–101. *National Economy of the USSR in 1973,* Moscow, 1975. *Pravda,* 1976 and 1977.

Most East Russian coal is mined in the Urals, central Siberia, and north Central Asia, while Eastern steel is mainly smelted in the Urals. The vast majority of Eastern oil comes from the Urals and a new basin in West Siberia. All these areas are far from seacoasts or western frontiers, relatively safe from land invasion, and a long trip into Russia's heartland by air.

Of course, this eastward march of industry also had nonmilitary motives. Communist ideology proclaims all nationalities to be equal, so the Soviet government tries to build factories in each of the many racial regions of the multinational USSR. Soviet Asia contains much more mineral wealth than European Russia, and in industrializing, the Communists have opened many mines in the Siberian taiga and tundra, or the Central Asian mountains and deserts.

Yet the enormous industrial development of Eastern USSR can hardly be explained as mere modernization of colonial areas, or logical location of industry near its sources of raw materials. Even today over 70 per cent of the Soviet population still lives in European USSR, so for peaceful purposes it is unreasonable to build much of heavy industry in the East far from the European USSR market. Further proof of the military nature of Eastern heavy industry is the fact that light industry has had no similar Oriental growth. Most Soviet clothes, shoes, furniture, and other consumer goods are still manufactured in European USSR, then shipped at high costs to all parts of the Soviet Union.

During the Soviet-German war of 1941–1945, the Eastern heavy industry supplied the Red Army after Ukrainian industry had been lost to the Germans. All Soviet sources agree that the munitions manufactured by the Urals and Soviet Asia saved the USSR from wartime defeat. It is hardly surprising that Soviet Eastern industry has greatly expanded since World War II and is still increasing. The 1976-1980 Plan calls for Siberian industry to increase by 50 per cent, and for especially large gains in oil, natural gas, and coal mining, copper and aluminum smelting, and electric power production in the entire Soviet East.

The third major feature of Soviet economic preparedness is the drive for autarky, which is described as "technical and economic independence." USSR heavy industry could easily be stalled in wartime if dependent on supplies from abroad. Moreover, most Soviet foreign trade is carried on via the Black and Baltic Seas, both of which can be easily blockaded by European powers. Likewise, the trade routes to major Soviet ports on the Pacific run between Japanese islands. Frunze himself preached the military value of national self-sufficiency, and Soviet economists have echoed him ever since.

Of course, the Soviets began their drive for autarky with the advantage of a country already satisfying most of its own needs. Tsarist Russia was a world leader in growing wheat and sugar beets, and fed itself well except during drought or war. Prerevolutionary Russia also was self-sufficient in iron and steel, and actually exported oil, manganese, and chrome. This partial self-sufficiency explains why Tsarist foreign trade was smaller than the commerce of any other great power.

Though the Soviet era of the 1920's was primarily a period of economic reconstruction, substantial gains were made toward self-sufficiency. For example, by 1928 the USSR broke the Tsarist tradition of supplying Leningrad with British coal, and imports of this fuel were abandoned. But the big Soviet drive for autarky really began with the First Five-Year Plan of 1928–1932. Since all munitions are made from minerals, intense efforts were exerted to find and mine every variety of mineral in the USSR itself. Tsarist and NEP Russia had extracted 20 minerals. By the late

1930's, USSR mines were yielding as many as 80 minerals. Today about 90 are being extracted and used in production. The military importance is obvious, since 30 minerals are needed to make a tank, and 46 to build a jet plane. Soviet production of most minerals is now sufficient for armament needs. The few shortages are usually filled by imports from the Soviet satellites.

But the Soviet concept of self-sufficiency goes far beyond minerals. Since farm collectivization, the entire sown acreage has been altered to produce greater amounts of strategic crops like cotton (uniforms and ammunition) and silk (parachutes). Attempts are made to produce every type of industrial machine within the country. By now, this attempt has largely succeeded. Huge synthetic industries have been built to produce items which nature has denied the homeland.

In the 1920's, all Soviet rubber was imported from distant Southeast Asia, because the Russian winters are too cold to grow rubber trees. Attempts to extract rubber from an unusual variety of Central Asian dandelion were a costly failure. Therefore in the 1930's a huge synthetic industry was set up, making artificial rubber at first from limestone and potatoes, and now also from coal and oil. Today this is the world's second largest rubber industry, excelled only by its American counterpart. Some natural rubber still has to be imported to blend with the synthetic product, but the Soviet rubber supply is far different from that of 50 years ago.

The drive for autarky is reflected in Soviet foreign trade. Though the USSR has the largest population of any industrial nation, and is second only to the United States in factory and farm production, its foreign trade—like that of Tsarist Russia—is smaller than the commerce of any other major power. Despite an increase in trading since Stalin's death, Russia's share in total world trade is still only some 7 per cent.

The fourth feature of USSR military-economic preparedness is little-known outside Russia. But Soviet laws, economic journals, and industrial tables of organization indicate a peacetime mobilization of all industry for future war.

Of course, the USSR organizes in peacetime for war with one great advantage—a planned economy. The huge central and regional planning apparatus that charts peacetime production can just as easily plan for war. But the Kremlin has not been content to rely on ordinary economic planning. Starting in 1927, USSR industry has been labyrinthed by a military mobilization system so intricate that one can find neither beginning nor end. Russia has the secret weapon of mobilization, which—like the know-how of a skilled engineer—is an advantage impossible to measure. But good mobilization makes weak countries strong, and cannot be underestimated. Well-mobilized Japan with an industry of medium size fought hard for four years during World War II before being defeated by the USA, an industrial giant.

To plan mobilization properly, the Soviet government has created a network of military offices attached to every major economic organization. These offices have had various names such as military sections, mobilization departments, anti-aircraft defense sections, or mobilization groups. Although these titles are frequently changed, such offices are staffed with military officers who learn how to mobilize the economic system by living with it. Military officers permeate the entire Soviet government and economy from top to bottom.

At the peak of the mobilization pyramid stands the USSR State Planning Committee, which makes plans for the entire national economy. Army officers in the Committee apparatus plan armament production, armed forces' supply, industrial mobilization, and economic warfare. Just below this top-level planning organization is the USSR governmental cabinet. Every civilian cabinet ministry also has military offices and units. Incidentally this cabinet includes six war-industry ministries.

Other military sections operate right down to the factory level in heavy industry. The army officers in these sections require their factories to plan camouflage, install bombshelters, and practice blackouts and air raid drills. Many factories are now digging large bombshelters into the sides of nearby hills.

But the chief work of military sections is mobilization planning. Working inside the plant, the army officers learn to know it intimately. They discover just what the factory can and cannot do. The officers draft practical and realistic plans to convert the plant to war production.

The advantage of this system is that civilian factories can be converted to war production rapidly. In wartime, all industrial nations have to convert most of their heavy industry to armament output. During future atomic war the speed of conversion may be vital. Many factories will be destroyed by air raids and rockets in the first days of war, and the remaining plants must convert quickly to production of the proper armament or the war will be lost.

Soviet army officers in a civilian factory have other duties. If the armed forces order any product from the factory in peacetime, the plant military section is responsible for filling the orders. The army officers ensure fast compliance. Engineers in Soviet factories have described to me how their plants stopped all other work when an army order arrived. The whole factory labors day and night until the defense job is done. Of course, the military section also serves as army inspector and buyer of the finished goods.

Morale espionage is another duty of the military section. Army officers in a plant listen secretly to the workers' conversations and forward reports to the Defense Ministry. Finally, the military section decides who shall be drafted into the armed forces from the factory in case of war, and who cannot be spared.

Soviet communications have a mobilization system as thorough as in heavy industry. Each individual railway has its army mobilization office, and every river or ocean steamship company has its naval mobilization group. A similar naval office exists in each seaport. Army officers are on duty in all large telephone, telegraph, radio, and television stations throughout the USSR.

Light industry is nowhere nearly as important for war as heavy industry. Nonetheless, the Soviet textile, shoe, and food-processing industries all have mobilization offices. Wood would normally not be considered a strategic raw material. Yet the timber industry has war mobilization departments.

Russia's movie industry has a military section which produces training films for the Soviet and satellite armed forces, and movies on war themes for the general public. The US Army captured several million feet of these training films during the Korean War of 1950–1953. One of the most interesting showed—by scenes of actual torment—how to torture enemy prisoners. The annual USSR plan for general movie production always orders several war movies. These war films for the general public glorify army and navy life, and make military service seem interesting.

Many war movies have catchy theme songs which become Soviet hit tunes.

The Ministry of Agriculture has mobilization offices which prepare farms for war. All state and collective farms must loan their trucks to the Soviet Army when it requests them. The Foreign Trade Ministry, which monopolizes almost all Soviet imports and exports, has a mobilization section, as does the Public Health Ministry that supervises doctors, clinics, hospitals, and sanitoria.

The weather service, whose data are so valuable for war, has both military sections and secret codes. Even in peacetime, many Soviet weather reports are secret, although the USSR has one of the best weather services in the world. Only local weather forecasts are published, not national summaries.

In comparison, the United States has some economic mobilization plans for war, but they are nowhere as thorough or complete. And American plans are largely drafted in Washington, not factory by factory as in the USSR.

During World War II, when American knowledge of the USSR was still slight, I told a US Army officer how most Soviet factories have mobilization offices staffed by military men. He listened carefully, then said:

> I don't think that is a good system. What does an army officer know about factories?

Of course, the Kremlin has thought of this aspect too. Military men are placed in Soviet factories because civilian engineers may lack munitions experience. Yet most army officers are trained to lead troops into battle, not to be at home among a maze of factory machinery. Mobilization and conversion of a large factory demand real industrial skill.

As early as the 1920's and 1930's, the Kremlin found a solution to this difficult problem. A whole new type of military engineers has been created. They are dual personalities, equally at home in the army or industry. To train them, the Soviet armed forces operate a network of about ten unusual military academies, which teach officers not just to use military equipment, but also to manufacture it. Among these military-industrial schools are the Military Electro-Technical Academy, the Military Transport

Academy, the Artilery Engineering Academy, the Military Chemical Academy, the Military Engineering Academy, the Academy for Mechanized and Tank Troops, the Air Force Engineering Academy, and the Naval Shipbuilding Academy.

Part of the graduating class from such schools joins the regular armed forces. The others are assigned to detached duty in industry and communications. There they work for several years, then return to military service. These military industrialists spend their entire career rotating back and forth between military and civilian work. During this rotation, some military men achieve top posts in civilian bureaucracy.

The recently deceased Tupolev, a top designer of giant planes, was an air general, yet he was not exceptional. The Military Aviation Academy has long boasted that most managers and chief engineers of Soviet aircraft factories are its alumni.

The advantage of these schools is tremendous. The same academic background brings together the producers and consumers of armament. For example, an air officer on active duty does not make impossible demands on the aircraft factory, because he knows the production problems involved. In turn, the military engineer in the factory understands what the air corps needs.

Thus Soviet heavy industry is infiltrated by military engineers who know how to operate civilian factories for war. What better way could be found to staff the mobilization offices in Soviet factories?

The Soviet Union is the only country in the world with special civilian colleges for the sole purpose of teaching armament production. Each of the war-industry ministries in the cabinet has its own engineering institutes, which train civilian students to mass-produce modern weapons. Many of these institutes are located in Moscow and Leningrad, while others are scattered in various provincial cities.

To conceal their purpose, the approximately 20 armament colleges usually have commonplace civilian names. Apparently innocuous institutes of "chemical technology" train civilian engineers to manufacture explosives. Few inhabitants of Leningrad are aware that their city's Industrial Academy is a war-industry school. One of the most famous engineering colleges in Russia is the Moscow Steel Institute, which is often described as the

Soviet equivalent of America's Massachusetts Institute of Technology. Yet this is not a general engineering school like MIT, but is another defense industry college.

Students in these war-industry colleges receive cost-of-living allowances more generous than the usual stipend for a Soviet university student. For example, in Moscow I talked with a Russian who described himself as a tank engineer. After graduating from a tank college in the Siberian city of Novosibirsk, he had worked about 15 years in the tank industry. Now the government was paying him the full equivalent of his engineering salary to return to college and obtain a doctoral degree in tank engineering.

Since 1935, another large group of Soviet civilian youths have been required to study armament production. They are students in certain colleges and technical high schools of nonmilitary heavy industry. These educational institutions primarily train youths to be experts in civilian chemistry, metalworking, or machinebuilding. Though the students major in civilian skills, they have to minor in munitions manufacture.

This study of war production is compulsory, and is the industrial equivalent of college ROTC. If students receive good marks in munitions, they serve only one year in the military training of peacetime conscription. This armament study is not a brief one-semester course. In a typical engineering college or technical high school of this type, a student averages two to three hours of classroom instruction per week in munitions manufacture throughout his three to five years of school.

Upon graduating, the student receives a reserve army commission in armament production. If war comes, all alumni of these militarized schools have to leave civilian work and transfer into war production plants. Thus many young civilian engineers and technicians, who never studied in an army academy or war-industry institute, are trained in munitions manufacture.

But no matter how many engineers are trained for armament, experience is always the best teacher.

Many convertible civilian factories have military workshops to practice weapon-making in peacetime. These workshops are usually organized in one of two ways. The civilian factory may have two assembly lines: a large conveyor manufacturing the peaceful product, and its little brother (the military workshop) grinding out armament. This method is used by the Kirov machinery plant in Leningrad, with separate assembly lines for tractors and for tanks. When war starts, the tractor conveyor simply switches to tanks, which the factory already knows how to build.

Or next door to a large civilian plant may be a small munitions factory producing the type of weapon to which the large plant can convert. This second method is used by the Volgograd (formerly Stalingrad) tractor plant. Among the many buildings within its huge factory compound is a small tank plant. The tanks are usually transported out of the factory at night, when a tourist would not see them.

A large convertible plant leads a double life, like an industrial Dr. Jekyll and Mr. Hyde. Tractor factories normally produce tanks. Parts for light tanks and amphibious tanks come primarily from automobile plants. Shipyards build more submarines than freighters. Farm machinery plants manufacture casings for rockets and bombs. Of course, the USSR has some factories which were built primarily to produce munitions. These war plants often have civilian workshops manufacturing commonplace industrial items. These workshops keep the defense industry operating at full capacity when demand for munitions is slack. It is no easy matter to tell which USSR factories are military, and which are civilian. Both do each other's work. But conventional pairings in Soviet factories are: automobiles and armored cars, machine tools and artillery, oil pipe and rocket barrels, fertilizers and explosive, railway cars and tanks. The end result is just what modern war demands: quick, easy, industrial conversion.

Armament production is dispersed far and wide throughout most of heavy industry. This may explain why the USSR at disarmament conferences objects strenuously to foreign inspection of Soviet factories. Munitions come from everywhere in the USSR, hiding behind the most innocent of factory names.

Few people outside Russia realize how vital this peacetime industrial preparedness was for the Soviet victory over Germany in World War II. The popular misconception in America is that Russia won by sheer manpower and Lend-Lease aid.

In fact, Lend-Lease did not reach Russia in large quantities until after the battle of Stalingrad, which is now generally conceded to have been the turning point of the European phase of World War II. This Lend-Lease consisted mainly of machinery, strategic raw materials, ships, and trucks, rather than armament.

It was mid-1941 when the Germans invaded Russia. By autumn of that year, after devastating Soviet losses during the first few months of the war, the German forces on the eastern front possessed three times as many airplanes and tanks as the opposing Red Army. This was the period of the greatest Soviet losses in manpower. Half a million men a month were sacrificed to slow down the German mechanized advance.

Just a year later, at the battle of Stalingrad, the Red Army was as well supplied with weapons as the Germans. This was the result of hard work by a Soviet industry itself suffering enormous war losses. At this time the Russian industry still intact was only one fourth the size of the production machine at Hitler's disposal.

Of course, Hitler's production machine—including Nazi satellite factories—at best was only half the size of American wartime industry. How did Soviet wartime armament output compare with America? To compare US and USSR wartime armament output and be fair to both sides, the last three years of World War II can be taken as an honest measuring stick. At this period both countries reached their peak wartime production. The comparison in Table 28 is based on official American and Soviet sources. In this instance, the latter appear accurate because they conform closely to Nazi German estimates of Soviet war production. Since they fought Russia on a wide front, the Germans could ascertain how much Soviet armament was thrown into battle, how great Soviet battle losses were, and how fast these losses were replaced.

The comparison of Soviet and American wartime production is hardly comforting to the West. Russia manufactured more machine guns and five times as many mortars as the United States. Of course, the American army did not use mortars as much as the Russians, who also preferred submachine guns to rifles for infantry armament. But the United States concentrated on artillery, and Soviet output of cannon was double that of America. The US led in rifle production, but the USSR rolled out more tanks. Only in naval ships and airplanes did Russia lag far

Table 28. *US and USSR Production of Certain Munitions During the Last Three Years of World War II*

Type of Armament	Soviet Union	United States
Tanks	90,000	86,000
Airplanes*	120,000	333,000
Mortars	300,000	61,000
Artillery**	360,000	173,000
Machine guns***	7,350,000	4,980,000
Rifles	9,000,000	10,700,000

Ames, Edward, "Soviet War Potential, an Alternative Approach," *American Economic Review,* Vol. XLI, No. 2, May 1951.

* In equivalent of fighter-plane weight, since America built many large warplanes, while most Soviet wartime planes were single-engine fighters.

** No breakdown of USSR artillery output by types is available. Thus only totals may be compared.

*** Including submachine guns.

behind. At this time Soviet industry was no more than one sixth the size of America's production machine.

The Kremlin has to consider other factors besides war in economic planning. The oversized heavy industry makes some contribution to the Soviet standard of living by producing such equipment as farm tractors, streetcars, buses, radios, television sets, railway passenger trains, electricity, gas, and coal. The insufficient light industry does expand slightly from year to year, gradually improving the modest standard of living.

But war planning always dominates any other consideration. The Kremlin would probably like to give its people a high standard of living, especially since this would be excellent propaganda for Communism. Yet thus far the Soviet leadership has assumed that the governments of most nations outside the Iron Curtain are active or passive enemies. Soviet economic planning is conducted accordingly. Communist faith in the correctness of its military-industrial methods was confirmed by the Soviet victory in the Nazi-Soviet War. In Kremlin belief, economic planning is not just a means of avoiding depressions as in America, but is the road to survival of the Soviet state.

The weak light industry of the USSR is no immediate threat to its huge American competitor. At present rates of growth of

Soviet and American standards of living, the USSR would not equal United States prosperity until the year 2000. This conclusion was reached by the US government after painstaking analysis of past and current Soviet statistics.

But Soviet heavy industry is a different matter. In 1940, on the eve of the Soviet-German War, this capital-goods industry was only one third the size of America's. Today it has increased to approximately four fifths. And its rate of growth is faster than the expansion of US heavy industry.

Since the rate of growth of Soviet industry is of vast international importance, one must note that industrial expansion has tended to slow down during the post-Stalin period. One reason is possibly the Soviet government's longtime neglect of the transportation system, which cannot move all the goods that industry creates. Another may be the disruptive changes in industrial administration from Stalinist centralized management to Khrushchev's decentralization, then recentralization by Brezhnev and Kosygin. Still another explanation could be that industry has grown too large to be efficiently planned. Table 29 depicts the slowdown by citing official Soviet statistics, which exaggerate the rate of USSR industrial growth but are still relevant.

Table 29. *Annual Growth of Soviet Industry in Percent Over the Previous Year*

	Year	Percentage of Growth
Stalin	1947	22
	1950	23
Khrushchev	1955	13
	1960	9
Brezhnev	1965	9
	1970	8
	1975	7
	1976	5

Despite this slowdown, even by 1960 USSR heavy industry was as large as that of the United States in 1940, just before the USA entered World War II. In this war, America was the arsenal of democracy, winning most victories by sheer weight of armament.

At present rates of growth, by 1980 USSR heavy industry could be as large as America's heavy industry today. Even now, Soviet industry is far better organized for war.

Suggestions for Further Reading

CLARK, M. GARDNER, *The Economics of Soviet Steel,* Cambridge: Harvard University Press, 1956.

CLINE, RAY S., *World Power Assessment, A Calculus of Strategic Drift.* Boulder: Westview, 1975.

GALLAGHER, MATTHEW P., and SPIELMANN, KARL F., *Soviet Decision-Making for Defense.* New York: Praeger, 1972.

GALLIK, DANIEL, *The Soviet Aircraft Industry,* Chapel Hill: North Carolina University Press, 1955.

KOROL, ALEXANDER G., *Soviet Research and Development: Its Organization, Personnel and Funds,* Cambridge: Massachusetts Institute of Technology, 1964.

KRAMISH, ARNOLD, *Atomic Energy in the Soviet Union,* Stanford: Stanford University Press, 1959.

KRUZHIN, PETER, "The Streamlining of Civil Defense in the USSR," *Radio Liberty Research Bulletin, No. 38.* Washington: Radio Liberty, Sept. 24, 1976.

RAYMOND, ELLSWORTH L., *Soviet Preparation for Total War,* (doctoral dissertation), Ann Arbor: University of Michigan, 1952.

SOKOLOVSKY, MARSHAL V. D., ed., *Military Strategy, Soviet Doctrine and Concepts.* New York: Praeger, 1963.

VOZNESENSKI, N., *The Economy of the USSR during World War II,* Washington: Public Affairs Press, 1949.

Chapter 20

The Standard of Living

Every American tourist is astonished by the high prices of most goods in Soviet stores. It is not easy to convert these prices into dollar equivalents. The official exchange rate of one ruble equaling $1.33 is artificial and overvalues the purchasing power of the ruble. On the black market along Moscow streets, a tourist can obtain 2 to 3 rubles per dollar.

Soviet citizens buy dollars to hoard, to purchase goods cheaply at USSR foreign-currency stores, or to resell to Soviet diplomats, sailors, and tourists who are going abroad. Soviet citizens traveling abroad receive small foreign-currency allotments, but desire more foreign cash to buy Western consumer goods.

CEMA, the Soviet-East European-Cuban-Mongolian Communist common market, conducts its transactions mostly by barter, with the bartered goods evaluated in bookkeeping rubles worth two rubles to the dollar.

For the sake of convenience, let's accept the official rate that a 1977 ruble equals $1.33. Most Soviet food prices are quite high. One egg costs 17 cents, and a chicken sells for $3.70. Per pound, butter costs $2.00, and meat $1.20 to $2.00.

Prices of nonedible consumer goods run even higher. In male apparel a suit costs $200, an overcoat also $200, a shirt $12, and a pair of shoes $40. To be even modestly dressed, a Soviet woman must pay $130 for a suit, also $130 for a coat, and over $50 for a pair of shoes.

Durable consumer goods other than apparel are priced very

high. Standard prices are $86 for a bicycle, $360 for a medium-sized black-and-white television set, $1,000 for a color TV, and $7,300 to $12,200 for passenger automobiles of small to medium size.

A few staple foods are reasonably priced. Per pound, sugar costs 54 cents, bread 24 cents, and potatoes 6 cents. A quart of milk is only 53 cents. Some services are also very cheap. A subway or bus ride costs 7 cents, a trolley trip 4 cents, a haircut 66 cents, and a postage stamp 5 cents. Mass transit has to be cheap, since few Soviet citizens own automobiles.

If Soviet wages were as high as American, most store prices would still strain the family budget. But wages, though constantly rising, are far below the American.

The lowest city wage for a full-time Soviet worker is $93 a month; $201 per month is the average city wage. Skilled workers in construction, transportation, industry, and scientific research receive above-average salaries. Office workers, bank clerks, teachers, and postal personnel earn less than the average wage. Poorest paid are janitors, store clerks, art workers, and medical personnel. At the very bottom are army soldiers, with cash pay of only $5 per month.

As already indicated, rural income averages lower than city wages. Collective farmers receive average monthly wages of $122, and state farm pay is only a little higher.

The average well-paid Soviet citizen rarely receives more than $1,000 per month. For example, a collective farm chairman is paid about $315 monthly, an ordinary ballerina $530, a factory foreman also $530, an industrial engineer $665, and the director of a small factory $800. According to official Soviet statistics, only one per cent of the entire USSR labor force earn ruble salaries equivalent to several hundred dollars or more per month. Yet most of the 1,300,000 job-holders in this well-paid one per cent are not receiving salaries which would be considered high in the United States, despite performing work of great skill or responsibility.

The Soviet elite receive fabulous salaries compared to the average citizen. A college professor may earn up to $1,300 per month, the director of a large plant $1,300, and a scientist $2,300. A member of the Communist Party Politburo earns $5,000 or more monthly. In addition, such people often receive free housing, free summer cottages, and free automobiles. But this elite is a tiny minority of the total working population.

The average Soviet citizen does not know the level of wages and prices in the West. But he is annoyed that Soviet prices are so high and wages so low. For example, an Intourist guide complained to me that a good dress cost more than half of her monthly salary. In private conversations many USSR citizens have tried to give me the following price explanation:

> Russia has too many people. We can't produce enough goods for all of them, and that makes our prices so high.

This explanation is partly correct. Not enough consumer goods are produced, and the high prices prevent low-paid Soviet citizens from buying too much at one time. Yet the main explanation is that the Soviet population is the most heavily taxed in the world.

The Kremlin can borrow from the West only a small fraction of the enormous funds needed for fast Soviet industrialization. Tsarist Russia had the largest foreign debt of any nation in the world in 1917, when about half of Russian industry and banks were foreign owned. After the Bolshevik Revolution, the Soviet government refused to settle Tsarist foreign debts, and nationalized foreign-owned banks, factories, and mines without compensation. American and West European banks were left holding huge stacks of worthless Tsarist bonds. Western governments could not even collect interest on old loans to the Tsarist and Provisional governments of Russia.

Therefore, for many years, no Western bank or government that had loaned money to Tsarist Russia would grant a large long-term loan to its Soviet successor. Only during the Khrushchev era did Western banks begin to grant such loans, which today total $17 billion. Yet even these loans are far from sufficient to cover Soviet financial needs.

Hence the Soviet public has to subsidize most industrialization. Taxation must be enormous to pay for the double burden of large-scale armament and fast expansion of heavy industry. Of every five rubles the average Soviet citizen earns, he must return three to the state in taxes. In comparison, taxes consume one of every three dollars earned by the average American.

Soviet income taxes are kept very low, and the highest tax rate for a state employee is only 13 per cent. Therefore income taxes constitute only 10 per cent of USSR budget revenues.

In addition to income taxes, Soviet citizens pay peripheral taxes, mostly concealed and largely indirect. Such taxes are levied on bachelors, spinsters, childless couples, gas, water, electricity, firewood, land, buildings, handicraft and consumer cooperatives, collective farms, private horses, and private gardens. All these taxes, taken together, provide about one fifth of Soviet budget revenue.

Trade with the Soviet satellites contributes a small percentage of Soviet budget income. Barter agreements with each country supposedly provide for an exchange of goods of equal value. But the Soviet goods are priced high, while satellite wares are valued low. The USSR also acts as a middleman, buying goods cheap, and reselling them to the West at a profit. Russia also imports Western goods at normal world prices, then retails them to the satellites at a high mark-up. Russia has exported to the free world such diverse items as Bulgarian rose oil, Chinese tin, Rumanian petroleum, and Tibetan medicinal herbs.

But most budget money comes from a hidden 150 per cent sales tax on everything the Soviet public buys. Everyone, even the poorest Soviet citizen, can't help paying this tax which siphons off the majority of his salary. Soviet finance books never call this a sales tax. Instead it is described as the "turnover tax" and "industrial profits."

The turnover tax is usually added to the price of consumer goods at light-industry factories, then passed on to the consumer, who pays a higher price to reimburse the factory for the cost of the tax. The industrial profits are mainly collected from light industry too. Again the factory makes the customer pay more, so the factory can absorb the tax. In recent years the turnover tax has been the largest source of budget revenue, with the industrial profits providing almost as much tax money. Taken together, they contribute about 70 per cent of budgetary income.

This double sales tax hits the poor more than the rich. Both pay it, but the rich can afford such expense. And since income taxes are low, a high-salaried person loses little money in this form of taxation. Soviet books explain that rich incomes are not highly taxed, so that there will be an incentive to work well and achieve a highly paid job. This contradicts the precepts of Karl Marx, who demanded that large incomes be heavily taxed until all earnings became equal.

All these tax revenues flow into one central budget, for there is no local taxation in the USSR. The central government collects all taxes, then decides how much money each republic, region, and locality shall receive. The central budget includes about 60,000 regional and local budgets. As a result of this centralization, regions and localities cannot spend large funds on local needs, and prosperous areas like the Ukraine can be forced to subsidize underdeveloped areas such as Central Asia.

But the main purpose of budgetary unity is to concentrate budget expenditures on the main goals of the Soviet regime. Ever since the Five-Year Plans began in 1928, the majority of budget expenses have been allocated to economic development and defense. About half of the funds for economic development have always gone to heavy industry. About half of the defense monies purchase armament, while the remainder pay for housing, feeding, clothing, and general upkeep of the armed forces. The concentration of the USSR on economic development and defense is shown in Table 30.

Table 30 shows the steep rise of budget funds for economic development as the First Five-Year Plan began in 1928. Also clear is the rise of defense expenditures during the late 1930's, at the expense of economic allocations, as the danger of war increased. In 1943, at the height of the Soviet-German War, defense expenditures alone comprised the majority of the budget. After the war, economic funds increased, while defense expenses decreased.

The other major items of budget expenditure in order of decreasing importance are education, propaganda and science, social security and social insurance, public health and organized sport, secret, and administration. Taken together these items amount to some two fifths of budget expenses. The strong Soviet emphasis on education, propaganda, and scientific research is clear. All state employees and collective farmers get old-age pensions, which are paid from the budget alloca-

Table 30. *Where the Soviet Budget Goes*

Year	Economic Development	Defense	Both taken together
	(in per cent of total expenditures)		
1927	18	13	31
1928	68	14	82
1932	71	4	75
1934	60	11	71
1940	34	33	67
1943	16	60	76
1950	38	20	58
1955	44	21	65
1960	44	13	57
1967	43	13	56
1970	46	12	58
1973	48	10	58
1976	51	8	59
1977	52	7	59

Source: Raymond, Ellsworth L., *Soviet Preparation for Total War,* (microfilmed doctoral dissertation), Ann Arbor: University of Michigan, 1952, p. 155.
National Economy of the USSR in 1974, Moscow, 1976.
USSR—Questions and Answers, Moscow, 1975.
Moscow News, 1975-1977.

tion to social security and social insurance. Medical treatment and some hospitalization are free to all Soviet citizens, and the expense is covered by the budget's appropriation for public health. The same appropriation supports a very extensive network of sport clubs for schools, trade unions, and youth organizations. The administration allotment goes mainly to the police and courts.

Besides the open defense expenditure, hidden military appropriations exist throughout the budget. The economic development funds contain allotments to build and subsidize war industry. The education appropriation includes the expense of compulsory military training in civilian schools. Funds for science are largely devoted to armament research. Social security and social insurance pay both civilian and military pensions. The allotment for organized sport is partly military, since Soviet athletes learn rifle shooting and army infantry tactics. The secret allotment is probably either military or military-economic. Many Western experts on Russia believe that this budget item covers expenses for military rockets and nuclear bombs. Thus, approximately half of the entire budget is devoted directly or indirectly to preparation for war.

No Soviet citizen can have a checking account in a bank or pay his bills by personal check. The only bank account he can open is a savings account. He is forbidden to maintain a charge account in a store, and only rarely can purchase goods on the installment plan. A personal loan cannot be obtained from a bank except to build a house. The housing shortage is so acute that the government has to encourage private homebuilding.

In many respects Russians live somewhat better today than in the Tsarist or early Soviet eras. But urban housing is more crowded than in the past.

The explanation is simple. Since fast industrialization began in 1928, large numbers of Soviet peasants have moved into the cities to work in the newly built factories. The present urban population is about five times what it was then. But the government has built insufficient new urban housing to provide shelter for these many millions of extra city dwellers. As a result, more people were squeezed into the same space.

Under the low Tsarist standard of living, an average of one person occupied each city room. With the coming of Communism, this ratio rose to two people, and finally three on the eve of the Soviet-German War. About 25 million persons had their homes destroyed in wartime, and housing construction had to concentrate for many postwar years on them. So today, at least two persons still share the average city room. This situation has been revealed by fragmentary statistics published throughout the years in the Soviet press.

Meanwhile, the relentless flow of peasants into the cities continues at a rate of two million a year. Higher city salaries are a great lure, besides such urban advantages as high schools, colleges, theaters, movies, and circuses, which are out of reach of most collective farms.

It would be a mistake to assume that only poor people are badly housed. On a lengthy trip through the USSR, one of my guides was the wife of a high-ranking journalist. She boasted that every family in her apartment had a television set. But when I asked how many families shared her apartment, she blushed and whispered: "Three."

Such city housing is commonplace throughout the USSR. The average apartment contains a kitchen, bathroom, and several bedrooms. Each of the latter is usually occupied by a different family, unless a family is large enough to be assigned two rooms. Three or more families normally occupy each apartment, all sharing the bathroom and kitchen, which often has more than one stove. The apartment, as a rule, has only one doorbell. Beside it is a hand-printed placard with this type of message: Praiko—one ring; Romanov—two; Gurtsev—three; Gorvich—four; and Kontsov—five. This multiring system for the doorbell is efficient, helps visitors contact the right person, and is used throughout the USSR.

The building superintendent of each apartment house appoints a housewife in each apartment as the custodian to keep order. Nevertheless, with such overcrowding, quarrels between different families in the same apartment are inevitable. An entire body of Soviet law exists to cope with apartment feuds. The overcrowding also breeds much tuberculosis, speeds the spread of other communicable diseases, and contributes to juvenile delinquency because teenagers relax on the streets from the cramped quarters of a one-room home.

The average upper-class Soviet citizen fares somewhat better, but is still poorly housed by Western standards. A Russian movie actress told me that she had only a three-room apartment. A tourist of Russian descent, whom I met, recently visited the home of a distant cousin—a top Soviet scientist with a salary of $2,000 per month. The scientist also had a three-room Moscow apartment where he has been living for 40 years. The main improvement since World War II was that he now had an icebox.

Of course, Soviet leaders have huge apartments or town houses in Moscow, and magnificent country estates as well. Most of these estates are located along a heavily policed road which no Moscow tourist map shows. The huge stone mansions and surrounding green grounds remind one of estates on Long Island's north shore.

But the average city family crowds into its one room in a poorly maintained apartment house. Outside walls of the building are neither painted nor cleaned for many years. Stairways are unpainted and dusty. Often roofs leak and elevators don't work. Fortunately rent is cheap, amounting to only about 5 per cent of a person's income. Without this low rental, the average Soviet family could not survive on their small salaries and low pensions. Heat, electricity, gas, and telephone are not included in the rent, but the additional cost is not excessive.

Old apartment houses are often preferable to new communal dwellings, which are poorly built. A new apartment house is usually constructed with bricks, and there rarely are steel girders to reinforce the brick walls. To save construction material, broken bricks are inserted in the walls, and the empty space around the half-bricks is plugged with mortar. In general, mortar work is very uneven.

Construction workers, who are mostly women, have trouble fitting the bricks around windows and doors. A common sight is a one-inch gap between the wall and the top, side, or bottom of a window frame. Such illfitted windows can be seen throughout the USSR, making rooms very chilly during winters.

The poor brickwork is quite visible in ordinary apartment houses, which have plain brick walls with no decorative surface. In upper-class neighborhoods the brick walls may be surfaced with large slabs of colored stone, but the bad brickwork still exists behind the facade. The result of this careless construction is that apartment houses start falling apart about two years after they are built. Battle damage during World War II was so great in Volgograd (Stalingrad) that the entire city was built anew after the war. Yet Volgograd, an almost completely new city with many large apartment houses, is already aging. Many buildings are sagging and have large cracks running down their walls.

Poor Soviet construction is not confined to apartment houses. The famed Lenin stadium in Moscow, where large sport meets and political rallies are held, is also deteriorating, although it was completed only in 1956. Yet the Tsarist-built railway bridges across the Moscow River in the Soviet capital are just as good as when they were first constructed 65 or more years ago. In contrast, the Soviet-built highway bridges of Moscow are often sagging. Wooden pillars have been erected under some of them to help hold them up.

Soviet construction is so poor because planners, engineers, and workers are better paid in heavy industry than in construction work. Naturally the best brains and most skillful hands gravitate into heavy industry. The combination of shortage of funds, uninspired architects, poor engineers, and unskilled workers produces poor construction.

Some Soviet construction is superb, however. The Volga-Don Canal, and Leningrad and Moscow subways are masterpieces of engineering. The Soviet government can accomplish construction miracles when it so desires. But the government has never truly concentrated on housing, which always has a low priority in state planning. Hence most new dwellings in USSR cities are already prematurely old. In future years, this deterioration of current construction may become a grave economic problem.

Almost all apartment houses in the USSR are state-owned and state-built. The few exceptions are cooperatives owned in common by their inhabitants. But each city also has many small private homes. The householder rents the land from the government at a low price, and can obtain a state loan for construction. Tired of living in one room of a city apartment, many families have built little huts on the city outskirts. Miles around each city stretch these one-story huts—log cabins in the north, adobe huts with thatched roofs in the Ukraine, and mud hovels with sod roofs in Central Asia. These hut suburbs have always existed, but have greatly expanded since World War II.

The average suburban hut often has electricity, but lacks the running water and sewers that exist in many apartment houses. But the hut with its three or four rooms is more spacious than an apartment room and much more private. The hut yard is usually planted with vegetables and berry bushes, providing cheap extra food for the suburban family.

Besides the suburban homeowners, many people rent rooms at suburban state and collective farms, then commute to urban work. One third of the inhabitants on a collective farm I visited nearby a large Russian city were not collective farmers, but workers in the city factories. Two million people commute into Moscow each weekday to reach their place of work.

To house more than 150 million urban people properly, the Kremlin must give top priority to housing construction at the expense of armament and fast industrialization. According to the 1976-1980 Plan, this will not be done.

Besides the high prices, low wages, and poor housing endured by the Soviet population, inadequate transport contributes to the modest standard of living. A nation must not only produce sufficient consumer goods but transport them easily to large cities. A typical New York breakfast may include Michigan cornflakes, Minnesota butter, Florida grapefruit, and Iowa bacon. And the breakfast is usually cooked on a stove burning Texas natural gas. The weakness of Soviet transport is revealed in Table 31.

Table 31. *Comparison of Transport in the USSR and US (1975)*

	Length in miles	
Type of Transport	*Soviet Union*	*United States*
Railways	84,000	206,000
Paved roads	365,000	1,700,000

Source: *Americana Annuals,* 1974-1976. *Current Abstracts,* 1977. *USSR—Questions and Answers,* Moscow, 1975

The USSR has a territory about two and a half times as large as that of the United States. Yet the USA has two and a half times more railways and four and a half more paved roads.

Good roads are difficult to build in the USSR, which mainly consists of great plains covered by a layer of dirt several hundred feet deep. Stone for road foundations must be quarried in the few mountain ranges, which are located mostly along the Asian frontier far from the large centers of Soviet civilization. Highways are often built without a proper foundation. Even a well-constructed road may be severely damaged by weather, for in winter the paved surfaces freeze. An abrupt spring thaw will crack them wide open. The average highway is no more than a two-lane asphalt road, already full of potholes and rather bumpy. Construction difficulties have discouraged the Soviet government from building a large road network. The entire European USSR only has about ten paved long-distance highways.

The USSR has constructed several spectacular oil pipelines, including one across Siberia and another from the Volga valley into the East European satellites. Major gas pipelines also provide natural gas to the larger cities. Soviet pipeline transport is comparatively new, and thus far plays a minor but constantly increasing role in Russia's overall transportation picture. The USSR has difficulty in producing large steel pipe for these lines, and has to import pipes from Japan and Germany.

The Volga is the longest river in Europe, while the Ob-Irtysh, Yenesei, and Lena in Siberia are among the largest rivers in the world. Altogether the USSR contains 82,000 miles of inland waterways. Huge canals have been dug during the Soviet era such as the Baltic-White Sea, Volga-Baltic, and Volga-Don, so that medium-sized seagoing ships can sail via river and canal between the Baltic, White, and Black seas. The largest canal of all is now being constructed between rivers flowing into the Black and Baltic seas.

Yet most of these inland waterways are insufficiently used. Slow river and canal transport cannot compete with the faster Soviet railways, even though waterway haulage is much cheaper. But speed is not the sole difference. Because of the severe Russian winter, most rivers and canals are frozen half of every year. Soviet firms become accustomed to using rail transport in winter, and find it awkward to shift to waterways during the summer. For decades the Soviet government has ordered more summer freight to be transported by water, and these orders have consistently been disobeyed.

Since nature is so unkind to roadbuilding and inland waterways, the railways are the main form of long-distance transportation. They too sometimes become snowbound in winter, but frosts and thaws don't tear them apart. By American standards these Soviet railways are slow. Because of shortage of crushed rock, the roadbed is often made of gravel which doesn't hold the rails firmly. If a train runs too fast, the rail vibration will throw it off the track. So 40 to 50 miles per hour is top speed for most Soviet trains.

The dependence of the USSR upon its railways is depicted in Table 32:

Table 32. *USSR Internal Freight Haulage by Major Types of Transport (1975)*

Type of Transportation	Per Cent of Internal Freight Traffic
Railways	77
Inland Waterways	5
Motor trucks	2
Oil pipelines	16
	100

Source: *Moscow News,* 1976.

Because of its vast distances, the USSR has two fifths more internal freight traffic yearly than the USA. In the United States three fifths of this traffic is carried by motor trucks, pipelines, and inland waterways (including the Great Lakes). In the USSR the railways bear most of the burden, hauling five times as much freight per mile of track as in the United States.

Since World War II, and particularly after Stalin's death, the USSR has done much to improve its overburdened railways. Most of the Trans-Siberian railway has been electrified, and an alternate line—the South Siberian—has been completed. Steam locomotives are being replaced by the more efficient diesel and electric engines, which now haul more than 90 per cent of rail freight. Nevertheless, insufficient funds are still allocated from the annual budget for modernization and development of transport.

Inevitably the overworked railways must establish priorities for various types of freight, since railroad capacity is not enough to carry all the freight which should be hauled. As might be expected, the top priority is assigned to raw materials, fuel, and machinery for heavy industry. Consumer goods and food are low priority. Hence the Soviet public suffers from inadequate distribution of simple household goods. For example, fruit is often scarce in Moscow and Leningrad while part of the fruit harvest rots in the southern citrus areas (the Crimea, Caucasus, and south Central Asia). A tourist in Russia might overhear the following whispered joke:

"The new Five-Year Plan will give every Soviet family an airplane."

"But why does every family need a plane?"

"If there are no needles on sale in Moscow, you can fly to Leningrad to look for them."

A crucial question, difficult to answer, is how the present standard of living compares with the Tsarist and early Soviet past. If the Kremlin can improve living standards despite its tremendous taxation to build heavy industry, Communism gains adherents at home and abroad. Conversely, few Russians or foreigners will forever be enthusiastic about an economy of "rockets instead of butter."

An honest answer must take into account the historical background, as described both by Russian writers and Western travelers. The standard of living has never been high. Tsarist Russia had a small rich upper class, a slightly larger middle class, and impoverished workers. The great bulk of the population were peasants who were even poorer.

The Bolshevik Revolution of 1917 came after four years of World War I, which had thrown Russia into economic collapse. Then the first three years of Soviet rule consisted of civil war between the Communists and White Russians. This civil war depressed living standards even further.

During the 1920's, the living standard slowly recovered to the low Tsarist level partly because of peace after seven years of combined world and civil war, and partly because of the early Soviet policy of tolerating private farming and small private business. Private enterprise and absence of war were sound economic stimulants.

Then in 1928 the First Five-Year Plan started. The new heavy taxes to support industrialization immediately depressed the standard of living. To make matters worse, the peasants sabotaged collectivization of agriculture by reducing crops and killing livestock. Food and clothing were strictly rationed, and were sold by ration cards until 1935. In American terms, this was the second Soviet depression.

By the close of the 1930's, the living standard had partially recovered. In education and medical care, the average Soviet citizen was much better off than ever before. He now had about four years of grade-school education, compared to little or none in the Tsarist or early Soviet period. He was safely inoculated against many epidemic diseases which had killed millions in the past. But in physical comforts, the average citizen had not regained the Tsarist or late 1920's level. Because of peasant slowdowns on collective farms, less food was available, particularly in livestock products such as meat, milk, butter, and cheese. Urban housing was more crowded, as peasants constantly swarmed into the cities to man the ever-growing heavy industry. But 1940, the last year of peace between two world wars, was the most prosperous time of the period of industrialization prior to the Soviet-German war.

Then Hitler attacked the USSR in 1941, and a new wartime depression began. Again food and clothing were strictly rationed. Full-scale rationing continued until postwar 1947, and bread was semirationed till 1956. Historically, this was the third Soviet economic depression.

In this latter period, I was an eyewitness. Living in the USSR from 1938 through 1943, I saw the improvement of 1940 and the economic slump of World War II. Wartime Moscow was blacked out, had no taxies, and suffered shortages of everything, even cigarettes. I cannot easily forget how an angry mother killed her 10-year-old daughter by hitting her on the head with a big wooden spoon, because the girl had lost the bread ration cards for the whole family.

Today most of the tremendous war damage in European USSR has been repaired. Some skeleton buildings, roofless, windowless and badly burned, can still be seen on the outskirts of cities in the war zone. But when one remembers that one fourth of European USSR was ravaged by bombs, shells, and scorched earth, the incomplete reconstruction of war damage has been no easy feat.

Past history proves that after each depression, the Soviet standard of living at least partially recovers. Let's compare present living conditions with prewar 1940, the best year before the wartime economic slump. Today Soviet heavy industry is eight times larger than in 1940.

But the standard of living is not eight times greater. Prices of consumer goods today are somewhat higher than in 1940. As a definite improvement, wages are over 170 per cent higher. Soviet clothes and shoes are sturdier and more colorful than in 1940, though both quality and style are medium by Western standards. The average Soviet woman wears a print dress, or a white blouse and dark skirt. Both costumes are in a loose-fitting style, hardly flattering to the figure.

In 1940 one way to recognize a Soviet police detective was by his raincoat, because almost nobody else had one. Raincoats are still not abundant, but many urban civilians wear them on damp days.

In 1940, a watch or fountain pen were luxuries the average Russian could never afford. Even if he had the rubles, there were few on sale. Today many middle-class Russians wear watches and carry fountain pens. The watches are thin, accurate, and sufficiently attractive to be exported abroad at the rate of several million per year. Presentday Soviet pens are good copies of Western ballpoints.

During 1940, Soviet municipal transport was so poor that many Russians had to walk miles to their place of work. Many provincial cities lacked both taxies and buses. Trolleys were packed full of people with latecomers clinging outside on the streetcar steps. Often one outrider would hang desperately to the car doorknob, a second would cling to his shoulders, and a third stranger would embrace them both. If the first rider lost his grip, all three fell and rolled along the pavement a few inches from the streetcar's wheels. I saw one Muscovite lose a foot in such a fall.

Today even the provincial cities have taxies, and many buses augment the old trolley lines. The buses are all shapes, sizes, and colors, apparently being copies of the autobuses of a dozen European nations. Trolleys and buses are still overcrowded. But rarely does one see a group of Russians wrapped round each other on the outside of a streetcar.

The average city side-street is still narrow, made of cobblestones or entirely unpaved, with stone or dirt sidewalks only two feet wide. In summer such roads are incredibly dusty. Despite this dust, the cities are much cleaner than in the past. Before World War II, each city literally smelled, even in the central part of Moscow. Today huge sprinkler trucks keep city centers clean.

Trying to take all factors into consideration, official Soviet statistics rate the USSR standard of living today at about half the level existing in the United States. In housing space per person, the ratio is also one half.

Living standards today in the USSR are better than in Asia, Africa, and most of Latin America, perhaps equal to southern Europe, but inferior to West Europe and far below the United States. Even in industrialized Soviet satellites like Poland, Hungary, Czechoslovakia, and East Germany, people live a little better than in the USSR.

Suggestions for Further Reading

BERGSON, ABRAM, *The Real National Income of Soviet Russia since 1928*, Cambridge: Harvard University Press, 1961.

BROWN, EMILY CLARK, *Soviet Trade Unions and Labor Relations*. Cambridge: Harvard University Press. 1966.

CHAPMAN, JANET G., *Real Wages in Soviet Russia since 1928*, Cambridge: Harvard University Press, 1963.

DODGE, NORTON T., *Women in the Soviet Economy*, Baltimore: Johns Hopkins University Press, 1966.

GOLDMAN, MARSHALL I., *Soviet Marketing: Distribution in a Controlled Society*, New York: The Free Press, 1963.

GOLDMAN, MARSHALL I., *The Soviet Economy: Myth and Reality*. Englewood Cliffs: Prentice-Hall, 1968.

GRANICK, DAVID, *The Red Executive*, New York: Doubleday, 1960.

HUNTER, HOLLAND, *Soviet Transportation Policy*, Cambridge: Harvard University Press, 1957.

ROBERTS, PAUL C., *Alienation and the Soviet Economy*. Albuquerque: New Mexico University Press, 1971.

SCHWARTZ, HARRY, *The Soviet Economy Since Stalin*, Philadelphia: Lippincott, 1965.

SMITH, HEDRICK, *The Russians*, New York: Quadrangle, 1976.

SOSNOVY, TIMOTHY, *The Housing Problem in the Soviet Union*. New York: Columbia University Press, 1954.

SPULBER, NICOLAS, *Soviet Strategy for Economic Growth*, Bloomington: Indiana University Press, 1964.

Part IV

Foreign Relations

Stalin made the USSR a Eurasian power, but Khrushchev promoted Russia to global influence. Soviet foreign relations are today vast and complex, extending by diplomacy, trade, aid, or revolutionary assistance to every corner of the world. Chapter 21 first traces the development of Soviet foreign policy. The vastness of the Russian bureaucracy of foreign affairs is then described in Chapter 22. Satellization is a subtle device to ease new satellite nations into complete Communist control and is treated in Chapter 23. Soviet trade and aid are not only utilized for political gain, but have antagonized the Soviet satellites, which desire fairer trade and more aid from the USSR. These political-economic problems are discussed in detail in Chapter 24. Finally, national communism or Titoism is slowly dividing the Communist nations. The result is polycentrism—a world of many different and sometimes conflicting types of communism. Therefore our discussion of foreign affairs ends in Chapter 25 with this trend toward decentralization. Chapter 26, a brief conclusion, assesses the prospects for the future.

Chapter 21

Soviet Foreign Policy

The basic goal of Soviet foreign policy is simple: Marxist world revolution. Not so simple, however, is how to achieve this goal. Throughout Soviet history the Kremlin has tried various methods to communize the world, with one method often being contradictory to another. Meanwhile Russia had to be preserved as a Marxist nation, and in search for survival was often compelled to play nonrevolutionary power politics.

When Lenin seized power in Russia during 1917, he believed that Communist Russia was the start of a Marxist revolution which would soon engulf the world. Yet almost immediately, Lenin had to compromise with his revolutionary principles by concluding peace with Germany and Austro-Hungary through the humiliating treaty of Brest-Litovsk. This treaty, which withdrew Soviet Russia from World War I, was the first Soviet move to preserve Russia as a nation rather than sacrifice it for world revolution.

Still Lenin did not abandon his revolutionary ideals. He rationalized Brest-Litovsk by his need for peace to consolidate Soviet power within Russia, and by the probable defeat of Germany by the Entente in World War I, leaving Germany vulnerable to Marxist revolution. When Germany did surrender to the Entente in 1918 fall, Lenin was enthusiastic, writing:

> Bolshevism has . . . helped the development of the proletarian revolution in Europe and America more . . . than any party in

> any other country. . . . To the proletarian masses of the world it is every day becoming clearer that bolshevism has shown the way of escaping from . . . war and imperialism, that bolshevism can serve as a model of tactics for all.
>
> Not only European but world revolution is maturing, and it has been aided and accelerated by the proletarian victory in Russia.[1]

Meanwhile Lenin's government was already engaged in the life-or-death struggle of civil war. Lenin, the self-appointed leader of world revolution, found himself threatened by defeat in his own home territory.

Yet even during civil war, Lenin continued striving for revolution in Europe. Gathering together a group of foreign socialists, who happened to be visiting Russia in 1919, Lenin formed the Third Communist International (Comintern), an alliance of world Communist parties. At the time, few foreign Communist parties existed, but the Comintern founders went home and organized them later.

From its very start, the Comintern was manipulated to favor Russia. Its highest organ was an international congress, in which each Communist party in the world was represented by delegates in proportion to the party's size. Until World War II, the membership of the USSR Communist Party outnumbered the combined memberships of all other Communist parties, and Russia had no trouble dominating the infrequent Comintern congresses.

Each Russian-dominated congress elected an executive committee, which controlled the Comintern between congresses. This committee consisted of Soviet citizens and foreign Communists obedient to Moscow. Furthermore, Comintern rules stated that every foreign Communist must pledge allegiance to the Comintern, which in reality meant loyalty to Soviet Russia. At first, true to Marxist tradition, the Comintern stressed revolution in Europe, especially in Germany.

Almost simultaneously with the Comintern foundation, Lenin in 1919 again sought security for his homeland. To William Bullitt, an envoy from President Wilson, Lenin offered to let

---

[1] Lenin, V. I., *Collected Works,* Vol. 23, Moscow: 1926–1932.

White Russians keep the Russian territories they held, to repay Tsarist foreign debts, and to let foreign businessmen help develop Soviet resources. As already indicated, these offers were rejected by the Whites and the West.

When Hungary and the German province of Bavaria established Soviet republics in 1919, Lenin was overjoyed and again prophesied imminent European revolution. But the Bavarian Communist regime lasted only two weeks, and the Hungarian four months, the former being crushed by the German republic army and the latter by troops from Rumania.

In the meantime, a new Russian revolutionary strategy was proposed by a Volga Tatar named Sultan Galiev. The Volga Tatars, highly Russified and fairly well educated, were used by Lenin to govern Moslem Central Asia, where the population was largely illiterate. Galiev was one of these Asian rulers.

By Galiev's reasoning, Soviet Russia was wrong in striving for fast Communist revolution in industrial Europe. Revolution would succeed first in the underdeveloped nations, which were colonies or protectorates of the Western capitalist powers. Colonial revolution would economically weaken the West by depriving it of easy markets and cheap raw materials. Then Western workers would have an opportunity to overthrow their capitalist governments.

To assist colonial revolution, Galiev urged Russia to support the upper class of underdeveloped nations. He noted that colonies contain few industrial workers, because there is little industry. Hence the colonial proletariat could not be a strong revolutionary force. The desperately poor colonial peasants were not good revolutionary material because of their illiteracy, superstition, conservatism, and strong religious beliefs. To arouse the peasantry would be a long painful process. But the native upper class in colonial countries was educated, anti-Western, and eager for national independence. If the upper class joined forces with the Communists, the peasants would follow. Communists should infiltrate underdeveloped nations from the top through the national bourgeoisie, not from the bottom through the peasantry.

Galiev even proposed the formation of a Colonial International to unite underdeveloped nations in Marxist revolution. After this revolution succeeded, the Colonial International would communize the West.

Galiev was a revisionist of orthodox Marxism, which assumed Communist revolution would come first in the industrial West. Lenin was intrigued by Galiev's proposals, but did not accept all of them. Galiev was permitted to form a Moslem International for fomenting revolution in the Middle East. This Asian organization gained membership rapidly, at a time when the Comintern was floundering in Europe. But the Moslem International began to develop pan-Moslem tendencies, so Lenin ordered it to be disbanded. Galiev was expelled from the Russian Communist party in the early 1920's, removed from any position of power, and later executed by Stalin. Nevertheless, his idea of colonial revolution became part of Soviet foreign policy.

As soon as the Russian Civil War was won, the Soviet government tried Galiev's plan of infiltrating underdeveloped countries from the top. In the early 1920's, Russia became a close friend of the new reform governments of Iran and Turkey. By the mid-1920's, the Comintern was allied with the bourgeois Kuomintang conducting revolution against war lords in China. All three of these Communist endeavors eventually failed.

In the same period, a final attempt was made at European revolution, when the Kremlin ordered German Communists to seize power in 1923 after French troops had occupied the Rhineland. By Soviet reasoning, the German people were so upset by French aggression that Germany would turn Communist. But this Teutonic revolution also failed.

While trying vainly for colonial and German revolution, Russia in the early 1920's still had to survive as a nation. Simultaneously with revolutionary intrigue, the Soviet government was concluding trade pacts with capitalist countries, seeking diplomatic recognition from the West, and inviting Western businessmen to help develop nationalized Soviet industry. A year before the unsuccessful German revolution of 1923, the USSR and Germany concluded the Treaty of Rapallo, providing for mutual recognition, trade, joint armament, and cancellation of war debts.

A contradiction had arisen in Soviet foreign policy. How could Russia pursue world revolution against capitalism, and simultaneously conduct normal businesslike relations with capitalist countries? Lenin died in 1924 without solving this contradiction.

Stalin, Lenin's successor, solved this problem. Stalin conceived such a brilliant foreign program that his strategy—with slight modifications—has continued to the present day. Stalin, not Lenin, was the real architect of Soviet foreign policy.

In 1925 Stalin announced his new policy of "socialism in one country." Against bitter opposition, especially from Trotsky, the slogan was adopted as permanent Soviet strategy.

Marx believed that Communist revolution must occur almost simultaneously in several industrial countries, which would ally in a "socialist league." Only such an alliance would be sufficiently strong to prevent a restoration of capitalism.

"Socialism in one country" revised this theory. Stalin bluntly stated that Russia must stand alone, and could survive as a Communist nation in a capitalist world. Actually at the time, there were two other Communist countries: Mongolia and Tuva, both conquered by the Red Army in 1921. But these two underdeveloped Asian wastelands were appendages of Russia rather than allies. For all practical purposes, Stalin was correct in saying that Russia was on its own.

By socialism in one country, Stalin did not mean to abandon world revolution. After 1925, the revolutionary alliance of the Comintern and Kuomintang continued in China until 1927. At the end of the 1920's, unsuccessful Communist revolts erupted in both Dutch Indonesia and French Indochina. World revolution was not discarded. But Stalin stressed that, for awhile, revolution outside Russia might not succeed. Hence Russia must build up its military-economic power to be the fortress for future world revolution.

Partly this decision was motivated by finance. Since 1917, Soviet Russia had expended vast sums of money abroad for world revolution. Despite Soviet financial support, all these revolutions had failed. Why not divert such funds into Russia itself, to create military-industrial might?

After "socialism in one country" became Soviet policy, the USSR never endangered itself while aiding foreign Communist parties. If major war might ensue from USSR support to a Communist uprising abroad, Russia would quietly withdraw, letting the revolt fail. The foreign Communist party could always be rebuilt for possible victory in the future, but if the USSR were ever defeated in war, world revolution would be finished.

Along with socialism in one country, Stalin invented the slogan of "peaceful co-existence." Time was needed to build the Soviet revolutionary fortress into a great military-industrial power. While this buildup was taking place, Russia must avoid major war by trading and cooperating with Western capitalist states.

Meanwhile Russia would weaken its capitalist friends by aggravating frictions which already existed in the capitalist world. Of these frictions, Stalin described three as most important: capital versus labor, capital versus capital, and capital versus colonies. In his words:

> Lenin called imperialism "moribund capitalism." Why? Because imperialism carries the contradictions of capitalism to their last bounds, to the extreme limit, beyond which revolution begins. Of these contradictions, there are three which must be regarded as the most important.
>
> The *first contradiction* is the contradiction between labour and capital. Imperialism is the omnipotence of the monopolist trusts and syndicates, of the banks and the financial oligarchy, in the industrial countries. In the fight against this omnipotence, the customary methods of the working class—trade unions and cooperative organizations, parliamentary parties and the parliamentary struggle—have proved to be totally inadequate. Either place yourself at the mercy of capital, linger in misery as of old and sink lower and lower, or adopt a new weapon—this is the alternative imperialism puts before the vast masses of the proletariat. Imperialism brings the working class to revolution.
>
> The *second contradiction* is the contradiction among the various financial groups and imperialist powers in their struggle for sources of raw materials, for foreign territory. Imperialism is the export of capital to the sources of raw materials, the frenzied struggle for monopolist possession of these sources, the struggle for a redivision of the already divided world, a struggle waged with particular fury by new financial groups and powers seeking a "place in the sun" against the old groups and powers which cling tightly to what they have grabbed. This frenzied struggle among the various groups of capitalists is notable in that it includes as an inevitable element imperialist wars, wars for the annexation of foreign territories. This circumstance, in its turn, is notable in that it leads to the mutual weakening of the imperialists, to the weakening of the position of capitalism in gen-

eral, to the acceleration of the advent of the proletarian revolution and to the practical inevitability of this revolution.

The *third contradiction* is the contradiction between the handful of ruling "civilized" nations and the hundreds of millions of the colonial and dependent peoples of the world. Imperialism is the most barefaced exploitation and the most inhuman oppression of hundreds of millions of people inhabiting vast colonies and dependent countries. The purpose of this exploitation and of this oppression is to squeeze out super-profits. But in exploiting these countries imperialism is compelled to build railroads, factories and mills there, to create industrial and commercial centres. The appearance of a class of proletarians, the emergence of a native intelligentsia, the awakening of national consciousness, the growth of the movement for emancipation—such are the inevitable results of this "policy." The growth of the revolutionary movement in all colonies and dependent countries without exception clearly testifies to this fact. This circumstance is of importance for the proletariat in that it radically undermines the position of capitalism by converting the colonies and dependent countries from reserves of imperialism into reserves of the proletarian revolution.[2]

Capital versus labor, the first of the three capitalist contradictions listed by Stalin, is borrowed from orthodox Marxism. The second, capital versus capital, is power politics rather than Communist theory. Capitalist nations could be weakened by pitting them against each other. The third contradiction, capital versus colonies, is taken from Galiev's idea of colonial revolution, which Stalin further described:

. . . the road to victory of the revolution in the West lies through the revolutionary alliance with the liberation movement of the colonies and dependent countries against imperialism. . . .

This does not mean, of course, that the proletariat must support *every* national movement, everywhere and always, in every single concrete case. It means that support must be given to such national movements as tend to weaken, to overthrow imperialism, and not to strengthen and preserve it. Cases occur when the national movements in certain oppressed countries come into conflict with the interests of the development of the proletarian movement. In such cases support is, of course, entirely out of the question. . . .

[2] Stalin, Joseph, *Foundations of Leninism,* New York: International Publishers, 1939, pp. 13–14.

> . . . The revolutionary character of a national movement under the conditions of imperialist oppression does not necessarily presuppose the existence of proletarian elements in the movement, the existence of a revolutionary or a republican program of the movement, the existence of a democratic basis of the movement. The struggle the Emir of Afghanistan is waging for the independence of Afghanistan is objectively a *revolutionary* struggle, despite the monarchist views of the Emir and his associates, for it weakens, disintegrates and undermines imperialism. . . . For the same reasons the struggle the Egyptian merchants and bourgeois intellectuals are waging for the independence of Egypt is objectively a *revolutionary* struggle, despite the bourgeois origin and bourgeois title of the leaders of the Egyptian national movement . . . I need not speak of the national movement in other, larger, colonial and dependent countries, such as India and China, every step of which along the road to liberation, even if it runs counter to the demands of formal democracy, is a steam-hammer blow at imperialism. . . .[3]

In this last statement, Stalin indicates his willingness to pursue colonial revolution by going through the top, supporting non-Communist freedom leaders in underdeveloped nations. Later, however, he was inconsistent on this approach, at times going through the bottom by attempting to arouse the colonial peasantry.

Regardless of qualifications, the three contradictions became basic Soviet foreign policy, weakening the capitalist world with which Russia traded and tried to stay at peace. Both the Soviet Foreign Ministry and the Communist International attempted to aggravate these contradictions, sometimes stressing one more than the others. Actually more than these three contradictions were utilized by Communists, who strove to intensify any existing friction in capitalist society. For example, Communists have exploited the grievances of minorities in the United States, particularly among American Negroes.

By the late 1920's, Soviet foreign policy was operating in a framework of one-country socialism, peaceful coexistence, and aggravation of capitalist frictions. Meanwhile Russia was building up its military-industrial potential by importing vast quantities

---

[3] *Ibid.*, pp. 78–81.

of machinery and technical aid from the great Western powers. After Communist failures in Turkey, Iran, China, Indonesia, and Indochina, colonial revolution slackened. In Europe, Communist parties were ordered by Moscow to combat the socialist parties, which were accused of unwillingness to support European revolution. American Communists at first opposed President Franklin Roosevelt, fearing his welfare program would alleviate worker discontent during the 1930's depression.

So engrossed was the large German Communist party in combating socialists, that in 1933 it allowed Adolph Hitler to attain power. The USSR was again in grave danger. Confronted by a hostile Japan on the east and Nazi Germany in the West, Russia began a frantic search for security. Western Communists were ordered to stop quarreling with the socialists, and not to strive for revolution. Fascism was the main threat, so Communists and socialists should form "united fronts" against the Hitler-Mussolini alliance. Western Communist parties dutifully obeyed these Kremlin orders by allying with any socialist and liberal groups willing to cooperate. In the mid-1930's, a united-front government even held power briefly in France.

In the underdeveloped nations, Nazi Germany encouraged colonial revolution. Germany had no colonies, and revolution would weaken the Western democracies. The Comintern therefore ordered Communists in the colonies to postpone revolutionary efforts, support colonial regimes, and conduct anti-Fascist propaganda. The Chinese Communists reunited with the Kuomintang (after having fought them for ten years), so that both could battle the invading Japanese. At the time Moscow seemed to have abandoned world revolution, but later this interpretation proved incorrect.

Meanwhile by the mid-1930's, Russia conducted diplomatic maneuvering in search for security. Russia joined the League of Nations, vainly urging it to unite against Fascist aggression. While repeatedly requesting nonaggression pacts with Nazi Germany, the USSR allied with France and Czechoslovakia against the Third Reich. Soviet military aid helped the Kuomintang fight the Japanese, and slowed Spanish Republican defeat by Fascist Generalissimo Franco. Thus most of the 1930's was a period of little Communist revolutionary activity, the Soviet emphasis being on "capital versus capital."

Soviet maneuvering reached its climax in 1939 with the conclusion of the Nazi-Soviet Pact which freed Germany to start World War II, stopped the undeclared Soviet-Japanese war in Mongolia, and divided East Europe between Germany and Russia. The Comintern then had to make the most awkward reversal in its entire history. Western Communist parties were ordered to become pro-Fascist or at least neutral. Again the parties obeyed Moscow. For example, the French Communist Party almost openly sabotaged the French war effort against Germany. The US party appealed for America to stay neutral in World War II with the slogan: "The Yanks aren't coming!" By such propaganda, the US Communist Party was advocating the same policy as America First and other right-wing groups.

The united fronts quickly collapsed. Most Western socialists and liberals, who had collaborated with the Communists, were sincerely anti-Fascist. Moreover, many left-wingers resigned from Communist party membership rather than aid Fascism. In the long run, the Comintern probably suffered little from these emotional resignations. The Communists who remained were completely loyal to Moscow.

In the underdeveloped nations, the Communists again advocated colonial revolution, thus aiding Fascism. An exception was China. The Chinese Communist Party publicly approved the Nazi-Soviet Pact, but continued to ally with the Kuomintang in fighting the Japanese. And Russia still sent arms to the Kuomintang for use in the Sino-Japanese war.

Fascist-Comintern collaboration ended abruptly when Hitler invaded Russia during 1941. The USSR quickly sought British and American material aid for wartime use against European Axis countries. The Comintern had to make another policy reversal.

Throughout the world, Communist parties again tried to organize anti-Fascist united fronts. Actual Communist operation depended on the situation in a particular country. In an Allied but uninvaded nation like England, the Communists aided the war effort, which they had previously weakened. In a neutral nation, such as America was during most of 1941, the Communists agitated for participation in the war on the Allied side. Overnight the US Communist Party changed its slogan from "The Yanks aren't coming" to "the Yanks are coming."

If the country were Nazi-occupied, like France, a Communist front organized underground activity harassing the enemy. The same was done in Japanese-occupied Southeast Asia, where Communist-nationalist coalitions fought the Japanese by jungle guerrilla warfare. Meanwhile the Chinese Communists continued war against Japan. During World War II, the Comintern was abolished, so Russia could pretend to have abandoned world revolution and have a free hand in Allied negotiations.

But world revolution was far from ended. When Germany collapsed at the close of World War II, Russia occupied most of East Europe, setting up satellite Communist regimes. In the Far East, the USSR also satellized North Korea by direct military occupation.

These Soviet actions started the Cold War, during which Stalin's diplomacy relied on force or threats of force. Russia tried threats to gain control of north Iran, the Turkish Straits, East Austria and West Berlin. When this policy failed, the USSR had to desist in Europe and the Near East for fear of major war.

Communist united fronts in Western nations collapsed under the impact of Cold War. For a time Stalin had great hopes that the French and Italian Communist parties might be voted into power, since they were the largest political parties in each of their countries. But without widespread socialist support, the Communists could not gain a majority in the French and Italian parliaments. As West Europe began to recover from war devastation, living conditions improved and Communist parties began to lose membership. Many European Communists also resigned from their Marxist parties because of sympathy for Tito in the Soviet-Yugoslav dispute.

Frustrated in Europe, Stalin again placed his hopes on Asia. At the end of World War II, civil war started in China between the Communists and Kuomintang, and in Indochina between a Communist-led front and the French. Communist-led guerrillas were harassing the legal governments of colonial Malaya and the newly independent Philippines. Burma and Indonesia were achieving independence through freedom movements led by

Communist-nationalist coalitions. Once the two latter countries were free, Russia apparently ordered the local Communists to overthrow the nationalists. In 1950, with Soviet material aid, North Korea invaded South Korea.

Asian Communists tried to seize power by sheer force, and eventually succeeded in China and North Vietnam. Elsewhere the Communists overestimated their own strength. America intervened in South Korea and the British in Malaya. In Burma, Indonesia, and the Philippines, the nationalists defeated the Communists.

In Asia at the time, Stalin ignored Galiev's advice of going through the top. Aside from Korea, where there was real undeclared war, Communist guerrillas operated in the East Asian countryside trying to rely on the local peasantry for support. Though successful in China and North Indochina, this revolutionary approach was not suited to other areas, where the local nationalists were strong.

But Stalin considered the nationalist leaders of newly freed colonies to be bourgeois and unreliable as allies. He took the same attitude toward Asian countries where there were no Communist revolutions. For example, Stalin considered Indian Premier Nehru to be a British agent. Thus Russia lost an opportunity to make friends with the leaders of many underdeveloped nations. Only in Latin America did Communists continue trying to infiltrate from the top.

Shortly before his death, Stalin seemed to realize that his foreign policy was going awry. He proposed "cold peace" to France and Italy, and his officials spoke of a "Stalin Plan" of technical aid to underdeveloped nations. In his last published writings of 1952, Stalin predicted that World War III would start among capitalist countries rather than between the West and the USSR. In his opinion, the revival of German and Japanese military-economic power would cause an inter-capitalist conflict. Stalin died in 1953 with the germ of new foreign strategy, but apparently placing his main hopes on "capital versus capital."

After Stalin's death, he was succeeded by a collective leadership, which preferred "capital versus colonies" to "capital versus capital." But Stalin's cold peace and technical aid were adopted and elaborated. As part of cold peace, Russia helped mediate the

Korean and Indochinese wars. Technical aid started in 1954 with a Soviet offer to build an Indian steel mill. There was still no clear public enunciation of post-Stalin foreign policy until 1956, when Khrushchev described the new strategy in detail.

Khrushchev redefined "peaceful coexistence," which under Stalin had been a device for Russia to gain time to arm. Going further than Stalin, Khrushchev indicated that Russia must avoid atomic war with the West because there would be no victor. While the West would be destroyed, so would the Soviet Union. Instead of war, there would be peaceful competition between the USSR and the West in economic development and ideology. As the Soviet Union began winning this competition, Western Communist parties would expand, might win parliamentary elections, and thus assume power peaceably. Soviet literature explained:

> At a certain stage of development of human society new socialist [Communist] states and old capitalist states will simultaneously co-exist. . . .
>
> This is not simply the co-existence of states of two different social systems, but is co-existence of states of two opposing social systems. . . .
>
> Peaceful co-existence is a specific form of class struggle between socialism and capitalism. In peaceful competition with capitalism, the socialist system will be victorious. . . . There is no contradiction between the policy of peaceful co-existence and the Marxist-Leninist stand concerning the inevitable victory of Communism in the entire world.[4]

Communist takeover of the West by peaceful competition was actually impossible in the Khrushchev period. Though Soviet industry grew, USSR agriculture suffered repeated failures. As long as the Soviet standard of living remained low, most Westerners were not attracted to Communist ideology. Obviously Khrushchev greatly over-estimated the growth capabilities of his economy. Since Russia would not risk atomic war to communize the West, in reality Khrushchev was abandoning Western countries to long-time capitalism. Many Western Communists were disappointed by this new version of "peaceful coexistence."

As part of peace with the West, Khrushchev threw Russia open

---

[4] "Peaceful Co-existence," *Diplomatic Dictionary,* Moscow: State Printing House for Political Literature, 1961, pp. 297–299.

to foreign tourists, visited Western countries, became accessible to foreign newsmen, developed cultural exchange, and increased Soviet trade with Western Europe. At times he reverted to Stalinism by creating or aggravating international crises in the Near East, Far East, Berlin, and finally Cuba. Such crises usually resulted in "capital versus capital," since the NATO allies would often disagree on the solution. But in each crisis, Russia retreated short of war.

Khrushchev ended his political career by concluding a number of agreements with the United States; the ban on above-ground nuclear tests, a consular agreement, the purchase of American wheat, and installation of direct radio-telegraph communication between the Kremlin and the White House.

However, Khrushchev placed his immediate hopes on "capital versus colonies." For the first time in many years, Russia republished the writings of Sultan Galiev. And like Galiev, Khrushchev believed in approaching underdeveloped nations through the top by making friends with bourgeois-nationalist leaders.

Khrushchev wooed the newly freed nations of Asia and Africa with trade, technical and military aid, cultural exchange, and diplomatic support. It did not matter if the underdeveloped nation would not immediately turn Communist. As long as Khrushchev could sever economic and political ties linking the underdeveloped country with the West, he would be weakening Western power. Eventually the isolated West would be thrown into depression, and there could be opportunity for Western internal revolution. Once the West fell, the weak underdeveloped nations could be easily communized.

By Khrushchev's reasoning, this slow process was the only safe method of world revolution in the atomic age. He hoped that Communists might infiltrate and control the governments of some underdeveloped nations before the West fell. And he did not discard violence as a Communist tactic in developing nations where the national-bourgeois leaders were extremely pro-Western. In such countries guerrilla warfare, civil war, armed insurrection or coup d'états would be permissible. Russia sent military aid to North Vietnam and the Viet Cong in the Vietnamese war, to pro-Communist rebels in the Congo, and to Marxist revolutionaries in Latin America.

Khrushchev's successors have continued his foreign policies with two major changes: First, international crises tend to be avoided. Second, the Brezhnev regime has instituted a policy of detente with both West Europe and the United States.

Detente began in 1968 when the United States, the USSR and Britain drafted and signed a worldwide treaty on non-proliferation of nuclear weapons. All nations on earth were invited to join this pact, and most have done so. By treaty terms, any signatory country now lacking nuclear bombs agrees never to purchase or produce them. If a signatory nation be threatened by atomic attack, Russia and America promise jointly to defend it. Thus in an unusual type of possible future war, the United States and USSR might again fight side by side.

A second landmark detente treaty was concluded in 1971 between the USSR, Britain, France, and the United States, allowing the three latter countries to continue stationing troops in West Berlin, which also would be freely accessible to civilian traffic from West Germany. Thus the USSR abandoned the West Berlin which Khrushchev had tried to seize.

Then in 1972 came a US-Soviet treaty limiting each country to 200 antiballistic missiles apiece, and a second agreement limiting each nation to its current number of intercontinental nuclear missiles, submarine-based nuclear missiles, and atomic-powered missile-firing submarines either in operation or being built. For the first time in history, the nuclear arms race was quantitatively curbed.

In 1974 US President Ford and Secretary-General Brezhnev met in the Siberian city of Vladivostok, concluding an agreement limiting the USA and USSR each to a total of 2,400 intercontinental rockets, submarine-based missiles, and bombers with 1,320 of the missiles permitted to have multiple hydrogen-bomb warheads.

An unprecedented international space feat occurred in 1975, when a US manned rocket docked with a Soviet spaceship, and the American and Russian crews visited each others' space vehicles. To achieve this joint-docking, the USA and USSR had to exchange technical data about their rockets, thus helping both nations to lead the world in space research.

As part of detente, the Soviet Union has greatly increased its trade, cultural exchanges, and scientific cooperation with both West Europe and the United States. Brezhnev has promised that detente will continue for at least 30 years, during which Western business firms will allegedly profit from the "stability" of the Soviet market.

The motives behind the Soviet desire for detente are complex. First, the Soviet press admits that Russian industrial technology lags behind that of the West, so machinery imports are needed to modernize USSR industry.

Second, the Brezhnev regime seems truly to fear that small nations might manufacture nuclear bombs, and have some means of delivery. Bomb production is not so difficult, since the fuel for atomic power stations is the same explosive as for weapons. Dictators of small nations might not be as cautious with atomic bombs as the leaders of the present "nuclear club" of the US, USSR, Britain, France, China and India.

Third, Russia realizes that a US-USSR atomic war would be a disaster for both countries, with no victors, only "losers."

Fourth, Brezhnev has openly claimed that better Soviet relations with the USA will help Russia control the Soviet satellite countries of East Europe. In his opinion, a more friendly United States would not encourage any future East European unrest.

Last but not least, the Soviet leaders fear a possible future war against China. During the quarter-century of cold war, the American and Soviet armies never fought each other. But in the past 17 years Chinese and Russian troops have tested each other's strength in at least 9,000 skirmishes along the Sino-Soviet frontier. Moscow and Peking are also deadly rivals in wooing the Third World with technical aid.

Though Brezhnev has predicted that detente will be long-lasting, the Soviet press indicates that it is a temporary strategy protecting the USSR from nuclear war while Communists try to take over the entire world. According to *Pravda,* detente makes it easier for Communists to spread world revolution. During detente, when relations are friendly with Russia, Western governments allegedly cannot use the excuse of a Communist threat to suppress Communist parties in the West or left-wing rebellion in the Third World. Meanwhile the Soviet Union will never "pay for detente" by "liberalization" of its internal regime.

Russia does not maintain peaceful coexistence to preserve capitalism, says *Pravda,* but the West still gains something from detente. "Detente and peaceful coexistence ensure the main thing for all countries and peoples, namely, the prevention of nuclear war."[5]

[5] *Pravda,* Dec. 27, 1975.

Suggestions for Further Reading

DEGRAS, JANE, ed., *The Communist International, 1919–1943,* New York: Oxford University Press, 1960.

KAUSHIK, DEVENDRA, *Soviet Relations with India and Pakistan.* New York: Harper and Row, 1972.

LANDIS, LINCOLN, *Politics and Oil: Moscow in the Middle East.* New York: Dunellan, 1974.

LEDERER, IVO J., and VUCINICH, WAYNE S., eds., *The Soviet Union and the Middle East.* Stanford: Stanford University Press, 1974.

MCLANE, CHARLES B., *Soviet-African Relations.* New York: Columbia University Press, 1974.

PAGE, STANLEY W., *Lenin and World Revolution,* New York: New York University Press, 1959.

PIPES, RICHARD, ed., *Soviet Strategy in Europe.* New York: Crane, Russak, 1976.

SETON-WATSON, HUGH, *The New Imperialism.* New York: Putnam, 1971.

SHULMAN, MARSHALL D., *Stalin's Foreign Policy Reappraised,* Cambridge: Harvard University Press. 1963.

STEIBEL, GERALD L., *Detente: Promises and Pitfalls.* New York: Crane, Russak, 1975.

TAI SUNG AN, *The Sino-Soviet Territorial Dispute,* Philadelphia: Westminster, 1973.

THEBERGE, JAMES D., *The Soviet Presence in Latin America.* New York: Crane, Russak, 1974.

ULAM, ADAM B., *Expansion and Coexistence: The History of Soviet Foreign Policy, 1917-1973*. New York: Praeger, 1974.

VIGOR, P. H., *The Soviet View of War, Peace and Neutrality*. Boston: Routledge, 1975.

Chapter 22

Administration of Soviet Foreign Policy

Who actually determines Soviet foreign policy? According to the Soviet Constitution, foreign affairs are decided by the Presidium of the USSR Supreme Soviet, the USSR Council of Ministers, and the Foreign Affairs Ministries of the 15 Soviet Republics comprising the Soviet Union. Thus the Constitution states:

> The Presidium of the Supreme Soviet of the USSR . . . :
>
> In the intervals between sessions of the Supreme Soviet of the USSR, proclaims a state of war in the event of military attack on the USSR, or when necessary to fulfill international treaty obligations concerning mutual defence against aggression. . . .
>
> Ratifies and denounces international treaties of the USSR;
>
> Appoints and recalls plenipotentiary representatives of the USSR to foreign states;
>
> Receives the letters of credence and recall of diplomatic representatives accredited to it by foreign states. (Article 119)
>
> The Council of Ministers of the USSR . . . :
>
> Exercises general guidance in the sphere of relations with foreign states. (Article 130)
>
> Each Union Republic has the right to enter into direct relations with foreign states and to conclude agreements and exchange diplomatic and consular representatives with them. (Article 80)

These paragraphs of the Soviet Constitution are misleading. The Presidium of the USSR Supreme Soviet does indeed ratify and denounce treaties, declare war and conclude peace, not to mention appointing ambassadors and other high diplomatic officials. However, few Presidium members participate directly in diplomatic negotiations. As already indicated, 15 members of the 39-man USSR Presidium are the chairmen of the Presidiums of the 15 Soviet Republics constituting the USSR. These republic presidents spend most of their time away from Moscow in the republic capitals, apparently not even attending most USSR Presidium meetings. (The USSR Presidium is believed to meet at least once a week.) Many other members of the USSR Presidium are distinguished old Bolsheviks who have outlived their usefulness but who are honored by being awarded a Presidium membership involving little responsibility or work. Such Presidium members rarely attend diplomatic receptions, almost never negotiate, and often do not even perform the ceremonial function of greeting foreign diplomats arriving in the USSR.

Until the Khrushchev period even the chairman of the USSR Presidium (President of the USSR) limited his diplomatic functions to greeting foreign delegations and receiving the credentials of new foreign ambassadors. But increasingly active Soviet diplomacy in the post-Stalin era required the USSR President to become a hard-working diplomat. As Moscow was inundated by visits from innumerable foreign delegations, Soviet diplomats were swamped in negotiations, so the USSR President had to help by assuming part of the negotiation burden. When the post-Stalin Soviet leaders started traveling abroad under a new policy of personal diplomacy, the USSR President paid official visits to many countries, sometimes negotiating trade or aid agreements in the foreign capitals.

During several periods of Soviet history the top leader of the USSR headed the Communist Party but was not governmental Premier. By international law, party leadership does not entitle a politician to participate in diplomatic negotiations. Before assuming the premiership, both Stalin and Khrushchev served as members of the USSR Presidium, thus gaining the governmental rank necessary for foreign negotiations. For example, Stalin was a Presidium member when he negotiated the Nazi-Soviet Pact of 1939, and Khrushchev had similar rank while attending the Geneva summit conference of France, Britain, the United States, and the USSR during 1955. In the post-Khrushchev period, party chief Brezhnev was first a member, then chairman, of the State

Presidium for the same reason. The USSR President and one or two members of his Presidium are real working diplomats. But the USSR Presidium as a whole takes little part in foreign affairs.

As for the Council of Ministers, or USSR governmental cabinet, the Premier has always been active in diplomatic negotiations, whether he was top Soviet leader or not. Premiers Molotov in the 1930's and Bulganin in the late 1950's both participated personally in foreign affairs. Premiers Lenin, Stalin, and Khrushchev achieved diplomatic coups which are landmarks in Soviet history.

The Minister of Foreign Affairs, his entire Ministry, and his embassies and consulates abroad are in the daily business of professional diplomacy. The extent of this Ministry's operations is indicated by Table 33.

Many nations do not maintain diplomatic relations with the USSR. This international vacuum creates grave difficulties for Soviet diplomacy. One might expect Soviet Russia not to be recognized by strongly anti-Communist nations such as South Africa and Rhodesia in Africa; and Qatar, Oman, Saudi Arabia, South Korea, and Taiwan in Asia.

But part of Latin America lacks diplomatic relations with the USSR. During World War II, the majority of Latin American governments recognized the Soviet Union, then broke relations after this war's armistice. There appear to be three reasons for the postwar divorce of Latin America and Russia: little trade, anti-Communist preachings of Catholic churches predominant in Latin America, and the emotional reaction of Latin American governments toward mistreatment of their diplomats stationed in the USSR. For example, Chile, which trades mainly with the West, severed relations with Moscow because the Russian wife of the Chilean Ambassador was not permitted to join her husband in departing from the Soviet Union.

In addition to the Ministry of Foreign Affairs, the USSR cabinet contains other ministries and committees which are ostensibly domestic, yet engage in activities abroad. The Soviet Ministry of Railways operates freight and passenger trains deep into the territory of Soviet-orbit nations. Sometimes this international railroading is achieved by using railway cars with movable wheels, which at the Soviet border are narrowed from the

Table 33. *Foreign Countries with Which the USSR Maintains Diplomatic Relations*

	Africa		
Algeria	Equatorial Guinea	Malagasy	Senegal
Angola	Ethiopia	Mali	Sierra Leone
Botswana	Gabon	Mauritania	Somalia
Burundi	Gambia	Mauritius	Sudan
Cameroon	Ghana	Morocco	Tanzania
Central Africa	Guinea	Mozambique	Togo
Chad	Guinea-Bissau	Niger	Tunisia
Congo	Kenya	Nigeria	Uganda
Dahomey	Liberia	Rwanda	Upper Volta
Egypt	Libya	Sao Tome	Zaire
			Zambia
	Americas		
Argentina	Colombia	Mexico	Uruguay
Bolivia	Cuba	Peru	Venezuela
Brazil	Ecuador	Trinidad	
Canada	Guyana	United States	
	Asia		
Afghanistan	Indonesia	Maldives	South Yemen
Australia	Iran	Mongolia	Sri Lanka
Bahrain	Iraq	Nepal	Syria
Bangladesh	Japan	New Zealand	Thailand
Burma	Jordan	North Korea	Turkey
Cambodia	Kuwait	Pakistan	West Samoa
Communist China	Laos	Philippines	Yemen
Fiji	Lebanon	Singapore	Vietnam
India	Malaysia		
	Europe		
Austria	Finland	Luxembourg	Switzerland
Belgium	France	Malta	West Germany
Britain	Greece	Norway	Yugoslavia
Bulgaria	Holland	Poland	
Cyprus	Hungary	Portugal	
Czechoslovakia	Iceland	Rumania	
Denmark	Ireland	Spain	
East Germany	Italy	Sweden	

Source: *US Department of State.*

5-foot Russian gauge to the smaller 4-foot 8.5-inch gauge, which is standard for most of the rest of the world. Since locomotive wheels cannot easily be altered, a change of engines takes place at the frontier.

To streamline transportation of freight and passengers within the Soviet orbit, the USSR has widened some railway tracks into satellite countries, or has built broad tracks abroad, so Soviet trains can roll into neighboring Communist nations without adjustment of car wheels.

By either method of crossing the Soviet frontier, travel of USSR trains into the Soviet orbit is far-reaching. Since 1954, direct rail communication has existed between Moscow and the city of Canton in southern China. Express trains have linked Moscow since 1955 with East Berlin and with the North Korean capital of Pyongyang. During 1966 a new broad-gauge railway was completed from the Soviet border to the Czechoslovak city of Kosice to transport USSR iron ore to the East Slovak Steel Plant.

Another Soviet organization engaged partially in foreign affairs is the USSR Ministry for Oil Refining, which since 1964 has operated the "Friendship Pipeline" pumping oil and petroleum products from the Volga valley more than 1,000 miles into Poland, Czechoslovakia, Hungary, and East Germany. Besides making these four East European nations dependent on Soviet oil, the Friendship Pipeline has created bitter economic debates in non-Communist West Europe. The USSR has offered to extend the pipeline beyond East Germany into West Europe, which lacks oil fields and which pays high prices for Near Eastern and African petroleum. Many West European nations would like to import the Soviet pipeline oil, which would be cheaper, but do not want to become dependent on Moscow for such strategic fuel. However, by the late 1970's international pipelines were supplying Soviet natural gas not only to Communist Bulgaria and Czechoslovakia, but also to non-Communist Austria, Finland, Italy, and West Germany. Apparently West Europe considers gas a less vital fuel than petroleum, which is essential for transport.

Similar economic pressure over part of East Europe can be applied by the USSR Ministry for Electric Power Stations. Since 1963, all the large electric power stations of Czechoslovakia, East Germany, Hungary, Poland, and the Soviet western Ukraine have been linked together by cables forming an international grid. If any of the five participants is short of electricity, the others help by wiring additional current to the nation in need. Russia has the opportunity to chastise Czechoslovakia, East Germany, Hungary, or Poland at any moment by switching off electricity from the USSR.

Seemingly only economic, but fast becoming political, is the USSR Ministry for Maritime Transport. This Soviet governmental office controls USSR ports, plus servicing and repairing visiting foreign ships. Much more important, however, is the fast post-Stalin growth of the Soviet merchant marine, which the ministry owns and operates. For decades after the Bolshevik Revolution the Soviet merchant marine was too small to transport USSR exports and imports, most of which arrive and depart via the Black and Baltic seas.

By the late 1970's the USSR had purchased many new freighters and tankers from West Europe, East Europe, and Japan, but the vastly expanded Soviet merchant marine still could only haul 60 per cent of all USSR overseas freight. Western ships are chartered to carry the other 40 per cent. Statistics on the Soviet merchant marine are fragmentary and estimated, but Table 34 shows USSR maritime growth in recent years:

Table 34. *Size of the USSR Merchant Marine*

Year	Tonnage (deadweight tons)
1951	1,898,000
1963	5,900,000
1966	9,400,000
1973	13,000,000
1975	15,000,000

Source: *Americana Annual*, 1952-1976.

The Soviet merchant marine is now among the largest in the world. The USSR is already participating in the world shipping market by offering many boats for shipments between non-Communist countries.

Aeroflot, the Soviet civil aviation company, is another cabinet ministry which has developed extensive foreign operations. Until 1950 Aeroflot was mostly confined to internal airlines, though at times there had been regular Soviet flights to Germany, Sweden, and pre-Communist China. Since 1950, and especially after Stalin's death in 1953, Aeroflot has established routes to many foreign countries. By the late 1970's, Soviet planes flew 218,000 miles of foreign air routes, and linked Moscow to the countries shown in Table 35.

Table 35. *Foreign Countries Served by Aeroflot*

		Africa		
Algeria	Guinea	Sudan	Nigeria	
Egypt	Mali	Tunisia	Senegal	
Ghana	Morocco	Gambia	Tanzania	
Angola	Somalia	Guinea-Bissau	Uganda	
Benin	Congo	Kenya	Zaire	
Cape Verde	Equatorial Guinea	Libya	Madagascar	
Chad	Ethiopia	Mauritania		
		Asia		
Afghanistan	Indonesia	Mongolia	Jordan	
Burma	Iran	North Korea	Laos	
Communist China	Iraq	Pakistan	Malaysia	
India	Japan	Syria	Singapore	
South Yemen	Lebanon	Turkey	Yemen	
Sri Lanka	Thailand	Bangladesh	Vietnam	
		Europe		
Austria	East Germany	Norway	Luxembourg	
Belgium	England	Poland	Portugal	
Bulgaria	Finland	Rumania	Spain	
Cyprus	France	Sweden		
Czechoslovakia	Holland	Switzerland		
Denmark	Hungary	Yugoslavia		
Greece	Italy	West Germany		
		North America		
Canada	Peru	Cuba	Mexico	United States

Source: *Aeroflot advertisements.*

The list of USSR foreign flights indicates that Aeroflot's international operations are as much political as economic. Logically most of the Communist countries are linked to Russia by air, the exception being Albania. Aerial transport of freight, mail, and passengers among Communist nations is probably considerable. There is less justification for the number of Soviet air routes into West Europe, since neither the tourist or commercial traffic on these lines is large. Often Aeroflot planes fly half-empty to and from West European cities. And only politics can explain the great expense of regular Aeroflot flights to distant underdeveloped nations like tropical Guinea. In such instances, Aeroflot's political value is rapid communication between Russia and a nonaligned country, plus the prestige of displaying modern Soviet planes to underdeveloped countries.

The USSR Ministry of Fishing conducts worldwide operations of two types. First, to provide fish for a nation which always has shortages of meat, the Ministry's fleet of trawlers catches huge quantities of fish along the west and east coasts of North America, South America and Africa as well as along Soviet shores. Second, some of the Soviet fishing boats are equipped with electronic devices, which chart foreign coastal waters and eavesdrop on foreign radio communications. One third of all fishing ships in the world belong to the USSR, which owns and operates the largest fishing fleet of any nation, and is exceeded in fish catch only by Japan.

Once Khrushchev became top Soviet leader in 1955, Russia was opened to large numbers of foreign tourists. Khrushchev also realized the propaganda value of cultural exchange with non-Communist countries; and numerous cultural agreements were concluded with Western and underdeveloped nations. This cultural exchange is conducted by the USSR Ministry of Foreign Affairs, which formed a special section to arrange foreign cultural tours within Russia, and to send Soviet artists, ballets, musicians, students, professors, and scientists abroad. At present the USSR conducts cultural exchange with the non-Communist countries shown in Table 36.

A typical cultural pact between the USSR and a non-Communist nation provides for mutual visits by cultural, economic, and parliamentary delegations, and by artists, professors, scientists, and students. In addition there are joint sport contests, and exchange of exhibits, movies, publications, radio broadcasts, and television programs. Soviet ballet has been prominently displayed in the

Table 36. *Existing Cultural Exchange Between the USSR and Non-Communist Countries*

		Africa	
Algeria	Ghana	Angola	Senegal
Burundi	Guinea	Benin	Sierra Leone
Cameroon	Kenya	Congo	Somalia
Central Africa	Mali	Guinea-Bissau	Sudan
Chad	Morocco	Libya	Tanzania
Egypt	Niger	Mozambique	Togo
Ethiopia	Nigeria	Sao Tome	Tunisia
Rwanda			Uganda
		Asia	
Afghanistan	India	Yemen	Syria
Burma	Indonesia	Malaysia	Turkey
Cambodia	Iran	Sri Lanka	
Australia	Iraq	Turkey	
Japan	Nepal	Pakistan	
		Europe	
Belgium	France	Austria	Norway
Britain	Holland	Luxembourg	West Germany
Denmark	Iceland	Portugal	Yugoslavia
Finland	Italy	Sweden	
		America	
Argentina	Canada	United States	Mexico

Source: *US Department of State.*

USA, because Americans love dancing and no knowledge of the Russian language is needed. For the more sophisticated West European audiences, the USSR relies heavily on classical music. And in Asian and African nations, where Western culture is alien, Russia stresses sport contests and vaudeville.

It is difficult to evaluate the impact of Soviet cultural exchange upon non-Communist nations. Certainly the USSR must make a strong impression on underdeveloped countries, where the Russian contribution is great and little can be offered in return. But cultural exchange between the USSR and any Western nation is relatively equal in quantity, so in propaganda Russia may lose as much or more than it gains. For example, the American jazz orchestra of Benny Goodman was just as popular in Russia as the Bolshoi Ballet in the United States. Western motion pictures draw larger audiences in the USSR than Soviet movies in the West. American student groups touring the USSR are often depressed by the uncomfortable hotels, unsanitary college camps, and obvious regimentation of Soviet youth. While touring abroad, a number of USSR artists and athletes have defected to the West. Soviet cultural exchange cannot be considered an unqualified success in terms of Soviet objectives.

Also involved in cultural exchange is the USSR Ministry for Higher and Special Secondary Education, operating all teacher training institutes in the Soviet Union, and supervising all professional colleges such as law, medicine, dentistry, science, and engineering, which are usually managed by the ministry for which the student will eventually work.

This educational ministry is in charge of a growing contingent of foreign college students studying in the USSR. There have always been such international students, but before World War II they numbered no more than a few hundred persons per year, mostly Communists, fellow-travelers, or students of Soviet affairs. After the war, large groups of students came to Russia from the Soviet satellite nations of both Europe and Asia. Then during the Khrushchev era, a major effort was made to attract college students from the non-Communist countries of Asia, Africa, and Latin America. In 1960 the USSR opened a "University of International Friendship" in Moscow only for students from underdeveloped nations of the non-Communist world. A year later this university was renamed "Patrice Lumumba" in honor of the assassinated Congo Premier who had been friendly to the USSR.

Relatively few students are invited to Russia from Western nations. Hence the USA is allowed only a few dozen college students per year in Russia, and the Soviet government screens each applicant. In contrast, almost any African can study in the USSR by merely applying to the local Soviet Embassy or Communist party headquarters.

Since Soviet college students pay no tuition, foreign students in the USSR study free of charge. Students from the underdeveloped nations also receive stipends (cost-of-living allowances) three times larger than those for Soviet students. Most foreign students in the USSR reside in Moscow or Leningrad, but some are located in other major cities. The majority of students from Asia, Africa, and Latin America enroll in professional college programs like economics, medicine, agronomy, and engineering, which provide practical skills for development of their backward countries. Though all foreign students in the USSR are taught Marxism, few major in Communist philosophy. Table 37 shows the consistent growth in the number of college students studying in the USSR from Communist and non-Communist countries:

Table 37. *Number of College Students in the USSR from Communist and non-Communist Nations*

Year	Number of students
1960	13,000
1962	15,000
1973	36,000
1976	44,000

Source: *Pravda,* 1960-1976.

Many foreign students become dissatisfied with the Soviet way of life. Most underdeveloped nations are located in the tropics, and their students find the frigid Russian winter difficult to endure. Africans suffer considerable racial discrimination in the USSR, some having been beaten up for dating Russian girls. Frequent complaints from foreign students in the USSR are that too much time is wasted studying Marxism, that they are kept apart from Russian youth (especially in Lumumba University), and that course programs are inferior to those in Western universities.

Each year several dozen foreign students transfer from Soviet to West European colleges, or simply go home and do not return.

Involved heavily in foreign news is TASS—the Telegraph Agency of the Soviet Union, which is a cabinet ministry whose minister often accompanies Soviet leaders when they visit foreign countries. Like the Associated Press or United Press in the USA, TASS collects and disseminates internal news throughout the USSR. But also similar to any large Western news agency, TASS has correspondents and offices throughout the Communist and non-Communist world. Some TASS personnel abroad are Soviet citizens, while others are local inhabitants, usually pro-Soviet. TASS provides, and heavily censors, most of the foreign news published in the Soviet press.

But TASS has other functions. Many important pronouncements from the Kremlin are issued by TASS radio broadcasts from Moscow. For example, during the Vietnam war TASS denied a Chinese Communist rumor that the Soviet government was informed in advance about American bombing of the North Vietnamese capital city of Hanoi. TASS also issues to high Soviet officials daily secret memoranda containing uncensored foreign news, both pro- and anti-Soviet.

The Soviet government in 1961 ordered already existing societies of USSR intellectuals, journalists, writers and foreign friendship to form the Novosti (News) agency, to compete with TASS in sending Soviet news abroad. By various channels, Novosti attempts to influence the intellectuals and artistic circles of foreign nations.

Each year during the late 1970's, the USSR was visited by some 4 million foreign tourists, mostly from nations of the Soviet orbit. About 3 million Soviet citizens travel abroad annually, mainly to East European countries. The Administration for Foreign Tourism, a department of the USSR governmental cabinet, controls Intourist, the official travel agency for adult tourists. Also under the Administration is Vneshposyltorg, through which foreigners can send gift packages to friends and relatives in the USSR. Student tourist groups are booked by Sputnik, a branch of the Komsomol. Neither Intourist nor Sputnik maintain many offices abroad. Instead the average foreign tourist contacts his local travel agency, which then negotiates with Intourist or Sputnik. The tours are usually prearranged, and payment is made in advance. In Russia Intourist or Sputnik provides transportation, hotels, meals, and guides.

The USSR desires foreign tourists for two reasons: to display

Soviet achievements and to gain Western currency. To make tourism easier, the post-Khrushchev regime reduced the time for issuing Soviet entry visas, built new hotels, and opened special stores where Russian goods and appliances are sold below cost if purchased with Western currency.

However, Soviet tourism is admittedly beset with many problems. Both Intourist and Sputnik are inefficient. Foreign tourists are often more impressed by Soviet poverty than achievements. Russia also tries to isolate tourists from the Soviet people, for fear the latter may be infected with bourgeois ideas. A few foreign tourists are arrested by Soviet police each year, apparently as a warning to the others. Under such circumstances, Russia cannot attract the enormous number of tourists which Western Europe has long enjoyed.

Soviet foreign trade is planned and conducted by the USSR Ministry for Foreign Trade, which has a network of trade missions and agents throughout the world. If possible, the Ministry tries to gain diplomatic status for its trade missions, which then cannot be sued for breach of contract except in Soviet courts. Should this diplomatic status be refused, the Ministry opens a Soviet-owned trading company in the foreign country, such as Amtorg in the United States. The Ministry controls the USSR Bank for Foreign Trade, which is the main Soviet depository for foreign currency. Cooperating closely with the Ministry is the All-Union Chamber of Commerce which organizes Soviet industrial exhibits in foreign countries. The Chamber also has an arbitration court, which judges disputes between the Ministry and foreign business concerns.

Besides conducting commerce, the Foreign Trade Ministry performs technological intelligence by purchasing foreign patents, blueprints, and new technical devices. If possible, this is done legally. If not, the trade agents resort to espionage, for which they are frequently arrested. By careful accumulation of data, the Ministry maintains a card file describing every factory in the outside world.

Soviet foreign aid is administered not by the Foreign Trade Ministry, but by the State Committee for Foreign Economic Relations, which has the rank of a cabinet ministry. By the late 1970's the USSR had concluded technical aid agreements with the non-Communist nations shown in Table 38. For most African and Near Eastern countries listed in this table, the Soviet technical aid also included armament.

Table 38. *Non-Communist Countries Receiving USSR Technical Aid*

Africa			
Algeria	Guinea	Sierra Leone	Malagasy
Cameroon	Kenya	Somalia	Mauritania
Egypt	Mali	Sudan	Mozambique
Ethiopia	Morocco	Tanzania	Rwanda
Ghana	Niger	Togo	Sao Tome
Angola	Nigeria	Tunisia	Upper Volta
Benin	Senegal	Uganda	Zambia
Burundi	Congo	Guinea-Bissau	Botswana
Central Africa	Equatorial Guinea	Libya	
Chad	Gambia	Madagascar	
America			
Argentina	Brazil	Colombia	Mexico
Peru	Trinidad	Venezuela	
Asia			
Afghanistan	Iran	Bangladesh	Pakistan
Burma	Iraq	Jordan	Singapore
Cambodia	Kuwait	Malaysia	Syria
India	Laos	South Yemen	Turkey
Thailand	Nepal	Sri Lanka	Yemen

Europe		
Cyprus	Greece	Iceland
Finland	Portugal	

Source: *US Department of State.*

The USSR concentrates its foreign aid to non-Communist countries mainly on Asia and Africa, and renders such assistance to some very remote and tiny nations. Soviet technical aid to Latin America is still in its infancy.

Communist countries also render technical aid to each other. The USSR supplies technical assistance to North Korea, Mongolia, Vietnam, Laos, and Cuba, and receives technical aid from all of the East European Soviet satellites.

Chapter 15 has already mentioned that the two USSR police ministries participate in foreign affairs. The Ministry of Internal Affairs (MVD) officially processes most applications for Soviet passports and visas. In every Soviet city, MVD also registers all foreigners residing or traveling in the USSR. MVD has the power to expel individual foreigners from the Soviet Union and occasionally does so.

The other police ministry, the Committee for State Security (KGB), patrols the Soviet borders, and provides the customs inspectors at seaports, land border stations, and international airports. KGB also watches and may attempt to blackmail resident foreigners and tourists from abroad. Periodically KGB arrests individual foreigners on charges usually involving theft, blackmarketing, or espionage. At times the charges appear to be true, and in some cases, to be concocted.

But the greatest international importance of KGB is its international spy ring, which operates from Soviet embassies, consulates, and trade missions, and also through foreign Communist parties which are pro-Moscow. In the past many spies were foreign Communists, because Russians found it difficult to conceal their identity abroad. During recent years, the foreigners are being replaced by Soviet citizens, who have been trained in foreign languages and customs.

KGB also plants saboteurs in foreign countries for future use. These agents do not spy, and therefore are difficult to apprehend. They marry, take jobs, and in general live normal lives. But their homes are usually located near a reservoir, pipeline, railroad track, factory, or other industrial installation which must be wrecked when war starts against the Soviet Union. A KGB agent defecting in West Germany during the 1950's revealed the names of several dozen of these hidden saboteurs residing in Western Europe. Once known, they were quickly rounded up by European police.

Along with KGB, the USSR Ministry of Defense is of international importance. Its General Staff prepares the war plans of the USSR. Since 1955, the Ministry has controlled the Warsaw Pact military alliance of Poland, East Germany, Czechoslovakia, Hungary, Rumania, Bulgaria, and the USSR. In the late 1970's the ministry issued orders to no less than 31 Soviet army divisions stationed abroad: 20 in East Germany, 4 in Hungary, 5 in Czechoslovakia, and 2 in Poland. Military advisors also accompany Soviet arms shipments abroad, which today are quite large to Cuba, Syria, Libya, and India.

Like the KGB, the Defense Ministry operates a worldwide spy ring, operating mainly out of Soviet diplomatic missions. The two espionage networks, KGB and military, are kept separate, so that if one is caught the other may escape unscathed. For example, soon after World War II the Canadian government arrested some 200 members of the Soviet military spy ring in Canada, but could not find the USSR police spies. Several years later, the United States trapped the main Soviet police spies in America, but failed to apprehend the agents of USSR military intelligence. Penkovskiy, a high Soviet official who spied for the West, estimates that three fifths of all USSR diplomatic personnel stationed abroad are agents of either military or police intelligence.

Though KGB and Soviet military intelligence read the foreign press carefully, and employ mechanical devices like wire-tapping and spy satellites, Soviet espionage prides itself on planting operatives in top agencies of capitalist governments. Thus far, the record of such high-level infiltration has been impressive. Leaving aside wild accusations that a Communist is hiding behind every capitalist bush, Soviet spies have been caught and convicted, or have hurriedly fled behind the Iron Curtain, from the foreign ministries, intelligence agencies, and atomic energy commissions of most Western powers. Presumably the same infiltration takes place within state chambers of newly developing nations.

Along with the USSR governmental departments engaged in foreign affairs, at least three sections of the Central Committee secretariat of the Soviet Communist Party are concerned with international work. One is the office for "Relations with Communist Parties of Socialist Countries,"—i.e., the bureau for coordination of the Soviet orbit.

A second international section of the secretariat is the office for "Relations with the Communist and Labor Parties of Non-Socialist Countries." This bureau is the successor to the old Communist International, and issues orders to all Moscow-oriented Communist parties and Communist-front organizations throughout the world.

Also the "Foreign Section" of the secretariat processes diplomatic memoranda from foreign governments. So secretive are all three international bureaus of the secretariat that the names of their chiefs are rarely published in the Soviet press.

Obviously the USSR has a large network of organizations dealing with foreign affairs. They are needed because the Soviet Union has truly become a world power. Still the question arises: Who determines USSR foreign policy?

Numerous refugee diplomats from the Soviet foreign service describe the decision-making procedure, which appears to have remained unchanged since the 1920's:

The USSR Foreign Ministry has almost no power to make decisions, as is true for other Soviet agencies which foreigners directly contact. The Foreign Ministry does not determine replies to diplomatic notes, Intourist and Sputnik do not grant tourist visas, and the Foreign Trade Ministry cannot freely negotiate commercial pacts abroad.

As in most countries, the majority of foreign requests to the USSR are channeled into its Foreign Ministry. The latter, however, only serves as a message center. Minor matters are forwarded from the ministry to the police, who apparently handle the bulk of the passport and visa requests. Because the Foreign Ministry must make international friends, the police suspect the ministry's loyalty and therefore often delay answers to routine foreign queries.

When the international affair is of medium importance, such as the US forbidding a Soviet merchant ship from sailing through the Panama Canal, the Foreign Ministry sends the problem to the appropriate section of the Central Committee secretariat, which decides what to do. Since the secretariat considers all foreigners to be enemies, its decisions often create needless hostility abroad.

Major international decisions are made by the Politburo of the USSR Communist Party. Though gradually increasing in size from 5 to 20 men during Soviet history, the Politburo has always been a small brain trust of top Communist party leaders, some of whom hold no governmental positions other than nominal membership in the Supreme Soviet. Yet, according to past Politburo agenda, these party officials determine Soviet foreign trade, foreign currency plans, national defense, and foreign affairs ranging from war crises and military alliances down to the treatment of foreign newsmen within the USSR. At times the Politburo has even served as an international court, arbitrating disputes between foreign Communist parties.

After the police, party secretariat, or Politburo make a foreign affairs decision, this judgment is sent to the Foreign Ministry for transmittal abroad. In some instances, the Foreign Ministry may delegate another USSR governmental agency to make the announcement. For example, it was more convenient in 1966 for the Soviet Red Cross to complain about mistreatment of Kurds by Iraq, than have the ministry do so.

This system of party and police policy-making, with the Soviet government acting as messenger, explains the long delay in answering many foreign queries. It also explains why Soviet delegations at international conferences can decide nothing new until receiving instructions from Moscow.

Although the Politburo determines top foreign policy, until recently this supreme body had no member trained specially for diplomacy. Of the Soviet foreign ministers who served 10 or more years in office, Chicherin (1920's) and Litvinov (1930's) were not even Politburo candidates. Molotov, serving 1939-1949 and 1953-1955, was a Politburo member untrained for foreign affairs. But in 1973 Andrei Gromyko, a professional diplomat and longtime foreign minister, gained full Politburo membership.

Throughout Soviet history, most Politburo members have been recruited among USSR regional party leaders. Yet these provincial amateurs have achieved worldwide diplomatic success.

Suggestions for Further Reading

ATHAY, ROBERT E., *The Economics of Soviet Merchant Shipping Policy*. Chapel Hill: North Carolina University Press, 1971.

COHN, HELEN DESFOSSES, *Soviet Policy Toward Black Africa*. New York: Praeger, 1972.

FLETCHER, WILLIAM C., *Religion and Soviet Foreign Policy, 1945-1970*. New York: Oxford University Press, 1973.

HAZAN, BARUCH A., *Soviet Propaganda, A Case Study of the Middle East Conflict*. New Brunswick: Transaction, 1976.

Hoffmann, Erik P., and Fleron, Frederic J., *The Conduct of Soviet Foreign Policy*. Chicago: Aldine-Atherton, 1972.

Penkovskiy, Oleg, *The Penkovskiy Papers,* New York: Doubleday, 1965.

Rubinstein, Alvin Z. and Ginsburgs, George, eds., *Soviet and American Policies in the United Nations*. New York: New York University Press, 1971.

Chapter 23

Communist Expansion

After World War II while the British, French, Dutch, and Belgian empires were falling apart, the USSR and its Marxist allies created the largest empire in modern history. By the late 1970's, one of every three human beings on earth lived under Communist rule. Taken together, 16 Communist nations covered one fourth of the land surface of the world, and operated two fifths of global industry. Dwarfing Hitler's short-lived Greater Reich and Japan's brief East Asian Co-Prosperity Sphere, Communist empire-building in the twentieth century has been a great achievement.

The Soviet orbit of nations quickly developed its own heretics, in the form of Communist governments which did not obey all Moscow orders. Today the Communist bloc of countries is evolving from a Russian empire into a loose alliance, with some Communist lands already expelled from the Marxist league of nations. But not a single Communist country, whether pro-Moscow or not, has returned to a completely capitalist system of economy or a democratic form of government.

Today there is diversity among Communist nations, each seeking its own road to socialism. Some Marxist countries such as Poland and Yugoslavia have developed an economy including much small-scale private enterprise, very similar to Soviet Russia's NEP of the 1920's. Communist China permits little private enterprise, but has decentralized state economic administration. Others, like the USSR, Rumania and Bulgaria, still continue with Stalinist centralized economic planning.

Communist diversity also exists in political fields, though to a lesser extent. Nowhere in the Communist world is there a Western type of representative government. But the average Pole or Yugoslav enjoys considerable personal and artistic freedom. Meanwhile the average Russian has less liberty, and the average Chinese none.

What explains the speed with which Communist nations arose after World War II, and their success in remaining Communist? Mass popular belief in Marxism is not the answer, for in no country has a Communist party ever won a free national election. Today the strongest Western Communist parties, as in Finland, France and Italy, obtain no more than one fourth or one third of the national vote in free elections. There have been Communist majorities in some local elections, as in the French capital of Paris or the Indian state of Kerala, but such Marxist victories have not been decisive. Even in Communist countries, Marxist idealism is not strong among the masses. For years the official press of both Russia and East Europe has complained about the cynicism and political nihilism among many youths, who were born and educated under Marxist regimes.

The first step in satellization is military force. Soviet army officers are taught that the USSR armed forces have two main functions: to safeguard Communism within the USSR, and to spread Communism abroad by the sword. Thus far every Communist government in the world has been placed in power by force, either by the Soviet army or local Communist troops, or both fighting as a team. Tuva and Outer Mongolia were conquered and communized by the Soviet army during 1921. As a result of military victories in World War II, the Soviet army installed Communist governments in Poland, East Germany, Hungary, Rumania, Bulgaria, and North Korea. Tito gained power in Yugoslavia through joint operations of his own Communist guerrillas and the Soviet army. Czechoslovakia adopted Communism peaceably in 1948, but under the threat of the Soviet army stationed around its frontiers. Soviet armament helped the Chinese Red Army to seize mainland China and Tibet, and the Indochinese Communists to win control over North Vietnam, South Vietnam, Cambodia, and Laos. Castro's guerrilla army overthrew Cuba's capitalist regime. Mongolia, East Germany, and

Hungary have all rebelled against Communist rule, and all have been crushed by USSR armed forces when native Communist troops failed.

Communist military force is sometimes applied with great cunning. A good example was when the Soviet army entered Poland late in World War II, driving the Germans back toward Berlin. As the Soviet army neared the Polish capital of Warsaw, Moscow radio asked the powerful Warsaw underground to rebel, and from the inside to help Soviet troops liberate the city from the Germans. The underground was anxious to rebel, hoping to free Warsaw and establish their own non-Communist Polish government before the Russians arrived. So the underground revolted, as Moscow had requested. Then the Soviet army sat motionless, just seven miles away, while the angry Nazis destroyed Warsaw with bombs and artillery, block by block. Without firing a shot, Russia crushed the Warsaw underground, which later would have opposed the communization of Poland.

But Communist control of non-USSR territories would be weak, if it relied on force alone. So military force is only the first step, destroying all major centers of possible opposition, as in Poland's Warsaw where 200,000 patriots were exterminated by the Nazis before the Red Army belatedly arrived.

Then comes a deceptive "lull." A coalition government of left-wing and liberal parties is set up. Often the prime minister and most of the governmental cabinet are not Communists. But three key cabinet ministries are usually in the hands of the Communist Party: armed forces, police, and education. The nation is officially proclaimed to be a "People's Democracy," not like the Communist USSR or the capitalist West, but a bridge between the two competing systems.

In the satellite nation, at first only mild socialist reforms are made. Large estates are broken up into small private farms, and the peasants are assured that there will be no agricultural collectivization. Big business is nationalized, but small storekeepers and artisans are told to conduct their private business as usual. Promises of job security and full employment are made to industrial workers.

In East Europe immediately after World War II, the largest political parties usually were the agrarian—demanding land reform, or the city socialist—urging nationalization of large-scale industry. Thus the "lull" government did no more than fulfill the economic desires of the agrarian or socialist parties, which would have assumed power, had Communist military force not been present.

Mass desire for peace aided the acceptance of lull governments. East Europe had just suffered through five years of World War II, was tired of fighting and war destruction, and felt betrayed by the Western Great Powers. China was in even worse condition having endured 22 years of civil war and war against Japan, before the Communists seized power. The majority of the population in each satellite nation accepted the lull government which at least would bring peace and quiet. The People's Democracy is launched with almost no resistance, just when Communist control is weakest.

The lull lasts as long as needed, the average period in East Europe being three years. In China the lull continued seven years, because of that Asian nation's vast size, backwardness, and poor communications. During the lull, almost no overt Communist action is taken. But the Communists and their supporters slowly and secretly infiltrate every organization which could exert political power.

Naturally one of the first targets for infiltration is the police. Many older police officers are retired, and replaced by new personnel loyal to Communism. In East Europe a large number of Soviet police arrived and became local police chiefs. Eventually the entire satellite police force consists of Communists and pro-Communists.

A similar process takes place in the armed forces, with older officers being retired and replaced by commanders whom Communism can trust. Meanwhile the enlisted men, who are often peasants conscripted into service, are subjected to two hours of Marxist indoctrination each day. Many of the peasant youths are converted to Communism by this intense propaganda.

Another key target for infiltration is the courts, where the judges are gradually replaced or retrained. The same process occurs in the school system, from universities down to kindergartens, with anti-Communist teachers being weeded out. Trade union leadership is infiltrated from the national level down to the shop stewards. Youth organizations and sport societies are slowly taken over by Communists or Communist sympathizers. The entire apparatus of government is infiltrated: ministries, town halls, county seats, village committees, and even city block leaders.

Anti-Communist political parties are often infiltrated in various ways. Certain party leaders may become secret Communist agents, and then maneuver their party into supporting the Communist program. This, for example, happened in Czechoslovakia, where the head of the socialist party was a pro-Communist. Or the socialist party may be pressured to join the Communists in a combined party, which will not take the name of Communist. But the new joint party, taking a name such as Socialist Unity in East Germany or United Workers in Poland, is dominated by Communists who quickly purge the strong anti-Communists. If a party cannot be infiltrated, an opposition party may be established by pro-Communists to split the old party's membership. In Poland, pro-Communists established a new peasant party to weaken the existing large anti-Communist agrarian party.

Sometimes churches are infiltrated. In East Europe, the Orthodox and Uniate (Catholic with the Orthodox rite) priests were required to accept the leadership of the Moscow Patriarch of the Russian Orthodox Church. The Patriarch, in turn, is a spokesman for Soviet foreign policy. For example, he condemned the Hungarian anti-Communist revolution of 1956. The political importance is obvious in countries such as Rumania, Bulgaria, and Yugoslavia, which have large Orthodox congregations.

Where the satellite church is not Orthodox or Uniate, the lull government may succeed in winning over some priests and bishops to the Communist cause. Such churchmen will then use the pulpit to solicit support for pro-Communist policies. Church infiltration has had some success in Czechoslovakia, Hungary, East Germany, and Albania.

A problem for the lull government in Poland was the existence of a large anti-Communist underground, which had been formed to harass the Nazi occupation regime of World War II. The Warsaw headquarters of the underground had been destroyed by the Nazis, but large numbers of Polish nationalist guerrillas still survived in provincial cities and rural regions. Outside Warsaw, the Nazis had never been able to crush this underground during all five years of German occupation.

Perhaps the mistake of the Nazis was their extreme cruelty. For the Polish lull government quickly and easily disarmed the underground by kindness. The Polish government simply published an amnesty, promising that any member of the underground would be unharmed, if he would surrender his arms to the infiltrated police. Many, tired of endless guerrilla fighting, did surrender. Mostly the government kept its word, and did not punish them. Only a few underground leaders were arrested, sent to Moscow, and tried there for wartime treason against the USSR. Since all of the underground had still not surrendered, a second amnesty was issued. Impressed by the government's leniency, most of the remaining guerrillas reported to the police. Only a few diehards continued fighting in the Carpathian mountains, where they tended to become bandits who eventually died from lack of proper medical care.

After the two amnesties, not only was most of the Polish underground disarmed, but the police knew the names and addresses of the surrendering members. These former guerrillas were kept under close police watch, so that they could never form an underground again. If anti-Communists should attempt to organize a new underground, the personnel would have to be completely new.

One of the smoothest lulls was conducted in early Communist China. In East Europe, big business was usually nationalized overnight, and the People's Democracy then had trouble finding competent state managers. Often the result was a temporary industrial slowdown. Instead of nationalizing most big business overnight, the Chinese government would usually enter into partnership with the big businessman. At first the state share of the private enterprise would be small, perhaps 10 per cent. Meanwhile the private owner would remain as skilled manager, but the state collected part of the profits. Gradually the state share of ownership was increased, but the private owner-manager remained in charge. After several years the state took the enterprise over completely, the private owner was out, but the government had had time to train state managers for the enterprise. Hence the early industrial slowdown was avoided.

The universal infiltration of society during a People's Democratic lull is accompanied by some force and terror. Soviet occupation authorities intervened strongly in Hungarian and Rumanian politics soon after World War II, when the lull governments in both countries became too democratic and nationalistic. During the Polish lull, several anti-Communist politicians were arrested, tried, and sentenced to imprisonment or death. In many villages of China during the Communist land reform, rich peasants were tried by a mob court, which often punished the prosperous farmer by cutting off his hands. Peking officially admitted that two million Chinese had been executed during the lull period. But force and terror are used only when individuals object to being quietly purged by the lull's infiltration. And this mass infiltration, rather than terror, firmly establishes long-lasting Communist rule.

Where do Communists obtain the millions of helpers to infiltrate the police, army, courts, government, unions, mass societies, churches, and opposition parties? The Chinese Communist party was good-sized when it seized power. But the East European Communists were small in number at the end of World War II, having been largely exterminated by Nazi German occupation.

Therefore, every possible method was used by Communists to recruit assistants during lulls. Some people are simply converted to belief in Communism by Marxist propaganda. These, however, are usually a small minority of the total population.

Opportunists are more important than the converts. In any nation at any time, opportunists will try to join the apparently winning political side. Many in the satellites become fervent Marxists, like the Chinese leader who first was prominent in the Kuomintang national movement, then became a puppet ruler for the Japanese occupation authorities, and finally ended his life as a high official of the Chinese Communists.

Former Fascists are eager to join Communist parties, and are usually welcomed into membership. Of course, prominent Nazis have been tried in Communist courts and sentenced to death. But the rank-and-file Fascist is accustomed to obeying orders, and finds it easy to substitute Communist discipline for previous Hitlerite commands. Usually a former Nazi is a very reliable Communist, because he knows that at any moment he could be sentenced to death because of his past Fascist record. Many of the Gestapo later were loyal members of the East German Communist police. Even more startling is the fact that as many as five ex-Nazis have served simultaneously as cabinet ministers in the East German government.

While Marxist believers, opportunists, and former Fascists are happy to aid satellite Communist parties, many other people are recruited against their will. In each satellite thus far, the lull followed a destructive war or civil war. Therefore living conditions were very bad, with rationing of food, housing and other necessities. Under such circumstances, political belief becomes less important than mere physical survival. Communist offer of a milk ration to a sick child may easily convert the parents into ardent Communist helpers. Hence many people are literally bribed into pro-Communism not by money but by food, medicine, clothes, or a room with running water and heat. Many are unhappy about surrendering to Communism for personal comfort, but feel they have no choice. Others are frankly cynical, like the young East European widow who boasted: "I don't care if most people are living badly in Czechoslovakia. A few always live well, and I am going to be one of them!"

Communist police also have a trick, not unknown in the West, of not imprisoning a minor criminal, if he will agree to become a secret police spy. So many satellite citizens are arrested for political or economic misdemeanors, and released to become faithful Communist assistants.

Lack of racial bias helps the Communists in their recruiting. For example, if a Pole wanted to become a Nazi during the German occupation of Poland in World War II, he was usually rejected because Hitler considered Poles an inferior race. In Nazi opinion, Poles were entitled only to be slaves of Germans, not equals. Naturally few Poles became Fascists, and most Poles employed by the German occupation government were spies for the anti-Nazi underground. In contrast, the Communists were happy to recruit Polish supporters, as well as persons from minorities within Poland such as Ukrainians, Belorussians, Lithuanians, or Jews. The same equality of nationalities was used to Communist advantage in other East European countries.

Many of the pro-Communists do not immediately reveal their

assistance to Communism. Soon anti-Communist citizens don't know whom to trust, for former capitalists, nobility, Fascists, and priests, generals, professors, politicians, even close personal friends may have become secret Communist helpers. During the Polish lull, an American diplomat heard the following complaint from a young anti-Soviet Pole:

> Here across the restaurant dining room sits a man, who once was my dearest friend. As children we were next-door neighbors. We were in the same classes in grade and high school, studied at home together, and when old enough, we double-dated with girls. We attended the same college, where we roomed together. I considered him more like a brother than a friend.
>
> Now I cannot trust him. His sister is reporting to the police. I don't know why, but believe that the police threatened to arrest her fiance, unless she became a spy.
>
> I am a member of the new Polish underground, where we cannot use old underground personnel. Normally I would try to recruit my boyhood friend into this new underground, which is just starting. But I dare not confide in him.

Thus Communists use the lull to split the nation, winning over large numbers of diverse people to aid the Communist cause.

After several years the subtle infiltration is virtually complete. Communists and their helpers now control most high and low positions of power throughout satellite government and society. Then the mask of a mild reformist regime is dropped. Communists openly take command of the entire nation. The formerly secret pro-Communists, now safe, reveal their true political function.

Lull propaganda ceases. It is now explained that "People's Democracy" is not a permanent system, but a transition from capitalism to complete socialism. Ended is all official talk about the satellite being a bridge between East and West. It is made clear that the satellite is in the Communist family of nations.

Small storekeepers, who had been previously told to conduct business as usual, are now put out of business by heavy taxation, unfair state competition, imprisonment, or even execution. Peasants, who had been assured of no collectivization, are now collectivized by tax pressure or force. In Poland at the end of lull, an unofficial joke was: "Once we could be jailed for saying collectivization would come. Now we can be imprisoned for opposing collectivization."

Meanwhile industrial workers discover that the government managers of the nationalized factories are worse exploiters of labor than the old private owners. But the trade unions are now controlled by Communists. Instead of protecting workers, the unions have become enforcers of state-imposed low wages.

In general, after the lull, the satellite was forced to copy the USSR. During the Stalin period, some of the copying was amazing. Most satellites, including North Korea, modeled their constitutions on that of the USSR, even to the point of translating whole constitutional paragraphs from Russian into the satellite language. Satellite hero-worship of Stalin became intense. Bulgaria changed the name of its main seaport from Varna to Stalin. Czechoslovakia's highest Carpathian peak was rechristened Mount Stalin. *Rude Pravo,* the chief Czech newspaper, mentioned Stalin's name 600 times in a single issue. It is too late for organized anti-Communist rebellion, because during the lull the Communists established an all-persuasive apparatus of control. Spontaneous rebellion, like the Hungarian of 1956, is possible but rare. The Czechoslovak liberalization of 1968 was not a revolt, but an attempt to make Communism more humane.

In the late 1930's and 1940's when the Chinese Communists had not seized complete power, but ruled a large area of provincial China, many British and American experts described Mao Tse Tung as a mere agrarian reformer. Later in the 1950's, when Mao ruled the entire Chinese mainland, Western and Indian books were published stating that the Chinese Communists called themselves Communists, but were moderate and did not behave like Communists. At the time, a Chinese businessman in America boasted that he was returning to China, where his factory would earn more private profit under Communism than during the capitalist regime of Chiang Kai Shek.

In East Europe an anti-Communist Czech politician, who was a cabinet minister during the Czechoslovak lull and later escaped to the West, has confessed that he didn't know that his own ministry was being infiltrated by Communists during the lull period. An experienced American foreign correspondent, who was stationed in Prague just as the Czech lull ended, has stated that he had no suspicion that the Communists were taking over. One evening in 1948, three years after World War II, he quietly retired for the night. As he walked to work the next morning, some people on the streets seemed excited. When he reached his office, his Czech assistants informed him that the Communists had assumed complete control.

Premier Fidel Castro conducted one of the smoothest Communist lulls during 1959–1961 in Cuba, just 70 miles away from the southern coast of the United States. In 1960 the US State Department officially declared that Castro was not a Communist. A year later, Castro announced that he had long been a Marxist. Among the thousands of anti-Communist Cuban refugees who have fled to the United States, at least hundreds helped Castro seize power. I have interviewed a professor, an engineer, a big businessman, and the first president of Cuba's lull government. All four had aided Castro at first, because they believed him to be similar to a liberal Republican in the United States. Gradually these pro-Castroites realized their political error, then fled to the USA.

In analyzing Communist lull techniques, blanket infiltration still depends on the initial presence of Red military power. Ever since the Russian Civil War of 1918–1920, Communists and their agents have tried to infiltrate Western and Eastern governments and societies. Thus far the infiltration of countries which are not under Communist military control has been marginal. For example, in Western Europe and the United States some Communists have controlled labor unions; led liberal parties and groups; held high positions in the arts, radio, television, journalism, and publishing; and been spies within Western foreign ministries and intelligence services. Yet this infiltration has not been decisive, because the infiltrators cannot gain control of the army and police.

Till now the West has been able to cope with Communist infiltration, or successfully suppress it. Even most of the weak underdeveloped countries may withstand future Communist infiltration, mainly because of their highly nationalistic armies. In Asia, Africa and Latin America, several Communist attempts to attain power have been stopped by military coups.

Meanwhile lull propaganda should not be underestimated.

Today the Italian Communist Party is bidding for power by promising a Communist regime of free elections, a multiparty parliament, a coalition cabinet, artistic freedom, and good church-state relations. One cannot forget that similar promises were made, at first kept, but eventually broken by the People's Democracies.

Suggestions for Further Reading

BARNETT, A. DOAK, ed., *Communist Strategies in Asia.* New York: Praeger, 1963.

BORKENAU, FRANZ, *European Communism,* New York: Harper, 1953.

CRETZIANU, ALEXANDRE, *Captive Rumania: A Decade of Soviet Rule,* New York: Praeger, 1956.

JAMES, DANIEL, *Cuba: The First Soviet Satellite in the Americas,* New York: Avon Books, 1961.

SCALAPINO, ROBERT A., ed., *The Communist Revolution in Asia: Tactics, Goals and Achievements.* Englewood Cliffs: Prentice-Hall, 1965.

SETON-WATSON, HUGH, *The East European Revolution,* New York: Praeger, 1951.

Soviet Security Agencies in Postwar Poland, New York: Columbia University Press, 1953.

TANG, PETER S. H., *Communist China Today,* New York: Praeger, 1956.

ZASLOFF, J. J., *The Pathet Lao.* Lexington: Heath, 1972.

Chapter 24

Soviet Foreign Trade

On the eve of World War II the Soviet government published a book of foreign trade statistics with a preface which boasted:

> Look how our foreign trade policy is succeeding. Every year we have less and less foreign trade!

Can you imagine a US Chamber of Commerce printing anything like that? But the book was not meant to be funny, because until World War II, autarky was the cornerstone of Soviet trade policy. As early as 1918, Premier Lenin nationalized all foreign trade, which henceforth was a monopoly of the state Council (later ministry) for Foreign Trade. Originally the main motive for autarky was to prevent foreign capitalists from upsetting Soviet economic planning. Unless restrained, the West might ship into Russia many goods desired by the Soviet public but not by the Soviet state. Free trade would have permitted Western businessmen to siphon away Russian goods needed for internal Soviet development.

Soviet economic divorce from the capitalist world came more quickly than Lenin had anticipated. During the Russian Civil War of 1918–1920, a blockade by the Entente Powers reduced Soviet foreign trade almost to zero. In 1919 imports sank to an all-time low of $2,640,000—2 per cent of the Tsarist level.

After civil war ended in Soviet victory, the Entente blockade was lifted, but the Kremlin feared that economic strangulation might be attempted in the future. Thus in the early 1920's Soviet Russia had an additional motive for autarky—fear of blockade in future war.

Of course, the Soviets began their drive for autarky with the advantage of a country already satisfying most of its own needs. Unlike Germany, England, or Japan, Russia never was a trade-or-die nation. Tsarist Russia could hardly be described as a wealthy country, when most of its population lived in crude cabins on wooden-plow farms. Yet along with China, India, and the United States, Tsarist Russia was one of the largest agricultural producers in the world. The Tsarist population ate well, except in years of war or drought. Prerevolutionary Russia mined all its iron, most of its coal, and could even export oil. Siberia and north European Russia contain the world's largest forests, so there was no lack of wood. Hence pre-Soviet Russia was already more economically independent than West European Powers. Tsarist imports and exports never amounted to more than 3 per cent of world foreign trade—a smaller share than for any other Great Power. Most of Russia's autarky was won before the Soviets seized control.

To achieve more autarky, however, Soviet Russia had to import equipment for new industries which would expand domestic production of goods normally purchased abroad. Thus paradoxically, some trade was necessary in order to improve economic independence. And in the early 1920's, foreign trade was difficult to revive. War-devastated Russia could produce few surplus goods to export in exchange for imports. Another grave handicap was the Soviet cancellation of Tsarist foreign debts.

Prerevolutionary Russia had the largest foreign debt of any government in the world. In addition, about half of Russian private industry and banks were foreign-owned. Then the Bolshevik Revolution erupted. The new Soviet regime refused to pay Tsarist governmental debts and nationalized foreign-owned banks, factories and mines without compensation. Western governments, banks, and private investors suffered a total loss of about 23 billion dollars.

Most of this debt was owed to the governments and nationals of Britain, France, Belgium, and Germany. The American loss was relatively small. The US government was left unpaid $70,000,000 which had been loaned not to the Tsarist, but to the

Provisional Russian government. Even so, most large New York banks still hold obsolete Tsarist bonds, now worth about a quarter of a cent per dollar.

In the early 1920's, Soviet Russia begged for large, long-term loans from Western banks to finance a revival of Russian trade. Small short-term loans were obtained, such as the $20,000,000 credit advanced by the Chase Bank of New York to start Soviet-American trade. The USSR repaid this loan in a few months, and in gratitude has kept its dollar account in east-coast America at Chase ever since. (The west-coast account is at the Bank of America.) But in the early 1920's, and for decades thereafter, no Western bank that loaned money to Tsarist Russia would grant a large long-term loan to its Soviet successor. Thus from the very start, the Kremlin had to tighten its belt, forcing exports to pay for necessary imports.

In the midst of this early struggle for foreign trade, the USSR found itself in dire need. Drought struck the breadbaskets of the Ukraine and lower Volga valley, and millions of Soviet citizens were threatened by death from famine. The Soviet government appealed for aid from the American Relief Administration (ARA), headed by future President Herbert Hoover.

The Kremlin requested that ARA feed only pro-Communist Russians, not the anti-Soviets. Hoover replied that no aid would be given unless all were fed, regardless of their political convictions. Faced by famine, the Soviet government had to accept Hoover's terms. During 1922–1923, millions of Soviet citizens in the Ukraine and Volga valley were given American food and inoculated with vaccines, thus being saved from almost certain death. This kindness was financed by an appropriation of $20,000,000 from the US government, which refused to grant diplomatic recognition to the Soviet government. Possibly the American Relief Administration helped keep the early Soviet regime in power. At any rate, American aid spread much good will among Soviet citizens. Old people in the Ukraine and Volga valley are still grateful to ARA for saving their lives. To counteract such sentiment, the Kremlin later accused Hoover of being a master spy, whose relief workers were intelligence agents. The basis for this accusation is that Hoover feared revolutionary Russia might degenerate into chaos, and therefore asked his agents to collect current documents which might later be lost. These documents became the basic collection of Stanford University's Hoover Library, which today contains some materials unavailable in the USSR. During the period of ARA work in Russia, Soviet President Kalinin remarked:

> The Americans have failed to conquer us by force of arms, but I fear that they will conquer us by kindness.

During the late 1920's the Soviet government made foreign trade more difficult by forbidding the export of rubles (1926) and import of the same currency (1928). A currency reform of 1922 had tried to stabilize the ruble, exchanging new rubles for old at the fantastic rate of 1 to 12,000,000. The new currency was backed both by gold and stocks of exportable goods. Nonetheless, the new money fluctuated in value, and foreign speculators began to profit from buying rubles cheap and selling them dear. The Kremlin could hardly be expected to encourage capitalist profit in Communist rubles. So by 1928, the ruble became a purely internal currency valueless abroad. To the present day, the USSR has been unable to apply ruble purchases in international trade. Instead, the Kremlin if possible strives for barter pacts of an exchange of goods of equal value priced in American dollars. If the trading partner refuses to barter, Russia has to sell enough goods abroad for hard currency like American dollars or British pounds to pay for the needed imports. The Soviet trading problem is complicated by the fact that quite a few of these dollars and pounds must be used for noncommercial purposes like maintenance of embassies and consulates, espionage, and promotion of revolution abroad. Thus trade must more than balance, but this excess of sales over purchases is not easily achieved. Almost every year, the Soviet Union has to export some gold to bring trade back into a favorable balance. Since the USSR is the world's second largest miner of gold (following South Africa), such gold sales are easy. The appearance of Soviet gold on the world market usually creates excitement on Western stock exchanges, who immediately fear that Russia will flood the world with gold. Thus far, such fears have proven groundless. Just enough Soviet gold is sold to bring USSR foreign trade back into balance.

Throughout the 1920's the USSR tried to obtain foreign investment in Russia by leasing some Soviet enterprises to Western businessmen called concessionaires, who could provide capital and engineering skill for restoration of Russian industry. But few foreign businessmen were willing to accept the harsh concession contracts offered by the USSR government, which severely taxed profits. By the late 1920's when the concession system reached its greatest height, only a small percentage of Russian industrial output was produced by concessionaires. The Kremlin learned that the USSR had no hope of attracting large amounts of foreign capital, and that future industrial expansion would be financed from Russia's own resources.

Under these difficult circumstances Soviet foreign trade in the 1920's had a slow erratic growth. Imports increased from a value of \$23,700,000 in 1920 to \$790,000,000 by 1928, the final year of the New Economic Policy. Some autarkal successes were achieved even this early. By the late 1920's Russia was self-sufficient in coal, and nearly self-sufficient in copper and cotton. But all rubber was imported from distant Southeast Asia, and many nonferrous metals were entirely or mostly purchased abroad. When a new factory was built, the Soviets constructed the walls and roof, but most of the machines in the plant were British, German, or American.

Then the Five-Year Plans of 1928–1941 put the drive for autarky into high gear. Imports above all were machines for fast expansion of mining, metallurgy, machinebuilding, and other war-potential industries. Just as heavy industry dominated industrialization, so it dominated foreign trade. At the close of the First Five-Year Plan, Stalin explained why:

> Surely from the billion and a half rubles worth of foreign currency spent during this period to equip our heavy industry, we could have diverted half to importing cotton, leather, wool, rubber, etc. We would then have had more thread, shoes and clothes. But we would then have neither a tractor nor an auto industry, no real iron and steel metallurgy, and no metal to make machines. We would then be disarmed before the capitalist encirclement armed with new equipment. . . . Our position would

> then be more or less similar to that of presentday China, which does not have its own heavy industry or war industry, and at which all peck who are not lazy.[1]

Thus the main purpose of USSR foreign trade in the 1930's was to strengthen Soviet defense.

During the 1930's thousands of American engineers and technicians worked in the USSR, helping build the industries of the early Five-Year Plans. Many older Soviet engineers and industrialists well remember this technical aid and the Americans who administered it. This aid, of course, was no gift. The Soviet government paid the Americans high salaries in dollars deposited at New York banks. This was the second time that the United States gave great help to the USSR.

To get the money to pay for imported Western machines, Soviet Russia in the 1930's exported mostly products of the mines and products of the soil. The drive for autarky aimed at stopping the USSR from being an economic colony of the West. Yet paradoxically the Soviet Union was trading just like a colony, exporting raw materials in exchange for machines. Even Tsarist Russia had exported manganese and chrome, which the Soviets continued. For some years in the 1930's, the whole American steel industry depended on USSR manganese, since a certain amount of this metal goes into the steelmaking furnace mix. Another big Soviet money-earner was lumber, mostly shipped from north European Russia to England. The great forests of Siberia and north European Russia abound in fur-bearing animals, so still another major export was furs. Each year a fur fair was held in Leningrad, with most of the pelts sold to American, British, and West European buyers.

In good harvest years, grain was also sent to West Europe to feed people and hogs. Linen was a big export, since the USSR had the largest flax crops in the world. Many American housewives stocked their linen closets with the low-priced Soviet cloth. Other export odds and ends included platinum for jewelry, mica for telephone receiver diaphragms, sheepskins, and animal intestines for use as sausage casings. At times, anthracite coal was

---

[1] Stalin, Joseph, "Results of the First Five-Year Plan," *Izvestia,* Jan. 10, 1933.

shipped out from the Ukraine to the United States. In the 1930's American cigarettes labeled "Finest blend of Virginia and Turkish tobaccos" more honestly should have been labeled "Finest blend of Virginia and Soviet tobaccos." For the USSR grew large quantities of Turkish tobacco, exporting much of it to the USA. And no export list should omit the luxury items—Pacific coast crabmeat and Caspian Sea caviar.

No effort was made in the 1930's to trade heavily. Just enough was exported to pay for the industrialization imports. In 1931, Soviet imports hit their peacetime peak between World Wars I and II. Yet this peak amounted to less than a billion dollars, and was no more than four fifths of Tsarist 1913 trade. As Soviet industry grew during the early Five-Year Plans, more strategic minerals, materials, and machines were produced at home, so there was less need to import them from abroad. As the 1930's wore on, Soviet economy became increasingly self-reliant, and foreign trade was deliberately reduced. From the 1931 peak of nearly a billion dollars, the value of imports shrunk to hardly more than a quarter billion by 1940, last year of peace. By then, Russia accounted for less than 1 per cent of world trade. Russia was less dependent on the outside world than ever before.

After World War II began in 1939, trade channels to the Allied Powers of West Europe were blocked by military operations, so neutral Russia traded mainly with Nazi Germany. During late 1939, all of 1940, and early 1941, the USSR sent Germany large quantities of grain, oil, cotton, flax, rubber, and various metals useful for the Nazi war effort. In return Germany was supposed to supply machine tools and military equipment to the USSR, but quickly fell behind in its deliveries. Russia, however, continued its shipments to Germany, thus attempting to bribe Hitler away from attacking the USSR. A trainload of Soviet oil was sent into German-occupied Poland the night before Hitler's Wehrmacht invaded Russia.

As soon as the Soviet-German War began, Britain and the United States offered Russia material aid. As early as July 1941, one month after Hitler had invaded Russia, Premier Stalin begged US Lend-Lease administrator Harry Hopkins for large quantities of rifles, machine guns, anti-aircraft artillery, tanks, tank steel, aviation gasoline, and aluminum. In 1940, last year of peace, the money value of Soviet imports was $272,000,000 with exports nearly in balance. But under the impact of war the USSR had to increase imports by 1943 to a gigantic $1,600,000,000. Thus 1943 imports amounted to more than six years' imports of the middle and late 1930's, and exceeded the Tsarist level for the first time in Soviet history. Meanwhile wartime USSR had little to spare for exports, which by 1943 fell to $70,500,000—less than one third of the 1940 level.

The majority of wartime imports came from the United States in the form of Lend-Lease, which the USSR refused to repay until the U.S.-Soviet detente of 1972, when the Kremlin agreed to pay $722,000,000 in settlement in the next 30 years. During the Soviet-German War the United States, Britain, and Canada sent Russia 10,000 tanks, 14,500 planes, 10,000 cannon, more than two million tons of food, hundreds of ships, nearly half a million trucks, half a million tons of nonferrous metals, enough cloth for three million uniforms, and three billion dollars worth of machinery including several complete factories.

Most of these shipments came from the United States, which sent wartime Russia a total of 11 billion dollars worth of aid. One billion dollars worth was sunk at sea, but the rest arrived safely. Again America had rendered great help to the Soviet Union. And like the American Relief Administration of the 1920's and the U.S. engineers of the 1930's, this aid created much good-will among the Soviet people. On a recent trip to Russia, a Soviet librarian volunteered the following statement to me:

> The younger generation doesn't remember, but we older people know how America helped us during the Soviet-German war. Every store in Russia had American food. We are very grateful.

Table 39 compares Soviet imports from 1918 to 1943 with Russian imports of 1913, the last peacetime year of Tsarist rule. These statistics summarize Soviet foreign trade in the period when autarky was the main goal.

As the Red Army pushed into East Europe late in World War II, a new Soviet import was possible: machinery and goods captured in Hitler's satellites, protectorates, and homeland. During 1944 the Soviet government formed a Special Committee

Table 39. *Value of Russian Imports in the Late Tsarist and Early Soviet Periods*

Year	Imports in Million Dollars
1913	1,140
1918	87
1919	3
1920	24
1921	174
1922	223
1923	118
1924	214
1925	684
1926	570
1927	625
1928	790
1929	730
1930	875
1931	910
1932	580
1933	288
1934	192
1935	199
1936	256
1937	253
1940	272
1942	520
1943	1,600

charged with removing factories, manufactured goods, raw materials, livestock, farm machinery, fertilizer, crops, laboratories, libraries, museums, scientific archives, engineers, and scientists from all of Eastern Europe. After years of devastating war, the Soviet Union was in desperate need of such items and experts. It also wanted to make sure that Germany would never again be a military and industrial power. The economic looting was done in haste, for Stalin was unsure whether Britain and America would permit the Red Army to remain in postwar East Europe.

Tens of thousands of Soviet engineers and technicians were hurriedly mobilized by the Special Committee, given army uniforms and officer ranks, and dispatched with the Red Army into the Hitler empire. Partly because of American delay, the Red

Army conquered the German capital city of Berlin, which was to be divided into Russian, British, French, and American sectors. Before turning over West Berlin to the western Allies, Soviet engineering troops removed factories, trolley tracks, sewer pipes, and even toilet seats. Besides countless factories, and half of east German printing presses, tens of thousands of Nazi tractors, horses, cows, and plows were railroaded into war-devastated Russia. And this planned looting was far from confined to East Germany alone. The economies of Nazi satellite Rumania, Bulgaria, Hungary, and Austria were plundered, along with Czechoslovakia and Poland, who were Soviet allies.

Thanks to American carelessness, Soviet rocket technology was aided at the close of World War II. Driving deep into Germany, the US Army had captured the provinces of Saxony and Thuringia. In this area near the city of Nordhausen was a mine containing the factory and research laboratory for the German V-2 rockets. Several months after the Nazi surrender, the US Army withdrew from this region, taking along many of the German rocket scientists. But the factory and laboratory were left intact for the Soviet army when the region became part of the USSR zone of occupation.

Soviet police troops moved the entire V-2 factory and laboratory into the USSR. Every piece of machinery, every spare part, every scrap of raw material, and each complete or incomplete rocket was carefully packed in boxes and sent to the Volga city of Stalingrad. Many workers and engineers of the rocket plant were found around Nordhausen and forced to accompany the factory into Russia. Most of the top German rocket scientists had left Nordhausen with the US Army. Yet by combing East Germany, the USSR found some space experts. Others were shanghaied from West Germany by bribery, blackmail, threats, or outright kidnapping. Once in Soviet hands, these experts were treated with care. According to an eyewitness, they enplaned to Russia taking along wife, children, mother, furniture, belongings, and even dogs and cats. In the USSR both pay and fringe benefits were high. For example, the chief German rocket scientist received a free house, free food, a private automobile and the ruble equivalent of $2,500 per month.

One year later, in 1946, the USSR was firing V-2 rockets in

tests across the Baltic Sea. A journal of the Soviet defense ministry already boasted that Russian long-range rockets would play a tremendous role in future war. German emigre rocket scientists in America estimate that the Soviet acquisition of the Nordhausen rocket plant and laboratory contributed 15 per cent to 20 per cent to the successful USSR 1957 launching of the world's first sputnik. For the fourth time the United States had rendered great assistance to the USSR—adding to the famine relief of the early 1920's, sale of machinery and technical know-how during the 1930's, and Lend-Lease of World War II.

At the time the Red Army discovered Nordhausen, a Soviet colonel spoke these prophetic words:

> The Americans gave us this. But in five or ten years, they will cry. Imagine when our rockets fly across the ocean![2]

Legal authorization for USSR looting of East Europe was granted by US President Truman and British Prime Minister Attlee to Stalin at the 1945 Potsdam Conference, which allowed Russia to obtain immediate war reparations by removing machinery and goods from East Germany and by seizing Nazi German property in other Soviet-occupied countries. Thus American abandonment of the V-2 factory to the Red Army was technically correct, since this rocket plant was in a German area assigned to the Soviet zone of occupation. But the Kremlin interpreted the Potsdam Agreement very broadly, taking as Nazi assets both Allied and Jewish properties which had been nationalized by wartime Germany. Neither the Allied nor Jewish owners were given any compensation. Similar machinery evacuation occurred from Manchuria and North Korea, where there was no legal justification. Only the Kremlin knows how many billions of dollars worth of immediate reparations moved during 1944–1946 from East Europe and the northern Far East into the USSR.

By 1947, Britain and America had demobilized most of their wartime armed forces, and obviously had no intention of wresting

---

[2] Shabinsky, Vladimir, "How I Found the Nazi Missile Secrets," *Look,* Feb. 4, 1958.

Also see Sokolov, V. L., *Soviet Use of German Science and Technology, 1945–1946,* New York: Columbia University Press, 1955.

East Europe, Manchuria, and North Korea from the USSR. Once certain of this Allied intent, Stalin ordered the machinery looting to cease. In both East Europe and the Far East, Russia began to rebuild the satellite industries which it had half-destroyed. Some machinery was actually returned from the USSR to its satellites, or new Soviet machines were sent to aid satellite industrialization. For example, at first the huge Meissen chinaware factory was deported from East Germany to Russia. But the plant machinery was old, and Meissen world fame actually depended not on machines but on the skill of its highly trained workers. The aged machines were sent to a small Soviet city, where unskilled Russian labor ruined them. A year later, Russia painfully rebuilt the Meissen factory in Germany.

From 1947 till Stalin's death in 1953, USSR policy toward its satellites changed from outright looting to subtle exploitation, which assumed various forms. First, Hitler's allies (Austria, Bulgaria, East Germany, Finland, Hungary, and Rumania) were forced to pay heavy reparations to the USSR. East Germany alone was ordered to deliver $10 billion dollars worth of reparations, and by 1953 announced that actual deliveries totaled $22,500,000,000. Finland, which the Red Army never occupied, had to build a whole new machinery industry to fulfill its $300 million worth of reparations, one third of which were wood products, one third, ships, and the remaining one third, machines. Some relief came in 1948 when the remaining reparations were cut in half for Finland, Hungary, and Rumania because they signed military alliances with the USSR. Similar reduction of the rest of reparations was granted to East Germany in 1950.

Unfair trade was the second Soviet method of exploiting its satellites. Each satellite was required to conclude with the USSR an annual barter pact theoretically providing for an exchange of goods of equal value. But the Soviet goods were priced high, while satellite wares were assigned a low value. Russia acted as a middleman between two satellites, or between a satellite and the free world. The USSR bought mining machinery from East Germany, and sold it at a higher price to Hungary, a neighbor of East Germany. Rubber imported from Britain was resold by the USSR to its East European satellites, with Russia pocketing the middleman's profit.

Still another device for exploitation were joint-stock companies owned half and half by the Soviet and satellite governments. Such international concerns were formed in each satellite, the Soviet government usually supplying the equipment while the satellite provided raw materials and labor. However, the equipment offered by Russia often was Nazi or Japanese war booty, so the Soviet investment cost nothing to the USSR, which then took half the company profits. Let's take the example of the Rumanian oil fields.

Before World War II three fifths of the Rumanian oil fields were German-owned, and one fourth was controlled by British, French, and Belgian companies. During the war Germany seized the Allied petroleum property as enemy assets. At the war's end the Soviet government confiscated both the German and ex-Allied fields as Nazi war booty. Then Russia forced Rumania to form a joint oil company, the former providing the fields and the latter the labor. Oil mined from Rumanian soil by the company was sold throughout Europe, with the Soviet government taking half of the profits. Thus Russia assumed control of most of the Rumanian oil fields, which are the largest in Europe. The Rumanian Communist government was so angry that its press barely mentioned the joint oil company's formation. Soviet-Rumanian joint companies also existed for transport, timber, chemicals, metallurgy, gas, insurance, banking, coal mining, construction, tractor industry, movie making and airlines. Rumania had more such companies than any other satellite.

All of these reparations, unfair trading, and joint companies gave a great boost to the USSR economy. Reliable Western estimates state that the Soviet Union during 1944–1956 made a total profit of $20 to $25 billion from East Europe alone, without counting material gain from the Far East. These profits, of course, were not in money but in the form of machinery, manufactured goods, and certain raw materials and foods scarce in the USSR. Though most of these imports from the satellites helped Soviet postwar industrial recovery and growth, USSR consumers also benefited. Satellite consumer goods became common in USSR stores. Even in Soviet provincial cities the stores began to sell Chinese tea and silks, Bulgarian and Czech cigarettes, and a variety of useful gadgets from Poland, East Germany, and

Czechoslovakia. Many a Soviet citizen was able to buy Czech wristwatches and fountain pens. Thus the shortage of consumer goods in the USSR was eased by imports from the satellites.

A Western tourist cannot help noticing the variety of satellite contributions to the Soviet economy. A large tourist boat on the Volga-Don canal was built in Hungary. The Volgograd planetarium, which is the biggest in the USSR, is a gift from East Germany. The gayest pictorial magazine is Hungarian or Polish, while a supposedly Soviet jazz record turns out to be Czech.

To achieve this satellite aid, Russia had to undertake a reorientation of its foreign trade. Instead of trading mainly with West Europe as in the 1920's and 1930's, most Soviet trade was diverted to East Europe and China. In turn both East Europe and China were forced to trade largely with the USSR, which had taken only a small percentage of their exports between World Wars I and II. The past policy of autarky for Russia alone had to be replaced by a campaign to make the entire Soviet bloc of nations economically independent from the outside world. No longer was it practical to reduce Soviet foreign trade, for tiny commerce would yield a meager profit from the satellites. So USSR trade quickly expanded, and by 1950 was already above the Tsarist level. The growth of post-World War II Soviet commerce is depicted in Table 40.

While total USSR foreign trade began its postwar increase, Soviet-American trade sharply declined. The causes were political. By American law, Lend-Lease to Russia had to end with the cessation of hostilities. The Lend-Lease flow of goods abruptly stopped, some American ships even turning back on the high seas. Russia then requested and was granted a US credit of $250,000,000 to purchase Lend-Lease equipment already manufactured by American industry, but not delivered before the war's end. Since this equipment had been built to Soviet specifications, there was no market for it in the United States. In the immediate postwar period UNRRA (United Nations Relief and Rehabilitation Administration) sent to Russia such supplies as food, clothing, seed, and farm machinery altogether worth about $200,000,000, of which $191,000,000 was provided by the United States. America thus continued to aid the USSR, though on a much smaller scale than during World War II. In 1947 the

Table 40. *Growth of Soviet Foreign Trade (Imports Plus Exports) After World War II, Compared with Prewar and Wartime Commerce*

Year	Value of Trade (in billion dollars)
1940	.5
1942	.6
1943	1.7
1950	3.2
1953	5.7
1955	6.5
1957	8.3
1959	10.5
1961	11.8
1963	14.3
1965	16.0
1968	19.8
1971	28.3
1973	42.9
1975	67.4

Source: U.S. Congress, Joint Economic Committee, *Annual Economic Indicators for the U.S.S.R.*, Washington: US Government, 1964.
Pravda, 1965-1976.

United States even invited Russia to participate in the European Recovery Program (Marshall Plan), which offered American loans to war-damaged European nations for economic reconstruction. Russia refused this invitation, and forced Poland and Czechoslovakia also to refuse.

After Russia began a blockade of west Berlin in 1948, President Truman retaliated by proclaiming the Truman Embargo, which forbade the shipment of American strategic materials or war-potential machinery to the USSR. Within a year, American exports to Russia had decreased almost 90 per cent, and amounted to less than $10 million per annum. When the North Atlantic Treaty Organization (NATO) was formed in 1949, all NATO members agreed to observe the embargo, which was applied to the Soviet satellites as well as Russia proper. Other US allies not in NATO, such as Japan, Formosa, and the Philippines, also participated in embargo measures. Though still in existence today, the embargo after its first few years was gradually less and less enforced by West European nations, and is now violated even by the U.S.A. Nevertheless, this incomplete embargo slowed Soviet acquisition of new Western industrial technique.

In 1952, less than a year before his death, Stalin tried to break the Truman Embargo by convening an international economic conference in Moscow. Boycotted by the United States but well attended by West European and Asian businessmen, the conference heard a Soviet offer of 2.5–3.75 billion dollars worth of trade with non-Communist countries. Promises were made that the USSR would accept payment in any foreign currency, import consumer goods, and export machinery to underdeveloped nations. Little new trade materialized before Stalin's death, but his successors fulfilled the 1952 promises by increasing commerce with the non-Communist world to more than four billion dollars by the 1960's.

Also at the 1952 international economic conference in Moscow, Soviet spokesmen talked about a Stalin Plan of technical aid to underdeveloped non-Communist nations. Stalin died too soon to implement this policy, but his successors began technical aid a month after his death by an economic agreement with Afghanistan. A year later in 1954, the USSR formally announced its technical aid program at the United Nations economic conference on Asia, promising long-term Soviet trade agreements on favorable terms, Russian loans, and technical aid to neutral Asian nations. Immediately several Asian countries applied for Soviet aid, which later was also extended to a number of nations in Africa and Latin America. By 1976 the USSR had granted about $10 billion worth of credits and loans for technical aid to underdeveloped free nations. About one fourth of this aid was in the form of arms shipments, which usually arrived quickly in contrast to economic commitments still only partially fulfilled. Egypt, Syria and India have been especially big recipients of Soviet armament. Though the total USSR aid program is only about one sixth that of the United States during the years since 1953, some Asian nations like Afghanistan now receive more technical aid from the USSR than from the USA. In general the

Soviet aid concentrates mainly on a few strategic nations, such as India, Egypt, Afghanistan, Iran, Iraq, and Turkey, all of which receive massive assistance. Minor aid is also rendered to more than 60 other nations. Altogether the USSR is supervising about 900 construction projects in underdeveloped nations. Most of these projects are large, like the already completed Indian steel mills and Egypt's Aswan dam.

The main aim of Soviet trade with and aid to underdeveloped neutral nations is more political than economic. Arms shipments create tension and local wars which may ease eventual Communist revolutions. Both military and economic aid please neutral governmental leaders, who usually are already anti-Western. Soviet economists also express the hope that the Soviet orbit of nations will slowly capture foreign markets in the underdeveloped countries.

Thanks to shrewd administration, USSR economic warfare is no financial drain on the Russian treasury. Trade with neutral underdeveloped nations is conducted by barter, which thus far has brought Russia more goods than it has exported in return. Soviet technical aid is usually not a grant, but long-term, low-interest loans which the underdeveloped nations must eventually repay.

Moreover, the USSR continues to profit from unfair trade with the Soviet satellites, although exploitation has been less severe since Stalin's death. The Soviet-satellite joint-stock companies have been disbanded, the satellite government being permitted to buy out the Soviet share. Technical aid from Russia to the satellites increased, particularly after the Hungarian revolution. Despite these concessions from the Soviet Union, trade statistics indicate that Russia made a profit of over $8 billion during 1955-1962 from the East European satellites alone. In 1975 this profit was at a lower rate, but still amounted to a sizeable $655,000,000. Naturally the East European Communist countries resent being so exploited. This involuntary satellite contribution to the Kremlin treasury more than pays for the technical aid granted by Russia to neutral underdeveloped nations. Under these circumstances it is little wonder that some Communist countries, particularly China, are very critical of the Soviet Point-Four program.

Chapter 25

National Communism

In 1948 when Premier Broz Tito of Yugoslavia defied Russia, the Kremlin seemed surprised. One wonders why, for national communism had caused trouble within Communist Russia almost since the Bolshevik Revolution. Today national communism, which is often called Titoism, is slowly dismembering the Soviet orbit of nations.

A national communist is a non-Russian who believes in Marxism-Leninism, but refuses to accept complete control from Moscow. Such Communist heretics first appeared in the land of Soviets during the Russian Civil War, when two Communist governments fought each other to rule the Ukraine. One of these Marxist opponents was truly Ukrainian, while the second consisted of Russians residing in the Ukraine. Eventually the Russo-Ukrainian Communist government triumphed, and the Ukrainian Communist nationalists were suppressed.

In the early 1920's Tatar and Turkish Communists tried to establish a Soviet Republic in Turkestan separate from the Russian Republic. Many of these Central Asian nationalists were expelled from the Russian Communist Party by Lenin, and later executed by Stalin. Hundreds of nationalistic Communist party officials were imprisoned or executed in Belorussia and the Ukraine during the early 1930's, and in all non-Russian republics of the USSR during 1937–1939.

Similar purges of local Communist officialdom occurred after World War II in the Ukraine, Caucasus, and Central Asia during the premierships of both Stalin and Malenkov. Latvian, Tadzhik, and Kazakh Communists suffered harsh treatment during the era of Premier Khrushchev.

Many non-Communists among Russia's minority nationalities were purged, along with their local leaders, but non-Communist resistance to the Kremlin is easy to understand. For example, an un-Marxist Soviet Turk might dislike many features of the Communist regime such as Russification, socialization, police brutality, censorship, or atheism. But a truly Communist Turk is an atheist socialist, who believes in the necessity of totalitarian dictatorship and accepts Russification as modernization and economic improvement. Still the Turkish Marxist may start resisting some Moscow policies, like his non-Communist Moslem neighbor. Why?

An answer is racism or nationalism. Both are tremendous forces throughout the modern world, and not difficult to inflame. But there is something more: struggle for power. If Kremlin leaders quarrel ruthlessly for personal power, there is nothing strange in a similar power struggle between Moscow and provincial Communist governors.

Perhaps the intensity of quest for power is due not to Communism itself, much less Marxism, but to Soviet reliance on a dictatorial form of government. A democracy has similar quarrels in its capital, and between the capital city and outlying areas. The democratic disputes are generally settled within a recognized framework of legality. Also a democracy has the traditional role of "loyal opposition" for the loser, who serves the useful function of publicly criticizing faults in the winner's governmental policy.

Once the USSR began to accumulate an empire of satellite countries, a power struggle between satellite dictators and Moscow became inevitable. Long before the Tito-Stalin split, the first Soviet-satellite disputes occurred between Russia and Outer Mongolia.

A desert and semi-desert two and a half times as large as the state of Texas, Outer Mongolia entered the twentieth century as a medieval nation. One third of Mongol males were Buddhist monks residing in Lama monasteries, which owned the vast herds of sheep, goats, cattle, and ponies constituting the main wealth of an almost treeless country. The remainder of the population were mostly nomadic tent-dwellers, shepherding the monastic livestock. A theocratic government was headed by a high priest, the Grand Lama.

Landlocked and isolated from the outside world, Mongolia was nominally a province of China, but in 1910 fell under the influence of Tsarist Russia. During the Russian Civil War of 1918–1920, thanks to Russia's collapse and China's weakness, Mongolia achieved independence from both. Then two White Russian armies fled from Siberia into the Mongol desert, and in 1921 Lenin's Red Army followed in pursuit. With the invading Red Army, which defeated the Whites, came Mongol Communists who were a mixed group of Russian-born Mongols and people from Mongolia trained in Soviet Russia.

The Red Army remained, installing the Mongol Communists as Russia's puppet rulers. Mongolia became a constitutional monarchy, still headed by the now powerless Grand Lama. When he died in 1924, the Mongol Communists abolished the kingdom, and established a Mongolian People's Republic. Almost immediately, national communism appeared among some Mongolian leaders. The War Minister of the new republic was killed for objecting to Soviet Russian control.

When Russia collectivized its peasants during 1929–1930, the Kremlin ordered Mongolia to collectivize its herdsmen, who in 1925 had been given the livestock formerly owned by the Buddhist monasteries. The Mongol nomads resisted so violently that Mongolia was hurled into a civil war causing enormous casualties. Mongolian collectivization had to be abandoned until after World War II, but meanwhile several Mongolian Communist leaders were purged for opposing Russia's agricultural orders.

Later in the mid-1930's, the Mongolian government was purged twice to eliminate leaders who allegedly were conspiring with Russia's enemy, Japan. Nor did evidences of Mongolian national communism disappear after World War II. Late in Khrushchev's premiership of the USSR, a secretary of Mongolia's Communist Party was removed for writing that Mongol conquest of medieval Russia brought the blessings of Oriental civilization to the then primitive Russians.

Meanwhile back in the 1920's and 1930's, Russia indicated its unwillingness to let Communist satellites unite with each other rather than with the USSR. Tuva, a tiny mountainous area separating northwest Mongolia from Siberia, was also satellized by Russia's Red Army during 1921. Inhabited mainly by Mongols, the Tuvan People's Republic created by Russia repeatedly requested permission to unite with the Mongolian People's Republic in a single Mongol Communist state. Russia always refused, and in 1944 forced Tuva to become part of the USSR.

All these little-noticed Mongol-Russian disputes of the 1920's and 1930's were a mere prelude for the violent Soviet-satellite quarrels after World War II. An un-Marxist law of Marxist human behavior became quite clear: The larger the Soviet orbit of nations grew, the greater were the feuds among Communist nations.

When the Soviet-German war ended in Russian victory, most of East Europe fell under Soviet control. Left unprotected by the Western Allies, eight small East European nations became Soviet satellites. Of these, mountainous agricultural Yugoslavia was unique in having a Communist government enjoying some popularity among its people. Most satellite leaders had spent World War II in Moscow or in East European prisons. Meanwhile Marshal Tito led a guerrilla army in the Yugoslav mountains, alternately fighting Germans, Italians, and non-Communist Serbo-Croatians. Geographically unable to obtain Soviet wartime aid, Tito had accepted Anglo-American arms and ammunition, negotiating with the Western Allies without always consulting Moscow.

Thus Tito became accustomed to making his own decisions, and was a hero of Yugoslav resistance to Axis occupation. Late in the war, Russia's Red Army joined forces with Tito's guerrillas to rid Yugoslavia of Nazi and Fascist intruders, crush Yugoslav anti-Communists, and install Tito into power.

At first after World War II, Tito was Moscow's favorite satellite leader. Because he was strong and enjoyed some popular support, the Kremlin asked Yugoslavia to socialize fast as a pace-setter and example to other satellites with less secure rulers. Of all East European Communist countries, Yugoslavia alone was permitted to have its own satellite, little Albania. Another sign of Soviet trust was making Belgrade the headquarters of the Communist Information Bureau (Cominform), organized in 1947 as an European successor to the worldwide Communist International abolished during 1943. In response, Tito seemed to justify Soviet confidence by establishing an oppressive Stalinist regime, which proved its hostility toward the West by shooting down two American transport planes.

Yet by early 1948 a quarrel had developed between Belgrade and Moscow, resulting in Yugoslavia's expulsion from the Soviet orbit of nations. Yugoslavia later published the Stalin-Tito correspondence preceding the break, providing an excellent case-history of Soviet-satellite tensions. From this correspondence, plus mutual recriminations between the Soviet and Yugoslav press, the causes of the dispute appear to be both political and economic.

Economically, Tito resented the unfair trade with the USSR by which a supposedly equal barter of goods was taking place, all wares being priced in American dollars. But the Yugoslav goods were valued at prewar low dollar prices, while Soviet commodities were listed at high postwar dollar costs. Tito also disliked the Soviet-Yugoslav joint companies in which the USSR monopolized management, then illegally collected more than half of joint profits. Most discouraging to Tito's pride was the Soviet demand that mineral-rich Yugoslavia should not develop manufacturing but concentrate on mining, and obtain its manufactured goods by imports from industrial satellites and the USSR.

Russia also demanded that Yugoslavia collectivize agriculture fast as an example for other East European satellites. Tito tried to comply, but soon encountered strong peasant resistance. Tito realized he was endangering his own bases of power—the Yugoslav army and Communist Party, both of which were predominantly peasant. So Yugoslavia slowed collectivization, much to Soviet displeasure.

Another dispute was over the high wages of the Soviet military and economic advisors sent into Yugoslavia. These alien technicians received three times the salaries of Yugoslav experts of equivalent rank, and were paid not by Russia but from the Belgrade treasury. Soviet military specialists also tried to train the Yugoslav army for fighting on open plains like the Red Army, whereas Tito's troops preferred to improve their skill in guerrilla warfare amid Balkan mountains.

Both military and industrial advisors from the USSR attempted to spy upon Yugoslavia. Thus USSR economic and military aid became politically dangerous. Tito's police promptly shadowed the Soviet advisors, whom the Kremlin called home in protest against Yugoslav counter-espionage.

Another sore point was the large Russian émigré colony in Yugoslavia—the descendants of White Russian armies defeated along the Black Sea coast in the Russian Civil War. At Soviet request, Tito had forced these émigrés to renounce Yugoslav citizenship and accept Soviet passports. Terrified by the prospect of possible repatriation to an unfriendly USSR, many Russian émigrés became Soviet spies within Yugoslavia. Naturally, Tito began to mistrust all Russians, White or Red.

Tito and Stalin also quarreled over foreign policy. Yugoslavia desired to annex the large seaport of Trieste, inhabited by a mixed Italo-Yugoslav population and serving as a maritime trade outlet for Austria, Hungary, northeast Italy, and northern Yugoslavia. Fearful of offending the huge Italian Communist Party, which controlled one fourth of Italy's electorate, the USSR refused to support Tito's claim to all of Trieste, which was eventually divided between Italy and Yugoslavia.

More serious was the plan of Bulgaria and Yugoslavia to unite, and form the nucleus of a Balkan federation of Communist nations which would eventually include Albania and Rumania. Such a federation had long been a dream of Balkan Communists for ending petty national rivalries and creating a Balkan multinational state large enough to be an European power. But, as earlier with Tuva and Mongolia, the USSR did not desire Bulgaria and Yugoslavia to unite.

Deployment of Yugoslav planes into Albania exhausted Kremlin patience. In June 1948 Russia induced the Cominform to issue a public statement condemning Tito's leadership of the Yugoslav Communist Party as excessively nationalistic, anti-Soviet, and procapitalist. Sternly the statement ordered Tito to repent and reform, or be removed from power by the Yugoslav Communist Party. Meanwhile Cominform headquarters hurriedly moved from Belgrade to the Rumanian capital of Bucharest, and USSR submarines sailed away from Yugoslav Adriatic ports to Albania.

Tito neither repented nor was overthrown by his Communist Party. Hence in 1949 Russia repudiated its military alliance with

Yugoslavia, and expelled the Yugoslav Ambassador from the USSR. But more dangerous to Yugoslavia was an economic blockade by the entire Soviet orbit of nations, depriving Tito of both Communist trade and aid. Yet no military invasion of Yugoslavia occurred, because the USSR was embroiled in a greater international crisis, the Berlin blockade which threatened to erupt into World War III.

Yugoslavia saved itself from Soviet economic strangulation by trading with the West, and receiving Anglo-American material aid. Arms shipments from the United States strengthened the Yugoslav mountaineer army, which at the time was second in size in Europe only to the huge Red Army of the USSR. Politically Tito stopped the spread of Communism in the Balkans by closing Yugoslavia's frontier to the Greek Communist rebel army, which had been fighting a stalemate civil war with the Greek government for three years. Deprived of Yugoslav supplies, and no longer permitted to retreat into Yugoslav border lands when hard pressed, the Greek Communists soon surrendered to Athens.

Failing to overthrow Tito, the Kremlin tried to prevent the rise of national communism elsewhere in the Soviet orbit of nations. East European satellites were ordered to purge leaders who were real or suspected pro-Titoists. During 1948–1952, the list of purged East European puppet rulers read like a Who's Who of satellite officialdom. Among those removed from power were Wladyslaw Gomulka, Polish Vice Premier and Communist party secretary-general (imprisoned); Bulgarian Vice-Premier Traicho Kostov (executed); Albanian police minister Koci Xoxe (executed); Czechoslovak foreign minister Vladimir Clementis and Communist party secretary-general Rudolf Slansky (both executed); Rumanian foreign minister Ana Pauker (disappeared); and Hungarian foreign minister Laszlo Rajk (executed). Most of these purge victims and the numerous high-ranking officials punished as their accomplices were Communists who spent World War II not in Moscow, but in their native countries. Along with high satellite officials, masses of lower ranking Communists were also purged. Thus during 1949 alone, 100,000 suspects were expelled from the Czechoslovak Communist Party, and 200,000 Hungarian Communists lost their party cards. These repressive measures were apparently successful. No serious case of new Titoism occurred as long as Stalin lived.

During these years of satellite purging, the USSR employed more than terror to hold together the Soviet orbit of nations. While the Cominform was criticizing Yugoslavia in June 1948, Russia cut in half the remaining reparation payments owed to the USSR by Hungary and Rumania. To please the new Asian satellites, the Kremlin granted technical aid on credit to North Korea during 1950 and to Communist China in 1951, much of this assistance probably being armament for the Korean War. Without any compensation Russia in 1952 returned to China the Manchurian port of Dairen, all Japanese property seized by Soviet troops in Manchuria, and the Russian army barracks in Peking. Included in this transfer were 44 factories, 2 power stations, 363 houses, and an unspecified number of warehouses, offices, theaters, hospitals, and schools. Meanwhile Albania was rewarded for remaining pro-Soviet by obtaining USSR goods on credit during 1949–1955, plus large-scale Russian technical aid. Remaining reparations were cut in half from East Germany in 1950, and the USSR during 1952 sold 135 former Nazi industrial enterprises to the governments of East Germany and Hungary. By this sale alone, East Germany acquired important lignite and potash mines, cable and railway carbuilding plants, steel mills, and the huge Rostok shipyard, all of which had been operated by postwar Russia at great Soviet profit. Stalin died in 1953 without regaining Yugoslavia, but having held the remainder of the Soviet orbit intact by a mixture of economic concessions and terror.

Stalin's death in March 1953 weakened Moscow control over the satellites. Just three months later in June 1953, East Berlin workers rioted against a rise in piecework production norms, which required more work to receive the same pay as before. When West Berlin radio stations broadcast the riot news, most other East German cities rebelled against Communist rule. The German satellite police and army hesitated to attack their own people, so Soviet troops stationed in East Germany had to suppress the widespread proletarian revolt. Since the West refused to aid the rebels, the revolt collapsed after two days of street fighting. Of course this German outburst was not Titoism, but anti-Communism.

However, Soviet-orbit reaction to the East German riots unintentionally provoked the rise of Titoism outside Yugoslavia. All governments and Communist parties of satellite East Europe unanimously condemned the East German revolt, but thereafter paid increasing and unprecedented attention to improving the lot of their own workers and peasants. Instead of satisfying the desires of satellite populations, these concessions only whetted appetites for further reform. Meanwhile the Kremlin purged police chief Beria, at least partly because his numerous agents in East Germany had failed to forestall the embarrassing riots. But Beria's arrest and execution weakened Soviet control over satellite police, which hitherto had almost been branches of the USSR secret police. For example, before 1953, an American diplomat traveling through Poland twice evaded Polish police detention by speaking Russian to his captors rather than Polish.

As Moscow police control slackened, the Kremlin made more economic concessions to satellite governments, which were permitted to buy out the Russian share in joint Soviet-satellite business enterprises. Also the USSR reduced its profit margin in barter trade with the satellites. But without police terror, such economic kindness gave the appearance of weakness rather than strength.

Perhaps the most awkward Kremlin maneuver after Stalin's death was the attempt to flatter Yugoslavia into rejoining the Soviet orbit. In 1954, at Soviet insistence, trade was resumed between the Soviet bloc and Yugoslavia. For the first time in six years, Tito was again quoted favorably in the Soviet and satellite press. The Cominform publicly urged Yugoslavia to rejoin the Communist orbit and again become a friend of the USSR. Then in 1955, Premier Bulganin and First Party Secretary Khrushchev of Russia made an apologetic visit to Yugoslavia, proclaiming friendship for Tito and respect for Yugoslav sovereignty, and blaming Beria for the 1948 Soviet-Yugoslav dispute. Almost immediately, the Soviet Union granted to Yugoslavia a technical aid credit which was as large as Soviet loans to India and Communist China.

Wooing a heretic is always a gamble, and in this case, the USSR lost. Tito gratefully accepted USSR trade and aid, but refused to rejoin the Soviet orbit of nations. Trading with and receiving aid from both Communism and capitalism, Yugoslavia was able to bargain with both East and West. This "neutral" bargaining still continues to Yugoslav profit.

Next to become a Communist heretic was Poland, which with its 34,400,000 inhabitants is the largest of all East European satellites in population. Located on a partly open and partly wooded plain between two great military powers—Russia and Germany—Poland has fought many wars against both. In medieval times Poland was strong, ruling an East European empire extending from the Baltic to the Black Sea. But Russia and Prussia became more powerful, and together with Austria partitioned and annexed the entire Polish kingdom late in the eighteenth century. For almost 150 years Poland disappeared from the map as a nation, becoming free again only in 1918 at the close of World War I. But freedom without military strength did not last long. In 1939 Nazi Germany started World War II by conquering West Poland, while the USSR seized Polish eastern provinces. Again Poland vanished from the map. Hitler invaded Russia in 1941, and all Poland fell under Nazi rule until 1944, when a new Soviet occupation began. After such a history, most Poles are both anti-German and anti-Russian.

The postwar Communist government, which Russia had installed in Poland, seemed solidly entrenched until the death of Stalin. Perhaps because of the purge of Beria, Josef Swiatlo—an assistant minister of Polish secret police—fled to the West at the end of 1953. Swiatlo published a book revealing the cruelties of the Polish Communist police. Radio Free Europe broadcast Swiatlo's memoirs into Poland, where an aroused public opinion forced the government to abolish the secret police ministry during 1954.

The de-Stalinization speeches by Khrushchev early in 1956 shocked the Polish Communist Party, which was already unnerved by the Swiatlo revelations. Then in mid-year, workers rioted in the city of Poznan for better living conditions. This unsuccessful uprising was perfectly timed to be seen by many Western newspapermen, who were visiting Poznan to describe its international trade fair. Stunned by the worldwide unfavorable publicity about turmoil in Poznan, the Polish government faltered, and the riot ringleaders were sentenced to a mere four and a half years in prison.

By the autumn of 1956, Russia became alarmed over Communist leniency in Poland. The Polish Titoist Gomulka had been released from prison, and was about to resume his old post of chief secretary of the Polish Communist Party. Soviet leader Khrushchev came personally to Warsaw for the purpose of restoring strict Communist discipline. To show USSR power, Soviet troops in Poland marched toward Warsaw, while Red Army forces in west European USSR and East Germany moved toward the Polish frontiers.

This show of force did not frighten Gomulka, who ordered the Polish Communist army to fight Soviet troops if necessary. Just in case, the Polish police began arming the workers of Warsaw. Gomulka had the support of most of the Polish nation, plus encouragement from the Polish Catholic church, which is a power in a predominantly Catholic country.

Khrushchev sent his troops back to their bases. Poland was allowed to control and liberalize its internal regime, as long as support was rendered to Soviet foreign policy. About $600 million of Polish debts to Russia were cancelled. Gomulka became head of the Polish Communist Party, allowing considerable personal liberty, some freedom of speech, the reopening of small private stores, and the dissolution of agricultural collectives into small private farms. Thus in a bloodless revolution during October 1956, Poland achieved a Titoist semi-independence without leaving the Soviet orbit of nations.

Important as the Polish revolution was, it was immediately overshadowed by the revolt of all Hungary against both Communist and Soviet rule. Hungary, a Magyar nation, has a greater tradition of past glory than Poland because there have been two Hungarian empires: in medieval times, and as equal partner with Austria in Imperial Austro-Hungary of the late nineteenth and early twentieth centuries. Bitter over loss of its empire after defeat in World War I, Hungary allied with Nazi Germany during World War II, only to be conquered again. Then came an unwanted Communist regime, dominated by Russia and headed mainly by Hungarian citizens from minority nationalities.

After Khrushchev electrified the Communist world in February

1956 by his open condemnation of Stalin, Hungary was the first Soviet satellite to de-Stalinize. During the following spring and summer, about 21,000 political prisoners were released from confinement, several dead leaders previously executed on charges of Titoism were posthumously rehabilitated, governmental bureaucracy was somewhat decentralized, police terror was reduced, and tyrannical Matyas Rakosi was forced to resign as first secretary of the Hungarian Workers (Communist) Party because of his "ideological errors." Barbed-wire fences and mine fields were dismantled along the Hungarian side of the Yugoslav and Austrian frontiers. Meanwhile a group of writers called the Petofi Circle attracted student and intellectual support by criticizing the Communist regime.

The Polish bloodless revolution of October 1956 excited Hungarian students, who began demonstrating in Hungary's capital city of Budapest. On October 23, police fired upon a Hungarian student parade proclaiming anti-Soviet slogans. This gunfire sparked a mass rebellion, which spread throughout Hungary largely because the Hungarian army refused to suppress the revolt. After some hesitation, Khrushchev ordered Russian armed forces of 200,000 men and 5,000 tanks to crush the anti-Soviet insurrection, which did not completely cease until two months after its outbreak. Soviet troops installed a new Hungarian Communist government headed by Janos Kadar, a former Titoist, who promised reforms, exiled thousands of young Hungarians to USSR prison camps, and cautiously began rebuilding Hungary's demoralized Communist Party and army. During this unsuccessful revolution, 25,000 Hungarians were killed and 155,000 others fled to Austria.

Already upset by Soviet de-Stalinization, Communist parties throughout the world were stunned by Hungary's revolution. Thousands of members resigned from West European Communist parties. The *Daily Worker,* newspaper of the usually pro-Moscow Communist Party of the United States, condemned Soviet military intervention in Hungary and never retracted this criticism of Kremlin policy. But more important were the reactions of Yugoslavia and Communist China.

Shortly before the Hungarian revolution, Yugoslavia's President Tito warned the Kremlin that trouble was brewing in

Budapest. After his prediction had come true, Tito publicly blamed "Stalinists" in East Europe and the USSR for harsh policies against which the Hungarians could not but rebel. The Soviet government promptly accused Tito of interfering in the affairs of other Communist nations, and during 1957 delayed Russian technical aid to Yugoslavia.

Probably because of this tension, Yugoslavia—not the USSR—started the second Soviet-Yugoslav dispute in 1958. At a Yugoslav Communist Party congress in April, various speakers accused the Soviet Union of trying to maintain an ideological monopoly over world communism, of dominating small Communist nations by force, of exploiting the economies of the Soviet satellites, and of dividing the world unnecessarily into Communist and capitalist military camps—a division harmful to world economy. Yugoslavs also described Soviet Communists as dogmatic and opportunistic, and criticized Russia's swollen bureaucracy. Tito personally praised the US government for its unselfish economic aid to Yugoslavia, and said Western Communist parties were divorced from the popular masses.

The Soviet press immediately attacked Yugoslavia for disrupting international Communist unity and for revision of true Marxism. Soviet economic aid to Yugoslavia was suspended during 1958 and was not resumed until 1972. The press of the Soviet satellites also criticized Yugoslavia, with especially vicious attacks from the newspapers of East Germany and Communist China. Poland and Hungary were relatively mild in their criticism, expressing the hope that some solution would be found for the new Soviet-Yugoslav dispute.

In reply to the Chinese Communists, Yugoslavia compared their attacks to the 1948 Cominform resolution expelling Yugoslavia from the Soviet bloc. According to Yugoslav research, the majority of East European Communist leaders who signed that resolution had by 1958 been executed, imprisoned, exiled, or demoted by their own Communist parties.

But the Chinese Communist reaction to the Hungarian revolution was more profound than new dislike of Yugoslavia. Publicly China supported Russia's forceful suppression of Hungary's revolt. But privately Peking blamed the Hungarian uprising on Khrushchev's inept de-Stalinization. Of all the countries in the Soviet orbit, only China supported the Polish independence movement of 1956. China politely but firmly refrained from copying the de-Stalinization campaign of the USSR, though Khrushchev accused Stalin of being anti-Chinese. Many Red Chinese speeches began to omit references to Russia. To appease China, Russia in 1957 started preparing Chinese industry for eventual production of nuclear bombs. But China continued to question basic tenets of post-Stalinist Soviet foreign policy.

Intense argument between Russia and China arose over the Soviet policy of "peaceful coexistence" with the capitalist West. According to the USSR, peaceful coexistence tended to divide and disarm the capitalist world, which thereby became weakened. Thus the Soviet orbit of nations could slowly extend Communist control over the entire world with no need to fight a major war.

China retorted that peaceful coexistence is useful propaganda for deceiving capitalist nations, but should never become actual Communist policy. As long as capitalist nations exist, they will use force to resist Communist expansion. Therefore, according to Peking, large-scale war between communism and capitalism is virtually inevitable. Nuclear warfare should not be feared, because communism would win, and in the postwar period would establish the greatest civilization ever known by mankind.

A second Sino-Soviet ideological dispute erupted over USSR military and technical aid to bourgeois governments of underdeveloped nations outside the Soviet orbit. The Russian viewpoint is that the Soviet bloc and the neutral underdeveloped nations will exert their combined influence to dissuade the capitalist West from warring against communism. Also by trade and aid, the Soviet bloc can slowly cut the underdeveloped nations off from Western markets, thus economically weakening the West.

In contrast, China mistrusts the bourgeois leaders of underdeveloped nations. Often such leaders suppress their local Communist parties, and profit from the cold war by obtaining material aid from both communism and the capitalist West. Rather than support such unreliable allies, China prefers Communist-led guerrilla revolution by workers and peasants against the bourgeois governments of underdeveloped nations.

The third ideological difference between the two giants of the Communist world concerned de-Stalinization. To the Kremlin,

Stalin was a villain who had inflicted great harm upon Soviet internal and foreign affairs. Peking replied that Stalin may have been a criminal, but Communists should not wash their dirty linen in public. By Chinese reasoning, de-Stalinization simply confused world communism and provided propaganda for the anti-Communist press of the capitalist West. China also declared that Stalin had been a great leader in a difficult period of Soviet history.

Here emotionalism entered the Sino-Soviet dispute. The hero-worship of Chinese Communist leader Mao Tse-Tung had traditionally been as great in China as that of Stalin in the Russia of 1929–1952. If China de-Stalinized, it must also downgrade Mao. Also during Stalin's last years, Mao had been elevated by the Soviet press to the status of a Marxist prophet, mainly because China had proved that a successful Communist revolution could be based on poor peasants rather than industrial workers. Thus postwar Stalinist Russia recognized five Marxist prophets: Marx, Engels, Lenin, Stalin, and Mao. When Khrushchev de-Stalinized in 1956, the list of Communist anointed shrank to four: Marx, Engels, Lenin, and Khrushchev. Mao could hardly be pleased by his demotion and replacement by Khrushchev, who in Chinese eyes was a Communist revisionist causing the embarrassing Hungarian revolution.

Very quickly the Sino-Soviet dispute changed from words to deeds. In 1958 Russia at first rendered diplomatic support to, then abandoned, Communist China in its effort to conquer the off-shore island of Quemoy from Nationalist China (Formosa). Russia's backdown, which forced a Chinese Communist retreat, came after the United States reaffirmed its support of Nationalist China.

Embarrassed by the Tibetan rebellion of 1959 against Chinese rule, Red China attacked India's border posts along the Indian-Tibetan frontier. Ostensibly the attack was made because Tibet's priest-king, the Dalai Lama, had been given refuge in India. However, the attack was timed to coincide with Khrushchev's crossing the Atlantic Ocean on a "peaceful coexistence" tour of the United States. Instead of supporting China, the Soviet government offered to mediate the Sino-Indian conflict.

Russia also ceased to aid China in developing nuclear bombs.

And during 1960, most Russian engineers were withdrawn from Communist China, often taking their blueprints with them so half-built Chinese factories could not be completed. Chinese industrial expansion was dealt a severe blow. Immediately, trade between Red China and Russia began a drastic decline.

During 1961, both China and Russia reported that their guards had been reinforced along the 2,000-mile Soviet-Chinese frontier. According to the Soviet press, no less than 5,000 border incidents occurred along this frontier during 1962, and 60,000 Chinese Moslems fled from Sinkiang into Soviet Central Asia in 1962 and 1963. Meanwhile both China and Russia maneuvered to secure left-wing support throughout the world. In Western countries, pro-Moscow Communist leaders appealed to socialists and labor unions for united fronts to gain leftist parliamentary majorities by peaceful elections. Using anti-white racial propaganda, China sought to unite the Mongoloid, brown-skinned, brunette, and Negroid peoples of Asia, Africa, and Latin America against the Caucasian nations of Europe, the United States, and the USSR.

When China again attacked India in 1962 along the Tibetan frontier, the USSR shipped fighter planes to the Indian air force. By 1964 China suggested that Russia give back to other Communist countries all areas which Tsarist or Soviet Russia had annexed by guile or force. The USSR angrily rejected this proposal, which would require Russia to surrender Bessarabia to Rumania, the western Ukraine and western Belorussia to Poland, and east Siberia, Tuva and part of Central Asia to China.

The enforced retirement of Khrushchev in 1964 failed to stop the Sino-Soviet dispute. By the late 1970's, Chinese and Russian troops had tested each other's strength in at least 9,000 skirmishes along the Sino-Soviet frontier. So great was Moscow-Peking hatred that the biggest border battle thus far was fought in 1969 over uninhabitable Damanski Island, which the Ussuri River floods each year. Meanwhile throughout the world, China promoted the formation of new Communist factions or splinter parties advocating violent revolution rather than peaceful coexistence with capitalism.

As the Sino-Soviet dispute emerged into the open during the 1960's, each Communist party throughout the world realized that it must eventually choose sides. Some parties made their decision quickly, others split into pro-Soviet and pro-Chinese factions, and still others vacillated. Most Communist parties in the Far East supported China. In addition, new Marxist parties loyal to Peking began operating in about 30 countries of Western Europe, Latin America, and South Asia. However the majority of Communists in west and east Europe supported Moscow, as also did the parties of North America and Outer Mongolia. Though nominally pro-Soviet, most Communists of Africa and the Near East tried to remain neutral.

As early as 1960, Yugoslavia publicly declared that China needed war to divert the Chinese people's attention from grave internal difficulties. In Yugoslav opinion, such a war would deform communism and strengthen capitalism. At first, both the Soviet and Chinese press criticized such Yugoslav intervention into the Sino-Soviet dispute. By 1962, however, the USSR needed every Communist ally it could get. Soviet-Yugoslav trade tripled, Tito again was a welcome guest in the USSR, and Russian tanks were sold to Yugoslavia for the first time since the Tito-Stalin break of 1948. Thus ended the second Soviet-Yugoslav dispute (1958–1961), but Yugoslavia still remained an independent Communist country outside the Soviet orbit of nations.

Tiny, primitive, mountainous Albania became the first Communist country in East Europe to take China's side in the Sino-Soviet dispute. This Albanian decision was motivated more by self-interest than by admiration for Oriental Marxism.

Tito and Stalin had split in 1948 when Yugoslavia tried to dominate its weak Albanian neighbor. At the time the Albanian government had the choice of becoming a satellite either of Yugoslavia or the USSR. The Albanian nation of mostly shepherds needed large-scale economic aid and could not survive alone. Logically Albania sided with Russia, which could offer immense assistance, rather than with poor underdeveloped Yugoslavia. Also the USSR was too remote to control Albanian internal politics, while Yugoslavia was uncomfortably near.

Delighted by Albanian friendship, Russia during 1949–1960 rewarded Albania with economic loans and grants exceeding $200,000,000—a vast sum for a small nation of 2,500,000 people. In Albania, Soviet instructors trained the local army, Russian professors largely staffed the colleges, and a Soviet submarine base arose at the seaport of Vlone. At least 3,000 Russians were supervising almost every important aspect of Albanian life.

Yet when Soviet leader Khrushchev made friends with Tito in 1955, Albania became fearful of Soviet intentions. By Albanian reasoning, Russia could easily surrender Albania to Belgrade as bait for Yugoslavia to rejoin the Soviet orbit of nations. Even the second Soviet-Yugoslav dispute did not allay the fears of Albania, which began to seek a new powerful Communist ally. Mutual understanding was achieved by 1959 with Red China, which granted Albania a small loan and was happy to find moral support in Russia's backyard of Eastern Europe.

By late 1960, Albania had become openly pro-Chinese in the Sino-Soviet dispute. Russia retaliated in 1961 by refusing to ship grain to Albania. which was suffering from crop failure. To the Albanian rescue came Communist China, which itself was buying Canadian wheat. At Chinese orders and expense, several Canadian grain ships were dispatched to Albania, thus saving the Balkan country from famine.

Having failed to starve Albania into submission, Russia in 1961 broke diplomatic relations, and suspended all trade and aid to its obstinate Balkan satellite. No longer was Albania invited to meetings of the Warsaw Pact or the Council of Economic Mutual Assistance, though legally holding membership in both. Albania became the second Communist country to be expelled from the Soviet orbit of nations.

Unlike Yugoslavia, Albania did not turn to the West for aid. Albania increased its trade with Italy, a historic economic partner, and with Afro-Asian nations. Offers of Yugoslav aid were rejected by Albania, as were several USSR attempts at Soviet-Albanian reconciliation. But real assistance came from Communist China, which loaned Albania more than $140,000,000, and sent Chinese technicians to replace former Soviet advisors. The East European Soviet satellites helped by refusing to stop trade with Albania despite Russo-Albanian friction.

After the Soviet-Albanian break, Russia tried to convert the Council of Economic Mutual Assistance (CEMA) into an East European common market. Khrushchev proposed a single economic plan for CEMA nations, joint Soviet-satellite enterprises in

East Europe, and economic specialization by all CEMA countries except the USSR. Viewing these USSR proposals as a new Soviet attempt to control their economies, all East European satellites refused to comply fully. Particularly angry was Rumania, which promptly increased its trade with Western capitalist countries, invited Western firms to help Rumanian industrialization, and became neutral in the Sino-Soviet dispute. Russia was angry, but dared not expel Rumania from the shrinking Soviet orbit.

The next Titoist Communist country was Czechoslovakia, which in early 1968 installed a liberal government headed by Communist party first secretary Alexander Dubcek, who ended police terror and press censorship. This Czech government strongly affirmed its loyalty to the USSR and to the Warsaw Pact military alliance, but the Soviet leaders feared that Czechoslovakia might leave the Warsaw Pact, divert its trade to the West, and inspire demands for liberalization within the USSR itself. Soviet troops began military maneuvers near the Czechoslovak frontiers, and Kremlin leaders visited Czechoslovakia to discourage liberalization.

On Aug. 20, 1968, suddenly and without warning Czechoslovakia was invaded by 200,000 Soviet troops plus small detachments from East Germany, Hungary, Poland, and Bulgaria. To save lives, Dubcek ordered the Czechoslovak people not to resist. The Czechoslovak government was forced to end its liberalization, and to permit some Soviet forces to remain in indefinite occupation. Within a year, Dubcek and all other Czech moderates were dismissed from power. The new leader, Gustav Husak, praised the Soviet occupation, liquidated all Czechoslovak recent liberty, and recreated a neo-Stalinist dictatorship.

Thus by the late 1970's, the former unity of the Soviet bloc and world communism had disintegrated. Both Yugoslavia and Albania remained outside the Soviet orbit. China and Russia were on the brink of open rupture. Because of national communism, CEMA could not achieve the teamwork of international labor which worked so well in its capitalist competitor, the European Common Market. Rumania was training its male and female youths to repulse any Soviet armed invasion. Both the French and Italian Communist parties, the two largest Marxist groups in the Western world, proclaimed their independence from Moscow policies, a defiant attitude shared by the Communist parties of Britain and Spain plus the Marxist governments of North Korea, Cambodia, and even the newly united Vietnam. Soviet attempts to form a new Communist International were rejected by China, East Europe, and the major Western Communist parties.

This fragmentation of world communism may be temporary, but appears permanent. Even Communists themselves have little hope of the disunity being overcome. In a frank conversation, a high-ranking Polish diplomat has told me:

> Titoism is the most important movement within the entire Soviet orbit. This is only the beginning, and no one knows how far Titoism will spread.

Suggestions for Further Reading

BRANT, STEFAN, *The East German Uprising,* New York: Praeger, 1957.

BRZEZINSKI, ZBIGNIEW K., *The Soviet Bloc: Unity and Conflict,* Cambridge: Harvard University Press, 1967.

CLISSOLD, STEPHEN, ed., *Yugoslavia and the Soviet Union 1939-1973, A Documentary Survey.* New York: Oxford University Press, 1975.

GITTINGS, JOHN, *Survey of the Sino-Soviet Dispute.* New York: Oxford University Press, 1971.

GRIFFITH, WILLIAM E., *Albania and the Sino-Soviet Rift,* Cambridge: Massachusetts Institute of Technology, 1963.

HAMM, HARRY, *Albania—China's Beachhead in Europe,* New York: Praeger, 1963.

IONESCU, GHITA, *The Breakup of the Soviet Empire in Eastern Europe.* Baltimore: Penguin, 1971.

LASKY, MELVIN, ed., *The Hungarian Revolution,* New York: Praeger, 1957.

LATTIMORE, OWEN, *Nomads and Commissars: Mongolia Revisited,* New York: Oxford University Press, 1962.

REMINGTON, ROBIN ALISON, *The Warsaw Pact, Case Studies in Communist Conflict.* Cambridge: Massachusetts Institute of Technology Press, 1971.

ZINNER, PAUL E., ed., *National Communism and Popular Revolt in Eastern Europe,* New York: Columbia University Press, 1956.

Chapter 26

Conclusion

It is difficult to predict the future of the USSR. Soviet leaders themselves have sometimes been incorrect in anticipating coming events. For example, the European Communist revolutions confidently predicted by Lenin did not materialize. Stalin was caught unawares by Hitler's invasion of Russia. Khrushchev did not foresee his removal from power by his closest associates. If Soviet leaders can be wrong, Western experts on Russia are likely to be even more inaccurate. The history of the USSR has been stormy, and storms can strike fast and hard without warning.

With these considerations in mind, let's examine certain trends.

Increasing urbanization created by industrialization has slowed the growth of the Soviet population, whose size may stabilize in the early 1980's. Therefore the USSR labor shortage will continue, and will require far greater mechanization of industry and agriculture than now exists. In turn this need for mechanization will necessitate largescale imports of Western technology, perhaps even bigger than at present. To continue heavy trading with the West, the Soviet Union will need to continue detente.

Meanwhile the enormous Soviet armament, even if limited or somewhat reduced by future detente agreements, will be a threat to both West Europe and China, who may be frightened into a foreign policy of appeasement.

Russia will .probably not risk a nuclear war with a USA equally well armed. Much of Soviet industry is concentrated in giant plants, which are ideal bombing targets. Thus nine electric power stations produce one eighth of all USSR electricity, and one tenth of all Soviet iron comes from one blast furnace. Russia is now building a truck plant, a railway car factory, and another power station, all of which will be the largest in the world. American industry is much more dispersed.

Moscow has lost control of the world communist movement, perhaps forever. Once a Communist country or party experiences independence, there is no desire to return to slavish obedience of Soviet orders. Thus the Sino-Soviet split is probably permanent.

Rebellion within the USSR is unlikely. Though there is much economic, racial and religious discontent, the police are strong and skilful. Most of the working population are civil servants, who hesitate to revolt against their employers. Also the low standard of living is slowly rising, thus creating hope that the Soviet system will provide a better future. Dissenting Russian intellectuals receive much publicity in the West, but at home have little contact with the general population. However, the post-Brezhnev regime might show more leniency than Brezhnev, like Khrushchev being milder than Stalin.

The Brezhnev regime is in its final years, because of the advanced age of its top leaders. In 1977 Secretary-General and USSR President Leonid Brezhnev was 70 years old, Premier Kosygin 73, and senior party secretary Suslov 75. In comparison, Stalin died at the age of 73, and Krushchev was ousted from power when he was 70. All three of the top leaders of the Brezhnev regime started their careers under Stalin, and were trained as Stalinists.

The post-Brezhnev regime will necessarily be led by younger men, probably middle-aged persons not trained as Stalinists and with a record of rising in the bureaucracy under Khrushchev and Brezhnev. At present, however, Brezhnev does not appear to be grooming anyone to succeed him.

Only time will tell who will inherit power from Brezhnev. But the next ruler will definitely inherit the world's second largest industry, immense armament, a sick agriculture, a restless Communist empire, and countless foreign-policy challenges.

Index